Revenge and Gender in Classical, Medieval and Renaissance Literature

Revenge and Gender in Classical, Medieval and Renaissance Literature

Edited by Lesel Dawson and Fiona McHardy

EDINBURGH
University Press

Edinburgh University Press is one of the leading university presses in the UK. We publish academic books and journals in our selected subject areas across the humanities and social sciences, combining cutting-edge scholarship with high editorial and production values to produce academic works of lasting importance. For more information visit our website: edinburghuniversitypress.com

© editorial matter and organisation Lesel Dawson and Fiona McHardy, 2018
© the chapters their several authors, 2018

Edinburgh University Press Ltd
The Tun – Holyrood Road, 12(2f) Jackson's Entry, Edinburgh EH8 8PJ

Typeset in 10/12 Sabon by
Servis Filmsetting Ltd, Stockport, Cheshire

A CIP record for this book is available from the British Library

ISBN 978 1 4744 1409 8 (hardback)
ISBN 978 1 4744 1410 4 (webready PDF)
ISBN 978 1 4744 1411 1 (epub)

The right of Lesel Dawson and Fiona McHardy to be identified as the editors of this work has been asserted in accordance with the Copyright, Designs and Patents Act 1988, and the Copyright and Related Rights Regulations 2003 (SI No. 2498).

Contents

List of Figures vii
Acknowledgements and Dedication viii

    Introduction: Female Fury and the Masculine Spirit of Vengeance   1
    Lesel Dawson

Part I The Gendering of Revenge
1. Why are the Erinyes Female? or, What is so Feminine about Revenge?   33
Edith Hall
2. Re-marking Revenge in Early Modern Drama   58
Alison Findlay

Part II Friends and Family – 'Revenging Home'
3. Vengeance and Male Devotion in *Laxdæla saga* and *Njáls saga*   85
Ian Felce
4. 'Now I am Medea': Gender, Identity and the Birth of Revenge in Seneca's *Medea*   97
Kathrin Winter
5. The Avenging Daughter in *King Lear*   111
Marguerite A. Tassi
6. 'Brother Unkind': Annabella's Heart in *'Tis Pity She's a Whore*   122
Sara Eaton

Part III Women's Weapons
7. Cursing-Prayers and Female Vengeance in the Ancient Greek World   141
Lydia Matthews and Irene Salvo
8. 'The Power of our Mouths': Gossip as a Female Mode of Revenge   160
Fiona McHardy

9 'Women's Weapons': Education and Female Revenge on the Early
   Modern Stage   181
   Chloe Kathleen Preedy

Part IV Women Transmogrified
10 The Vengeful Lioness in Greek Tragedy: A Posthumanist
   Perspective   203
   Alessandra Abbattista
11 'She's Turned Fury': Women Transmogrified in Revenge Plays   221
   Janet Clare

Part V Lamentation, Gender Roles and Vengeance
12 A Phrygian Tale of Love and Revenge: *Oenone Paridi* (Ovid
   Heroides 5)   239
   Andreas N. Michalopoulos
13 Lament and Vengeance in the Alliterative *Morte Arthure*   251
   Anne Baden-Daintree
14 What's Hecuba to Shakespeare?   264
   Tanya Pollard
15 'Nursed in Blood': Masculinity and Grief in Marston's *Antonio's
   Revenge*   295
   Rebecca Yearling
16 Outfacing Vengeance: Heroic Dying in Webster's *The Duchess of
   Malfi* and Ford's *The Broken Heart*   307
   Lesel Dawson

List of Contributors   326
Index   330

List of Figures

Figure I.1 William-Adolphe Bouguereau's *Orestes Pursued by the Furies* (1862), Chrysler Museum of Art, Norfolk, VA, USA. 2

Figure 1.1 Design from prothesis vase. From Jane Ellen Harrison, *Prolegomena to the Study of Greek Religion* (Cambridge: Cambridge University Press, 2012; first published in 1903). 39

Figure 1.2 Amphora fury. From Jane Ellen Harrison, *Prolegomena to the Study of Greek Religion* (Cambridge University Press, 2012; first published in 1903). 40

Figure 1.3 *Oresteia*-inspired scene. Detail from an Apulian red-figure bell-krater, 380–370 BC. Louvre Museum, Paris. 49

Acknowledgements and Dedication

Many of the essays in this volume were first given at the conference 'Female Fury and the Masculine Spirit of Vengeance' which took place in 2012 at Bristol University. The conference was generously supported by: Bristol's Institute for Research in the Humanities and Arts (BIRTHA); Bristol's Institute of Greece, Rome and the Classical Tradition (IGRCT); the Department of English; The Society for the Promotion of Hellenic Studies; and the assistance of Samantha Barlow. Bristol University's Faculty Fund supported the project in its final stages. Mark Curtis, Tamsin Badcoe, Ian Burrows, Ian Calvert, Ros Powell, Laurence Publicover and Rebecca Yearling offered valuable support and advice. Gratitude is also due to Samantha Matthews, who was a vigilant reader during the final stages of the volume and a wonderful friend throughout.

This book is dedicated to Sara Eaton, who sadly died before the volume came to completion. Sara was an inspirational scholar and teacher and we are honoured to include her work in this collection.

Introduction:
Female Fury and the Masculine Spirit of Vengeance

Lesel Dawson

In William Adolphe Bouguereau's *Orestes Pursued by the Furies* (1862) (Figure I.1), Orestes turns away from his mother, Clytemnestra, whom he has killed to avenge the murder of his father, Agamemnon. Horrified rather than triumphant, Orestes is pursued by the Erinyes, or Furies, the three snaky-haired chthonic deities responsible for punishing blood crimes. Bouguereau's Clytemnestra – draped in red fabric, more swooning than dying – is utterly unlike the ferocious, 'man-minded' woman portrayed by Aeschylus (ἀνδρόβουλος, *Ag.* 11), whose first thought on discovering that Orestes has returned is to defend herself with an axe (*Cho.* 889).[1] Her graceful, relatively bloodless death contrasts also with the queasy intimacy created in the corresponding scene of Euripides' *Electra*, in which Clytemnestra clings to her son, begging for mercy (1214–17) and showing him her breast (1207); in this version, Orestes describes how he hesitates, eventually covering his eyes with his cloak before slitting her throat (1221–3), as 'the legs which [he] was born through' (lit. her fruitful limbs - γόνιμα μέλεα, 1209) bend beneath her. Instead, Bouguereau romanticises and domesticates Clytemnestra, contrasting her pathetic figure with the ferocious energy of the Furies, a juxtaposition that recalls Nancy Sorkin Rabinowitz's claim that female characters in Greek tragedy are represented as either sacrificial or vengeful.[2]

This scene, and its many renditions and reinterpretations, expose some of the stereotypes and contradictions inherent in the complex interrelationship of revenge and gender. As in the case of Orestes, revenge is frequently depicted as a man's job: women incite and men act, performing the killings that establish their masculinity and protect their honour. Yet, while conceptualised as a quintessential masculine activity, revenge simultaneously unleashes the female Furies and the violent, 'feminine' emotions which threaten a man's reason and self-control. Hunted by the 'hounds of his mother's hate' (μητρὸς ἔγκοτοι κύνες, Aesch. *Cho.* 1054, cf. 924), Orestes is driven to near madness by their pursuit, his manliness undone by the same act that establishes it. Women, of course,

Figure I.1 William-Adolphe Bouguereau's *Orestes Pursued by the Furies* (1862), Chrysler Museum of Art, Norfolk, VA, USA.

also take revenge, as when Clytemnestra kills Agamemnon to requite the sacrifice of their daughter, Iphigenia. However, scholars are divided as to whether female avengers should be interpreted as honorary men, heroes in their own right, monstrous inversions of gender norms, or conduits through which male subjectivity is formed. Implicit in these debates are also questions about how revenge plots impact on wider constructions of gender, and whether such narratives reinforce conservative gender roles, interrogate the 'masculine' values that society prizes, or establish new ways of conceptualising women and men.

This collection takes up these questions, probing revenge's gendering, its role in consolidating and contesting gender norms, and its relation to friendship, family roles and kinship structures. Spanning Western ideas of revenge in literary works from ancient Greece to early modern England, it considers how writers respond to and reimagine inherited plots and characters, exploring continuities between historical periods as well as the ways in which texts and traditions diverge.[3] A collection of this scope cannot be comprehensive: it aims instead to encourage dialogue and debate, exposing areas of scholarly interest and controversy through methodologically diverse essays that, at times, advance conflicting arguments. This introductory essay takes account of these varied positions, arguing that while revenge functions as a repressive cultural script that reinforces conservative gender roles, it also repeatedly triggers events and actions that disturb and interrogate gender norms. Indeed, I argue here that revenge's unruly energies can blur conventional male/female and animal/human binaries, challenging cultural expectations about gender and provoking wider ontological questions.

This Introduction also examines lamentation, a female-gendered activity which enables women to play an important role in revenge narratives. Particularly in earlier periods, women use lamentation to express grievances and keep the past alive, directing revenge action and, at times, influencing wider political events. However, female lamentation becomes discredited in later periods and detached from the revenge process. In early modern tragedy, female mourning no longer incites revenge. Instead, the revenger is also the mourner, whose grief inhibits the revenge process. Vengeance becomes the occasion for a confrontation with the potential purposelessness of life and the inevitability of death, opening up wider ethical and metaphysical questions and creating a new kind of tragedy which reflects on and revises earlier models.[4] Drawing on several essays in this volume, I therefore argue that the change in lamentation's status and function has wider implications for women's roles and for the gendering of the male revenger.

REVENGE AND MASCULINITY

Revenge narratives represent manliness as a highly prized commodity that individuals acquire through retaliatory acts of violence, exposing the performative nature of gender in which, in Judith Butler's words, 'identity is ... constituted by the very "expressions" that are said to be its results'.[5] The revenger, in his role as an artist-figure enacting mimetic violence, draws attention to his self-fashioning: just as he devises plots, so too does he fabricate his masculinity. However, while the revenger's self-conscious theatricality can make him appear autonomous and self-authored, from another perspective he merely replicates conservative cultural scripts and gender roles. Performativity, as Butler has commented, 'is not radical choice' nor 'voluntarism', but more often 'the repetition of oppressive and painful gender norms'.[6] Revenge narratives frequently repeat and reinforce such oppressive gender norms, often with women acting as the guardians of a conservative ideal of manliness aligned with violent reprisal. Revenge, from this perspective, is not a liberating form of empowerment, but a repressive cultural script that men are expected to adhere to whatever the costs.

There are pragmatic opportunities and psychological benefits to vengeful self-fashioning, and most of the male characters discussed in the collection enthusiastically embrace vengeance. Vengeance can enhance status and frequently 'coincides admirably with calculations of expediency', serving a man's financial and political self-interests.[7] In Greek texts, revenge not only confirms

Orestes' manhood and fulfils his filial obligation, but also enables him to return from exile and regain his father's throne and wealth.[8] Vengeance can also relieve the avenger's sense of powerlessness and guilt: by transferring the pain experienced onto another, the avenger appears to cancel the loss of the past and is simultaneously transformed from the passive sufferer into the active avenger. Revengers, as John Kerrigan observes, are 'questers after psychic balance as well as ethical equivalence', tallying up their losses like careful accountants and repaying the suffering they have experienced in kind.[9]

The extent to which vengeance bolsters or undermines masculinity depends, in part, on the cultural value attached to revenge; its perceived relationship to justice; and how the competitive principle of requital is counterbalanced by other cooperative values such as compassion, forgiveness, self-restraint and steadfastness. In general, texts that promote a positive view of revenge also see it as manly. Anne Pippin Burnett argues that in ancient Greece the expectation that one should 'help friends and harm enemies' made revenge obligatory for men: it was 'not the opposite of order . . . but order itself in its original form, the community's power to punish being only a borrowed version of each man's ingrained right to retaliate'.[10] Recent critics have shown how this principle is explored and critiqued in Athenian literature, embedded in its legal system, and part of a culture of reparation.[11] Although some critics emphasise cooperative values, suggesting that men act with a 'civic restraint' that supersedes the code of vendetta, most agree that in ancient Greece ideas of manliness and justice are bound up with ideas of retaliation – as evident in the range of meanings of the word δίκη (*dikē*), from 'revenge' and 'punishment' to 'justice' and 'lawcase' – and see retaliation as central to masculinity.[12] Danielle Allen argues that in order to limit retaliatory violence and keep it outside the domestic sphere, revenge was restricted to 'one angry punisher per household – the male adult' and to the male, public domain, a space defined less by geography than by gendered values and the expectations attached to them.[13] Negative representations of female revengers as monstrous delegitimate women as revengers and thereby contain vendetta's inflammatory potential and threat to interfamilial conflict.

In a variation of this dynamic, Old Icelandic literature represents revenge as central to a man's honour and to the wider social order. However, critics have disagreed on the extent to which this construction of masculinity is being celebrated or critiqued. Whereas according to William Ian Miller, a man who neglected vengeance 'had to feel shame for not wanting to, or at least had to come up with a plausible account as to why it was not shameful for him not to seek revenge', David Clark argues that the Guðrún Poems in the *Poetic Edda* 'undermine the heroic ideal of vengeance' in which the hero '(whether male or female) is distanced and represented as belonging to the past'.[14] In this collection, Ian Felce's 'Vengeance and Male Devotion in *Laxdæla saga* and *Njáls saga*' addresses this debate, exploring the tensions between competitive and cooperative values and examining how these relate to, and conflict with, male homosocial bonds. Felce emphasises the performative and precarious nature of the saga-heroes' manliness, 'a finite commodity that is continually sought, bartered for and exchanged', in which men must choose either to betray a friendship in seeking revenge or risk 'forfeiting their manhood' by avoiding it. However, rather than coming down on one side of the debate, and interpreting the sagas as either a celebration of earlier honour codes or a means of criticising them as immoral and outdated, Felce instead argues that the sagas expose 'the conflict between competitive and cooperative virtues at the heart of saga society without proposing an answer to it'. The sagas thus highlight the irresolvable conflicts that result from clashing values, when men must choose either to honour homosocial friendships or prove their manliness through violence.

Similar debates about the relationship between revenge and justice and how far the former is beneficial to or destructive of masculinity and to social order[15] are to be found in discussions of Roman, medieval and early modern literature. While some Roman writings associate vengeance with masculinity, in other texts the obsession with revenge engenders a loss of self-control deemed effeminising; in Stoic philosophy in particular, power is reconceptualised as power over the self, and heroic masculinity is established through the ability to moderate passion and to remain steadfast and virtuous.[16] Senecan tragedy thus dramatises the dangers of passionate emotion,[17] showing, in the words of Seneca's Medea, 'How difficult it is to turn the soul from its anger when once it is aroused'.* In medieval literature, conflicting expectations of masculinity are embedded in chivalry: according to Nigel Saul, a noble man was expected to revenge any slight, thus displaying his 'prowess' and 'courage', but also to follow 'an elaborate code of restraint'.[18] And in Tudor England, while 'the blood-for-blood ethic ... was the basis of private, public and divine vengeance alike', the state sought to discredit personal vengeance, emphasising 'the antisocial nature of crime' in order to claim the right of retribution for itself.[19] Kristine Steenbergh attributes different views of vengeance to different social groups and discourses in this period, arguing that anger could variously be 'represented as an emotion that contributes to masculine selfhood' and one 'capable of transforming a man to such an extent that he loses his masculine identity'.[20] But the most important counter-discourse to revenge that emerged in the post-Roman world was Christianity, which gave moral purpose to the avoidance of revenge and suggested that retaliatory violence could be sinful. Although vengeance remained central to Christianity, displayed in God's punishments and the providential revelation of crimes, punishment was reserved for heaven ('Vengeance is mine; I will repay, saith the Lord', Romans 12:19), prompting those contemplating revenge to hesitate for fear of the spiritual consequences. The clash between classical and Christian discourses, and the divergent ways that vengeance is viewed within Christianity, has fuelled debates about the relation of revenge and justice,[21] the moral and psychological

---

* *difficile quam sit animum ab ira flectere / iam concitatum* (203–4).

condition of the revenger,[22] and the way that the revenge genre itself engages with early modern theological issues and the trauma of the reformation.[23]

REVENGE, INHERITANCE AND FAMILY ROLES

The idea it is a man's right and duty to seek revenge is derived in part from the way that revenge obligations are a form of inheritance, a structure which excludes women, particularly daughters. Just as property cannot be bequeathed to women, so too are women excluded from the obligations of blood feuds and its financial rewards, except in unusual circumstances.[24] Although women often function as the conduits that create kinship, generating the bonds between men, they are unable to inherit the rights and obligations of the kinship networks they foster. In the early medieval period, women were excluded from receiving *wergeld*, the money which could be paid in compensation for a relative's death.[25] Instead, women were often married to members of a warring tribe to forge alliances as peace-weavers (*friðusibb*), and consequently experienced painfully divided loyalties when hostilities broke out.[26] This structure is found beyond medieval literature, even in texts where the marriage or romantic relationship serves no political purpose, as in the case of Shakespeare's Ophelia, whose position as a revenging daughter is compromised by her love for Hamlet. The repetition of this pattern even when the relationship serves no political purpose suggests that, for many playwrights, wives and daughters in revenge narratives function primarily as figures of pathos, who make visible vendetta's self-destructive energies and entanglements of friend and foe.[27]

There are of course exceptions. Medea's own emphasis on her maternity and its centrality to her revenge masks the extent to which she is also an avenging daughter, repaying the crimes that she herself committed. In 'The Avenging Daughter in *King Lear*', Marguerite A. Tassi addresses the scarcity of revenging daughters, focusing on another exception to the paradigm, Shakespeare's Cordelia, who takes up the male role of revenger. Although *Lear* is rarely interpreted as a revenge play, Tassi demonstrates its structural affinities with the genre and engagement with ethically contrasting forms of requital: while Goneril and Regan pursue a path of 'harm for harm', Cordelia aims to restore Lear's kingdom and his 'right'. These different types of revenge are also gendered: while Goneril and Regan correspond to negative stereotypes about vengeful women, Shakespeare's Cordelia, particularly in the 1623 folio, resembles the 'male-like' Cordelia depicted in the historical chronicles and supports an idea of 'right' that is aligned with traditional patriarchal hierarchies. Tassi thus argues that revenge does a 'double-edged service for destructive and restorative ends', a tendency encapsulated in Kent's prediction that 'These injuries the King now bears will be revenged home' (3.3.10–11). While Kent's words are intended to offer a hopeful image of revenge as restorative payback, Tassi points out that they also evoke 'a darker, alternate vision of revenge that is unsparing and destructive of home', an image that corresponds to 'the estrangements, divisions, and disunities that have besieged the royal family and kingdom'.

Kent's image of 'reveng[ing] home' captures the ways in which revenge can entail families turning in on themselves, confusing the boundaries between friend and foe. Destructive and self-consuming, rather than nourishing and regenerative, such families are frequently described as cannibalistic and incestuous. These metaphors are literalised in Ford's *'Tis Pity She's a Whore* (1630), a play that centres on an incestuous brother–sister relationship that eventually turns murderous. Sara Eaton's '"Brother Unkind": Annabella's Heart in *'Tis Pity She's a Whore*' explores the nature of this incestuous relationship and Giovanni's motivation for killing his sister and ripping out her heart. Beginning with Giovanni's infamous revenge, Eaton explores his preoccupation with interpreting his sister-lover and her heart, arguing that Annabella embodies the contradictions inherent in the courtly love rhetoric found in the play. Just as descriptions of the heart as a repository of subjectivity led to worries about sincerity and the knowability of the self, so too Giovanni's attempts to inscribe Annabella's heart with meaning reinforce her opacity. Drawing on the Slavoj Žižek's seminal essay, 'Courtly Love, or, Woman as Thing', Eaton argues that 'Giovanni has all the marks of an abject masochist', and that his self-definition is achieved via a narcissistic fantasy of Annabella as a second self. Eaton's chapter thus provides a psychological reading of revenge's self-destructive energies and propensity to 'revenge home'.

THE GENDERING OF REVENGE AND THE FEMALE REVENGER

Although revenge is typically imagined as a quintessentially masculine activity, it is paradoxically gendered female and seen to be aligned with the female psyche. As Janet Clare observes: 'the impulse to revenge has been identified as a feminine one' and 'vengeance itself, "Vindicta", is personified and apostrophized as feminine'.[28] Edith Hall's 'Why are the Erinyes Female? or, What is so Feminine about Revenge?' explores this 'toxic patriarchal myth', asking why, given that men carried out more acts of revenge, the Greeks envisaged the supernatural agents of punishment as female. Examining the complex gendering of the Furies, monstrous females who 'destroy rather than nurture', Hall argues that their femininity derives from a variety of sources, including their association with chthonic, thanatological and maternal forces and their links to other mythological figures, such as the Gorgons and Harpies. Yet Hall also notes that in archaic vase-painting and Hesiod's *Theogony*, the Furies' gender is 'decidedly ambiguous': predominantly female in appearance, they are yet incapable of reproduction and can act 'as surrogates, representatives and even vicarious embodiments of the interests of wronged men'. Proposing that the furies should in fact be regarded as 'transgender', Hall concludes her essay by considering recent neurological studies that indicate a gendered distinction in how men and women experience punishment.

Hall's analysis of the transgender aspects of the Furies reminds us of revenge's ability to traverse and disturb expected cultural categories.[29] Like the Furies, female revengers are often depicted as monstrous, hybrid creatures who blur the distinction between masculine and feminine, human and animal. The female revenger's gender-bending aspects, and her function and meaning more generally, has been an area of controversy in literary criticism. While there have been a wide variety of responses to the female revenger, three significant approaches can be identified that cut across historical periods: those that emphasise the monstrosity of the female revenger and the corresponding misogyny of the genre; those that emphasise the female revenger's relation to male subjectivity; and those that see the female revenger as a heroic figure in her own right. Scholars who follow the first approach analyse negative depictions of female revengers, whose cruelty is perceived to render them frighteningly unnatural, concealing a 'tiger's heart wrapp'd in a woman's hide'.[30] Such interpretations explore wider fears about women, the ways that misogyny is embedded in intellectual traditions and political ideologies, and how revenge texts impact the viewing position of the spectator.[31] Eileen Allman, for example, considers the misogyny of Jacobean revenge plays in political terms, exploring how the tyrant's authority is based on a shared misogyny.[32]

Grendel's mother in *Beowulf* can be used as an example of how female revengers are depicted as monstrous, uncanny beings. She typifies the ontological uncertainty provoked by the female revenger, whose unknowable aspects are emphasised in the descriptions of her as an animal (*brimwylf* 'the wolf of the deep', 1599) and as a non-human alien being (*grund-wyrgenne* 'swamp-thing from hell', 1518) of uncertain gender.[33] Jane Chance sees Grendel's mother as 'a parodic inversion both of the Anglo-Saxon queen and mother' who simultaneously 'arrogates to herself the masculine role of the warrior or lord'.[34] Whereas Grendel has a hunger for human flesh, devouring his victims' bodies, his mother is instead 'Grief-racked and ravenous, desperate for revenge' (1278), tearing off Ashhere's head to display it rather than eat it.* Paul Acker argues that her '"powers of horror" ... partly reside in (or are attributed to) her maternal nature': Grendel's mother is the bringer of life and death, who crosses gender and geographical borders, living beyond the marshes in a strange watery lair that evokes the fascination and dread of the abject.[35] The connection between the generative processes of motherhood and revenge are brought out by Seamus Heaney's translation of *gemunde*.[36] In Heaney's translation, Grendel's mother '*brooded* on her wrongs',† a word which links her angry contemplation of her injuries to the creative process by which she hatches a plan.[37] Thus while Grendel's mother's ferocious strength is gendered masculine, it also derives from her dangerously procreative maternity.

A second critical approach to the female revenger considers the ways in which female characters in tragedy are central to male subjectivity, providing

---

* *gífre ond galgmód ... sunu déoð wrecan* (1277–8).
† *Grendles módor / ides áglaécwíf yrmþe gemunde* (1258–9).

a context in which men's civic, erotic and familial roles can be debated. Here tragedy is fundamentally about male homosocial and homoerotic relations; it offers a means of treating difficult political, social and philosophical problems at one remove. In the influential *Playing the Other: Gender and Society in Classical Greek Literature*, Froma Zeitlin argues that female characters' 'demands for identity and self-esteem are still designed primarily for exploring the male project of selfhood in the larger world'.[38] Victoria Wohl similarly views 'the tragic woman as a fantasy – fictional and ideologically invested – through which the male subject thinks about himself and his place in the world'.[39] While for Helene Foley, 'masculine identity and conflicts' are central; 'the texts often explore or query these issues through female characters and the culturally more marginal positions that they occupy'.[40] Linda Bamber takes up a related position in her interpretation of Shakespearean tragedy, a genre which she argues is centred on male subjectivity and its relation to 'the feminine as a principle of Otherness'.[41]

However, Alison Findlay rejects such approaches in *A Feminist Perspective on Renaissance Drama* and, by drawing attention to the female audience members in early modern theatres, rejects claims that early modern drama is chiefly concerned with the male self. Focusing on revenge's tendency to violate political hierarchies and gender norms, she argues that revenge tragedy is in fact 'a feminine genre' which has 'the power to consume and dissolve gendered identities, [and] to elevate women to new heights of self-determination in its pyrotechnic and destructive splendour', an argument she extends in this volume.[42] Findlay's work is related to a third approach which emphasises female revengers (and tragic figures more generally) as heroic figures in themselves. Naomi Conn Liebler challenges pejorative interpretations of female tragic characters, rejecting claims that female figures are predominantly depicted negatively in order to demonise female agency and promote conservative gender roles. She argues:

> The female tragic hero engages in a struggle exactly as rigorous, exactly as dangerous, and exactly as futile as that of any of her masculine counterparts. That the space where her *agon* is staged is sometimes (but not always) domestic rather than public does not in any way diminish either its rigor or its social and political significance. To assume, as many critics – including many feminists – have done, that the representation of the tragic agon in a domestic or interior setting is somehow degraded or trivialized is to impose a particular set of (de)valuations on that representation.[43]

Conn Liebler's emphasis on female tragic figures as heroic have been complemented by related reassessments of female revengers and of revenge. Woodbridge argues that female revengers, and revenge itself, are often positively portrayed in early modern texts, and maintains that 'to treat male revengers as fascinating, morally ambiguous heroes and female revengers as simple villainesses is merely sexist'.[44] Marguerite A. Tassi similarly argues that female characters play an important role in Shakespearean plays and are at times driven to acts of violence by a desire for justice.[45]

These different approaches to female revengers are evident in responses to Euripides' Medea, who has been interpreted, variously, as a monstrous, inhuman figure who inverts gender norms or as a tragic hero in her own right. Elizabeth Bongie argues that Medea becomes 'filled with an unrelenting resolve to destroy her enemies and to vindicate her honour' in a manner which aligns her 'with the great male heroes of Greek literature such as the Homeric Achilles and the Sophoclean Ajax'.[46] Helene Foley, however, regards Medea's use of a heroic discourse as the means through which the play interrogates Greek values: Medea is a terrifying embodiment of what that society prizes and the logical endpoint to the uncompromising adherence to such values, demonstrating its cost to the self and to society. As she argues:

> By choosing Medea, a barbarian woman, to display the contradictions inherent in this heroic ethic and behaviour, Euripides has achieved a particularly devastating and grotesque demonstration of the problematic nature of this archaic heroism – and one he might have hesitated to make through a Greek or male protagonist.[47]

Engaging in these debates, Alessandra Abbattista in 'The Vengeful Lioness in Greek Tragedy: A Posthumanist Perspective' reinterprets the animal metaphors used to describe revenging women from a posthumanist perspective. Whereas critics have commonly regarded such metaphors as indicating the female revenger's inhuman savagery and otherness (whereby a woman's attempt to assume a male heroic role transforms her instead into a monstrous beast), posthumanism challenges conventional distinctions between animal and human, male and female. Drawing on the work of Rosi Braidotti, Abbattista argues that female revengers similarly challenge these distinctions. The metaphorical metamorphosis of Aeschylus' Clytemnestra and Euripides' Medea into lionesses reveals their complex figuration as male–female hybrid beings, recalling the tragic suffering and protective violence of the Homeric lion within a new context of interfamilial conflicts. These transformations engender terror but also compassion, evoking new ways of conceptualising humans-as-animals that invite recognition of our own unstable and hybrid nature.

Kathrin Winter's '"Now, I am Medea": Gender, Identity and the Birth of Revenge in Seneca's *Medea*' also explores the way that female revengers complicate gendered categories, arguing that when Seneca's Medea aligns her vengeance to her maternal capacities, revenge is envisaged as a perverse form of self-creation. As Winter argues, Medea's birth metaphors are instrumental in her formulation of a new vengeful subjectivity, marking her distance from Euripides' version. In Zeitlin's account of Greek tragedy, female characters function as part of male self-definition, where 'the dialectic of self and other is consistently and insistently predicated on the distinctions between masculine and feminine'.⁴⁸ However, as Winter argues, Seneca's Medea radically appropriates masculine self-definition: as in the case of male tragic subjects, Medea also uses an other to define herself, but here the 'other' is her former self. As a consequence, Medea not only creates a new identity for herself, but is also 'the conceptual ground on which this new self is conceptualised and forged'. Winter thus provides evidence for Zeitlin's model as operating in Senecan tragedy while demonstrating how female characters can appropriate forms of self-definition assumed to be male.

Revenge tragedy's protean, gender-bending qualities is also considered in Alison Findlay's 'Re-marking Revenge in Early Modern Drama', which examines competing theories for revenge's appeal in a wide range of plays from 1580 to 1699. Focusing on the ways that early modern revengers reference and revise earlier classical texts and figures, Findlay examines revenge as a textual practice and affective performance and considers whether classical murderous mothers, such as Medea, 'embody ancient human anxieties about the uncanny feminine power of revenge to undo human subjects and societies'. Using Early English Books Online (EBBO), Findlay also examines different theories as to the genre's popularity. She surveys the frequency of the words 'revenge', 'avenge' and 'vengeance' (and their derivatives) in order to test whether it was a genre that peaked in the Elizabethan period and was followed by a period of decline, emerged particularly in periods of political crisis, or has an enduring appeal.

WOMEN'S WEAPONS

In Shakespeare's *Much Ado About Nothing*, Beatrice, furious that Hero has been slandered and humiliated before her family on her wedding day, tests her newly found relationship with Benedict, ordering him to 'Kill Claudio'.⁴⁹ In making this request, Beatrice falls into a typical pattern of revenge narratives in which women incite revenge and men do the killing. Indeed, either because of her own internalised understanding of gender norms or practical concerns about swordplay, Beatrice assumes that she cannot take vengeance, despite her passionate and bloodthirsty wish to see Claudio suffer: 'O God, that I were a man! I would eat his heart in the marketplace!' (4.1.304–5). When Benedick initially refuses to swear to her he will take revenge, her fallback position is to lament: 'I cannot be a man with wishing, therefore I will die a woman with grieving' (4.1.320–1).⁵⁰

Beatrice's response typifies the role of women in revenge plots: she goads and incites, but assumes that the role of revenger must be performed by a man. And when she finds her words do not work, she declares that she will die from grief, a response triggered less by Claudio's treatment of Hero, than by her own frustration and enforced passivity. Like Beatrice, women in revenge narratives across periods use words as weapons, either goading men into action or expressing their anger in other ways, such as through lament.⁵¹

Women could also seek revenge by cursing. However, while there is a readiness to see women as particularly able to practice illicit magic and likely to use words as weapons, the key factor in cursing is powerlessness rather than gender. This is particularly the case in classical Greece and imperial Rome, where curses and other forms of magic were a common feature of day-to-day life used by people of every status.[52] Esther Eidinow regards ancient Greek cursing as a form of risk management: 'curse-writers wrote their texts because they wanted to direct future events in their favour by managing sources of risk: they aimed to weaken and incapacitate their targets and thus neutralize the threat that they presented'.[53] Curses also could be motived by revenge, as evidenced by the curse tablets (*defixiones*) found throughout the ancient Mediterranean world and by examples of imprecations found in literary and religious texts.

Across the range of literary malefactions, curses are primarily the weapon of the weak against the strong. Women with power do not curse, and men who are disempowered do. In Euripides' *Hecuba* the blinded Polymestor crawls on the ground, demanding 'Tell me where she is so that I may seize her with my hands ... and tear her in pieces'[54] (Euripides *Hecuba* 1125–6).* Unable to find her, he curses the Trojan women instead, and predicts Hecuba's transformation into 'a dog with fiery eyes' (1265).† Shakespeare's Queen Margaret in the *Henry VI* trilogy, one of the most famous stage-cursers, revels in inflicting violence on her enemies, only turning to cursing when her attempted actions no longer have consequences. In a similar vein, Shakespeare's King Lear and Timon curse when they are frustrated and disempowered, as does Caliban when enslaved, and Aaron before being executed. Nevertheless, as most literary imprecations are fulfilled, cursing (like prophecy) can also empower the speaker and validate the justice of his or her complaints.[55] Cursing not only stands in place of the violence the speaker wishes to inflict at that moment, but also looks forward to the consummation of vengeance. Curses thus involve multiple temporalities, contributing to the way in which events (and time itself) can become layered, entangled and condensed in revenge narratives.

However, there are circumstances in which prayers for vengeance could be particularly useful for women. Lydia Matthews and Irene Salvo make this argument in their chapter, 'Cursing-Prayers and Female Vengeance in the Ancient Greek World', which analyses literary imprecations alongside thirteen prayers for justice written exclusively by women and found in Knidos (Caria, modern Turkey). They argue that because women did not have direct access to legal forms of retribution and often had complaints that fell outside the normal judicial system (such as a husband's adultery), cursing-prayers had 'an important psychological and social function' for women, 'providing a legitimate outlet for potentially disruptive feelings through an established ritual that was recognised as meaningful by the civic community'. That the

---

* σήμηνον, εἰπὲ ποῦ 'σθ', ἵν' ἁρπάσας χεροῖν / διασπάσωμαι καὶ καθαιμάξω χρόα.
† κύων ... πυρσ' ἔχουσα δέργματα.

Knidos prayers for justice were probably made during the annual festival of the Thesmophoria, in which women shared their complaints and performed their prayers, invites speculation on the rituals' therapeutic aspect. Like lamentation, cursing allowed women to express anger and hatred 'within socially acceptable roles and practices',[56] providing women with a legitimate, communal medium in which to air grievances and to rectify or revenge the injuries done to them.

Fiona McHardy's '"The Power of our Mouths": Gossip as a Female Mode of Revenge', explores another method by which women use words as weapons, examining how gossip is employed maliciously in ancient Greek literature and court trials. As McHardy demonstrates, gossip provides another mechanism by which women and other disempowered individuals, such as servants, can take revenge: either directly, by damaging an individual's reputation, or indirectly, by provoking others to violent behaviour. In court trials and literary texts – such as Aeschylus' *Choephori*, Euripides' *Andromache* and *Hippolytus*, and Chariton's novel *Chaereas and Callirhoe* – gossip and false reports are vital components of revenge, used either to incite violence directly or to set up situations in which revenge can take place. McHardy also demonstrates how legal revenge narratives recall literary plots and character archetypes, focusing in particular on Lysias' *On the Murder of Eratosthenes*, a speech in which Euphiletus, an Athenian man, defends himself for murdering his wife's lover, Eratosthenes. In Euphiletus' account, gossip is what instigates the revenge action: Euphiletus is told about his wife's affair by the servant of Eratosthenes' former lover. While the ostensible crime involves two men (a husband kills his wife's lover), from another perspective it is Eratosthenes' former lover who has achieved revenge indirectly through gossip. McHardy thus provides another way in which women find circuitous and covert ways of achieving revenge/requiting wrongs: she demonstrates the ability of individual women and wider female networks to 'incite, persuade or deceive', while simultaneously showing how women's reputation for gossip allows them to be used as scapegoats for men's violence.

While McHardy's analysis of gossip offers an example of how women can use covert and indirect methods to achieve revenge, Chloe Kathleen Preedy's '"Women's Weapons": Education and Female Revenge on the Early Modern Stage' examines some of the more direct ways that women participate in vengeance in early modern plays. Focusing on Lavinia from Shakespeare's *Titus Andronicus*, Bel-Imperia from Kyd's *The Spanish Tragedy*, and Tamyra and Charlotte from *The Revenge of Bussy D'Ambois*, Preedy argues that female characters' education and classical learning enable them to influence and take part in revenge plots rather than being 'banished to the margins'. Acknowledging how female revengers are often negatively constructed as 'an aberration against nature', she nevertheless finds that 'women's vengeance ... is simultaneously associated with learning and the revenger's meta-theatrical ability to script the action'. While acknowledging the problematic morality (and the high cost) of vengeance, Preedy proposes that female revengers are heroic tragic figures who, rather than being simply trapped within misogynistic stereotypes, are instead active agents who interrogate these stereotypes and determine their fates. Preedy thus contributes to studies that aim to recover the female tragic hero, foregrounding education as a means by which women employed revenge scripts for their own purposes.

LAMENTATION, GENDER ROLES AND VENGEANCE

Lamentation has long been regarded as women's work. As Margaret Alexiou asserted in her influential book, *The Ritual Lament in Greek Tradition*, 'From the earliest times the main responsibility for funeral ritual and lamentation has rested with [women].'[57] Recent critics agree: from the ancient to the early modern period, it was predominantly women who washed and dressed the dead, watched over the body and performed the rituals of mourning. However, not simply a sign of women's confinement and low status, this role allowed women to 'enhance their status as active individuals within the kin group'.[58] Moreover, Casey Dué argues that women use 'the language of lament to manipulate their listeners and to achieve various goals', and in some circumstances, lamentation 'is the only medium through which women have a sanctioned public voice'. Women can thus use lamentation to manipulate actions (both onstage and off) and to express dangerous views while 'stay[ing] well within their prescribed gender roles'.[59] Men lament too, in literary texts as in life; Ann Suter, for example, has demonstrated that men also lament in Greek tragedy. Nevertheless, lamentation can be a particularly useful activity for women prohibited from other ways of expressing discontent and inciting action. Moreover, there is often an expectation that men display moderation in their grief: when a man's mourning is perceived to be wild or all-consuming, he may be criticised for displaying an 'effeminate' lack of restraint.[60] Lamentation is not exclusive to women, but is nonetheless a female-gendered activity, especially passionate, excessive and unrestrained forms of grieving.

Lamentation is a central way that women participate in revenge, especially in ancient Greek and Icelandic literature. According to Alexiou, women's behaviour in funeral rites 'coincides exactly with the role of women in cases of vengeance. Although the act itself rested with the men ... the women maintained the consciousness for the need to take revenge by constant lamentation and invocation at the tomb.'[61] While from a psychological standpoint, the repetitive cries of the mourner suggest the emotional paralysis of trauma, in political terms lamentation offers women a powerful form of complaint. Thus in many literary texts lamentation is a deliberate, carefully crafted performance, with subversive meanings and consequences, maintained in the face of extreme pressure. In Seneca's *The Trojan Women*, Hecuba instructs the chorus of women to loosen their hair, beat their breasts, and 'outdo the usual style of mourning' (*solitum flendi vincite morem*, 97), commenting 'yes, this appearance is right' (*placet hic habitus, placet*, 94–5) when they comply.[62] Aiming to intensify (as well as perhaps to alleviate) the pain of loss, Hecuba reopens wounds that are physical as well as emotional; striking her arms, she tells her dead son Hector: 'Every scar I made at your funeral must burst open, flow and stream with copious blood' (121–3).* Lamentation keeps the past alive, resisting the process whereby the pain fades. To adopt Francis Bacon's famous words about revenge, lamentation keeps wounds green which otherwise would heal and do well – wounds that are social, familial and political as well as personal and psychic. For those parents, siblings, friends and rulers who want to forget or conceal their crimes, lamentation marks a return of the repressed which also seeks to reinstate the suppressed.

In ancient Greece and Rome, women's lamentation could include keening, singing, self-harm (such as scratching one's face) and exaggerated displays of grief at the tomb (performed by professional mourners as well as the bereaved).[63] The potentially dangerous consequences of such displays, which could whip up vengeful passions and fuel vendettas, is evident in laws in Athens and elsewhere from the sixth century BC that attempt to restrict funeral rites.[64] Plutarch describes how Solon forbade 'everything disorderly and excessive in women's festivals, processions and funeral rites', including the 'laceration of cheeks, singing of set dirges and lamentation at other people's tombs' (*Solon* 21.4).[65] However, it is likely that these laws were not entirely successful, and exaggerated displays of grief are a recurrent feature in ancient Greek literature. There are key scenes of individual and ritualised mourning in Homer's *Iliad*[66] and in tragedy, as is evident in the lamentations of Sophocles' Antigone, Tecmessa in *Ajax*, Euripides' Hecuba and Andromache in *The Trojan Women*, Hecuba in *Hecuba*, Iphigenia in *Iphigenia in Aulis*, and the female chorus in Euripides' *The Suppliants*.

The subversive potential of lamentation is dramatised in Sophocles' *Electra*, in which Electra's grief for her father, Agamemnon, functions as a form of political protest which threatens Clytemnestra and Aegisthus' rule over Mycenae. As Helena Foley argues, Electra 'aims to provoke revenge through the awakening of shared pain ... Electra keeps alive the cause of the dead Agamemnon, and awakens the citizens' longing for the return of Orestes'. Her behaviour is effective: over the course of the play, the chorus gradually align themselves with her, eventually acting as co-conspirators.[67] Clytemnestra recognises the potentially damaging impact of Electra's behaviour, worrying that her daughter's 'chattering tongue, wagging in malice' (σὺν φθόνῳ ... πολυγλώσσῳ βοῇ, 641) will 'sow in all the city bad reports' (σπείρῃ ματαίαν βάξιν εἰς πᾶσαν πόλιν, 642).[68] Indeed, so threatening are Electra's public displays of grief that Chrysothemis warns that Aegisthus will force Electra to live the rest of her life in an underground cave if she refuses to stop (379–82). Thus, while lamentation is sometimes regarded as a repetitive state of inaction, Electra's mourning shows how it can act as a powerful form of complaint and a spur to political action.

---

* *fluat et multo sanguine manet / quamcumque tuo funere feci / rupta cicatrix.*

Although lamentation typically works to provoke men to action, it can also prepare the female speaker to take vengeance herself,[69] or operate as a covert means of revenge.[70] Andreas N. Michalopoulos explores the latter aspects of lamentation in 'A Phrygian Tale of Love and Revenge: *Oenone Paridi* (Ovid *Heroides* 5)', which focuses on Ovid's *Heroides*, a collection of fictional epistolary poems written as though by women from Greek and Roman mythology to the lovers who abandoned and mistreated them (in several pairs of letters, the lovers reply). Michalopoulos interprets the fifth letter, in which the nymph Oenone writes to Paris, her former lover, as a 'letter of revenge' that expresses Oenone's 'frustration and anger'. Michalopoulos demonstrates how Ovid's language and imagery alludes to events that await Paris 'in the dramatic future of the letter', hinting at her revenge to come. Countering the view that the female speakers of the *Heroides* offer a consistent view of women as pathetic and passive victims, the chapter thus shows how Ovid's female letter writers can exploit socially prized roles as a means of expressing their anger and preparing for vengeful action.[71]

Oenone's careful control of the language of complaint and her passive-aggressive linguistic dexterity run counter to many Roman writers' assessments of lament as a behaviour that disrupts self-possession and rationality. For men in particular, it was held to undermine one's gender identity and heroic status. Petra Schierl argues that Cicero, who influenced Roman tragedy's moralising, promotes the superiority of Roman tragedy through a distinction between 'Greek / Roman' and 'lament / endurance'.[72] While Cicero censures the Greek tragedians 'for presenting heroes reduced to tears and for establishing negative examples that enfeeble the human soul', he instead praises Pacuvius' Odysseus who 'does not lament to excess' (*Tusculanae disputations* 2.19–25; 2.48–51).[73] Some critics find a similar distrust of lament in Roman poetry[74] and also in tragedy, where grief rarely advances the plot and must be overcome.[75] That lamentation has lost status and purpose in Roman tragedy is evident in *The Trojan Women*. Hecuba's expressions of grief may powerfully convey her suffering and articulate the wrongs done to her and to Troy, but they do not stimulate any revenge action.[76] Instead, it is Achilles' ghost who fulfils this function, demanding the sacrifice of his intended bride, Polyxena, to appease his wrath (Sen. *Tro*. 190–6). It is typical of Seneca's tragedies that the ghost incites revenge action and that the emotion that triggers vengeance is anger rather than grief. It is typical too that the shaky grounds for Achilles' request are explicitly questioned in the text (here by Agamemnon, who counsels Pyrrhus, Achilles' son, to ignore the ghost's request as unjust and intemperate, 250–91). Thus, while grief remains a language of complaint in Senecan tragedy, it is often portrayed as an ineffectual medium that does not provoke action.

In Old Icelandic literature, female lamentation does have a prominent role in the revenge process. However, here the term 'lament' refers to the formal speeches and symbolic gestures women use to incite vengeance. These are rather different from the emotive wailing at burial sites that characterise Greek and Roman lament, but serve the same function in vendetta.[77] Although, as in Greek tragedy, there are women who take revenge themselves,[78] the typical woman of the sagas acts as an inciter to revenge, goading men to retaliate. Miller suggests that the absence of 'males as grievants is consistent with and probably attributable to the sex-typing of women's roles in the bloodfeud. Just as they were not appropriate expiators, they were not appropriate avengers.'[79] This female provocation takes place during formal *hvǫt* scenes (from the verb *hvetja*, 'to whet') of 'ceremonial charge', which are found in the very earliest Eddic poetry and can be distinguished from mere goading.[80] *Hvǫt* scenes often take place during a meal and are carefully choreographed: emblematic and staged components emphasise the listener's kinship and duty to the dead as well as the shameful nature of his inaction. Women give formal speeches, display the bloody clothes or the head of the deceased, sit a guest down next to an empty chair, and sing songs. In *Heiðarvíga saga*, when Þuríðr's son, Hallr, is killed, she incites her three surviving sons to take revenge through a symbolic meal intended to unsettle and shame them. First she serves them 'a huge ox-leg cut into thirds, to remind them of Hallr's dismembered body; and second, three stones, which are as hard to digest as the fact of Hallr's death'.[81] Miller relates *hvǫt* scenes to shaming rituals in other cultures where the weaker members of a group incite others into acting on their behalf, arguing that while such performances rely on (and promote) traditional gender roles, nevertheless a woman could play 'a central role in organizing the actions which she was socially disabled from undertaking herself'.[82]

Medieval literature exhibits divided views about the extent to which lamentation evinced a laudable piety or lack of faith in God's grace. Wider Christian tradition interprets tears as an eloquent form of contrition that speaks directly to God: 'Adam, Abraham, Isaac, Jacob, Moses, David, and Jeremiah are made exemplary by their tears', observe Kimberley Christine Patten and John Stratton Hawley, a statement also applicable to Peter, Jesus and Mary Magdalene.[83] However, while the fact that 'Jesus wept' over the death of Lazarus suggests the value of grief, excessive mourning was seen as blasphemous by Christian church fathers such as St John Chrysostom, for whom it indicated a lack of faith that the dead will be redeemed. Focusing on visual representations of Mary Magdalene's tears, Diane Apostolos-Cappadona distinguishes between quiet, saintly weeping, which is controlled and signifies a faith in God, and unrestrained crying, which involves the whole body and suggests a lack of faith.[84] The Christian ambivalence about lamentation became even more pronounced with Reformation theology, which prohibited many rites of mourning and intercessions on behalf of the dead. According to Katharine Goodland, the early modern lamenting figure articulates 'the cultural trauma of the Reformation, especially that associated with eradication of the doctrine of Purgatory, the suppression of Catholic mourning ritual, and iconoclasm against the pieta and female saints'.[85] The 'wailing for the dead', as it was known, was also seen as a dangerously female and irrational activity. In a funeral sermon for Martin Bucer in 1551, Matthew Parker 'admonishes his English audience to refrain from "womanish wayling, and childish infirmities ... for it is both unseemly and wicked to use any howling or blubbering for him"'.[86]

The view that lamentation can be irrational and effeminising is evident in Old English and in medieval literature more broadly, which often distinguishes between grief that incites heroic action and grief that overwhelms and incapacitates.[87] Men frequently lament their fallen comrades-in-arms (especially in the prelude to a battle), but such demonstrative behaviour is only perceived as acceptable when it is moderate or can be quickly redirected into heroic action. In *Beowulf*, after King Hrothgar's beloved warrior, Aeschere, has been killed by Grendel's mother, Beowulf counsels the king: 'do not grieve. It is always better to avenge dear ones than to indulge in mourning' (1384–5).* He then advises him: 'Bear up / and be the man I expect you to be' (1395–6).† Being a man here thus involves a 'manly' control of grief and rechannelling loss into vengeance.

The complex relationship between lamentation, masculinity and heroic action is explored by Anne Baden-Daintree in 'Lament and Vengeance in the Alliterative *Morte Arthure*'. Baden-Daintree argues that the fourteenth-century poem's earlier sections seem to distinguish between the contained grief that prompts heroic action and the debilitating grief which shocks and overwhelms: the fighting men's formal laments for their fallen comrades are qualitatively different from the grief displayed by the widow after the duchess, her foster-daughter, is raped and killed. However, this gendered model of male, moderate grief, and female, overwhelming grief, breaks down when Gawain, Arthur's beloved nephew, is killed in battle. Arthur himself becomes the grief-stricken lamenter, displaying behaviour that his knights view as both ineffectual and unseemly. Overwhelmed by his grief, Arthur uses words and gestures redolent of the widow's grief, and even compares himself to a widow. While Arthur eventually recovers sufficiently from his grief to return to battle, Baden-Daintree argues that Arthur's lament also marks his return to male homosocial bonds and to a heroic role.

King Arthur's grief in the alliterative *Morte Arthure* anticipates the depiction of the revenger in early modern tragedy, for while there are women whose laments trigger revenge in such drama,[88] more frequently the revenger is also the mourner who grieves for his dead family member, beloved or friend. In some respects, this new structure simply follows a Senecan model of ghosts triggering revenge. However, in Seneca's plays the operative emotion is anger rather than grief – vengeance is only achieved after the revenger whips himself up into a state of readiness through fury. Like the Senecan figure, the early modern revenger also passes through a set of emotions in his or her journey to revenge, although, crucially, these are profound sorrow, despair and self-hate: emotions that inhibit rather than ignite the revenge process.

---

* Ne sorga, snotor guma sélre bið aéghwaém / þæt hé his fréond wrece þonne hé fela murne.

† ðýs dógor þú geþyld hafa / wéana gehwylces swá ic þé wéne tó.

Anger plays an important part, but often only at a later stage, countering the inertia brought on by grief. Early modern revenge plays tend to focus on the protagonist's overwhelming grief as the central emotional experience, fusing the Senecan model of fury-driven vengeance with modes of channelling grief and despair inherited from medieval cultures of feeling and devotion, validating grief as an appropriate response to loss as well as an obstacle that must be overcome.

This new configuration of grief and revenge is examined in Rebecca Yearling's '"Nursed in Blood": Masculinity and Grief in Marston's *Antonio's Revenge*'. Yearling proposes that Antonio, the revenger, is also a mourner who sees his grief as an emasculating threat to the revenge task. Following convention, Antonio is urged to take revenge by a ghost (here the ghost of his father), but unlike other contemporary revenge dramas, the play ends with Antonio alive and unpunished. Critics have puzzled over this unusual ending, seeing it either as evidence of Marston's lack of artistic skill or as a uniquely positive depiction of revenge as necessary and just. Yearling rejects both interpretations, arguing instead that the jarring ending is characteristic of Marston, who frequently pitches genre conventions against perplexing ethical questions in order to unsettle the spectator's aesthetic expectations and moral judgements. In Yearling's account, the play questions whether revenge can be beneficial, allowing victimised men to recover from trauma and 'to reclaim their lost masculinity'. Antonio may indeed pass from 'tears to blood', coming to embody a vengeful hyper-masculinity; yet Antonio's new version of manliness is monstrous and 'not far from psychosis'.

Yearling's proposition raises wider questions about the gendering and value of grief in the period. As Patricia Phillippy argues:

> Sixteenth- and seventeenth-century death manuals, representational forms, and cultural practices revised women's long association with ritualistic acts of mourning to portray feminine sorrow as excessive, violent, and immoderate, while representing men's grief – both stoic and short-lived – as correcting and improving upon 'wivishe' mourning.[89]

While *Antonio's Revenge* follows this model (representing Antonio's grief as a 'feminine' form of excessive mourning which he must overcome), it nonetheless simultaneously suggests the destructive consequences of taking such cultural values to their logical conclusion. Antonio articulates and embodies the period's negative view of feminine mourning, but the play also provides a framework through which to interrogate these values, representing the movement from sorrow to anger as neither psychologically beneficial nor morally right.

Tanya Pollard's 'What's Hecuba to Shakespeare?' explores the marginalisation of female mourning through Shakespeare's engagements with Euripides' *Hecuba*, the most popular Greek play in sixteenth-century Europe. Whereas Euripides' play provides a model 'of emotionally affecting tragedy that was female-centered, rooted in lament, and culminating in triumphant action', *Hamlet* sidelines female mourning, offering instead a male protagonist who remains distant, observing and commenting on these figures and the action of the play. Hecuba's passionate laments contrasts with Gertrude's inadequate mourning and Hamlet's ambivalent grief. As Pollard argues: Hamlet 'refuses to follow the genre's conventions, modelled on Hecuba, of transforming lament into revenge'. Instead he occupies a position than is akin to the Greek chorus, which is 'predicated more on watching and reflecting than on action', offering a 'new model of tragedy' centred on male suffering, indecision and introspection.

Janet Clare's '"She's Turned Fury": Women Transmogrified in Revenge Plays' also explores early modern responses to Hecuba, arguing that whereas Euripides' Hecuba is a sympathetic tragic heroine and successful avenger, this model could not be replicated in early modern plays. Instead the two aspects of Hecuba's role, that of lamenting mother and ruthless avenger, 'bifurcate in English revenge tragedy'. Pitiful, mourning mothers such as Isabella from *The Spanish Tragedy* are unsuccessful, while savage ones, such as Tamora from *Titus Andronicus* and Queen Margaret in the *Henry VI* trilogy, are 'abhorrent and aberrant', inflicting violence from a position of power. Contrasting the English tradition with that of Germany and France – where artistic treatments of the Biblical Judith decapitating General Holofernes offer a heroic, political image of female vengeance – Clare concludes that in England 'revenge was quite definitely not a woman's business'.

In readings by Yearling and Pollard, early modern playwrights challenge the idea of heroic masculinity as being bound up with retaliatory violence: while Yearling maintains that Marston sees the transfiguration of grief into revenge action as ethically and psychically corrosive, Pollard maintains that Hamlet advances an alternative, contemplative, detached position for the male revenger. Lesel Dawson's 'Outfacing Vengeance: Heroic Dying in Webster's *The Duchess of Malfi* and Ford's *The Broken Heart*' suggests that this reconfiguration of tragic masculinity corresponds to a new vision of the heroic, outlined by Mary Beth Rose, which privileges 'not the active confrontation with danger, but the capacity to endure it, to resist and suffer with patience and fortitude'.[90] While this 'heroism of endurance' reinforces the denigration of female, 'excessive' mourning, it simultaneously celebrates values traditionally thought of as feminine, contributing to the positive value given to 'feminised' male figures and opening up a space for female heroes. Within revenge narratives, Dawson argues that the heroics of endurance allows the victim to resist the revenger's tyrannous 'script', acting as a form of personal and political resistance. However, while 'heroic dying may provide even the most downtrodden revenge victims with a powerful means to outface vengeance', differences in how the duchess' and Ithocles' deaths are represented 'suggests the persistence of a model in which masochistic self-sacrifice is seen as essential to women, and bad for men'.

In the essays that follow, the assembled group of scholars examine both enduring archetypes and exceptions; in tracing both patterns and deviations, their readings outline the ways in which the relationships between revenge and gender have been configured and reconfigured in literature, and the ways in which gendered structures persist, sometimes in unexpected ways. This work is still ongoing: as in Bouguereau's *Orestes Pursued by the Furies* (1862), the image with which I started, the action, arrested momentarily by the viewer's gaze, is still in motion.

NOTES

1. For reinterpretations of Clytemnestra, see: Edith Hall, 'Aeschylus' Clytemnestra versus her Senecan Tradition', in Fiona Macintosh, Pantelis Michelakis, Edith Hall and Oliver Taplin (eds), *Agamemnon in Performance: 458 BC to AD 2004* (Oxford: Oxford University Press, 2005), pp. 53–76.
2. Nancy Sorkin Rabinowitz, *Anxiety Veiled: Euripides and the Traffic in Women* (London: Cornell University Press, 1993).
3. There are a number of excellent studies that examine the wider revenge tradition or specific examples of influence and intertextuality. Examples include: Gordon Braden, *Renaissance Tragedy and the Senecan Tradition: Anger's Privilege* (London: Yale University Press, 1985); Charles Martindale and Michelle Martindale, *Shakespeare and the Uses of Antiquity* (London: Routledge, 1990); Robert S. Miola, *Shakespeare and Classical Tragedy: The Influence of Seneca* (Oxford: Clarendon Press, 1992); Jonathan Bate, *Shakespeare and Ovid* (Oxford: Clarendon Press, 1994); John Kerrigan, *Revenge Tragedy: Aeschylus to Armageddon* (Oxford: Clarendon Press, 1996); Charles Martindale and A. B. Taylor (eds), *Shakespeare and the Classics* (Cambridge: Cambridge University Press, 2004); Colin Burrow, *Shakespeare and Classical Antiquity* (Oxford: Oxford University Press, 2013); and Tanya Pollard, *Greek Tragic Women on Shakespearean Stages* (Oxford: Oxford University Press, 2017).
4. See, for example, Robert N. Watson, *The Rest is Silence: Death as Annihilation in the English Renaissance* (Berkeley: University of California Press, 1994); and Michael Neill, *Issues of Death: Mortality and Identity in English Renaissance Tragedy* (Oxford: Clarendon Press, 1997).
5. Judith Butler, *Gender Trouble: Feminism and the Subversion of Identity* (New York: Routledge, 1990), p. 25.
6. Judith Butler, 'The Body You Want: Liz Kotz Interviews Judith Butler', *Artforum* (November, 1992), p. 84.
7. Gabriel Herman, *Ritualised Friendship and the Greek City* (Cambridge: Cambridge University Press, 1987), p. 126. Cf. Fiona McHardy, *Revenge in Athenian Culture* (London: Bloomsbury, 2008), p. 115.
8. McHardy, *Revenge*, pp. 104, 107, discusses the pragmatic social and political reasons that Orestes takes revenge in Homer and in ancient tragedy.

9. Kerrigan, *Revenge Tragedy*, p. 10. See also, Deborah Willis, '"The Gnawing Vulture": Revenge, Trauma Theory, and *Titus Andronicus*', *Shakespeare Quarterly* 53.1 (2002), pp. 21–52; and Linda Woodbridge, *English Revenge Drama: Money, Resistance, Equality* (Cambridge: Cambridge University Press, 2010), who emphasises revenge's relationship to economic models of payment and equivalency.
10. Anne Pippin Burnett, *Revenge in Attic and Later Tragedy* (Berkeley: University of California Press, 1998), p. 64. See also Mary Whitlock Blundell, *Helping Friends and Harming Enemies: A Study in Sophocles and Greek Ethics* (Cambridge: Cambridge University Press, 1989).
11. See, for example, Richard Seaford, *Reciprocity and Ritual: Homer and Tragedy in the Developing City-State* (Oxford: Clarendon Press, 1994); David Cohen, *Law, Violence and Community in Classical Athens* (Cambridge: Cambridge University Press, 1995); Matthew R. Christ, *The Litigious Athenian* (Baltimore: Johns Hopkins University Press, 1998); Elizabeth S. Belfiore, *Murder Among Friends: Violation of 'Philia' in Greek Tragedy* (Oxford: Oxford University Press, 2000); Donna Wilson, *Ransom, Revenge and Heroic Identity in the* Iliad (Cambridge: Cambridge University Press, 2002).
12. Gabriel Herman, *Morality and Behaviour in Democratic Athens: A Social History* (Cambridge: Cambridge University Press, 2006), sees 'civic restraint' as an Athenian ideal that counters the ideology of vendetta. Against this view, Cohen, *Law, Violence and Community*, argues that Athens was a feuding society and that ideas of retaliatory violence were central to Athenian law. Christ, *Litigious Athenian*, attempts to reconcile these views. For dikē's range of meanings, see Simon Goldhill, *Reading Greek Tragedy* (Cambridge: Cambridge University Press, 1986), pp. 33–56.
13. Danielle S. Allen, *The World of Prometheus: The Politics of Punishment in Democratic Athens* (Princeton: Princeton University Press, 2000), p. 135. Allen further comments that 'Anger had to be kept out of the family if its valorisation in the realm of politics was not to have negative implications' (p. 135).
14. William Ian Miller, 'In Defense of Revenge', in Barbara Hanawalt and David Wallace (eds), *Medieval Crime and Social Control* (London: University of Minnesota Press, 1999), pp. 70–89 (p. 70); David Clark, *Gender, Violence, and the Past in Edda and Saga* (Oxford: Oxford University Press, 2012), p. 17. Miller maintains that for the inhabitants of Icelandic sagas, 'revenge was constitutive of much of their public, personal and moral order' (ibid. 70). Ólafur Briem, *Íslendinga sögur og nútíminn* (Reykjavík: Almenna bókafélagð, 1972), pp. 32–3, also sees male honour codes as central. Hermann Pálsson, *Art and Ethics in Hrafnkel's Saga* (Copenhagen: Munksgaard, 1971), rejects this view, arguing that the sagas offer moral lessons about the dangers of vengeance and should be read in relation to medieval Christianity. Vilhjálmur Árnason, 'Morality and Social Structure in the Icelandic Sagas', *The Journal of English and*

Germanic Philology 90.2 (1991), pp. 157–74, summarises ethical debates about the sagas; in a more recent article, 'An Ethos in Transformation: Conflicting Values in the Sagas', *Gripla* 20 (2009), pp. 217–40, Árnason argues that 'the saga describes an ethos in the process of transformation from heathen values to Christian values' (p. 237).

15. See Daniel Lord Smail, 'Factions and Vengeance in Renaissance Italy: A Review Article', *Comparative Studies in Society and History* 38.4 (1996), pp. 781–9, for an overview of the debate as to whether revenge is 'an irrational system of legal redress located in primitive societies and destined to be cast aside with the advance of law' or 'both rational and effective when practiced by members of stateless societies' (p. 782).

16. For discussion of Stoicism and subjectivity, see: John G. Fitch (ed.), *Seneca* (Oxford: Oxford University Press, 2008); Shadi Bartsch and David Wray (eds), *Seneca and the Self* (Cambridge: Cambridge University Press, 2009); and Sesse Tateo, 'Angry Women and Men in German Drama', in Karl A. E. Enenkel and Anita Traninger (eds), *Discourses of Anger in the Early Modern Period* (Leiden: Brill, 2015), pp. 97–125, who discusses the gendering of anger in Seneca and in German drama.

17. Martha Nussbaum, 'Serpents in the Soul: A Reading of Seneca's *Medea*', in James J. Clauss and Sarah Iles Johnston (eds), *Medea: Essays on Medea in Myth, Literature, Philosophy, and Art* (Princeton: Princeton University Press, 1997), pp. 219–52.

18. Nigel Saul, *Chivalry in Medieval England* (Cambridge, MA: Harvard University Press, 2011), pp. 183, 190.

19. Ronald Broude, 'Revenge and Revenge Tragedy in Renaissance England', *Renaissance Quarterly* 28.1 (1975), pp. 38–58 (p. 43). Broude argues that revenge tragedy 'mediate(s) between the elegant simplicity of Tudor-Stuart theory and the demoralizing inconsistency of Tudor-Stuart justice' (p. 58). Focusing on Kyd's rendition of the vegetative soul, Christopher Crosbie, '*Oeconomia* and the Vegetative Soul: Rethinking Revenge in *The Spanish Tragedy*', *English Literary Renaissance* 38.1 (2008), pp. 3–33, argues that revenge is 'not merely sensationally brutish but also coherent, the natural outgrowth of a middling sort circumscribed by an artificial yet entrenched system of preferment and advancement' (p. 33).

20. Kristine Steenbergh, 'Emotions and Gender: The Case of Anger in Early Modern Revenge Tragedies', in Jonas Liliequist (ed.), *A History of Emotions 1200–1800* (London: Pickering & Chatto, 2012), pp. 119–34 (p. 122). Steenbergh argues that positive views of revenge and anger were associated with 'aristocratic traditions of blood revenge' whereas pejorative representations belonged to 'a younger generation of middle-class administrators who sought to expand the legal system and eradicate practices of private revenge' (p. 122). See Stuart Carroll, *Blood and Vengeance in Early Modern France* (Oxford: Oxford University Press, 2006), for an excellent overview of intrafamilial disputes over property and inheritance in early modern France.

21. Lily B. Campbell, 'Theories of Revenge in Renaissance England', *Modern Philology* 28.3 (1931), pp. 281–96, argues that revenge was unequivocally condemned, a view backed up by Fredson Bowers' *Elizabethan Revenge Tragedy, 1587–1642* (Princeton: Princeton University Press, 1940). However, Philip J. Ayres, 'Degrees of Heresy: Justified Revenge and Elizabethan Narratives', *Studies in Philology* 69.4 (1972), pp. 461–74, suggests that attitudes were more mixed and that texts differentiate between types of revenge and the moral culpability of the revenger. Harry Keyishian, *The Shapes of Revenge: Victimization, Vengeance, and Vindictiveness in Shakespeare* (Atlantic Highlands, NJ: Humanities Press, 1995), distinguishes between just forms of revenge, which can be redemptive, and vindictiveness. Woodbridge, *English Revenge Drama*, emphasises revenge as a tool for justice.
22. See, for example, Charles A. Hallett and Elaine S. Hallett, *The Revenger's Madness: A Study of Revenge Tragedy Motifs* (London: University of Nebraska Press, 1980), who argue that the revenger's madness is necessary in getting over the prohibition against murder; R. A. Foakes, *Shakespeare and Violence* (Cambridge: Cambridge University Press, 2003), explores 'the dramatic possibilities arising from the disparities between classical and Christian values' (p. 135).
23. For example, Heather Hirschfeld, *The End of Satisfaction: Drama and Repentance in the Age of Shakespeare* (London: Cornell University Press, 2014), explores the 'special reciprocity, even entanglement, between revenge and repentance' (p. 65); and Steven Mullaney, *The Reformation of Emotions in the Age of Shakespeare* (Chicago: The University of Chicago Press, 2015) argues that revenge tragedy was one of the literary genres that allowed Elizabethans to understand the affective upheavals and cognitive gaps that resulted from Reformation.
24. See, for example, Carol J. Clover, 'Maiden Warriors and Other Sons', *The Journal of English and Germanic Philology* 85.1 (1986), pp. 35–49. Carol J. Clover, 'Regardless of Sex: Men, Women, and Power in Early Northern Europe', *Representations* 44 (1993), pp. 1–28, argues that in Old Icelandic literature's manliness is based 'to an extraordinary extent on winnable and losable attributes', rendering gender a permeable category in which 'a physical woman could become a social man' (pp. 13, 19).
25. William Ian Miller, 'Choosing the Avenger: Some Aspects of the Bloodfeud in Medieval Iceland and England', *Law and History Review* 1.2 (1983), pp. 159–204 (p. 185).
26. Jane Chance, *Woman as Hero in Old English Literature* (Syracuse: Syracuse University Press, 1986), pp. 1–12; Carol Parrish Jamison, 'Traffic of Women in Germanic Literature: The Role of the Peace Pledge in Marital Exchanges', *Women in German Yearbook* 20 (2004), pp. 13–36.
27. See also, for example, Elizabeth Cary, *The Tragedy of Mariam* (1613), in David Bevington, Lars Engle, Katharine Eisaman Maus and Eric Rasmussen (eds), *English Renaissance Drama* (London: W. W. Norton &

Company, 2002) and Harding, S[amuel], *Sicily and Naples, or, the Fatall Union*, ed. Joan Warthling Roberts (New York and London, 1986).
28. Janet Clare, *Revenge Tragedies of the Renaissance* (Horndon: Northcote House Publishers, 2006), pp. 116, 117.
29. Wendy Griswold, *Renaissance Revivals: City Comedy and Revenge Tragedy in the London Theatre 1576–1980* (Chicago: The University of Chicago Press, 1986), sees this as integral to revenge tragedy's ongoing appeal; by 'mixing categories that are customarily separate', such as living and dead, friend and enemy, and violating sacred bonds, such narratives induce fascination and horror' (p. 78).
30. William Shakespeare, *3 Henry VI*, ed. Andrew S. Cairncross, Arden Shakespeare (London: Arden Shakespeare, 1969), 1.4.137.
31. See, for example, Karin S. Coddon, '"For Show or Useless Property": Necrophilia and *The Revengers Tragedy*', *English Literary History* 61.1 (1994), pp. 71–88; Cynthia Marshall, *The Shattering of the Self: Violence, Subjectivity, and Early Modern Texts* (London: Johns Hopkins University Press, 2002), explores the ways that violence towards women is enhanced and complicated by the 'masochistic viewing position' of the spectator (p. 122).
32. Eileen Allman, *Jacobean Revenge Tragedy and the Politics of Virtue* (Newark, DE: University of Delaware Press, 1999), argues that 'the tyrant's power over his male subjects relies, in fact, on their mutual misogyny in understanding signifiers of femaleness as degrading to men' (p. 41).
33. *Beowulf: A Student Edition*, ed. George Jack (Oxford: Clarendon Press, 1994). My translations are from *Beowulf*, trans. Seamus Heaney (London: Faber and Faber, 1999), pp. 52, 50. Grendel and his mother are also described as *ellorgaéstas* (1349; 'from some other world', p. 45). Grendel's mother is said to look like a woman, *idese onlícnæs*, rather than be one. As Jane C. Nitzsche [also known as Jane Chance], 'The Structural Unity of *Beowulf*: The Problem of Grendel's Mother', *Texas Studies in Literature and Language* 22.3 (1980), pp. 287–303, points out, she is frequently described in masculine terms even as her role as mother is emphasised throughout the poem (pp. 288–9).
34. Chance, *Woman as Hero*, p. 97.
35. Paul Acker, 'Horror and the Maternal in *Beowulf*', *PMLA* 121.3 (2006), pp. 702–16 (p. 708).
36. Jack (ed.), *Beowulf*, translates as to 'have in mind' (p. 104).
37. Heaney, *Beowulf*, p. 42.
38. Froma Zeitlin, *Playing the Other: Gender and Society in Classical Greek Literature* (Chicago: The University of Chicago Press, 1996), p. 347. Edith Hall, *Inventing the Barbarian: Greek Self-Definition through Tragedy* (Oxford: Clarendon Press, 1989), explores, in a related fashion, how foreign others are also crucial to Athenian self-definition.
39. Victoria Wohl, *Intimate Commerce: Exchange, Gender, and Subjectivity in Greek Tragedy* (Austin: University of Texas Press, 1997), p. xxvi.

40. Helene P. Foley, *Female Acts in Greek Tragedy* (Princeton: Princeton University Press, 2001), p. 3.
41. Linda Bamber, *Comic Women, Tragic Men: A Study of Gender and Genre in Shakespeare* (Stanford: Stanford University Press, 1982), p. 4. Critics have found ways of subverting this aspect of early modern tragedy. In an important study, Pascale Aebischer, *Shakespeare's Violated Bodies: Stage and Screen Performance* (Cambridge: Cambridge University Press, 2004), uses performance and performance studies to enable female characters who are 'evacuated, mutilated or killed into silence' to take centre stage (p. 5).
42. Alison Findlay, *A Feminist Perspective on Renaissance Drama* (Oxford: Blackwell Publishers, 1998), pp. 49, 83.
43. Naomi Conn Liebler, 'Introduction: Wonder Woman, or the Female Tragic Hero', in Naomi Conn Liebler (ed.), *The Female Tragic Hero in Renaissance Drama* (Basingstoke: Palgrave Macmillan, 2002), p. 2. See also Lisa Hopkins, *The Female Hero in English Renaissance Tragedy* (Houndmills: Palgrave Macmillan, 2002).
44. Woodbridge, *English Revenge Drama*, p. 28.
45. Marguerite A. Tassi, *Women and Revenge in Shakespeare: Gender, Genre, and Ethics* (Selinsgrove: Susquehanna University Press, 2011).
46. Elizabeth Bryson Bongie, 'Heroic Elements in the *Medea* of Euripides', *Transactions of the American Philological Association* 107 (1977), pp. 27–56 (pp. 38, 27). Bernard M. W. Knox, 'The *Medea* of Euripides', *Yale Classical Studies* 25 (1977) 193–225, also argues for her heroic status and resemblance to Sophoclean heroes; Deborah Boedeker, 'Euripides' Medea and the Vanity of ΛΟΓΟΙ', *Classical Philology* 86.2 (1991), pp. 95–112, demonstrates how 'Medea appropriates and uses against her enemies each of the forms of discourse which she accuses Jason of having abused' (pp. 97–8).
47. Helene Foley, 'Medea's Divided Self', *Classical Antiquity* 8.1 (1989), pp. 61–85 (p. 81).
48. Zeitlin, *Playing the Other*, p. 347, n. 13.
49. William Shakespeare, *Much Ado About Nothing*, ed. Claire McEachern, Arden Shakespeare (London: Arden Shakespeare, 2006), 4.1.288.
50. Raymond J. Rice, 'Cannibalism and the Act of Revenge in Tudor-Stuart Drama', *Studies in English Literature* 44.2 (2004), pp. 279–316, explores this scene in relation to images of cannibalism in revenge plays.
51. McHardy, *Revenge*, has argued that women were in fact the more vengeful gender (pp. 37–41).
52. John G. Gager, *Curse Tablets and Binding Spells from the Ancient World* (Oxford: Oxford University Press, 1992), observes that 'just as *defixiones* cut across all social categories, they were not respecters of gender' (p. 119).
53. Esther Eidinow, *Oracles, Curses, and Risk among the Ancient Greeks* (Oxford: Oxford University Press, 2007), p. 227. For a compendium of ancient curses see: Gager, *Curse Tablets*, pp. 175–99.

54. Euripides, *Hecuba*, trans. David Kovacs, in David Kovacs (ed.), *Children of Heracles; Hippolytus; Andromache; Hecuba*, revised edition, Loeb Classical Library 484 (London: Harvard University Press, 2005).
55. Laurel Bowman, 'The Curse of Oedipus in *Oedipus at Colonus*', *Scholia: Studies in Classical Antiquity*, ns 16 (2007), pp. 1–11, argues that Oedipus' 'change in status from refugee to saviour hero is produced by his gradual comprehension and ultimate use of his power to curse his sons' (p. 2). See also, Rebecca W. Bushnell, *Prophesying Tragedy: Sign and Voice in Sophocles' Theban Plays* (Ithaca: Cornell University Press, 1988), p. 98.
56. In a complementary study, Pauline Ripat, 'Cheating Women: Curse Tablets and Roman Wives', in Kimberly B. Stratton and Dayna S. Kalleres (eds), *Daughters of Hecate: Women and Magic in the Ancient World* (Oxford: Oxford University Press, 2014), pp. 341–65, argues that Roman wives used curse tablets to protect their marriage and household status when threatened by a husband's adulterous relationship with a slave, a relationship 'not considered adultery by law or social custom' (p. 345).
57. Margaret Alexiou, *The Ritual Lament in Greek Tradition* (Cambridge: Cambridge University Press, 1974), p. 21.
58. Karen Stears, 'Death Becomes Her: Gender and Athenian Death Ritual', in Ann Suter (ed.), *Lament: Studies in the Ancient Mediterranean and Beyond* (Oxford: Oxford University Press, 2008), pp. 139–55, makes this comment relation to ancient practices (p. 151). See also Ann Suter, 'Introduction', in Suter (ed.), *Lament*.
59. Casey Dué, 'Lament as Speech Act in Sophocles', in Kirk Ormand (ed.), *A Companion to Sophocles* (Oxford: Wiley-Blackwell, 2012), pp. 236–50 (pp. 236–7). See also, Casey Dué, *The Captive Woman's Lament in Greek Tragedy* (Austin: University of Texas Press, 2006); Foley, *Female Acts*, pp. 19–56.
60. Ann Suter, 'Male Lament in Greek Tragedy', in Suter (ed.), *Lament*, pp. 156–80, rejects this view, arguing that that male characters frequently lament in Athenian tragedy and that 'there is no difference between male and female laments in occasion, strophic structures, meters, topoi, or linguistic features' (p. 165). Katharine Derderian, *Leaving Words to Remember: Greek Mourning and the Advent of Literacy* (Leiden: Brill, 2001), on the other hand, argues that in the Homeric poems there is a clear distinction between men's and women's forms of grief and their impact: while men's mourning leads to action and glory, women's mourning is passive and ineffectual.
61. Alexiou, *Ritual Lament*, p. 22.
62. Seneca, *Hercules; Trojan Women; Phoenician Women; Medea; Phaedra*, ed. and trans. by John G. Fitch (London: Harvard University Press, 2002).
63. For an overview of ancient Greek lament and its relation to funeral ritual and contemporary Greek practice, see: Alexiou, *Ritual Lament*. Alexiou makes a distinction between thrênos, 'the set dirge composed and performed by the professional mourners', which was professional and more

restrained, and góos 'the spontaneous weeping of the kinswomen', which was passionate and unrestrained (p. 103). See also Suter (ed.), *Lament*.

64. According to Ann Suter, 'Introduction', in Suter (ed.), *Lament*, the laws in Athens and elsewhere attempting to restrict lamentation have been 'interpreted as efforts to control women's public activity or to curb the power of aristocratic families in the developing democracy in the polis' (p. 4).
65. Alexiou, *Ritual Lament*, pp. 15, 12. Nicole Loraux, *The Mourning Voice: An Essay on Greek Tragedy*, trans. Elizabeth Trapnell Rawlings (London: Cornell University Press, 2002), argues that within such a climate, plays take on a particularly powerful role, allowing an outlet for the expression of tragic suffering.
66. Critics are divided as to whether female lamentation in the Homeric poems is portrayed as ineffectual or whether it provides a framework through which to critique the heroic male codes of honour. For example, whereas Hélène Monsacré, *Les larmes d'Achille: le héros, la femme et la souffrance dans la poésie d'Homère* (Paris: Albin Michel, 1984) and Derderian, *Leaving Words*, see women's laments as impotent and infantilising (unlike men's displays of grief that lead to action), Christine Perkell, 'Reading the Laments of *Iliad* 24', in Suter (ed.), *Lament*, pp. 93–117, argues that women's laments 'function to put heroic ideology into question' (p. 94).
67. Foley, *Female Acts*, pp. 151, 157.
68. Sophocles, *Electra*, trans. and ed. David Grene, in David Grene and Richmond Lattimore (eds), *Greek Tragedies* (London: The University of Chicago Press, 1960), vol. 2.
69. As in the case of Sophocles' Electra, who resolves to take revenge herself when she believes (wrongly) that Orestes is dead.
70. The debates about the enigmatic ending of the medieval poem 'The Wife's Lament' testify to the difficulty at distinguishing between self-abnegating lamentation and manipulative revenge. Critics remain divided as to whether the poem ends with the speaker's stoical acceptance of her husband's abandonment or with a curse. See, for example, Anne L. Klinck, *The Old English Elegies: A Critical Edition and Genre Study* (London: McGill-Queen's University Press, 1992), pp. 50–1; Barrie Ruth Straus, 'Women's Words as Weapons: Speech as Action in "The Wife's Lament"', *Texas Studies in Literature and Language* 23.2 (1981), pp. 268–85; and John D. Niles, 'The Problem of the Ending of the Wife's Lament', *Speculum* 78.4 (2003), pp. 1107–50, which contains an excellent overview of medieval cursing practices.
71. Judith Goodsell, 'Generic Experimentation in Ovid's *Heroides*', in Michelle Borg and Graeme Miles (eds), *Approaches to Genre in the Ancient World* (Newcastle upon Tyne: Cambridge Scholars Publishing, 2013), pp. 59–78, also argues that Ovid's poems incorporate lamentation as language of 'protest and challenge' (p. 74).
72. Petra Schierl, 'Roman Tragedy – Ciceronian Tragedy? Cicero's Influence on

Our Perception of Republican Tragedy', in George W. M. Harrison (ed.), *Brill's Companion to Roman Tragedy* (Leiden: Brill, 2015), pp. 45–62 (p. 62).
73. Ibid. pp. 51, 53.
74. Vassiliki Panoussi, *Vergil's Aeneid and Greek Tragedy: Ritual, Empire, and Intertext* (Cambridge: Cambridge University Press, 2009), p. 6. Panoussi suggests that the *Aeneid* contrasts 'death and mourning ... and the successful control of grief, which eventually benefits humanity' (p. 159).
75. A similar pattern is evident in other contemporary plays. Christine M. King 'Seneca's *Hercules Oetaeus*: A Stoic Interpretation of the Greek Myth', *Greece & Rome* 18.2 (1971), pp. 215–22, argues that in *Hercules Oetaeus* (no longer attributed to Seneca) 'the injunction not to lament ... is because Hercules is trying to rouse a Stoic attitude in his mother', unlike the Sophoclean Hercules, who is worried that his ghost will haunt Hyllus (p. 220).
76. Wolfgang Clemen, *English Tragedy before Shakespeare: The Development of Dramatic Speech* (Abingdon: Routledge, 2011; first published in 1961), observes that unlike in Greek tragedy, Seneca's speeches of lamentation are 'entirely divorced from the sphere of concrete action' (p. 220).
77. William Ian Miller 'Emotions and the Sagas', in Gísli Pálsson (ed.), *From Sagas to Society: Comparative Approaches to Early Iceland* (Middlesex: Hisarlik Press, 1992), pp. 89–109, argues that the emotions in the sagas are not directly expressed but implied. While women use symbolic actions to display their loss, they speak in a matter-of-fact manner (p. 107). See also Sif Rikhardsdottir, 'Translating Emotion: Vocalisation and Embodiment in *Yvain* and *Ívens Saga*', in Frank Brandsma, Carolyne Larrington and Corinne Saunders (eds), *Emotions in Medieval Arthurian Literature: Body, Mind, Voice* (Cambridge: Boydell and Brewer, 2015), pp. 161–80, who argues that 'dialogue is, in fact, frequently used to *obscure* internal emotive life in the sagas, rather than *expressing* it' (p. 168).
78. Clover, 'Maiden Warriors'.
79. Miller, 'Choosing the Avenger', p. 185.
80. Ibid. pp. 176, 181.
81. Sandra Ballif Straubhaar, *Old Norse Women's Poetry: The Voices of Female Skalds* (Cambridge: D. S. Brewer, 2011), p. 20. See also *The Saga of the Slayings on the Heath*, trans. Keneva Kunz, in *The Complete Sagas of Icelanders*, Viðar Hreinsson (ed.), vol. 4 (Reykjavík: Leifur Eiríksson, 1997), p. 105.
82. William Ian Miller, *Bloodtaking and Peacemaking: Feud, Law and Society in Saga Iceland* (London: The University of Chicago Press, 1990), p. 212. A woman in such scenes acts as 'the self-appointed guardian of the honor of her men and as such she generally sees honor as unnuanced heroism' (p. 212).
83. Kimberley Christine Patton and John Stratton Hawley, 'Introduction', in Kimberley Christine Patton and John Stratton Hawley (eds), *Holy Tears*:

Weeping in the Religious Imagination (Oxford: Princeton University Press, 2005), p. 13.
84. Diane Apostolos-Cappadona, '"Pray with Tears and Your Request Will Find a Hearing": On the Iconology of the Magdalene's Tears', in Patton and Hawley (eds), *Holy Tears*, pp. 201–28. In the same volume, Santha Bhattacharji, 'Tears and Screaming: Weeping in the Spirituality of Margery Kempe', argues that these distinctions do not hold in the case of Kempe, who represents her noisy public weeping as divinely authorised, transcendent and efficacious (pp. 229–41).
85. Katharine Goodland, *Female Mourning and Tragedy in Medieval and Renaissance English Drama: From the Raising of Lazarus to King Lear* (Aldershot: Ashgate, 2005), p. 1.
86. Quoted in Katharine Goodland, '"Vs for to wepe no man may let": Accommodating Female Grief in the Medieval English Lazarus Plays', *Early Theatre* 8.1 (2005), p. 71.
87. Rikhardsdottir, 'Translating Emotion', in Brandsma, Larrington and Saunders (eds), *Emotions in Medieval Arthurian Literature*, argues that there is no such correlation between whetting and lamenting in medieval romance. These cries are dissociated from 'the social obligations of the blood-feud society' allowing for 'an emphasis on the emotional itself' (p. 178).
88. See, for example, the opening of John Fletcher and William Shakespeare's *The Two Noble Kinsmen* (c.1613–14), 1.1.
89. Patricia Phillippy, *Women, Death and Literature in Post-Reformation England* (Cambridge: Cambridge University Press, 2002), p. 1. Phillippy draws on Juliana Schiesari, *The Gendering of Melancholia: Feminism, Psychoanalysis, and the Symbolics of Loss in Renaissance Literature* (London: Cornell University Press, 1992), who argues that early modern period (and beyond) advances a view of grief which celebrates male melancholia (as intellectual and controlled) and denigrates feminine practices of mourning (as excessive and irrational). See also Goodland, *Female Mourning*, who argues that these changes result in part from the Reformation, which radically curtailed established practices in mourning and offered a different conception of the afterlife.
90. Mary Beth Rose, *Gender and Heroism in Early Modern English Literature* (London: The University of Chicago Press, 2002), pp. xii, xxi.

PART I

THE GENDERING OF REVENGE

CHAPTER I

Why are the Erinyes Female? or, What is so Feminine about Revenge?

Edith Hall

Sweet is revenge – especially to women. (Byron, *Don Juan*, 1.124)

Females have been routinely associated in the Western tradition with vindictive emotions and vengeful crimes. Colourful examples of the stereotypical vengeful female can be identified all the way from Aeschylus' Clytemnestra, whose spectre wakens the chorus of foul Erinyes (Latin Furies) to avenge her murder in *Eumenides*, to Alex Forrest in Adrian Lyne's dismally sexist 1987 revenge movie *Fatal Attraction* and beyond. This essay explores the role played in this triumphant feat of patriarchal ideology by the identity, gender and role of the Erinys.

One stalwart of the Renaissance tragic stage was the vengeful female – and especially the retaliatory mother – and she was fundamentally informed by the classical models, especially Clytemnestra and Medea.[1] Tamora in the late sixteenth-century Shakespearean *Titus Andronicus* actually dresses up to accost her enemy, Titus, in the costume of 'the dread Fury' (5.2.82), called also 'Revenge, sent forth from th' infernal kingdom' (5.2.30).[2] Or remember Tamyra's terrifying speech in George Chapman's *The Revenge of Bussy d'Ambois* of 1613, 'Revenge, that ever red sitt'st in the eyes / Of injured ladies, till we crown thy brows / With bloody laurel, and receive from thee / Justice for all our honour's injury' (1.2.1–4).[3] Few invectives have gone so far as the nineteenth-century Swiss-French satirical poet Jean-Antoine Petit-Sens who was believed to have said that an angry woman is vindictive beyond measure, and hesitates at nothing in her bitterness, but many would recognise the sentiments expressed in Rudyard Kipling's famous lines from 'The female of the species' (1911), 'But when hunter meets with husbands, each confirms the other's tale / The female of the species is more deadly than the male' (15–16).[4]

She-avengers lurk in diverse genres and media at all levels of culture, cumulatively affirming the ideological shibboleth that women are especially vengeful. The subtitle of an anonymous novella purporting to recount a true story, published in London in 1732 as *The Perjur'd Citizen*, is simply *Female Revenge*. It is a lurid account of the psychological subjectivity of a slighted woman, a figure 'actuated by a Fury'. Matilda is spoilt, rich, and outraged when her fiancé Calamus absconds. He prefers a (much nicer) bride called Lucy. Matilda is now 'ready to burst with Rage and Envy; a thousand different strategems ran thro' her Mind, to poison the Felicity of this happy Pair'.[5] She is invited to a dinner party, along with her parents, at the newly-weds' house. She manages to conceal her contorted feelings until Calamus begins to look just too happy. Matilda, seeing this

> as a new Insult to her, had, in a moment, all Hell within her Bosom: All Considerations of Fame, and even of common Humanity, were stifled by over-powering Rage; and as if actuated by a Fury, she snatch'd up a large Carving-Knife that lay near here, and starting suddenly from her Chair, struck it into the Throat of Calamus, as he was drinking, with so well-aimed and forcible a Blow, that it cut his Wind-Pipe quite thro', and he fell instantly dead at her feet.[6]

Matilda is with difficulty restrained from now murdering Lucy, and vents her frustration at being prevented from doubling the death toll:

> But Matilda, quite mad to have been prevented from her purpose, cry'd aloud, May all perfidious Villains, who like Calamus, triumph in the Ruin of our Sex, fall as he has done! – I glory in having sent his Soul to Perdition, and am only grieved, that I had not the Power to dispatch his Minion the same way.

The novella ends with Matilda being taken for trial, and the stress caused by the catastrophic episode threatening the health and even the lives of everyone else involved. The author rams home the moral of the piece in the closing sentence, 'For the desire of Revenge once kindled in the Soul, is a Fire not to be extinguish'd but in a general Devastation.' But the epigraph on the title page is Zara's famous couplet from Congreve's *The Mourning Bride* (1697):[7] 'Heaven has no Rage like Love to Hatred turn'd, / Nor Hell a Fury like a Woman scorn'd.' The profit-seeking author of this novella chooses for this case study the revenge of a *female*, and one sexually motivated at that, in what purports to be a Christian morality tale illustrating the importance of suppressing vindictive emotions *for men and women alike*. Females have regularly shouldered the ideological load in *symbolic* explorations of the dark side of revenge. In making the Erinyes female, the Greeks guaranteed it would be impossible to dislocate our thinking about revenge from our negative cultural constructions of the female psyche.

Even the more positive recent feminist constructions of the female mind, in psychoanalytical literature, often fall back on the association of revenge desires with femininity. In a book based on her own experiences with women patients,

New York psychoanalyst Lucy Holmes resorts to that hackneyed Congreve quotation when entitling her chapter on revenge: 'Hell Hath no Fury: how Women seek Revenge'.[8] Holmes says that her patients have taught her that women are indeed 'excellent at revenge', but 'get even in a uniquely feminine way'.[9] She argues that they favour three (even if strikingly *non-aggressive*) modes of wreaking it: suffering (especially effective if directed at a spouse who lavishes money and attention upon a woman who remains resolutely miserable), seducing but withholding (using sex appeal to create desire but not satisfying it), and re-enactment of trauma through unconscious manipulation of relationships with other people in later life.[10] I shall return briefly to these 'uniquely feminine' ways of wreaking revenge in my concluding paragraph.

Since the ancient Greek embodiment of reprisal in histrionic, snaky-haired females has a substantial ideological legacy to answer for, this essay conducts an enquiry into their gender. It looks at the contribution of language, ritual, thought patterns, mythopoeia, and the requirements of visual arts and poetic genre, especially epic and tragic theatre, to the multi-faceted but highly irregular femininity of the Erinyes. It pays particular attention to Hesiod's account of their genesis. Its aim is not to offer a comprehensive review of the enormous bibliography on reciprocity, retaliation and penology in prehistoric Greek society. It is intended, rather, to be a 'think-piece' introducing this volume's discrete case studies in femininity's relationship with revenge. It concludes with a short review of the 'truth' as established by neuroscience comparing the responses of male and female human brains, at least those in twenty-first-century experiments, to reprisal and the pain of the punished.

Men have always carried out more acts of the violent reprisal which the Erinyes symbolise than women. It must have been obvious, given the patriarchal and warlike nature of archaic Mediterranean society, that violent revenge and physical punishment, far from being a female monopoly, were more likely to be exacted by men. In the heroic world of the *Iliad*, women feature less as avengers than as goods to be exchanged as part of restitution packages between male adversaries.[11] Yet the ancient Greek mythopoeic imagination, in generating the gruesome Erinyes, bestowed on the idea and principle of revenge a feminine gender. In a general sense, it is helpful to remember that anthropological symbolism, ever since a landmark discussion by Sherry Ortner, has explored how cultures use the figures of women, even when they are not visible in public life, to help them imagine their social order.[12] But the conceptualisation of the Erinyes developed its own momentum, as some of their unforgettable manifestations in art, ritual and literature exerted a dialectical pressure on the ways in which narratives and iconography were subsequently shaped.

Other aspects of Greek culture enriched the nexus of associations informing the conceptualisation of the Erinyes. Philosophically speaking, the ancient Greek habits of polarised and analogical structures of thought suggested a whole range of associations: most of the principles and qualities allied with femininity rather than masculinity in the Pythagoreans' 'table of opposites' (Table 1.1), as cited by Aristotle (*Metaphysics* 986a22–7), elucidate aspects of

Table 1.1 *The Pythagoreans' 'table of opposites'.*

limit	odd	unity	right	male	rest	straight	light	good	square
unlimited	even	plurality	left	female	motion	crooked	dark	bad	oblong

the Erinyes' representation in classical poetry and art.[13] The Erinyes are plural, female, motile, dark, bad and the cycles of escalating reprisals they symbolise are potentially unlimited.

Ritual is also illuminating. Women uttered the ritual cry when the first blood was spilt on the earth in sacrifices, re-enacting the perceived attraction of the blood of the slain to the chthonic realm. They physically handled corpses of kin as they prepared them for funeral rites, washing, dressing and anointing the bodies of both men and women. They were thus felt to have an intimate psychological and physical relationship with the dead. They also led the lamentations which drew blood from their own cheeks and in the case of murdered or mistreated kin included imprecations against the perpetrator. The lament in some traditional societies which practise blood feuds serves to keep alive the family's memory and prepare the next generation for revenge.[14]

The evolution of the Erinyes was also affected by the syncretic way that figures with similar functions and attributes invariably cross-fertilise one another in Greek mythopoeia. Besides reflecting the 'dark side', of other, less repellent, feminine divine collectives – the Charites and Eumenides or Semnae Theae – and sometimes absorbing their beauty, they merge at other times with the Poinae (Penalties) and the Curses or Oaths (Ἀραί, as at Aesch. *Eum.* 417) and share features with the Gorgons and Harpies. With the Gorgons, Fates (Moirae) and Graces, they often share the 'magic' number three, and as a trio receive the names Allecto, Megaera and Tisiphone. Indeed, they are closely associated with magic. On one curse tablet an Erinys is actually invoked alongside Hecate,[15] and in *Eumenides*, as Faraone has shown, the Erinyes sing a 'binding song', attempting to use magic to control the performance of their adversaries in court.[16] On an Attic lekythos, an Erinys appears in an underworld scene alongside Hecate, an *eidōlon*, and dogs.[17] And the chthonic, triple-faced Hecate is not the only individual goddess with whom the Erinyes share features. Besides Demeter (as we shall see below), their representation as hunters 'on the scent' of their prey brought them into the conceptual sphere inhabited by both Artemis, who hunts with hounds, and Lyssa, the 'dog-faced' goddess of berserk hyper-masculine violence. Lyssa, indeed, was at least a half-sister of theirs: in Euripides' *Hercules Furens*, Lyssa introduces herself as 'the daughter of Night, sprung from the blood of Ouranos' after his castration (Νυκτὸς Οὐρανοῦ τ' ἀφ' αἵματος, 844).

Criminologists, cultural anthropologists, social and evolutionary psychologists alike are unanimous that reciprocal anger and aggression, across the planet and across time, are most frequently seen amongst men, especially young men. Acts of revenge are integrated in a web of masculine behaviours including insults and attempts to save face or attain status by fighting. In non-police societies, it is thus crucial to social organisation.[18] Where crime and punishment become responsibilities of the society as a whole, rather than individuals or families, men have also carried out most 'official' reprisals against criminals, through officially sanctioned punishment, of the type associated with the Erinyes – pursuit, execution, use of goads, whips, and flames or brands and so on. These elements are depicted in several underworld scenes in ancient Greek vase-painting where offenders are punished by an Erinys, such as Pirithous (who colluded in the abduction and rape of Persephone), Ixion who lusted after Hera[19] and Sisyphus, flogged by an Erinys while rolling his boulder in punishment (for multiple offences including murder, and niece seduction) on a famous vase in Munich by the Underworld Painter.[20] That the Erinyes are female may have added to the sensational effect of such punishments, and even eroticised them at some bizarre level of sado-masochistic fantasy. But in reality, at least, there is no evidence that in ancient Greek society the pursuit of criminals and the implementation of their punishment were ever female responsibilities. At Athens, for example, they were performed by the male Scythian slave archers owned by the state.[21] So why were the Greeks convinced that the supernatural agents of reprisal and punishment were feminine?

The Erinyes received scant scholarly attention until the late nineteenth century, and it comes as no surprise that one of the earliest voices to discuss the gender of the Erinys intelligently was the female classical scholar Jane Ellen Harrison. In an important article published in 1899, she argued that the Erinyes were *inevitably* female because they are chthonic, and chthonic 'genii' in any anthropomorphic vision of gods – not only in ancient Greece but in primitive human communities everywhere – are almost inevitably imagined to be daughters born of Mother Earth:

> With the first dawn of anthropomorphism appears the notion that the earth is the mother, and the earth genii tend to be conceived of as her daughters. This notion is helped out by the fact that in primitive communities, agriculture, and thence the ritual attendant on it, is largely in the hands of women. Hence the sex of the Erinyes – a monstrous anomaly when they are regarded as avengers of blood – is naturally determined.[22]

For Harrison, the Erinyes are not only vengeance spirits, but imaginary avatars of the women who, in primitive societies, are in charge of the rituals that ensure the fertility of the soil. Harrison knows, long before biological 'sex' had been distinguished from culturally imposed 'gender' by Margaret Mead in the 1930s and subsequently by Simone de Beauvoir, and before Lévi-Straussian anthropological structuralism, that the polarisation of male and female is a primary organising principle of human thought: 'If the first step in the making of a god is the attribution of human quality, the attribution of sex will not tarry long.'[23] Since earth pushes forth plants, it is universally gendered female in cultures, not just across the Mediterranean but across the planet. Harrison points out that in the Cretan dialect, the word for the land of one's birth was still *mētris* rather than *patris* (Plato, *Rep.* 9.575d). As Harrison trenchantly remarks, 'Mother-Earth is a conception too wide-spread to need comment. Father-Land is a late and monstrous patriarchalism.'[24]

Harrison distinguishes two ways in which gender is assigned to discrete phenomena by human thought patterns. The primitive thinking which makes Earth female applies a simple form of analogy to the material world. The analogy results from conceiving one material phenomenon as resembling another, in this case an adult female body which produces offspring. But a different kind of thinking, produced by societies organised in such a manner that men are dominant, can change the commonly agreed gender of any phenomenon if it so suits their ideological needs or imperatives. Harrison's line of argument could be challenged, therefore, by pointing out that if Land can change from a mother to a father under patriarchy, then an Erinys could at least theoretically change from a daughter to a son. But for the ancient Greeks, and those cultures who have inherited their mythology and symbolism, the Erinyes/Furies have remained emphatically and (almost) universally female.

This is strange since there is evidence that ancient Greek men could have their own *Erinys*. In Aeschylus' *Seven against Thebes*, Eteocles calls upon 'Zeus and Earth and the Gods who protect the City, and the Curse and extremely strong (μεγασθενής) Erinys of my father' (69–70). Towards the end, the chorus invoke 'Fate, giver of heavy suffering, and the solemn shade (σκιά) of Oedipus, the black Erinys, you who are extremely strong' (977–9); this entails what Harrison called 'an instructive *contaminatio* of two radically different conceptions, the Homeric phantom shadow idea and the powerful local ancestral ghost'.[25] Oedipus' *Erinys* is on both occasions grammatically feminine, but she is 'extremely strong' and there is no doubt as to the gender of her 'owner'. Harrison stressed that the Erinyes were originally 'angry souls' and that it is 'easy enough even to the modern mind to realise that the Erinys was primarily the angry ghost, and a ghost is never so angry as when he has been murdered'.[26] She may have been pushing her argument too far when she comes close to claiming that the Erinys could be conceived as a ghost resembling the dead individual, citing a dream diagnosis in the Hippocratic treatise *Dreams* (= *Regimen* 4, ch. 92). If one dreams about the dead (masculine plural, τους ἀποθανόντας) and they are clean and in white cloaks (ἱματίοισι λευκοῖσιν), it is a sign of good health, but to see them naked or dressed in black indicates disease. Since the Erinyes are customarily described in black when they are pursuing malefactors, including Orestes, but white when they are benign – in their 'Eumenidean' aspect – according to Pausanias (8.34.3), Harrison infers that they are almost indistinguishable from the actual dead individual whose interests they represent. It is also interesting that the 'Eumenidean' aspect of the Erinyes, in which by a typically Greek dialectical mythopoeic move they become blessings instead of curses and promote fertility and growth rather than sterility and destruction, is implied in the same Hippocratic text; those white-clad, benign masculine plural 'dead' are bestowers of nurture and growth and seeds.

Figure 1.1 Design from prothesis vase. From Jane Ellen Harrison, *Prolegomena to the Study of Greek Religion* (Cambridge: Cambridge University Press, 2012; first published in 1903).

But in their black, angry aspect, according to Harrison, the Erinyes were originally envisaged as actual snakes, and only later became imagined anthropomorphically, which required more attention to their gender. They then accrued features from other archaic conceptions of the forms taken by human life after death.[27] The Erinyes may have inherited wings from the idea of the fluttering, feeble *eidōlon* of the departed person familiar from Homer. Harrison points to the combination of snake and flitting images depicted on the grave tumulus on an archaic prothesis vase, and provides a drawing of the image (Figure 1.1).[28] No indication is given of the gender of the dead person, the snake or the fluttering beings. Even more fascinating is the winged being on a black-figure amphora of which she also reproduces a drawing (Figure 1.2): the conspicuous snake suggests it must be an Erinys, yet the figure is informed by the familiar type of the Gorgon; the muscular legs, thick waist and lack of emphasis on either breasts or long hair make the gender of this Erinys decidedly ambiguous.[29] Indeed, if considered in conjunction with the Pythian priestess' description of the repellent Erinyes in Aeschylus' *Eumenides*, s/he offers a clue to the huge contribution which the theatre made

Figure 1.2 Amphora fury. From Jane Ellen Harrison, *Prolegomena to the Study of Greek Religion* (Cambridge University Press, 2012; first published in 1903).

to the complex, but compromised femininity of the Erinyes in art thereafter. The Pythia says that they are not women, 'but Gorgons; / nor indeed shall I compare them to images (τύποις) of Gorgons / ... / once before now I saw some painted female creatures / carrying off Phineus's meal' (48–51). Her memory provides her with images of sculpted Gorgons,[30] and then of painted Harpies. In the cultural encyclopedia of her audience there were certainly various Harpy images, for example on the Cypselus chest (Paus. 5.17.11), on Apollo's throne at Amyclae (Paus. 3.18.15), and in archaic vase-painting.[31] But several vases dating from around 470 portray Harpies. They include a fascinating red-figure amphora in London (E 302 = ARV^2 652.2); here not only is Phineus presented wearing a mask (there is a discernible line connecting beard to ear), but beneath the Harpy wings are youths, labelled *kalos* and therefore masculine by the painter, which could 'refer to the young men who play the parts'.[32] This vase-painting, along with others of similar date, is probably connected with the painted Harpies of another kind who had appeared in a previous tragedy by Aeschylus, his *Phineus*, performed in 472 BC as the first play in the prizewinning group comprising *Phineus*, *Persians*, *Glaukos Potnieus* and a satyric *Prometheus*.[33]

In three of the four fragments of *Phineus*, the Harpies and the stolen meals provide the subject matter. One reports 'and many a deceitful meal with greedy jaws did they snatch away amid the first delight of appetite' (fr. 258 *TgrF*). Harpy roles would be consonant with Aeschylus' reputation for having been the first to stage 'terrifying masks painted with colours' (Aesch. T 2 *TgrF* = Suda s.v. αι 357). The masks worn by the Erinyes that the audience were about to glimpse, when the Pythia compared them with painted Harpies, may therefore have resembled those which Aeschylus' Harpies had worn fourteen years previously in *Phineus*.[34] An allusion to works of visual art may well 'mask' a specific inter-performative reference.[35]

The efforts of costume- and mask-makers seem, therefore, to have been instrumental in defining and settling the classical iconography of the conspicuously female Erinys. But the Phineus vase-painting reminds us how clear audiences were that it was young men dancing in the guise of terrifying females, and this consciousness must have affected the way that images of Erinyes, especially the more obviously theatrical ones, were read as in some sense gender-ambiguous outside the theatre as well. Moreover, even in the fifth century, the ancient Greek imagination *was* capable of bestowing some kind of masculine gender identity on this supernatural avatar of the dead. Finglass, on whom I here depend, argues that three lacunose lines of a fascinating fragment of Pindar, narrating the contents of the dream experienced by Hecuba before she gave birth to Paris, suggest this strongly:[36] 'for it seemed to her / that she would deliver a firebearing Eri[/ hundred-hander'. Although the original editors assumed that the correct supplement of Eri[was Eri[nun,[37] others have objected to this on the ground that Paris, as a male, could not be represented even in a dream by a female creature such as an Erinys. The first objector proposed that Hecuba dreamed she gave birth to a Hundred-hander, one of the repulsive giants whom Ouranos begat with Earth (see below), and that he was described by an adjective beginning with eri-.[38] This strange proposal has been widely accepted. But there are several arguments against it besides its inherent incongruity: the suitability of the adjective 'fire-bearing' for an Erinys, especially since Paris in some other versions of Hecuba's dream is symbolised by a torch, and the widespread comparison of individuals who cause damage (especially Paris' lover Helen) to Erinyes.[39] Moreover, Finglass points out that in Sophocles' *Electra*, Aegisthus and Clytemnestra are jointly described as a 'double Erinys' (1080), and that in Aeschylus' *Agamemnon*, the two male Atreidae are 'formally parallel' to the Erinys sent by a god as reprisal for the stolen eaglets (55–62).[40]

But if a man can have or even 'be' an Erinys or Erinyes, as the nineteenth-century scholar of Greek religion, Karl Otfried Müller, believed, are such Erinyes actually masculine? I feel that they are, rather, 'transgender'. They are predominantly female in outward appearance, although incapable of biological reproduction, but capable of acting as surrogates, representatives and even vicarious embodiments of the interests of wronged men. Müller pointed to the passage in the *Odyssey* where Odysseus, in beggar's disguise, effectively curses Antinous, who has thrown a footstool at him. 'If there are gods and vengeance spirits (θεοὶ καὶ Ἐρινύες) for beggars, then may death doom Antinous before ever he marries!' (17.475–6). Müller is approving: 'the poor man, the beggar as well we the suppliant, being from his situation entitled to a hospitable reception in more wealthy families, if instead of that he meet with insolent treatment, also has his Erinnyes [sic]'.[41] But we cannot infer from this passage that the Erinyes Odysseus invokes are in any sense his own avatars or indeed male. Odysseus sees them, rather, as independent retributive agents, working alongside the gods to uphold the laws of hospitality.

The explanation usually given for the prevalent ancient Greek practice of gendering abstractions as feminine points to the linguistic gender of many abstract concepts in the Greek language. This phenomenon is thought to have developed from a proto-Indo-European suffix that could indicate both abstract and collective senses (as in the English noun 'youth'), the first gendered feminine and the latter indicated by the neuter plural.[42] While this can help to explain why, for example, Eirene, Dike, Eunomia, Poine or Philia (Peace, Justice, Good Government, Penalty and Friendship) and literary genres such as *Tragōidia* and *Kōmōidia* are personified by female figures in classical Greek iconography,[43] it is less clear that an Erinys needed inevitably to be feminine. Indeed, the term Erinys is one of a tiny group of nouns which end in -nus (-νυς, genitive singular –νυος); although most of them are feminine, they are not all (ὁ θρῆνυς = ho thrēnus, footstool).

The Erinyes are *not* etymologically connected with Eris, the female personification of strife. In Eris, the iota is short, but it is long in Erinyes (apparent from both metrical position in all verse forms and from the variant ancient spellings: Erinnus = Ἐριννύς and Erinuas = Ἐρινύας are attested). This did not mean that ancient Greeks did not hear an acoustic similarity, and play with it in their poetry and proverbs. Hesiod's *Works and Days* warns against conducting business on the fifth day of the month, because it was then that 'the Erinyes assisted at the birth of Horkos (Oath) whom Eris bore to inflict woe on perjurers' (803–4). Conflict, oaths, perjury and its punishment are thus connected both by poetic assonance and ethical synergy.[44]

The term *e-ri-nu* does appear in Linear B in a poorly understood cultic context, but little can be surmised from this controversial Mycenaean word that does not risk anachronistic reading back of assumptions from the Erinyes of ancient Greek literature.[45] We need to go forward more than a millennium and a half to find an ancient writer addressing the etymology of *Erinys*. When Pausanias (8.25.4–6) visited Thelpousa, a remote village in western Arcadia, he followed the local river downhill to a sanctuary of 'Demeter Erinys'. He explains that the goddess acquired this name because she became angry with Poseidon. He had pursued her sexually when she was looking for Persephone, and when she changed herself into a mare to avoid him, he raped her in the form of a stallion. Pausanias says that Demeter became furious, and 'the Arcadian word for "be angry" is *erinuein*' (ἐρινύειν).[46]

Pausanias' explanation is plausible, since the Arcadian dialect preserved some otherwise obsolete Greek words.[47] And the context might be thought to be telling in terms of the wider associations of the Erinyes: it involves the violation of sacred rights of an individual at a vulnerable time by someone socially close who ought most to have respected them.[48] But the derivation from an active verb reminds us that the Erinyes are *not* precisely abstract personifications of revenge in the way that, for example, Eirene is a personification of the abstract principle of peace, or Eunomia of good government. The Erinyes are concrete, albeit supernatural, *agents* of reprisal. They may come to denote something similar to a personification when they appear on vase-paintings manifesting the incidence or imminence of reprisal in scenes from myths prominent in tragic theatre – at the sacrifice of Iphigenia, or the murders of Agamemnon, Aegisthus or Clytemnestra, or with Orestes and Electra, or with Bellerophon and Stheneboea, or Eteocles and Polynices, or Oenomaus and Pelops. In a sense, they 'mean' that this is a situation in which revenge is actual or potential.[49] But they will also be active and instrumental in ensuring that the retaliation takes place. Such scenes are dominated by their substance and case-specific agency rather than a universal, abstract signification.[50]

Ancient Greeks used genealogies and aetiologies, set in the past, to explain the nature of the presents they inhabited. The earliest origin of the Erinyes might therefore be hoped to illuminate all aspects of their nature in the Greek imaginary, including their gender. One of the earliest narratives, disseminated by Greek-speakers as part of their core identity and cultural curriculum everywhere they spread from the late eighth century onwards,[51] occurs early in Hesiod's *Theogony*. This curiously under-investigated passage rewards detailed analysis. The Erinyes are some of the youngest in the long line of siblings produced in the first sexual mating, between Gaea and the son she has produced alone, Ouranos. They are primeval, but they are also low-status among this primordial generation: they are framed, forever, as the junior, little sisters of mighty beings.

The *Theogony* describes how the Erinyes originate materially in blood and/or semen falling on Gaea, and socially in a crisis within a phenomenally dysfunctional family *already* encompassing incest, inter-generational violence, conflict between sexual partners and co-parents, mother–son collusion, castration and child abuse. Its complexity in terms of both ethics and gender ideology can be seen from a comparison with its Hittite/Hurrian precursor; when Kumarbi bit off and swallowed his father Anu's genitals, before spitting out the blood, Earth was inseminated. She gave birth to a male god Tasmisu (connected with the important male Weather-God) and a female, a rather straightforward personification of the river Tigris. There is no sense of a conflicted nuclear family and the engendering (in both senses) of the cosmic principle of retribution for kinship-group crimes.[52] Similarly, when Enkidu comes back from below after his katabasis in the Sumerian text *Bilgames and the Netherworld*, he reports the eternal punishment of groups whom the Greeks certainly later saw as the responsibility of the Erinyes – those who disrespected or were cursed by a parent, and oath-breakers.[53] But there is no sense that the punishment was carried out by supernatural females. Reprisal and revenge have not yet been gendered feminine.

Here I provide my translation of the (slightly compressed) text of *Theogony* 132–92, with the words important to my argument in bold font:

> She lay with Ouranos and gave birth to deep-churning Oceanos, Coeus and Crius and Hyperion and Iapetus, Theia and Rhea, **Themis and Mnemosyne** and gold-crowned Phoebe and lovely Tethys. After them Cronos of the crooked counsel was born, the youngest and most terrible of her children, **and he hated his vigorous father.**
>
> Then she bore the Cyclopes, overbearing in spirit, Brontes, and Steropes and stubborn Arges ... And again, three other sons were born of Earth and Heaven, indescribable in size and power, Cottus and Briareos and Gyes, presumptuous children. From their shoulders sprang a hundred arms, not to be approached, and fifty heads grew from the shoulders upon the strong limbs of each, and irresistible was the stubborn strength that was in their great forms. For of all the children that were born of Gaea and Ouranos, these were the most terrible, **and they were hated by their own father from the first.** And he used to hide them all away in a secret place of Gaea as soon as each was born, and would not let them out into the light: and he rejoiced in his evil doing. But vast Gaea was put under strain, and groaned inside, and thought up a cunning and evil plan. Straightaway she created the element of grey flint and shaped a great sickle, and told her plan to her dear sons ... 'My children, offspring of an evil father, if you obey me, **we could punish (τισαίμεθα)** the vile outrage of your father; for he **first (πρότερος)** thought of doing shameful things.' So she said; but fear seized them all, and none of them uttered a word. But great Cronos the wily took courage and answered his dear mother: 'Mother, I will undertake to do this deed, for I do not revere our father of evil name, for he **first (πρότερος)** thought of doing shameful things.'
>
> So he said: and vast Gaea rejoiced greatly in her heart, and set and hid him in an ambush, and put in his hands a jagged sickle ... And Ouranos arrived, bringing on night and desiring for love, and he lay about Gaea, spreading himself all over her. Then from the place of ambush, the son stretched forth his left hand and in his right took the great long sickle with jagged teeth, and swiftly sheared off his own father's genitals and cast them away to fall behind him. And they did not fall from his hand in vain, for **Gaea received all the bloody droplets (ῥαθάμιγγες ... αἱματόεσσαι)** that gushed forth, and as the seasons moved round she bore the **powerful (κρατεράς)** Erinyes and the great Giants with gleaming armour, holding long spears in their hands and the nymphs whom they call Meliae (Ash-Tree Nymphs) all over the boundless earth. And so soon as Cronos had cut off the genitals with flint and cast them from the land into the surging sea, they were swept away over the waters a long time:

and a white foam spread around them from the immortal flesh, and in it there grew a maiden [Aphrodite].

In this primal scene of crime and counter-crime, the first felon is the patriarch. Ouranos represses all except one of his younger group of children (all boys) and their mother. The oldest of this group, although not himself oppressed by his father, castrates him. *It is at this pivotal moment that the Erinyes are born*. It is between the second and third act of violence in what is to become an infinite cycle. They somehow mark the very moment when the process, rather than finding a solution in finding a punishment to fit a crime, forever loses all possibility of being limited and indeed escalates.[54] It is also the moment when reciprocal violence is no longer a matter of straightforward tit for tat, with the perpetrator being punished by the actual victim: Cronos' intervention, and the genesis of the unlimited, plural Erinyes, underline the potential for revenge to be redirected, and for confusion about who is guilty of what, to spiral out of control.[55] The symbolic importance of the threefold movement establishing an irreversible process of crime and counter-crime, escalating in scale as dazzlingly dramatised in Aeschylus' *Oresteia*,[56] found expression in the distillation of the archaic Erinyes into the classical triad of three named Erinyes.[57] For the upshot of the castration, just after the birth of the Erinyes, is Ouranos' displeasure. He declares that on Cronos and the other hidden-away sons (whom he called Titans, 'Strainers') there will later come vengeance (τίσις) for their evil deed. His speech is the first, primal and primordial *curse*. This as we know will expand in significance beyond the family to become the first great *political* struggle for power in the universe.

The Erinyes' position within the first ever dysfunctional, strife-ridden family is therefore precise. They are generated just before the threat of the *counter*-counter-crime is made and an unending cycle or pendulum swing thus inaugurated. All this takes place *before* the Olympians, let alone humans, come into being. This critical moment establishes a primordial law of cosmic penology. The Erinyes have a sinister aspect, but they are also part of the *universal moral order*;[58] one of their elder sisters is 'Right Way of Doing Things' (*Themis*); another is Memory (*Mnemosyne*), who prevents malefactors from going unpunished simply because their crimes are forgotten or erased by some primeval Statute of Limitations. Justice may come late in the world of archaic Greek, but it is foolish to hope that it will never come at all.

The Erinyes' closest siblings, besides the Giants and those mysterious Ash-Tree nymphs, is their younger half-sister Aphrodite, the goddess of sexual impulses. The Hesiodic genealogy thus implies the alliance between the destructive feelings engendered in the soul by sexual infatuation with another person (especially if s/he rejects the lover or abandons them in favour of another) and by a desire to inflict reciprocal damage. Moreover, this group of siblings is not born unambiguously from Ouranos' semen. The passage describing the drops which fell from Ouranos' genitals when Cronos tossed them behind is explicit that the genitals 'did not fall from his hand in vain, for Gaea received all the bloody droplets that gushed forth, and as the seasons moved round she bore the powerful Erinyes'. The word translated as 'droplets' here (ῥαθάμιγγες) is used in the *Iliad* for drops of blood which issue from wounds with nothing to do with genitals (11.536) and of solid specks or flecks of dust or grains of ash or dust (23.502). The Erinyes are made of earth *inseminated by genitalia blood not by semen*. Ouranos' detached genitalia also contribute to the making of Aphrodite, but the material contribution in her case sounds more like semen than blood, since it is 'a white foam'. She is conceived when they are cast from the land into the sea, where 'a white foam spread around them from the immortal flesh, and in it there grew a maiden'.

Clarifying the exact genealogy of the Erinyes in the Hesiodic version shows that the male parent has not actually provided an exclusively male substance (semen) in their creation, but only the blood which is common to the bodies of both sexes, even if it is blood from his hacked-off genitals. Unlike their younger sister Aphrodite, born from genital foam in contact with seawater rather than genital blood in contact with earth, the Erinyes themselves are permanently sexually inactive and incapable of producing children of their own. Perhaps this is partly explained by the peculiar nature of their male parent's contribution to their genetic make-up. They are females but defective ones who do not give birth; their paternal physiological constituent is also deviant, indeed functionally disabled. From the perspective of their genesis, their gender identity is far less obviously 'female' than it appears on the surface.

This does not mean that the association of the Erinyes with hunting and tearing the flesh of those they pursue, and drinking or sucking their blood, does not have a gendered resonance. The alimentary or nutritive and the retaliatory seem fused at a deep subconscious psychological level, as Herman Melville saw in *Moby-Dick* (1851). The obsessive Captain Ahab wants revenge on the great white whale which had bitten off his leg; but Melville tellingly likens Ahab's anger and need for reprisal to an autophagous urge to devour *himself*:

> As the grizzly bear burying himself in the hollow of a tree, lived out the winter there, sucking his own paws, so, in his inclement, howling old age, Ahab's soul, shut up in the caved trunk of his body, there fed upon the sullen paws of its gloom.[59]

In the *Iliad*, revenge and eating the enemy are conceptually linked: two mothers and one male warrior are briefly imagined devouring the flesh of their deadliest enemy. Zeus suggests in a spirit of sarcastic hyperbole that the pro-Achaean Hera should glut her fury against Troy by devouring Priam, his sons and the other Trojans raw (4.35). Achilles tells the dying Hector of his gloating fantasy about carving him up and eating him raw (22.346–8). After Hector's death in the *Iliad*, Hecuba (whose female body has earlier been emphasised when she bared to Hector the breast he had suckled on) announces that she would like to get hold of Achilles' liver and gorge on it if she could (24.212–13).[60] The Erinyes are barren, distorted females, born from blood not semen, who destroy rather than nurture, but their mouths and nipples are focal points of their monstrosity. In one way, they are like the snakes they brandish in the faces of hapless kin-murderers and perjurers on so many vases: they inject venom but also drain their victims of blood.[61] Attention is also often drawn to their breasts in the iconography by breast-bands and sometimes partial nudity, but these are not breasts that will ever feed young.

The deviant but marked relationship of Erinyes/Eumenides with (in)fertility is inseparable from the fundamental analogy in Greek thought between the chthonic and the female, indeed between Earth and Mothers. In the *Iliad*, acts of violent revenge within the family are few, since the frame narrative consists of a formally declared war, on an international scale. The central (male) actors are motivated more by the need actively to demonstrate their prowess and retain their honour than by retributive urges. Violence is a matter for men in combat with other men, and the household and nuclear family are not the central social units under examination. There are a few exceptions, but they occur in embedded tales, 'digressions' or 'excursuses', tiny compressed 'proto-tragic' narratives of dramatic events which antedated the Trojan War. In these, we can see that revenge and the maternal feminine are already closely entwined. The inclusion of these feminine 'proto-tragedies' reminds us forcibly of the degree to which tragic theatre was itself perceived as a feminine genre, in which women and the *oikos* were prominent. The ancient Greeks were themselves uncomfortably aware of this. 'There are more females than males in these plays', remarked a character in a treatise, composed in the second century AD, on danced versions of Greek tragedy (Lucian, *On Dancing* 28); in a novel of similar date there is a discourse on the large number of plots which women have contributed to the stage (Achilles Tatius, *Leucippe and Clitophon* 1.8). Only one extant tragedy, Sophocles' *Philoctetes*, contains no women, and female tragic choruses outnumber male in a ratio of more than two to one. And the Erinyes, especially after they were sensationally staged in Aeschylus' *Oresteia*, come almost to symbolise the perceived 'femininity' of the tragic genre.[62] *Tragōidia* herself is often personified as a maenad in classical iconography, only later developing the more dignified persona of a matron which she shared with the Hellenistic tragic muse Melpomene.[63] But when the haggard, ill-kempt Poverty appears on stage to threaten Chremylus and Blepsidemus with death in Aristophanes' *Wealth*, the latter guesses that she is 'some Erinys from tragic theatre; the look in her eyes is crazed and like in a tragedy' (423–4). In the popular imagination, the Erinyes are almost symbols of the tragic genre and somehow represent the tragic mood and acting styles.

The context of one of the most significant of the embedded epic 'proto-tragedies' is the Calydonian boar hunt, recalled by the ageing Phoenix on his embassy to Achilles. After the boar had been slaughtered by Meleager, this rash young hero had also killed two of his maternal uncles in a quarrel about the division of the beast. His mother Althaea's reaction as described by Phoenix is the earliest detailed description of the psychological effect on a bereaved human individual of the need for revenge (9.566–72):

> For she made prayer to the gods, sorely aggrieved at the death of her brothers, and pounded the all-nurturing earth (*Gaean*) hard with her hands, calling as she knelt there on Hades and dread Persephone to bring death to her son, and she soaked her breast with her tears. From Erebos she was heard by the shadowy Erinys, by her of the ungentle heart.[64]

Here we have a clear articulation of the constituents of the cultural nexus where vengeance and femininity intertwine, later to achieve its consummate embodiment in a tragedy with Aeschylus' Clytemnestra. In archaic, Homeric Calydon, the agent who feels the need for revenge is likewise a woman. The context is the murder of kin (brothers) and the individual on whom she wants to be avenged is also a close blood relative (son). The appeal for revenge is connected with the lament for the dead, as the ritual actions which they share – weeping and earth-beating – demonstrate. There is a sense that revenge is somehow chthonic, in residence and perhaps in origins. Perhaps it is even to be understood here as a more personified 'Earth'-figure – the implication of the epithet 'all-nurturing'. The divinities who are directly addressed are Hades and Persephone. But the one who *responds* to Althaea's cries is the supernatural feminine agent of revenge in cases of kin-murder, the 'shadowy and ungentle' Erinys. Here we have an early example of the most familiar function of Erinyes, to act as representatives or surrogates of those felt to be unjustly slain at the hands of close kin.

The other principal function of the Erinyes is to witness and enforce certain kinds of oaths, and punish perjurers, but almost always in association with the supreme god who took ultimate responsibility for violation of the 'unwritten laws' including offences against kin, recipients of oaths, suppliants and vulnerable strangers – Zeus *horkios*, *hikesios* and *xeinios*, often in conjunction with Themis. The archetypal episode demonstrating this task is also recounted by Phoenix in *Iliad* 9 (446–77), when he recalls how he felt compelled to leave his father Amyntor's house. Amyntor had a concubine, and his adultery insulted his wife, Phoenix's mother. Phoenix's mother begged Phoenix to sleep with the concubine himself, to alienate the woman from Amyntor, and Phoenix eventually did what his mother wanted. But Amyntor was enraged, says Phoenix,

> and cursed me bitterly, calling the dread Erinyes to witness. He prayed that no son of mine might ever sit upon knees – and the gods, Zeus of the world below and awful Persephone, fulfilled his curse. I took counsel to kill him, but some god restrained by recklessness and made me consider men's evil tongues, and that I would be branded as the murderer of my father: nevertheless, I could not bear to stay in my father's house with him so bitter against me.

The Erinyes, rather than the more customary witnesses of oaths Helios and Earth, are probably here called to witness Amyntor's curse, which will actually be upheld by Zeus and Persephone, because Amyntor perceives his son's deed

Figure 1.3 *Oresteia*-inspired scene. Detail from an Apulian red-figure bell-krater, 380–370 BC. Louvre Museum, Paris.

as a crime against a close kin member; the curse is an attack on the whole kinship line through time. Phoenix's own impulse towards patricide in response reveals that he, too, sees the situation – a blighted *oikos* with sexual crimes being committed between spouses and fathers and sons – as one in which the Erinyes have an obvious part to play.

Unlike the Olympian gods, the Erinyes are usually asleep, often lying on the ground. This may be one reason why they are sometimes said to be (like Lyssa) daughters of Night (Aesch. *Eum.* 416) or of Darkness (Soph. *OC.* 40) rather than of Earth. They sleep unless one of their functions is activated, for example by the breaking of a vow which they have witnessed, or by the ghost of a murdered individual, as in Figure 1.3 when, in an *Oresteia*-inspired scene, the spectre of murdered Clytemnestra tries to awaken them to avenge her. Their appearance in early classical art is strikingly varied.[65] They are sometimes winged and sometimes wingless; they are occasionally black; they may wear, long, short and/or patterned dresses; they may be topless or bare-breasted but with cross-bands; their hair may be long or short; they are sometime ugly and sometimes beautiful; some sport snakes on their hair-bands, snakes as hair, snakes wound round their arms or waved in their hands; they hold torches, goads, whips, branding irons, even mirrors or scrolls; they may be barefoot, booted or wear elaborate fabric *endromides*. But the iconography becomes much more settled in fourth-century vase-painting, probably as a result of experiments in representing the Erinyes on stage producing a recognisable theatrical 'uniform'.[66] The numerous vase-paintings show the enormous creative inspiration their gender proved in imagining their more or less spectacular physiology, costume and hairstyles.

To sum up: the female gender of the Erinyes was not quite a foregone conclusion, and in Greek religion and thought it was possible to think in terms of a wronged male murder victim's ghost being 'his' Erinys, or of him being equivalent to an Erinys if he was the bringer of certain kinds of horrific destruction. The role of the theatre was crucial in the invention of the familiar ravening, canine, bloodletting, snake-brandishing repellent torturer figure of the girlish or haglike Erinys, winged or not, and the peculiar 'transvestite' nature of females represented on stage by male performers must have compounded their already peculiar version of aggressive, barren, orally fixated femininity. The femininity of revenge, emblematised by the femininity of the Erinyes, was consolidated in ritual, mythopoeia, literature and philosophy by their chthonic, thanatological and maternal associations, by the *oikos* plots and memorable female protagonists of tragedy, and their similarity and sometimes partial assimilation to other female figures including the Harpies, Gorgons, Hecate, Demeter, Artemis and Lyssa.

Understanding even one part of the longstanding ideological project of gendering revenge female is a valuable exercise in 'de-naturalising' a toxic patriarchal myth. But where, if anywhere, does it leave us in terms of understanding psychological 'reality'? Is there *no* evidence for females having a special talent for or proclivity towards revenge? When it comes to Renaissance tragedy's vengeful mothers, at any rate, Heather Hirschfield thinks not. In a fascinating article, she has explored the widespread figure of the 'maternal penitent' – older woman confessing to sins and crimes – in Renaissance and Jacobean revenge tragedies where the vindictive protagonists are actually male. She points out that this peculiar trope is indebted to a long tradition of medieval penitential manuals providing instructions, which are 'always ideologically fraught', for handling the sins of women.[67] But these penitential mothers function, argues Hirschfield, as a convenient emotional surrogate, somewhat like the female surrogates of the male citizen self which Zeitlin has argued was really at stake in the Athenian theatre.[68] They can articulate the feelings of guilt or shame or self-loathing which the Revenge Hero cannot face in himself. The crimes of these (fictional) women – sometimes including revenge crimes – are not the point at all. And contemporary psychoanalysts are increasingly interested in the ways that our subjective experience of emotions are conditioned by the gendered *cultural* representations of desire, passion and revenge which we have encountered; the 'dystonic' or negative representation of desiring, passionate or vengeful women must be related to the way girls learn to suppress or express their own impulses.[69] This makes it impossible for the idea of a 'universal' or 'natural' feminine propensity for, or avoidance of, revenge to be psychoanalytically posited or maintained.

But we should, finally, consider the possibility that somehow the cultural stereotype of revenge as a peculiarly feminine principle reflects at least *potential* reality. Perhaps women really are just vengeful, or even more so, than men, and is it *only* the contingent history of misogynistic ideology and the patriarchal monopoly on violence, warfare and weaponry that has prevented women from become supreme avengers? Here we can turn to behavioural neuroscience – the study of the relationship of the transhistorical biological human brain to feelings and conduct – even though it is still in its infancy. There have only been a few studies comparing male and female responses to reciprocal violence or the infliction of pain. But such results as are available uniformly suggest that we should definitely be gendering revenge as *masculine*.

It is not just that vastly more men than women are convicted of vengeance-motivated murder.[70] When it comes to pain, the male brain does seem to be hardwired, transculturally, in a different way from the female. Men have a far greater tendency to seek sensations of any kind – an intolerance of situations in which nothing is happening and no external sensations are to be felt – than women. In one famous experiment, the subjects were left on their own in a room with nothing to do except give themselves electric shocks. During a fifteen-minute period of such solitude, 67 per cent of men gave themselves at least one shock during the thinking period (with one administering no fewer than 190 shocks to himself!). But only 25 per cent of women did the same.[71]

More directly relevant to revenge is the study of a team based at the University of Connecticut, which stumbled on the surprise finding that the pleasure centres in male brains fire up when they watch people they believe deserve punishment being given electric shocks. What Colin Wayne Leach's experiment was actually designed to test was the difference between reactions in the *empathy* centres of the brain in subjects of both sexes witnessing pain being administered to actors they believed were guilty and not guilty. As Leach expected, people of both sexes showed more empathetic responses in the cases of the 'not guilty'. What they did not expect was that the male subjects' *pleasure* centres activated while watching the 'bad' people getting what they believed to be deserved.[72]

Similar results were published in a 2006 article in the journal *Nature* by a team led by Tania Singer at University College, London. They conducted sustained research using brain scans into empathy and retributive responses,[73] comparing the results gathered from male and female subjects. Men, once again, were seen to derive greater pleasure than women from watching retribution being enacted. The brains of thirty-two individuals were scanned when they watched actors who had previously cheated them receive painful electric shocks. Singer explained in an interview that, in women,

> the same pain regions of their brains were activated when they saw one of the actors get a shock as when they got a shock themselves; it was as

if they actually felt the other person's pain. But in men, these pain areas were not activated and instead, the pleasure centres of their brains lit up, meaning that they got pleasure, or at least satisfaction, from seeing the other person get a shock.[74]

Singer said that men 'expressed more desire for revenge and seemed to feel satisfaction when unfair people were given what they perceived as deserved physical punishment'.[75] The team speculated that men may have evolved to feel pleasure when they see what they perceive as just revenge being enacted, 'so they can more easily mete out punishments to help keep society cohesive'.[76]

Singer was prepared to entertain the possibility that the results 'could indicate a predominant role for men in maintaining justice and issuing punishment in human society', but insisted that more research was needed, especially since the punishment used in the experiment may have favoured masculine ideas about the best way to take revenge since it was physical rather than psychological. But her results remind me of New York psychoanalyst Lucy Holmes' description of the non-aggressive ways, centred *on their own psychological experience*, in which she has witnessed women wreaking revenge: by displaying their suffering, seducing but withholding, and re-enacting trauma. Perhaps Byron, who was obsessed with female revenge,[77] had it right, that women are so closely allied to revenge precisely because, as Neurological experiments have now shown, their empathetic capacities are indeed more highly developed. Woman's revenge, he claims in *Don Juan* (2.71), 'is as the tiger's spring, / Deadly, and quick, and crushing; yet, as real / Torture is theirs, **what they inflict they feel.**'

NOTES

1. Amidst a massive literature, Karen L. Raber, 'Murderous Mothers and the Family/State Analogy in Classical and Renaissance Drama', *Comparative Literature Studies*, 37 (2000), pp. 298–320, stands out for clarity and novel detail. On the performance history and influence of *Agamemnon*, see Fiona Macintosh, Pantelis Michelakis, Edith Hall and Oliver Taplin (eds), *Agamemnon in Performance 458 BC to AD 2004* (Oxford: Oxford University Press, 2005); for *Medea*, Edith Hall, Fiona Macintosh and Oliver Taplin (eds), *Medea in Performance* (Oxford: European Humanities Research Centre, 2000). The importance of the descriptions of the assault by the Erinyes in Euripides' *Iphigenia in Tauris* and its enormous influence on post-Renaissance opera and ballet are explored in Edith Hall, *Adventures with Iphigenia in Tauris: A Cultural History of Euripides' Black Sea Tragedy* (New York: Oxford University Press, 2013).
2. See Marguerite A. Tassi, *Women and Revenge in Shakespeare: Gender, Genre, and Ethics* (Selinsgrove: Susquehanna University Press, 2011), p. 42.

3. George Chapman, *The Revenge of Bussy D'Ambois*, in Katherine Eisaman Maus (ed.), *Four Revenge Tragedies* (Oxford and New York: Oxford University Press, 1995).
4. Rudyard Kipling, *Rudyard Kipling's Verse: Inclusive Edition, 1885–1918* (London: Hodder & Stoughton, 1919).
5. Anon., *The Perjur'd Citizen; or, Female Revenge* (London: Charles Corbett, 1732), p. 47.
6. Ibid. pp. 50–1.
7. It is itself a tragedy with a not-so-distant relationship to a Greek 'revenge' tragedy, Sophocles' *Electra*. See Edith Hall and Fiona Macintosh, *Greek Tragedy and the British Theatre 1660–1914* (Oxford: Oxford University Press, 2005), pp. 157–62.
8. Lucy Holmes, *The Internal Triangle: New Theories of Female Development* (Lanham, MD: Jason Aronson, 2008), pp. 113–23.
9. Ibid. p. 8.
10. Ibid. pp. 113–23.
11. Donna F. Wilson, *Ransom, Revenge and Heroic Identity in the* Iliad (Cambridge: Cambridge University Press, 2002), pp. 8, 26–7, 41–53. Yet women in Homer are still heavily associated with desiring revenge, see Fiona McHardy, *Revenge in Athenian Culture* (London: Duckworth, 2008), pp. 37–8. See further below n. 60 on Hecuba.
12. Sherry Ortner, 'Is Female to Male as Nature is to Culture?', in M. Z. Rosaldo and L. Lamphere (eds), *Woman, Culture, and Society* (Stanford: Stanford University Press, 1976), pp. 67–87.
13. On which see the fine discussion of Sabina Lovibond, 'An Ancient Theory of Gender: Plato and the Pythagorean Table', in Léonie J. Archer, Susan Fischler and Maria Wyke (eds), *Women in Ancient Societies: An Illusion of the Night* (Basingstoke: MacMillan, 1994), pp. 102–14.
14. M. Alexiou, *The Ritual Lament in Greek Tradition*, 2nd edition, revised by Dimitrios Yatromanolakis and Panagiotis Roilos (Lanham, MD: Rowman & Littlefield, 2002). Cf. Fiona McHardy 'Women's Influence on Revenge in Ancient Greece', in Fiona McHardy and Eireann Marshall (eds), *Women's Influence on Classical Civilization* (London: Routledge, 2004), pp. 92–114.
15. No. 108 in R. Wuensch (ed.), *Inscriptiones Atticae aetatis Romanae, Pars III, Appendix continens Defixionum tabellae Atticae* (Berlin: Georg Reimer, 1897).
16. Christopher A. Faraone, 'Aeschylus' ὕμνος δέσμιος (*Eum.* 306) and Attic Judicial Curse Tablets', *Journal of Hellenic Studies* 105 (1985), pp. 150–4. See Matthews and Salvo in this volume.
17. Athens, Mus. National 19765. See S. Karazou, 'An Underworld Scene on a Black-Figured Lekythos', *Journal of Hellenic Studies* 92 (1972), pp. 64–73.
18. Aaron Sell, 'Applying Adaptationism to Human Anger: the Recalibrational Theory', in Phillip R. Shaver and Mario Mikulincer (eds), *Human*

Aggression and Violence (Washington, DC: American Psychological Association, 2011), pp. 53–70 (p. 61).

19. For example, Haiganuch Sabian, 'Erinys', *Lexicon Iconographicum Mythologiae Classicae* 3.1 (1986), pp. 825–43, no. 9 = Naples Mus. Naz. 80854.
20. Munich, Antikensammlungen 3297.
21. Edith Hall, *The Theatrical Cast of Athens: Interactions between Ancient Greek Drama and Society* (Oxford: Oxford University Press, 2006), pp. 225–54.
22. Jane E. Harrison, 'Delphika.-(A) The Erinyes. (B) The Omphalos', *Journal of Hellenic Studies* 19 (1899), pp. 205–51 (p. 205).
23. Ibid. p. 211.
24. Ibid. p. 211.
25. Ibid. p. 208.
26. Ibid. pp. 207, 208.
27. Cf. Diana Burton, 'The Gender of Death', in Emma J. Stafford and Judith Herrin (eds), *Personification in the Greek World: From Antiquity to Byzantium* (Aldershot: Ashgate, 2005), pp. 45–68.
28. She has taken the drawing from the *Mittheilungen des Kaiserlich Deutschen Archaeologischen Instituts*, Athenische Abteilung, vol. 16 (1891).
29. J. B. Passerius, *Picturae Etruscorum in vasculis* (Rome: Monaldini, 1787), vol. 3, 279.
30. On this and other references to the terrifying impact of carved Gorgons in tragedy, see D. Steiner, *Images in Mind: Statues in Archaic and Classical Greek Literature and Thought* (Princeton: Princeton University Press, 2001), p. 176.
31. For example, a sixth-century black-figure amphora in the British Museum (BM 1894. 11-1.161) and a Hydria in the Getty Museum (85 AE 316). See L. Kahil, 'Harpyiai', *Lexicon Iconographicum Mythologiae Classicae* 4.1 (1988), pp. 445–50.
32. A. D. Trendall, and T. B. L. Webster, *Illustrations of Greek Drama* (London and New York: Phaidon, 1971), 3.1, p. 25.
33. Kahil, 'Harpyiai', p. 449; L. Kahil 'Phineus I', *Lexicon Iconographicum Mythologiae Classicae* 7.1 (1994), p. 388; E. Hall *Aeschylus' Persians, edited with Translation, Introduction and Commentary* (Trowbridge: Aris & Phillips, 1996), pp. 10–11.
34. Hall, *The Theatrical Cast of Athens*, pp. 116–18.
35. For some examples of the way that later tragedies visually reminded their audiences of earlier tragic spectacles, see Pat Easterling, 'Form and Performance', in Pat Easterling (ed.), *The Cambridge Companion to Greek Tragedy* (Cambridge: Cambridge University Press, 1997), pp. 151–77 (pp. 168–9).
36. Pindar fragment 52i(A). 19–21 Snell-Maehler = B3.25–7 Rutherford (Paean 8a); Patrick J. Finglass, 'Erinys or Hundred-hander? Pindar,

fr. 52i(a). 19–21 Snell-Maehler = B3.25–7 Rutherford', *Zeitschrift für Papyrologie und Epigraphik* 154 (2005), pp. 40–2.
37. B. P. Grenfell, and A. S. Hunt, 'Pindar, Paeans', in *The Oxyrhynchus Papyri*, Part V (1908), pp. 11–110 (p. 65).
38. C. Robert, 'Zu Pindars VIII. Paean', *Hermes* 49 (1914), pp. 315–19 (pp. 315–16).
39. Aesch. *Ag.* 748; Soph. *Trach.* 895, *El.* 1080; Eur. *Med.* 1260, *Or.* 1388.
40. Finglass, *Erinys or Hundred-hander*, p. 41.
41. C. O. Müller, *Dissertations on the Eumenides of Aeschylus*, English Translation, 2nd edition (London and Cambridge: John W. Parker and John Deighton, 1853), p. 156.
42. Silvia Luraghi, 'The Origin of the Feminine Gender in PIE. An Old Problem in a New Perspective', in V. Bubenik, J. Hewson and S. Rose (eds), *Grammatical Change in Indo-European Languages* (Amsterdam and Philadelphia: John Benjamins, 2009), pp. 3–13 (pp. 6–8).
43. Emma J. Stafford, *Worshipping Virtues: Personification and the Divine in Ancient Greece* (London: Duckworth, 2000); Hall, *The Theatrical Cast of Athens*, pp. 170–83.
44. A. Marchiando, 'Les Erinyes dans la poésie épique: essai de comparaison', in Menelaos Christopoulos and Machi Païzi-Apostolopoulou (eds), *Crime and Punishment in Homeric and Archaic Epic: Proceedings of the 12th International Symposium on the Odyssey* (Ithaca: Centre for Odyssean Studies, 2014), pp. 81–96 (pp. 82–4).
45. KN Fp 1, 8; see Sabian, *Erinys*, p. 825.
46. See Bernard C. Dietrich, 'Demeter, Erinys, Artemis', *Hermes* 90 (1962), pp. 129–48.
47. Müller, *Dissertations*, p. 155.
48. Ibid. pp. 155–6.
49. See especially numbers 102 (Meleager and Atalanta) and 107–9 (Pelops and Oenomaus) in Sabian, *Erinys*.
50. In antiquity, the story of another matricide pursued by the Erinyes, Alcmaeon, was also made famous through tragic theatre and was almost as popular as the myth of Orestes, although it does not feature on surviving vases.
51. See Edith Hall, *Introducing the Ancient Greeks. From Bronze-Age Seafarers to Navigators of the Western Mind* (New York: Norton, 2014), Ch. 2.
52. Hans Gustav Güterbock, 'The Hittite Version of the Hurrian Kumarbi Myths: Oriental Forerunners of Hesiod', *American Journal of Archaeology* 52 (1948), pp. 23–134 (p. 125); Carolina Lopez-Ruiz, *When the Gods Were Born: Greek Cosmogonies and the Near East* (Cambridge, MA and London: Harvard University Press, 2010), p. 92.
53. See the edition of A. R. George (ed.), *The Babylonian Gilgamesh Epic: Introduction, Critical Edition, and Cuneiform Texts* (Oxford: Oxford University Press, 2003), vol. 2, pp. 776–7 with the discussion of

W. Burkert, 'Pleading for Hell: Postulates, Fantasies, and the Senselessness of Punishment', *Numen* 56 (2009), pp. 141–60.
54. On escalation as a feature of revenge, see especially: C. Nathan DeWall and Craig A. Anderson, 'The General Aggression Model', in Phillip R. Shaver and Mario Mikulincer (eds), *Human Aggression and Violence: Causes, Manifestations, and Consequences* (Washington, DC: American Psychological Association, 2011), pp. 15–53. It is connected with the 'fundamental attribution error' in which individuals caught up in retaliatory behaviour begin to explain the causes of their opponents' behaviours as dispositional ('Ouranos is morally bad) and of their own as situational ('we children of Ouranos are oppressed and in an impossible situation'). On this see C. A. Anderson, D. S. Krull and B. Weiner, 'Explanations: Processes and Consequences', in E. T. Higgins and A. W. Kruglanski (eds) *Social Psychology: Handbook of Basic Principles* (New York: Guilford Press, 1996), pp. 271–96.
55. David P. Barash and Judith Eve Lipton, *Payback: Why We Retaliate, Redirect Aggression, and Take Revenge* (New York: Oxford University Press, 2011), pp. 15–18.
56. Edith Hall, 'Peaceful Conflict Resolution and Its Discontents in Aeschylus's *Eumenides*', *Common Knowledge* 21 (2015), pp. 253–63.
57. Tassi, *Women and Revenge*, p. 34.
58. But not, as sometimes alleged on the strength of *Iliad* 19.400–18 and Heraclitus fr. 94 DK, of the 'natural order': see the insightful discussion of Sarah Iles Johnston, 'Xanthus, Hera and the Erinyes (*Iliad* 19.400–18)', *Transactions of the American Philological Association* 122 (1992), pp. 85–98 (pp. 91–2).
59. See Barash and Lipton, *Payback*, pp. 125–6.
60. Edith Hall, *Inventing the Barbarian* (Oxford: Oxford University Press, 1989), p. 27. On gendered aspects of revenge in these instances, see Wilson, *Ransom, Revenge and Heroic Identity*, pp. 32–3 and McHardy, *Revenge*, pp. 37–8.
61. Cf. Harrison's argument, outlined previously, that the earliest Erinyes were actually envisaged in serpentine form, only later gaining their wings and associations with dogs. Harrison, 'Delphika', p. 205.
62. On which see Hall, *The Theatrical Cast of Athens*, pp. 99–169 and Edith Hall, *Greek Tragedy: Suffering under the Sun* (Oxford: Oxford University Press, 2010), pp. 126–8, 220–7.
63. Edith Hall, 'Tragedy Personified', in Chris Kraus, Simon Goldhill, Helene P. Foley and Jas Elsner (eds), *Visualizing the Tragic: Drama, Myth & Ritual in Greek Art & Literature* (Oxford: Oxford University Press, 2007), pp. 221–56.
64. See Matthews and Salvo in this volume.
65. Michael Junge, *Untersuchungen zur Ikonographie der Erinys in der griechischen Kunst* (Kiel: Christian-Albrechts-Universität, 1983).
66. Sabian, *Erinys*.

67. Heather Hirschfield, 'The Maternal Penitent in Early Modern Revenge Tragedy', in Dympna Callaghan (ed.), *The Impact of Feminism in English Renaissance Studies* (Basingstoke and New York: Palgrave MacMillan, 2007), pp. 53–66. For the way gender is formulated in these manuals, see Jacqueline Murray, *Handling Sin: Confession in the Middle Ages* (York: Medieval Press, 1998), pp. 79–94.
68. Froma I. Zeitlin, *Playing the Other: Gender and Society in Classical Greek Literature* (Chicago: The University of Chicago Press, 1996).
69. Leyla Navaro, 'The Passion of the "Bad Girls": Women's Struggles with Desire and Passion', in Leyla Navaro, Robi Friedman and Sharan L. Schwartzberg (eds), *Desire, Passion and Gender: Clinical Implications* (New York: Nova Science Publishers, 2011), pp. 47–60.
70. David F. Luckenbill, 'Criminal Homicide as a Situated Transaction', *Social Problems* 25 (1977), pp. 176–86.
71. T. D. Wilson, D. Reinhard, E. C. Westgate, D. T. Gilbert, N. Ellerbeck, C. Hahn, C. L. Brown and A. Shaked, 'Just Think: The Challenges of the Disengaged Mind', *Science* 345 (2014), pp. 75–7.
72. C. Leach, R. Spears, N. R. Branscombe and B. Doosje, 'Malicious Pleasure: Schadenfreude at the Suffering of another Group', *Journal of Personality and Social Psychology* 84 (2003), pp. 932–43.
73. T. Singer, B. Seymour, J. P. O'Doherty, K. E. Stephan, R. J. Dolan and C. D. Frith, 'Empathic Neural Responses are Modulated by the Perceived Fairness of Others', *Nature* 439 (2006), pp. 466–9.
74. Davina Bristow, 'Men Hungrier for Revenge than Women, Brain Scan Study Reveals', *The Telegraph*, 19 January 2006, <http://www.telegraph.co.uk/news/uknews/1508174/Men-hungrier-for-revenge-than-women-brain-scan-study-reveals.html> (last accessed 3 July 2017).
75. Singer quoted in Bristow, *Men Hungrier for Revenge*.
76. Bristow, *Men Hungrier for Revenge*.
77. Anna Camilleri, 'Sacrilegious Heroics: Biblical and Byronic Archetypes of the Vengeful Feminine', *Byron Journal* 43 (2015), pp. 109–20.

CHAPTER 2

Re-marking Revenge in Early Modern Drama[1]

Alison Findlay

In *The Tragedy of that Famous Roman Oratour Marcus Tullius Cicero* (1651) Antony's wife Fulvia longs to publish her revenge on Cicero who accused her of corruption against Rome: 'Had I his damned tongue within my clutches, / This bodkin should in bloody characters / Write my revenge.'[2] Writing in 'bloody characters' with a 'bodkin', a particularly female weapon, is a means for Fulvia to mark her revenge as part of a long tradition in which revenge is feminised. From the Erinyes, or Furies of Greek mythology, to the terrifying figure of Medea, and to Tamora's impersonation 'I am Revenge, sent from the infernal kingdom' in Shakespeare's *Titus Andronicus* (5.1.30), the sphere of vindictive action is defined as a passionate, feminine alternative to the masculine law. Vengeance is 'a kind of wild justice' as Bacon called it.[3] This chapter will extend the central argument I put forward previously about revenge being a feminine genre which overturns conventional appearances, gender identities and forms of behaviour and taps into fundamental fears about maternal power and female agency. I situate these arguments within the early modern practice of re-marking revenge tradition, and the affective power of performance.[4] Employing techniques from corpus linguistics to survey the rewriting of revenge from 1580 to 1700, I ask whether revenge tragedy is primarily an Elizabethan genre or whether it endures over time. I consider how revenge is self-consciously re-marked (rehearsed, repeated, rewritten) in performances across the seventeenth century that look back to the feminised figures of the Erinyes and Medea. I draw on neuroscience to explore how the affective power of performance engages with our own cognitive hardwiring, arguing that revenge involves a complex engagement of both human intellect and emotions. I then speculate on how its enactment in staged representations carries a heightened affective resonance for spectators, thus opening up questions about its ongoing appeal.

REVENGE INSCRIPTIONS

Over fifty years before Fulvia vowed to 'write my revenge', Bel-Imperia in Thomas Kyd's *The Spanish Tragedy* (1582–92) had sent Hieronimo a 'bloody writ', an injunction to 'revenge Horatio's death' penned in her own blood.[5] Hieronimo exacts revenge through a performance of his own dramatic writing, 'Soliman and Perseda', and concludes by biting out his own tongue. In *Marcus Tullius Cicero*, Fulvia reworks the earlier tragic climax and realises her wish to inscribe her revenge on Cicero's tongue, chopping it with her bodkin in return 'For your tart, nipping jeers' (E4). Speech, writing and silencing are intertwined in the pattern of repetition and reversal that characterises vengeance. The tradition of women writing revenge goes back to classical times. Prayers for revenge inscribed on lead tablets, dating from the first century BC and written exclusively by women, were discovered in the sanctuary of Demeter at Knidos.[6] Similarly, prayers for justice – in the form of revenge – are marked on tombstones of women at Rheneia in ancient Greece and at Alexandria in Egypt, as Irene Salvo has shown in her analysis of the inscriptions' affective power 'to channel feelings and to contain the negativity of the situation'.[7] Writing revenge indicates knowledge of – and subscription to – a tradition. As in the cases of Bel-Imperia and Fulvia, it also involves agency. Edith Hall's essay in this volume points out that men are far more likely to carry out aggressive acts of revenge but, nevertheless, the women who invoke it are active agents, following in the tradition of the Erinyes (Furies) of ancient Greek mythology. Unlike ghosts, the Erinyes are substantial, 'active and instrumental' presences who ensure that the correct retaliation takes place.[8] The Furies' dominant feminine influence continues to be instrumental, inspiring both male and female revengers in early modern drama. Kristine Steenberg notes the presence of the Erinyes in remodellings of Seneca's revenge tragedies at the Inns of Court, in translations and in plays like *Gorboduc* (1561) and *The Misfortunes of Arthur* (1587).[9] She argues that these rewritings of the Furies 'revived feminine vindictive fury to react to male traditions of blood revenge and not to aggressive women'.[10]

While the Erinyes are ambiguously gendered, and influence both men and women in tragic drama, the figure of Medea, arguably a terrifyingly aggressive woman, offers something different. She gives birth to a disturbingly independent female subjectivity through revenge, and so provides a model for active female revengers in early modern scripts. At the opening of Seneca's *Medea*, the eponymous protagonist declares 'I will become Medea', as if aware that her enactment of revenge through the script will be the means not only to construct a new identity, but also to claim her name.[11] In Act 5 she articulates the fulfilment of that goal. Paradoxically, by killing her children in revenge, she will give birth to a new self as Medea. In John Studley's 1566 translation, republished in *Seneca: His Tenne Tragedies* (1581), the tragic heroine narrates her growth to become Medea:

What durst my rude unskilfull hand assay that was of wayte?
What could the mallice of a Gyrle inuent her foes to bayte?
Still conuersaunt with wicked feates **Medea** am I made.
My blunt and dulled braynes hath so ben beate about this trade.[12]

Seneca's tragedy (unlike that of Euripides) and John Studley's translation thus configures Medea's revenge as both a rejection of motherhood and a quintessentially feminine generative act. Medea is made by revenge. As well as being highly self-conscious, Medea's lines are also deeply metatheatrical, as Ulrich von Wilamowitz-Moellendorff observed.[13] Seneca's Medea seems to be referring to the already-written tragedy in which she is determined to act, both in the sense of being self-determining and predetermined by the written script. The disturbing creative power of Seneca's *Medea* generates new stories of female revenge and selfhood by future generations of early modern writers and spectators. Katherine Heavey argues that writers have returned to Medea for thousands of years 'as a compelling woman, utterly resistant to male strictures of control, and to the obedience traditionally demanded of women in patriarchal societies, whether they are classical, medieval or early modern'.[14]

WRITING AND SURVEYING REVENGE

Writing has its own agency in the performance of revenge by incorporating characters and spectators into a tradition. Christopher Pye has argued that a 'mimetic crisis' animates revenge drama because the 'revenger becomes indistinguishable from the figure he sets himself against, and revenge becomes a matter of boundless surrogacy and substitution'. Writing, the substitution for speech, is where revenge's excess spills over into metatheatricality; a play's use of writing on stage thus points up its own repetition of a revenge script is a form 'self-incorporation', a means 'to translate itself into an allegory of its own condition'.[15] Thus, in *The Spanish Tragedy*, Bel-Imperia's letter written in blood seems 'to arrive from some phantasmatic site in and beyond the thematic logic of the play' as Pye argues. It is simultaneously a projection of Bel-Imperia's will, a materialisation of Hieronimo's dreams and desires, and a prescription from an ancient revenge tradition. Writing revenge on stage thus not only troubles the boundaries between right and wrong, between the law and the autonomy of the subject; it creates an ontological crisis for male and female characters on stage and spectators offstage. By forcing spectators to confront the paradox of absolute self-authorisation and self-annihilation demanded by revenge, the re-marking or inscription of vengeance on stage problematises spectators' own sovereignty as judges and as emotionally engaged participants.[16]

At a more literal level, Bel-Imperia and Fulvia's wish to mark their revenge through self-determining 'bloody characters', draws attention to the way 'revenge' is marked linguistically in early modern printed texts. Research in corpus linguistics has provided tools to survey the billion words from printed texts digitised in Early English Books Online (EEBO),[17] and allows us to recontextualise the orthodox view of revenge tragedy as an 'Elizabethan' genre that burst on the scene following the publication of Seneca's tragedies in 1581, and gradually declined in the following century. Fredson Bowers' definitive study, tellingly titled *Elizabethan Revenge Tragedy 1587–1642*, argued that in the early Jacobean period, the focus changed from revenge per se to a taste for violence and horror. After 1620, according to Bowers, a bourgeois disapproval of revenge and the avenging protagonist corrupted the form, so that by 1642 'Revenge has lost all power of true inspiration and remains only an artificial incentive to create and, in turn, to resolve strained and bewildering situations.'[18] Linda Woodbridge has challenged this assessment of revenge drama as decadent, arguing that vengeance was an essentially political phenomenon with very material roots in reckoning or bookkeeping, linked to the concepts of retribution and justice. Rather than becoming outmoded, revenge was used persistently 'in the service of resistance' by both Royalists and Parliamentarians throughout the English Civil Wars, she argues.[19] A third thesis proposes that revenge drama is an enduring form from classical times to the present, attracting 'writers as historically various as they are historically disparate', according to John Kerrigan.[20] Wendy Griswold's study *Renaissance Revivals* argues that the genre's enduring popularity into the late seventeenth century and beyond is due to its capacity to horrify by disturbing the symbolic boundaries between categories of living and dead, animal and human, self and environment (through dismembered body parts), and by violating cultural taboos relating to consumption (what can be eaten) and sex (incest and necrophilia).[21] Such views suggest that revenge drama may cater to our genetic legacy as human beings, allowing us to reflect on aspects of our social and psychological constitution. Women's traditional position as gatekeepers at the boundaries of human life, and their role in the pre-symbolic infantile state of vulnerable liminality, associates them with the traumatic effects caused by revenges that violate the symbolic boundaries ordering human existence. The classical prototypes of murderous mothers (Medea, Althaea and Procne), may embody ancient human anxieties about the uncanny feminine power of revenge to undo human subjects and societies.

A corpus survey of instances of the words 'revenge', 'avenge' and 'vengeance' (and all their derivatives), occurring in texts published between 1580 and 1699 and digitised in EEBO, allows us to roughly test the opposing theses of decadence, political timeliness and durability.[22] While remembering that the figures are drawn from printed texts rather than oral culture or manuscript writings, EEBO does provide a bird's-eye view of the currency of 'revenge' in early modern discourse. Such a perspective is what revenge itself appears to give those who enact it. In Thomas Goffe's translation *Orestes* (1633), for example, the tragic protagonist imagines that he cannot prove himself 'if my revenge fly not with ample wing'.[23] The revenger's appropriation of God's autonomous right to judge and punish others gives him or her an illusion of panoptic control, derived from biblical images like that in Zechariah, where a flying roll of twenty cubits long and ten cubits wide (*Zechariah* 5:1) proclaims and visits revenge on the ungodly of Israel. Early modern ministers described it as the 'flying booke of Gods vengeance'.[24] In terms of how EEBO positions us, corpus searching might be regarded as a contemporary parallel with the 'flying booke' or roll of immense proportions. As twenty-first-century readers, we assume command over a vast number of texts, flying over them with 'ample wing' like the avenger who adopts the divine prerogative of omniscient judgement. Corpus analysis offers a 'surface' reading, a glimpse of the panoramic wide vista of a word or a concept across fragments of texts. It is akin to what French philosophy would call *survoler* – a term coined by Raymond Ruyer in 1952, meaning to fly over but also to self-survey – to become critically aware that we are sensationally embedded in what we appear to survey from outside.[25] Gilles Deleuze and Felix Guattari expand Ruyer's point about experiential process to regard *survoler* or survey as a concept defined by 'the inseparability of a finite number of heterogeneous components traversed by a point in absolute oversight, at infinite speed'.[26] This accurately describes the experience of reading revenge across EEBO using a corpus method and a tool like Andrew Hardie's CQPweb, where the results can be produced in seconds.[27]

From our position of surveying panoptically, we enjoy something of the revenger's illusion of control over the textual and dramatic world we survey. A corpus method allows us to access what Raymond Williams famously called a 'structure of feeling' about revenge in early modern society, and its changes from one generation to the next.[28] A decade by decade survey of occurrences of 'revenge' and its related terms in digitised texts from 1580 up to 1700 produces statistics of occurrences per million words (Table 2.1). We see an explosion of 'revenge' instances in 1590s following the pattern identified by

Table 2.1 Occurrences of 'revenge' and its associates in digitised texts, 1580–1700.

Years	Number of occurrences of 'revenge' and its associates
1580–9	130
1590–9	167
1600–9	134
1610–19	146
1620–9	126
1630–9	120
1640–9	112
1650–9	102
1660–9	108
1670–9	106
1680–9	109
1690–9	112

Bowers but thereafter a steady maintenance of interest in the term. Statistical evidence from the 1630s to 1660 supports Linda Woodbridge's thesis that revenge maintained its currency as a highly politicised form in the lead up to the English Civil Wars and their aftermath. The statistics from 1660 to 1699 demonstrate the sustained popularity of revenge until the end of the century, when theatrical practices and a ruling monarch were restored. A steady-state 'structure of feeling' about revenge, as revealed by its linguistic occurrences, may point to its capacity to probe and disturb enduring – universal – human values, as Wendy Griswold proposes. Indeed, extending the chronological survey of EEBO to the years preceding the advent of Elizabethan revenge tragedy shows comparable average occurrences for the years 1530–80 (127 per million words) with a peak of occurrences in the decade 1550–9 (155 per million words). The overall average indicates an established preoccupation with revenge, supporting the thesis of durability, while the peak in 1550–60, during the crises of succession after the deaths of Henry VIII (1547), Edward VI (1553), Lady Jane Grey, the nine-days queen (1553) and Mary I (1558), confirms revenge's 'timeliness' at moments of political instability.[29]

REVENGE AND AFFECT

Subjecting the data from 1580 to 1700 to a further corpus test of collocation reveals that the most common associations of revenge do cluster around apparently quintessential human concerns with desire, death, divinity and justice. If we discount the prepositions 'on' 'upon' 'to' and 'of', and the interesting reflexive 'himself', the remaining fifteen terms from the top twenty collocates fall into three groups. The first relate to divine beings: 'God' (twenty)', Gods' (seventeen), 'divine' (fifteen), and to ethics: injury (ten), 'injuries' (six), 'just' (eight) and 'wrongs' (nine). A second group relates to affect: 'wrath' (four), 'desire' (thirteen), 'malice' (sixteen), 'quarrel' (nineteen, predominantly as a noun) and to the body: 'blood' (eleven) and 'death' (fourteen); while the final category are active verbs: 'take' (three) and 'execute' (seven). If we narrow the chronological range to the years 1630–40 'execute', 'wrath', 'blood' and 'take' move up to the top four collocates (after 'upon' and 'on').[30]

These results support that view that revenge drama revives and re-circulates, like revenge itself, because its fundamental human concerns exert a tightly sprung, intractable grip on spectators' emotions. As we read or watch individual plays, we are embedded, in a tangible sense, in the peculiar emotional frisson of revenge. The Athenian Erinyes' affective power is tied to revenge's prehistoric raw emotion as Edith Hall's essay in this volume amply demonstrates. Even though the Erinyes were not originally gendered, 'females have always shouldered the ideological load in *symbolic* explorations of the dark side of revenge', she argues, citing Greek tragedy's representations of the Erinyes as snaky haired women (played by men) as instrumental in consolidating their femininity in ritual, mythopoeia, literature and philosophy due to their chthonic, thanatological and maternal associations.[31] The chthonic 'feminine' energies that drive revenge always threaten to erupt from within the civilised masculine superstructures, physical and cultural, that govern communities.

In the case of early modern revenge drama, excess threatens generic boundaries, producing shared jokes between spectators and conspiratorial revengers, or horrid laughter at the grotesque violence enacted as a result of their plots. John Kerrigan, Nicolas Brooke and Jonathan Dollimore all noted that revenge tragedy invariably spills over into comedy.[32] It is as though the feminine spirit of revenge deliberately imitates and deconstructs the masculine model of tragedy where the fall of an exceptional hero excites the pity, awe and fear of spectators. The twists of feeling spun in the weaving of a revenge plot are much more quizzical, involuntary and perverse as Aristotle and his early modern translators acknowledged. Thomas Hobbes' 1637 summary of his *Rhetoric* explained that anger was a 'desire of revenge, joyned with greefe' for neglect, and 'in *Anger* there is also pleasure proceeding from the imagination of revenge to come'.[33]

Aristotle recognises that the anticipation of re-enacting and reversing the direction of a felt injury gives the revenger a feeling of control, an important psychological counterbalance to their sense of neglect. Research using positron emission topography has offered scientific evidence to support Aristotle's thesis on 'pleasure proceeding from the imagination of revenge to come' by showing that 'altruistic punishment' activates the striatum, a subcortical region of the brain producing positive emotions, in place of another region of the brain producing negative emotions at having been violated. Good feelings continue to dominate even when the revenge is taken at a personal cost.[34] A 1686 translation of Aristotle's *Rhetoric* likewise observes that 'he that acts a piece of Revenge, does it to gratify himself'.[35]

The pleasure of revenge is expressed by protagonists across the period from Hieronimo's '*Vindicta mihi!*' (3.13.1) in *The Spanish Tragedy* where 'all shall be concluded in one scene' (4.1.190), through to Valerius in John Crown's *Caligula: A Tragedy* (1698) who kisses the corpse of Julia with the words 'Revenge! Revenge! Oh how it swells my heart!'[36] The ecstasy of claiming the godlike sovereignty of *vindicta mihi* and becoming a glorious exception to the law is produced by awareness that it is also the moment of self-destruction. Triumphant self-revelations like Vindice's ''Twas Vindice murdered thee! . . . murdered thy father! . . . And I am he!' are effectively, and paradoxically, acts of self-murder which will imminently sentence the revenger to death.[37] The transcendent passion that 'will make the murderer bring forth himself' (5.3.118) also kills him for, as Christopher Pye remarks, 'suicide supplicates sovereignty in the self-exceeding, self-completing gesture of a self-authorizing subjectivity'.[38]

How do the conflicting terms associated with revenge in the collocations – 'wrath', 'desire', 'blood', 'death', 'injuries', 'God', 'just', 'execute' – and the complex network of emotions they signify – communicate themselves to spectators when they are performed on the stage? Cognitive scientists' discovery of the so-called 'mirror neuron' provides a starting point to appreciate the peculiarly affective power of revenge drama in the theatre. Mirror neurons reveal a physiological basis to empathy, suggesting that humans make spontaneous *embodied* comprehension of the actions, emotions and intentions of others.[39] We 'see it feelingly' (*King Lear* 4.5.145), sensing others' intentions, actions and emotions physiologically and 'resonate' in empathy. Bruce McConachie and F. Elizabeth Hart recognised the relevance of such research to theatre practice, arguing that when an actor on stage performs feelings, the spectator involuntarily mirrors these him or herself, creating an affective bond with the character and possibly the actor. Moreover, the physiological likeness of human brains means that common mental processes can be assumed transhistorically, alongside 'the varying historical contingencies' that structure people's bodies and minds'.[40] An awareness of cognitive processes in early modern England can thus refine an analysis of revenge drama's appeal at the specific cultural and political moments of its production, while also suggesting its enduring popularity through the seventeenth century.

Actors and spectators at a performance of revenge drama are in a heightened echo chamber of empathetic resonance since revenge's basic pattern of repetition is endlessly circular and familiar. As a result of their mirror neurons, spectators resonate empathetic attachment to the revenger's sense of injury even though they know full well that the actor him or herself has no such emotions, and the external display of them as feelings is a practised skill. Toggling or oscillating[41] between resonant empathy and admiration of the actor's art is a typical feature of revenge that neatly mirrors the relationship spectators have to watching a revenger on stage. Revenge characters and their dramatists self-consciously play with the tension between a passion that drives the revenger and the poise with which he or she crafts a perfect revenge. Thus, Gaspar, the eponymous anti-hero of *The Bastard* (1652), can draw spectators to share his sense of justifiable rage against the 'treach'rous animals' who reject him and, simultaneously, to celebrate the artistry of his revenge. 'Have I not laboured finely? Has my brain / Not won the Laurell wreath?' he asks spectators, and cues his victims on stage with the dry observation 'More objects still of ruine? this will be / A bloudy Poppet-play'.[42]

An awareness of the concept of revenge is essential to its operation. Animals cannot take revenge because vengeance is, according to Robert J. Stainton, 'a social phenomenon like bidding three no trump or making a promise'.[43] The articulation of a commitment to revenge is an essentially performative act and on stage it invariably engages spectators' emotions. Looking back to Bacon's claim that 'vindictive persons live the lives of witches' (p. 8), we might say that dramatic revengers – male and female – cast a spell against their adversaries. Their ritualistic dedications to revenge invariably incorporate spectators as witnesses, and infect them with the passion and the charismatic sovereign agency enacted on stage. For example, in James Shirley's *The Maides Revenge* (1639), based on two sisters' tragic rivalry, spectators' ambiguous attitudes towards the legacy of powerful, female revenge going back to Medea, are deftly manipulated. Katherine Heavey has pointed out that Shirley referred to the tragic story of Medea's murder of her younger brother (and flight with Jason) in *The Schoole of Complement* (1625) and *The Triumph of Beautie* (1646) to test the boundaries between comedy and tragedy.[44] Shirley's tragedy, *The Maides Revenge* (1638), is a much fuller rewriting of the Elizabethan Senecan *Medea* that has, thus far, gone unnoticed.

Catalina, the jealous, elder sister, takes centre stage in the opening acts, determined to 'prove a wandering starre' in a course of maleficent plotting 'which I must finish for my selfe' (D2v).[45] When her lover, Antonio, is murdered, the younger sister Berinthia is driven to retaliate and betters her sister's instruction in embracing revenge. Berinthia vows to emerge from the 'icy Alpes of snow' which 'Have buried my whole nature' (I1v). Through the generative power of revenge 'it shall now / Turne Element of fire and fill the ayre / With bearded Comets, threatning death and horrour / For my wrong'd innocence' (I1v–I2). Such energetic incantation, like Medea's sorcery, excites a mood of anticipation. To enact her own metamorphosis, Berinthia invokes the Furies in a soliloquy that recognises the maternal origins of revenge:

> if there be
> Those furies which doe waite on desperate men,
> As some have thought, and guide their hands to mischiefe.
> Come from the wombe of night, assist a maide
> Ambitious to be made a monster like you;
> I will not dread your shapes, I am dispos'd
> To be at friendship with you, and want nought
> But your blacke aide to seale it. (I2)

As well as invoking the Erinyes, Berinthia's words recall and regenerate a tradition of female revengers going back to Seneca's *Medea*. The lines draw directly on John Studley's translation which adds an appeal to the Furies by Medea, as if she cannot murder her children without supernatural help. Berinthia's appeal for help to 'assist a maide / Ambitious to be made a monster like you' may thus be directed not just to the Furies, but also to the monstrous Senecan *Medea* as an earlier revenge 'script' that she is determined to follow. As a maid, Berinthia does not commit infanticide. Her status as a victim, as in many Elizabethan representations of Medea, makes her turn to revenge more sympathetic. Nevertheless, Berinthia wrestles with 'Nature' and transcends the 'tie of blood' (I3) to kill two members of her family: poisoning her sister (and rival) and stabbing her brother while he is at rest in the supposedly safe, domestic space of their father's house.

Like Seneca's Medea, Berinthia gives birth to a new self in preparing and enacting her revenge. Bloody deeds and subjectivity merge so that, one might say, revenge becomes her: 'she' emerges as a triumphant sovereign subject. Poison and passionate self-determination 'Make up the fire that *Berinthia* / And her revenge must bathe in' (I3) before stabbing herself (I3v). Her father

Villarezo offers a metatheatrical commentary on her performance, redefining his 'girle' as 'the Tragedian', and 'mother of all this / Horror' (I4). Berinthia thus shifts, like Studley's Senecan Medea, from the position of a relatively helpless virgin to the mother of a revenge tragedy whose children are her murderous deeds. Her generative power as 'author' depends upon her foreknowledge of Medea and earlier revenge traditions. As Chloe Kathleen Preedy's chapter in this volume shows, 'the female revenger who is knowledgeable about classical sources' can use her learning and eloquence to 'shape the plot of her tragedy'.[46] In *The Maides Revenge*, Berinthia's knowledge of her avenging foremothers allows her to recreate herself in their image.

A more recent model for Berinthia's speech is Lady Macbeth's appeal to the spirits. Inga-Stina Ewbank noted the influence of Medea's invocation of the Furies in John Studley's translation,[47] while Margaret Tassi identifies a 'latent revenge play centred on the myth of female ascendency and female heroic mettle' in Shakespeare's tragedy.[48] Robert S. Miola notes traces of Seneca's *Medea* in the play and observes that Lady Macbeth, like Medea, 'urges transcendent self-creation through terrible action' although, this time, it is Macbeth who must act.[49] Shirley's Berinthia recreates the Medean legacy more faithfully by translating words into action. She draws attention to herself as the full dramatic flowering of that female revenge fantasy, using Medea's incantatory power as sorceress to seduce spectators as well as transforming herself into a revenger.

How are spectators implicated in the revival of an ancient legacy of feminine vengeance in the present moment of performance? Like the snakes who cross the boundaries between the individual and the underworld, in the case of the Erinyes, Berinthia's invocation crosses temporal boundaries and, additionally, boundaries between the stage and playgoers in the performance context. Gina Bloom's book *Voice in Motion* has shown that the ear is vulnerably open; auditors cannot avoid hearing this invocation so the transformative power of vengeance penetrates their ears with contaminating affect.[50] For empathetic women spectators, the half-familiar words of Berinthia's spell summon a shared awareness of the long dramatic history of revenge tragedy, and combine it with their personal, immediate fantasies of, or desires for, revenge. May not this collective memory make them into Berinthia's accomplices, on both emotional and cognitive levels? In performance, the invocation to 'come from the wombe of night, assist a maide' is addressed to the audience. Spectators are petitioned and positioned *as* the Erinyes who transform Berinthia into their agent, while she is a figure who can exorcise their vengeful desires, enacting the positive, cathartic aspect of revenge. In an uncanny way, the repetition of familiar vows of vengeance transforms the audience from consumers to producers of Berinthia as a monstrous Medea: she is terrifyingly alien but simultaneously perilously close to home in a society approaching civil war. It is a moment of uncertain but undeniable 'becoming' for character (and possibly performer) and for spectators; a moment at which, Christopher Pye argues, spectatorial subjectivity consists in 'a reiterated border crossing and *aphansis*' a fading and thickening process of 'disappearance and reappearance to itself'.[51]

GENDERING REVENGE AND THE CIVIL WARS

It is unsurprising that, as a form of 'wild justice', revenge continued to flourish in drama during the English Civil Wars, when principles of law, justice and hierarchy were radically unsettled by revolutionary acts and texts. *The Rebellion of Naples* (1649), for example, shows that political institutions and gender conventions are equally fragile. Its political plot dramatises a recent, real life popular revolt that took place in Naples in the summer of 1647, which was led by a Neapolitan fisherman, Massanello. The rebellion and its consequences offer a direct allegory of political events England: what the Prologue calls 'seasonable things' or 'fightings twixt the people and their Kings' (A4v).[52] Massanello's form of wild justice against royalist oppression produces a feminised and darkly carnivalesque revolution or inversion of the symbolic order. Cultural taboos about consumption and the boundaries between human and animal are violated in action which replays the excesses of earlier revenge tragedy (particularly *Titus Andronicus*). Bakers are to be baked in their own ovens 'untill you see them all over of a crust, and their eies look like parch'd plumbs upon a plumb cake' (p. 36). Butchers are to be carried 'unto their own slaughter-house' knocked out like their oxen and have their throats cut like their calves. Such grotesque images materialise the maternal power of revenge to undo human subjects and social order.

Gender disorder where 'women preach and weare the britches' (p. 76) is particularised in the revenge subplot of Ursula, Massanello's elder daughter, who becomes jealous when her half-sister, Flora, is wooed by the Viceroy's son Antonio. Ursula tells spectators 'How I burn to be revenged' (p. 61). Ursula wants vengeance for her mother Agatha's death since Massanello had broken her neck when, like a 'Fury', she stabbed Flora in the face (p. 40). Ursula finds her half-sister's snow-white purity repugnant and identifies herself, by contrast, with spicy black pepper: which 'hath a good smacke' (p. 58). She poisons Flora on her wedding day and drags the prince into the revenge cycle. Any return to order under the new regime is thus rendered suspect: the prince's demand to see Ursula quartered and fed to the dogs suggests he is contaminated by her ravenous desire for wild justice and is destined to go to the dogs himself.

Revenge is also presented negatively as a politically destabilising and tyrannous passion in William Peaps' post-war pastoral *Love In Its Extasie* (1649), a play notable for its high frequency of instances of 'revenge' words (forty in total), although here it is the male characters who are vengeful.[53] Peaps disingenuously assures readers that his old play does not deal with 'common issues of this regnant age' (A2) but its politics clearly identify revenge with the dangerous power of ungoverned agency.[54] The play equates the self-centred quality of masculine revenge with absolutism and shows this to be inimical to the successful running of a kingdom or commonwealth. Likewise, the absolute passion driving male revenge is characterised as fanatical. Charastus (motivated partly by news of his sister's death) vows to recover his crown and descend on the usurper Bermudo (who has outlawed love) with apocalyptic fury:

> Charastus: I'le break upon him,
> Like some direfull Comet sparkling my vengeance
> 'Bout his Throne, or like a swelling channel long damn'd up
> Will I discharge my streams on all sides of him,
> Rushing forth with a strong and hideous torrent
> As mischievous as irresistible. (C4v)

Fidelio sagely cautions him that such tyrannical power would 'violate your Laws' and provide a dangerous example to subjects. The deputy Bermudo, equally impassioned, frantically attributes the escape of his royal prisoners to the work of 'damn'd Magitians', sent by the Furies 'To stupifie a Kings divinity'. The older deities of vengeance seem to have already taken (him) over; he admits that, 'Fury like lightning feeds upon my soul' (C3v).

The extravagance of male revenge for honour is held up for mockery in the duel between the romantic leads Virtusus and Fidelio, who enter with naked rapiers in Act 2 Scene 1. Fidelio who is angry with Virtusus for locking up his sister Constantia, warns the young man that a 'fierce and cruel beast' or 'hideous Monster' has appeared on the hill and threatens to swallow Virtusus alive. The monster is unequivocally male:

> Fidelio: Alas! it follows thee[.] Here, take this sword,
> And stand upon thy Guard: See, how he yawnes,
> As if he meant to swallow thee alive:
> His eyes are numberless from which proceeds
> Such a sulphureous flame, that alas, I fear,
> The very smell will kill thee: Oh what a black
> And noysome mist his gaping mouth sends forth?
> His tongues spit floods of venome, and his reaching tayle
> Sweeps down whole mountaines, on his
> Cristed back doth rise, so many and such massy spears,
> That you would swear whole Armies
> Came to thy destruction. (B4)

The invisible beast of Fidelio's imagination is 'Revenge' which has swallowed his whole being. Objectifying the consuming appetite of revenge rather than enunciating its energising frisson within himself dissolves its power to affect spectators through empathy. Playgoers cannot resonate with the passion of the revenger if it is an invisible monster. Peaps deconstructs revenge's affective power further through Virtusus' response. He is comically nonplussed by this hyperbolic performance. He cannot recognise the monster, or his challenger, or what is at stake:

> Fidelio: You must dye.
> Virtusus: It is acknowledged: So must we All.
> Fidelio: Nay, by this Hand I mean, Revenges Instrument.
> Virtusus: I am so innocent,
> I can't perswade my self to credit you. (B4–B4v)

Disbelief in revenge as a viable modus operandi for heroism or for governing a country is thus firmly encouraged amongst those watching.

The triad of female characters, Thesbia, Donatella and Catalina, imitate the Erinyes as 'The Kindly Ones', ensuring right is done to redeem the kingdom of Sicily from chaotic misgovernment. Their actions are restorative rather than vengeful in the conventional sense. Thesbia is praised for having 'dissolv'd this mass of Tyranny, / And brought our long-lost honors to their former lustre' (G2v). Donatella adopts the role of Echo to take a passive revenge on Bermudo (whose rejection apparently killed her), adopting the role of Echo to invoke his remorse and shame. She mimics his words, in the typical pattern of vengeance as imitation or repetition, before reappearing as Diana, the icily chaste, punitive goddess, and simultaneously a revenant of herself, fading and returning as Donatella (Act 3 Scene 4, D3–D4), until he is reformed. More assertively, Constantia shames all the men by being still more shameful. She fights Bermudo's ban on love by openly declaring her passion for Fidelio, earning the exclamation 'Oh, Audacity, This is she!' (E3v) Like the outspoken female sectaries who challenged the authority of established religion and patriarchy during the commonwealth, she tells the king plainly that a woman who 'loves most truly' and declares it publicly 'Ought to be thought most modest' (E3v). While her outrageous loquacity tips the play into comedy, dumbfounding the watching men, she makes a serious point: what is needed for harmonious society to work again in England is *not* the violence, anger and self-aggrandisement represented by revenge but the giving of self in love, understanding and cooperation. Peaps' pastoral thus optimistically re-marks feminine retaliation and restitution as just while critiquing the aggressive masculine forms of revenge from a former age as anachronistic.

GENDER HYBRIDITY AND REVENGE

Revenge tragedies of the later seventeenth century did not simply abandon past traditions, but often self-consciously reworked them in elaborate critiques of the form itself, or to unsettle assumptions about legitimacy, gender and race. Cosmo Manuche's *The Bastard* (1652) dramatises Edith Hall's suggestion that revenge is transgender – conceptualised as feminine, but enacted by men – through its hybrid protagonist. Indeed, the play itself is a bastardised palimpsest of borrowings from early modern revenge tragedies and feminised classical allusions that reflect the protagonist's own hybridity. Indeed, the play itself is a bastardised palimp-sest of borrowings from early modern revenge tragedies and feminised classical allusions that reflect the protagonist's own hybridity. The Prologue admits the play is 'A *Spanish BASTARD* in an *English* dresse', an appropriation of plot from Ford's *'Tis Pity She's A Whore* (also set in Seville) and Middleton and Rowley's *The Changeling* (set in Alicante).[55] As a bastard, the protagonist, Gaspar is feminised: he is a mother's son and draws naturally on the illegitimate, generative energies associated with the Erinyes. His role as a 'Cash-Keeper' (p. 13) to his master Alonzo, gives him the force of male reckoning to translate these feminine impulses into retributive action when Alonzo breaks his promises to marry his daughter Mariana to Gaspar. Unlike Berinthia or Lady Macbeth, Gaspar does not need to expel or reject the feminine in him. On the contrary, it is an empowering complementary force that transforms him from a helpless victim to a protagonist with full sovereign subjectivity. When Gaspar is betrayed a second time, he turns to the underworld, home of the Furies: 'I'm resolv'd / *Flectere si nequeo Superos, Acheronta movere*' [If I cannot order the world above, I will invoke Acheron] (p. 46). Gaspar uses Chaves as a Medea-like pawn to make his rival Picarro's wedding to Mariana 'Fatall as *Jasons*' (p. 49). Picarro sums up Gaspar's revenge as feminine in origin, the natural consequence of his identity as a mother's son:

> Who e're begot thee, sure thy mother drew
> Her blood from th *Bassarides*, or was
> Of near allyance to that cursed Hag,
> That into fritters slic'd her only son:
> Hell was thy Cradle, and some *Harpy* did
> Perform the office of a wretched nurse:
> Thy heart can study nought but treachery. (p. 77)

A host of madly impassioned female revengers are conjured up in these lines. The Bassarides or Maenads furiously tear Pentheus in pieces to avenge his ban against their worship of Dionysus, as dramatised in Euripides' *The Bacchae*. Pentheus' mother Agave, also a Maenad, rips off his head and takes it back to Thebes. In Greek mythology the Harpies, monstrous bird-like women, carry wrongdoers to the Erinyes, with whom they are often conflated. Gaspar is thus a son of collective feminine vengeance. Like the Erinyes, he is an agent, prompting men to defend their honour with revenge in order to serve his own interests to be 'rid of all' (p. 54) by setting one enemy off against another.

Gaspar's sense of injury is shared by the play's female characters. Varina and Mariana are credited with the potential for subversive action through their association with Medea. Varina, who wants to marry Roderiguez rather than the foolish Praepontio, refers in passing to '*Medea's* inchanting spels to

Aeson' (p. 7 Act 1 Scene 3). Mariana's lover Chaves notices her beauty might well captivate men like '*Medea's* charms and inchanted hearbs' (p. 10). Both women also use potions: Varina imitating Juliet to test her lover and Mariana following Beatrice-Joanna's trickery. Picarro tells Mariana 'Thou hast a place about thee, where the furies / Take up their mansion' (p. 62) and refers to her and her maid as 'Harpies' (p. 70).

It is Roderiguez' sister Eugenia who is most like Medea in exacting a bloody revenge on Chaves who has deserted her. Unable to 'stirre a fury' in her brother to 'devoure him up / Like some wild *Anthropophagus*' (p. 48) and so redeem the family honour, she cross-dresses and attempts to persuade Balthazar that 'gratious *Themis* / Has you decipherd for her instrument / Of vengeance' (p. 51). Themis, the elder sister of the Erinyes, is 'The Right Way of Doing Things', especially retaliation for broken oaths, so is an appropriate choice for the wronged Eugenia.[56] Appropriately, she assumes female dress again to let 'Some vengeance fall from my provoked hand' on Chaves' corpse: 'Now my disguise is uselesse, Heav'n hath own'd / My cause at length, and its due vengeance showr'd / Upon his perjur'd head' (p. 76). This is a symbolic act since Chaves is already dead. Nevertheless, it reverses the convention of woman as agent and man as actor of revenge since Eugenia rights the wrongs to her father and brother, stabbing Chaves once for each of them. Before she stabs herself, she rejoices that 'my rage now sits / Triumphant in her element'; her words bring together the feminine chthonic tropes of consumption and annihilation, and the masculine principle of reckoning. She feeds her rage with 'wounds' and makes Chaves' blood 'repay / Both principall and Interest of my tears!' (p. 76). *The Bastard* thus presents revenge as a gender-hybrid form by paralleling a mother's son and a cross-dressing woman as successful reckoners who manipulate others to craft the 'bloudy Poppet-play' (p. 76) of revenge.

Gender hybridity is taken further in Elkanah Settle's *Love and Revenge* (1675) which features a cross-dressed female revenger as protagonist. Anne Hermanson has argued that translations of Seneca in the mid-seventeenth century produced a revival of revenge tragedy that emphasised spectacle and horror. The play rewrites *Hamlet* as part of its grotesque scenes which pick up on the darkly comic nature of revenge tragedy. Hermanson reads post-Restoration 'horror plays' as 'troping [the] recurrent, deep-seated and unresolved anxieties' of a nation traumatised by civil war, and concerned with religious and political unrest caused by the Duke of York's Catholic sympathies.[57] Hermanson's view that the spectre of popery and the catastrophic consequences of its resurgence in post-Restoration England are represented in the villainous queens of post-Restoration tragedy[58] is borne out in *Love and Revenge*. Settle constructs a feminised rewriting of *Hamlet* which sets two female revengers, Queen Fredigond and the disguised Clothilda, in opposition.

Before the play begins Clothilda has been raped by Queen Fredigond's son, Clotair. Clothilda wants revenge for her rape, while Fredigond wants revenge on Clothilda's brothers who mistakenly killed Fredigond's brother to avenge the dishonour of their sister. Fredigond delights in the sense of empowerment vengeance lends her, asking 'Is not Revenge a Pastime for the Gods?' (p. 6). For all her bravado, however, she personifies Love rather than Revenge in the play's title. It is Clothilda, disguised as the black slave Nigrello, who embodies 'Revenge', and her vengeance, like Hamlet's, is 'one that moves most slowly' and 'is most wise' (p. 15). 'My Art', she claims, will right personal wrongs and cure a kingdom that is out of joint (p. 18). From the character's perspective, personal injury, being ruined by rape, is the motor: 'Revenge, / Does feed on Ruine. Ruines are / Its Food and Life' she declares in appropriately broken lines that draw spectators to empathise with her suffering (p. 13). Did spectators' senses resonate with the female body of the actress, Mary Lee, within the breeches role of Nigrello, or was the performance even more radical in eliding racial and gendered others as 'wracks' (p. 13) left on the shores of patriarchal imperialist conquest? The possibilities are suggestive.

Clothilda's revenge on Fredigond and Clotair is also a public service to France. As her brother recognises, 'the Ulcerous State is ripe and we must lance it' (p. 54). The accession of the virtuous Prince Lewis, 'Agent in my revenge' (p. 33), promises a new beginning. Nevertheless, as Clothilda's black disguise materially reminds spectators, she is also driven by darker motives. Like Hamlet, she wants her victims dead *and* damned: 'My Vengeance calls / For black and tainted blood', she insists, plotting to kill Fredigond while nothing 'may save her Soul which my Revenge would damn' (p. 49). Clothilda sadistically gives Fredigond and her lover Clarmount opportunity for 'unlawful Lust' and hope of life, only to massacre them moments later:

> Revenge, oh dear Revenge. Name me the man
> In story that e're prosecuted Vengeance
> So far as I have done . . . .
> To stop the Adulterous breath just in that minute
> As damn'd their Souls is a revenge so charming.
> But business now grows thick . . . .
> . . . . Burn on
> Burn on my best loved Rage. Ye infernal Furies
> Be kind, and heighten my weak gall; be but
> My slaves to day, and be my Saints tomorrow. (pp. 74–5)

In spite of her male disguise, Clothilda proclaims she outdoes Hamlet, or any other 'man in story' in prosecuting vengeance. She claims kinship with a more radical feminine tradition of self-transformation represented by Medea. By Act 5 Clothilda has proved she is no longer a sympathetic victim, a personification of 'Ruine'. She has given birth to a new identity as the bringer of ruin to others. Her repetition of 'Revenge' and 'Burn on', along with her appeal to the 'infernal Furies', recreates the generative power of revenge through its incantations. The mysterious, androgynous black slave in breeches with a siren's urgent voice must surely have intrigued and perhaps seduced any playgoer harbouring secret fantasies of revenge.

In line with its heroine's feminist agenda, the play hollows out masculine revenge through a parodic, highly metatheatrical rewriting of *Hamlet*. Prince Clotair knows his father's 'Fate calls down / For thoughts of Vengeance' but comically postpones revenge until tomorrow to satisfy his love or rather lust for Aphelia 'tonight' (p. 15).[59] The terrifying spectre of Old King Hamlet is reduced to a piece of theatrical trickery in *Love and Revenge* when Queen Fredigond makes Clarmount put on her dead husband's nightgown to avoid detection in her bedchamber. She testifies that Childrick's ghost, 'most terribly frightful', appeared to her and 'Thrice did he cry Revenge!' giving Clarmount chance to escape 'disguised in the habit of Childrick, his face discolour'd white' (p. 26). Far from urging the 'spirit' to conference, the unheroic Clotair is anxious to get rid of it, bidding 'Do but depart, thy presence does not please me' (p. 26).

Instead, the play celebrates Clothilda as 'thy Sexes champion' (p. 72). Her revenge is radical in rewriting and re-righting rape from the perspective of the victim. She also protects Aphelia from the tragedies that befall Ophelia, Philomel and countless other women. Clothilda's disguise as Nigrello the slave performatively critiques the denigration of the rape victim's body and actively redeems the wronged woman through revenge.[60] This is tempered by a conservative restraint. Clothilda will not kill her rapist, Clotair, because he is King, showing an enduring loyalty to royalist values amidst the chaos of wrongdoing. Her return to gender conformity is less conservative. She puts 'on my own Sex agen' to broadcast her purity, presumably donning the white wig she wears for the Epilogue. Clothilda asks that her deeds be judged as 'Revenge: A satisfaction due to an Injur'd Lady' (p.72), the emphasis on victimhood echoing early modern softenings of Medea's role. Revenge is thus morally and materially whitened. Its strange androgynous quality, as a means of righting wrongs for both men and women, is advertised in the play's remarkable Epilogue which is spoken by Mary Lee 'in a Mans Habit' (as Nigrello) and 'in a white Wig, and her Face discovered' as Clothilda (b2v). Although the dramatic character of Clothilda is dead, the masculine power and feminine spirit of revenge return together to the stage to speak to the 'Ladies' in the audience. It is their 'Anger' and 'Indulgence' that have created the production, testifying once again to the affective power of revenge (as well as love).

As these examples show, playwrights and revengers who self-consciously rewrite revenge as part of an ancient tradition, influence the gendering of revenge. The practice is illustrated right at the end of the seventeenth century by Mary Pix's *The False Friend or the Fate of Disobedience* (1699).[61] The play opens with the arrival to Sardinia of the newly married Emilus and Lovisa. Emilus is greeted by his friend and foster-sister, Appamia, who harbours a secret love for him. Although Appamia has never revealed her love for Emilius, her fury at having to attend to Lovisa and 'prepare the Bridal bed' makes her sound more like an abandoned wife than a foster-sister (p. 9). Refusing to accept a passive role as the 'injur'd Woman' (p. 24), Appamia turns instead to the regenerative power of revenge:

I begin to wake –
What was't but slighted Love, made *Medea*,
Prove a Fury? Doubtless her breast was
Once as soft, as Fond, as Innocent as mine
As free from black Revenge, or Dire Mischiefs –
Rise ye Furies! Instead of Tresses, Deck me
With your Curling Snakes! – For
I will sting 'em all to Death! (p. 10)

Appamia's words 'I begin to wake' replays the pattern in Seneca where Medea is 'made' a new woman through the transformative power of vengeance. Appamia conceives this creative process using metaphors of pregnancy and rebirth. She points out that the 'Seeds of Ruine grow pregnant, the very Moment / They are Sown' (p. 10). She dismisses her 'Expiring Love', and claims 'from the Death of that I Rise / Another Woman' (p. 12). Becoming 'Another Woman' ironically means becoming another Medea, enacting the *same* story of transformation from wronged victim to monstrous murderer. Appamia goes on to poison her rival, Lovisa, with barbarous cruelty.

Appamia's references to Medea and the Furies in this speech (drawing on the early modern translation), summarise revenge's matriarchal dynasty which has sown the seeds of her own actions. From the outset, she speaks with awareness of her role as actor in a tragedy predetermined by the female goddess of retribution. Nemesis has already 'Writ' Emilius' fate 'in Bloody Characters' (p. 12). Appamia is simply excelling in playing her part. She hopes that the infernal powers will 'turn o're their horrid Leaves / Of black Revenges: And set mine down most Exquisite' (p. 45).

As the subtitle of the tragedy suggests, Appamia's transgressive actions are explicitly condemned in line with the 1690s movement to moralise the stage. She presents herself as a cautionary tale against 'thoughts of Black Revenge' and 'Violent Passions' (I2) on the part of female spectators. However, like Seneca's Medea, who ascends from the scene of her crimes in a chariot, Appamia escapes punishment by the law (p. 60). Pix may be challenging the tide of early modern disapproval (and rewriting) of Seneca's supposedly immoral ending by staging brief moments of transcendent female passion or becoming. Lovisa perceives Appamia the revenger as an 'Airy Fantam' (p. 29). When Appamia poisons and contaminates the romantic heroine, Lovisa dies with a spectacular radiance that energises her whole being: 'My Breath is Flakes of Fire! My Eyes like flaming / Meteors Shoot! My Nerves, my Arteries, / Like Shrivel'd Parchment shrink in Fire – / I Burn; I Blaze: I Dye' (p. 57). Heavey remarks that 'the horror of Pix's scene is heightened' by 'the fact that it is staged' rather than being described as it is in Euripides' text.[62] The immediacy of performance heightens the physical effects of the poison and the speech of fire advertises an alarmingly embodied subjectivity, previously unseen in Lovisa's role. The ecstatic exclamations 'I Burn; I Blaze: I Dye' take actor and spectators beyond the 'Shrivel'd Parchment' of the prescribed text and its moralistic judgements on female revenge.

The recurrence of revenge in scripts from across the period 1580–1700 is thus explained not just by its timeliness at moments of political crisis or as a delayed and repeated expression of cultural trauma. The appeal of revenge is deeply rooted in the human psyche and history, and shared between actors and spectators as it is brought to life through the moment of performance. Early modern plays show that, like the Erinyes or Furies, revenge is ambiguously gendered. Its violation of symbolic and social (patriarchal) boundaries, along with its power to undo subjects – dissolving the identities of revengers and their victims, crossing the line between life and death – ally it with an unnerving chthonic female energy. Both male and female characters draw on its simultaneously creative and destructive forces, often addressing appeals for revenge to the Furies. Medea, the archetypal injured woman turned monstrous revenger, looks back to these ancient mothers and returns to haunt early modern drama. Transgressive female revengers in the texts draw, in turn, on her legacy. It should therefore come as no surprise that, in 1695, Edward Ward confidently asserted 'Nothing is so Revengeful as an injured Woman; for which Reason, the Poets have ordered the Furies to be put up in the Feminine Gender'.[63]

NOTES

1. I would like to thank Lesel Dawson, whose advice has been invaluable as I have worked to improve the essay as a whole and I offer her heartfelt thanks for her help.
2. *The Tragedy of that famous Roman oratour Marcus Tullius Cicero* (London, 1651), attributed to Fulke Greville, Lord Brooke, sig. B3v. See Janet Clare (ed.), *Drama of the English Republic, 1649–1660 Plays and Entertainments*, Revels Plays Companion Library (Manchester: Manchester University Press, 2005).
3. Francis Bacon, 'Of Revenge', in *The Essays of Lord Bacon* (London: Frederick Warne, 1889), p. 7.
4. Alison Findlay, *A Feminist Perspective on Renaissance Drama* (Oxford: Blackwell Publishers, 1998), p. 49.
5. Thomas Kyd, *The Spanish Tragedy*, ed. Philip Edwards, Revels Plays (Manchester: Manchester University Press, 1991), 3.2.26–31. All subsequent references will be to act, scene and line numbers in this edition.
6. See Matthews and Salvo in this volume.
7. Irene Salvo, 'Sweet Revenge: Emotional Factors in "Prayers for Justice"', in Angelos Chaniotis (ed.), *Unveiling Emotions: Sources and Methods for the Study of Emotions in the Greek World* (Stuttgart: Frans Steiner Verlag, 2012), pp. 235–66.
8. Hall, 'Why are the Erinyes Female?', p. 43.
9. Thomas Norton and Thomas Sackville, *Gorboduc* (London, 1561); Thomas Hughes, *The Misfortunes of Arthur* (London, 1587).

10. Kristine Steenberg, 'The Case of Anger in Early Modern Revenge Tragedies', in Jonas Liliequist (ed.), *A History of Emotions 1200–1800* (London: Pickering and Chatto, 2012), pp. 119–34.
11. John Fitch (ed.), *Seneca. Hercules, Trojan Women, Phoenician Women, Medea, Phaedra* (Cambridge, MA: Harvard University Press, 2002), p. 171. See also Winter in this volume on the way in which Seneca's Medea frequently returns to metaphors of birth and feminine generation even while she rejects conventional femininity to enact it.
12. *The seventh tragedie of Seneca*, in *Seneca: His Tenne Tragedies*, translated into English, ed. Thomas Newton (London, 1581), fol. 137v, emphaisis added.
13. Ulrich von Wilamowitz-Moellendorff, Griechische Tragödien. Band III (Berlin: Weidmann, 1906), p. 162.
14. Katherine Heavey, *Early Modern Medea: Medea in English Literature 1558–1688* (Basingstoke: Palgrave Macmillan, 2015), p. 4.
15. Christopher Pye, *The Storm at Sea: Political Aesthetics in the Time of Shakespeare* (New York: Fordham University Press, 2015), p. 86.
16. Ibid. pp. 89, 91.
17. Version 3 of EEBO, digitised by the Text Creation Partnership, contains 1,202,214,511 words in 44,422 texts. From 1580 to 1699, the period selected for this survey, the database contains 1,077,746,995 (one billion, seventy-seven million, seven hundred and forty-six thousand, nine hundred and ninety-five words) and 40,727 texts.
18. Fredson Bowers, *Elizabethan Revenge Tragedy 1587–1642* (Princeton: Princeton University Press, 1940), p. 283.
19. Linda Woodbridge, *English Revenge Drama: Money, Resistance, Equality* (Cambridge: Cambridge University Press, 2010), pp. 185, 189–222 (esp. pp. 193, 201).
20. John Kerrigan, *Revenge Tragedy: Aeschylus to Armageddon* (Oxford: Clarendon Press, 1996), p. 3.
21. Wendy Griswold, *Renaissance Revivals: City Comedy and Revenge Tragedy in the London Theatre 1576–1980* (Chicago: The University of Chicago Press, 1986), pp. 79–80.
22. Derivative forms of 'revenge' include revenges, revenged, revenging, revengeful, revengefulness. Avenge (listed by the *Oxford English Dictionary* (*OED*) as a verb meaning execution of vengeance; retributive punishment, retaliation (either upon an offender, or on account of a wrong) functions as a synonym to revenge in the period. The *OED* lists vengeance as a noun: 'The act of avenging oneself or another; retributive infliction of injury or punishment; hurt or harm done from vindictive motives' and less commonly in adjectival and adverbial phrases such as Beaumont's *The Knight of the Burning Pestle*, 'This sword is vengeance angry.' For details of the corpus survey see n. 27 below.
23. Thomas Goffe, *The tragedy of Orestes* (London, 1633), sig. C1v.
24. See, for example, William Sclater, *The ministers portion" By William*

Sclater. Batchelar of Diuinity and minister of the word of God at Pitmister in Somerset (Oxford, 1612), p. 47.
25. Raymond Ruyer, *Neo-Finalisme* (Paris: PUF, 1952), cited in Gilles Deleuze and Félix Guattari, *What Is Philosophy?*, trans. Hugh Tomlinson and Graham Burchell (New York: Columbia University Press, 1991), p. ix.
26. Ibid. p. 21.
27. Andrew Hardie, 'CQPweb – Combining Power, Flexibility and Usability in a Corpus Analysis Tool', *International Journal of Corpus Linguistics* 17:3 (2012), pp. 380–409. I am deeply indebted to Andrew Hardie for creating, maintaining and improving the CQPweb corpus tool and for advising me on how to use it. In a survey of EEBO using CQPweb, the variants of revenge, avenge and vengeance and the variant spellings with u and v were captured by the command "*[v,u]eng*" where the asterisks capture any prefix or suffix and the square brackets indicate a set of permitted alternatives. The search captured a negligible number of erroneous words: vengo (forty-eight matches in eleven different texts); scavenge and its derivatives (413 matches in 210 different texts); lueng (twenty-three matches in eleven different texts) and Swevengh (one match in one text).
28. Raymond Williams, *The Long Revolution* (London: Chatto and Windus, 1961, reprinted Peterborough, Canada, Broadview Press, 2001), pp. 64–5.
29. The same query *[v,u]eng* in texts from 1530 to 1579 returned 11,587 matches in 1,061 different texts (in 90,656,579 words [2,132 texts]; frequency: 127 instances per million words). A decade by decade survey produces the following instances per million words: 115 (1530–39); 138 (1540–49); 155 (1550–59); 118.30 (1560–69); and 125 (1570–79). In the peak decade, 1550–59, there were 1,700 matches in 179 different texts.
30. The collocation database was of texts from 1580 to 1700 captured with the search term "*[v,u]eng*" (as outlined in n. 27 above). It was subjected to a collocation search in CQPweb based on log-likelihood (a measure of word association based on statistical significance) and using a window of three words to the left and three words to the right. On collocation see: S. Hoffmann, S. Evert, N. Smith, D. Y. W. Lee and Y. Berglund Prytz, *Corpus Linguistics with BNCweb – a Practical Guide* (Frankfurt am Main: Peter Lang, 2008), pp. 149–58.
31. Hall, 'Why are the Erinyes Female?', refers to Jane E. Harrison's essay 'Delphika.-(A) The Erinyes. (B) The Omphalos', *Journal of Hellenic Studies* 19 (1899), pp. 205–51. See also Marguerite A. Tassi, *Women and Revenge in Shakespeare: Gender, Genre and Ethics* (Selinsgrove: Susquehanna University Press, 2011), pp. 31–4.
32. Kerrigan, *Revenge Tragedy*, p. 203, Nicholas Brooke, *Horrid Laughter in Jacobean Tragedy* (London: Open Books, 1979); and Jonathan Dollimore *Radical Tragedy*, second edition (Hemel Hempstead: Harvester Wheatsheaf, 1989).

33. Aristotle, *A Briefe of the Art of Rhetorique containing in substance all that Aristotle hath written in his three books of that subject*, trans. Thomas Hobbes (London, 1637), p. 69.
34. Dominique J.-F. de Quervain, Urs Fischbacher, Valerie Treyer, Melanie Schelhammer, Ulrich Schnyder, Alfred Buck and Ernst Fehr, 'The Neural Basis of Altruistic Punishment', *Science* 305.5568 (2004), pp. 1254–8, <http://science.sciencemag.org/content/305/5688/1254.full> (last accessed 22 September 2016) and Brian Knutson, 'Sweet Revenge?' *Science* 305.5688 (2004), pp. 1246–7, <http://science.sciencemag.org/content/305/5688/1246.full> (last accessed 22 September 2016).
35. Aristotle's rhetoric to Theodectes in *Aristotle's Rhetoric, or the True grounds and principles of oratory made English by the Translators of the Art of Thinking* (London, 1686), p. 56.
36. John Crown, *Caligula: A Tragedy, as it is acted at the Theatre Royal by His Majesty's Servants* (London, 1698) p. 42 (sig. G1v).
37. Cyril Tourneur [Thomas Middleton], *The Revenger's Tragedy*, ed. Brian Gibbons, New Mermaids (London: Benn, 1967), 5.3.78–9.
38. Pye, *The Storm at Sea*, p. 87.
39. Leonardo Fogassi, Vittorio Gallese, Giovanni Buccino, Laila Craighero, Luciano Fadiga and Giacomo Rizzolatti, 'Cortical Mechanism For the Visual Guidance of Hand Grasping Movements in the Monkey: A Reversible Inactivation Study', *Brain: A Journal of Neurology* 124 (2001), pp. 571–86. For an account of subsequent research on the applicability of mirror neuron theory see Richard Cook, Geoffrey Bird, Caroline Catmur et al., 'Confounding the Origin and Function of Mirror Neurons', *Behavioral and Brain Sciences* 37 (2014), pp. 177–241.
40. Bruce McConachie and F. Elizabeth Hart, 'Introduction', in *Performance and Cognition: Theatre Studies and the Cognitive Turn* (Routledge: Abingdon, 2006), pp. 7–8. Mirror neurons are discussed by George Lakoff and Mark Johnson, *Philosophy in the Flesh: The Embodied Mind and its Challenge to Western Thought* (New York: Basic Books, 1984).
41. John McGavin and Greg Walker, *Imagining Spectatorship from the Mysteries to the Shakespearean Stage* (Oxford: Oxford University Press, 2016), pp. 5–6, 46–8. The idea of switching between modes of perception comes from Gilles Fauconnier and Mark Turner, *The Way We Think: Conceptual Blending and the Mind's Hidden Complexities* (New York: Basic Books, 2003).
42. Cosmo Manuche, *The Bastard: A Tragedy* (London, 1652), pp. 42, 45, 76.
43. Robert J. Stainton, 'Revenge', *Critica: Revista Hispnoamerican de Filosofia* 38.112 (2006), pp. 3–20 (p. 6).
44. Heavey, *Early Modern Medea*, pp. 146–7.
45. James Shirley, *The Maides Revenge* (London: Printed by T[homas] C[otes], 1639), sig. D2v.
46. See Preedy in this volume (p. 184).

47. Inga-Stina Ewbank, 'The Fiend-like Queen', *Shakespeare Survey* 19 (1966), pp. 82–94 (p. 83).
48. Tassi, *Women and Revenge in Shakespeare*, p. 2.
49. Robert S. Miola, *Shakespeare and Classical Tragedy: The Influence of Seneca* (Oxford: Clarendon Press, 1992), pp. 92–121 (p. 101).
50. Gina Bloom, *Voice in Motion: Staging Gender, Shaping Sound in Early Modern England* (Philadelphia: University of Pennsylvania Press, 2007), pp. 111–17.
51. Pye, *The Storm at Sea*, p. 83.
52. T. B., *The Rebellion of Naples or The Tragedy of Massanello but rightly Tomaso Aniello di Malfa Generall of the Neopolitans* (London, 1649). For a reading of the play's politics, see Woodbridge, *English Revenge Drama*, pp. 212–13.
53. William Peaps, *Love In Its Extasie* (London: Printed by W. Wilson, 1649). In the aftermath of the civil wars, the play reuses the 1590s Inns of Court tradition noted by Steenberg, 'Case of Anger', where feminine vindictive fury is invoked to critique male traditions of blood revenge (pp. 119–34).
54. That this frequency count represents a highly remarkable feature of this particular text is clear from a comparison of relative frequencies: these forty instances of results for CQPweb query *[v,u]eng* as above, are equivalent to 1,187 instances per million words, in contrast to the background frequency in EEBO of 118 per million words, or even to *Seneca His Tenne Tragedies* (1581), where the relative frequency is 747 per million words.
55. It features a bed-trick, a virginity test and a fire like those in *The Changeling*. Preapontio's infantile preoccupation with food and murder resembles the fate of Bergetto in *'Tis Pity She's A Whore*. Gaspar wryly cues Alonzo's echoing of Soranzo's lines to Annabella (4.3.1.14) with the words 'such a passion would befit / A husband better than a father' (p. 41). Less candidly, the play's '*English* dresse' includes extensive unacknowledged (and some previously unnoticed) borrowings from Shakespeare. In addition to the wooing scene of *Richard III* (1.2.11–12, 46–150) reappearing in Act 5 (pp. 77–8) and 3.1 of *Romeo and Juliet* being transplanted wholesale in 5.1 of *The Bastard*, Alonzo speaks Henry VI's lines of grief over the murder of Gloucester (*2 Henry VI* 3.2.39–55), concluding with an injunction to Alvarez to 'fright thy soule / With a new *Gorgon*' (*Macbeth* 2.3.66–7). Act 2 Scene 4 of *The Bastard* plays out a version of the star-crossed lovers' tragic exchange of poison and daggers in *Romeo and Juliet*.
56. See Hall, 'Why are the Erinyes Female?' pp. 45 and 48.
57. Anne Hermanson, *The Horror Plays of the English Restoration* (Aldershot: Ashgate, 2014, reprinted Routledge, 2016), pp. 22–5.
58. Ibid. p. 7.
59. The book Aphelia reads is the tale of 'Ravisht Philomel', predicting the danger she will endure and perhaps alluding to *Cymbeline*.
60. On blackness in the play see Morwenna Carr, 'Material/Blackness: Race

and Its Material Reconstructions on the Seventeenth-century English Stage', *Early Theatre* 20.1 (2017), pp. 77–95.
61. Mary Pix, *The False Friend or the Fate of Disobedience, A Tragedy as it is acted in the New Theatre in Lincolns-Inn-Fields* (London, 1699). References are to page numbers in this edition.
62. Heavey, *Early Modern Medea*, p. 197.
63. Edward Ward, *Female Policy Detected. Or, the arts of a designing woman* (London, 1695), p. 24.

PART II

FRIENDS AND FAMILY – 'REVENGING HOME'

CHAPTER 3

Vengeance and Male Devotion in *Laxdæla saga* and *Njáls saga*

Ian Felce

At a climactic moment in *Laxdæla saga*, one of the most popular of the sagas of Icelanders (*Íslendingasögur*), the hero Kjartan Óláfsson challenges his beloved foster-brother and cousin Bolli Þorleiksson to decide whether or not to attempt to kill him in vengeance. The moment is the culmination of a feud that has developed between the kinsmen after Bolli steals Kjartan's lover Guðrún Ósvífrsdóttir from him. Following a series of increasingly humiliating slights, the two men finally stand before each other:[1]

> Then Bolli drew Fótbítr [his sword] and now turned towards Kjartan. Kjartan then said to Bolli, 'You are now, kinsman, certainly going to do a deed of a *níðingr* [shameful man], but it seems far better to me to receive my deathblow from you, kinsman, than deal one to you'. Then Kjartan threw his weapons down and did not want to defend himself at all ... Bolli gave no answer to Kjartan's words but instead dealt him his deathblow. Bolli at once placed himself under Kjartan's shoulders and Kjartan died in Bolli's lap; Bolli mourned the act immediately.*

The choreography of Bolli's act dramatically illustrates how the necessity for vengeance conflicts with homosocial bonds in the saga. Though Kjartan initially encourages Bolli to enter the fight (while addressing him as *frændi*, 'kinsman'), he throws down his weapon as soon as he turns on him. Bolli, for

---

* *Þá brá Bolli Fótbít ok snýr nú at Kjartani. Þá mælti Kjartan til Bolla: 'Víst ætlar þú nú, frændi, níðingsverk at gera, en miklu þykki mér betra at þiggja banaorð af þér, frændi, en veita þér þat'. Síðan kastaði Kjartan vápnum ok vildi þá eigi verja sik ... Engi veitti Bolli svǫr máli Kjartans, en þó veitti hann honum banasár. Bolli settisk þegar undir herðar honum, ok andaðisk Kjartan í knjám Bolla; iðraðisk Bolli þegar verksins.* Einar Ól. Sveinsson (ed.), *Laxdæla Saga. Halldórs þættir Snorrasonar. Stúfs þáttr*, Íslenzk Fornrit, 5 (Reykjavík: Hið íslenzka fornritafélag, 1934), pp. 153–4, ch. 49. Further references to this volume are given parenthetically.

his part, strikes Kjartan's deathblow before immediately sweeping him up, possibly in a single movement, so that his determination to kill his cousin and the love that he demonstrates by holding him as he dies appear almost concurrent. Bolli's oscillation makes visible the scene's central dilemma: whether it is a greater *níðingsverk* (deed of a shameful man) for a man to restore his manhood by killing his kinsman or to forbear vengeance for the sake of their kinship while enduring tarnished masculinity. In throwing down his weapons, Kjartan chooses forbearance at the risk of emasculation, while Bolli chooses the restitution of manliness at the cost of kin slaying.

Irresolvable ethical dilemmas such as this one, in which the male characters' inclinations are divided between upholding masculinity by maintaining honour and preserving devoted bonds by showing restraint are central to several of the sagas of Icelanders: the thirteenth- and fourteenth-century prose narratives that recount the lives of the first few generations of eminent (but not royal or aristocratic) families who settled Iceland from the late ninth century. The *Íslendingasögur* developed out of a geographically remote oral culture (which was, however, neither diplomatically nor economically isolated) into what Margaret Clunies Ross describes as 'crypto-noble biographies' influenced by contemporary romance traditions in Western Europe.[2] Certain sagas such as *Laxdæla saga* and *Njáls saga* appear simultaneously to portray blood vengeance as a natural response to dishonour (lacking the early modern problem of guilt) and as a major source of strife. In *Laxdæla saga*, the mutual hostility that arises from the competitive requirements of manhood gradually ruins the especially close relationship that Kjartan and Bolli enjoy from childhood, while in *Njáls saga* the series of assaults and reprisals that transpire between the wives of the central characters Gunnarr Hámundarson and Njáll Þorgeirsson increasingly threaten their steadfast friendship. Rather than explicitly endorsing either the impetus for vengeance or the desire for restraint, both *Laxdæla saga* and *Njáls saga* appear to present the dilemma between the two forces as impossible to resolve: if the male characters avenge a slight, they jeopardise their relationship, and if they show forbearance, they risk forfeiting their manhood. In Preben Meulengracht Sørensen's words:[3]

> In the course of one conflict after another, the dilemma in which the persons of the saga are placed is repeated and accentuated; the dilemma between the desire for peaceful co-existence on the one hand, and on the other the demand that a man shall maintain his right and his prestige at any price ... neither the audience nor the heroes of the saga had any hope of meeting the demand. If they did not respond to offence and oppression, not only would they have to live on in shame, but they also risked losing all that made life worthwhile.

As Meulengracht Sørensen intimates, at the heart of the dilemma in sagas such as these is a conflict between an ethos that esteems cooperative virtues, producing magnanimity and conciliation, and an ethos that esteems competitive virtues, producing a cycle of feud and vengeance. While in both *Laxdæla saga* and *Njáls saga* there are numerous examples of cooperative virtues bolstering a man's reputation,[4] when it comes to the crunch and the cooperative virtues conflict with the competitive ones, the competitive virtues are repeatedly deemed more manly. As a consequence, if a character's manliness is particularly impugned he resorts to the ethos of competition to reacquire honour. Given that this ethos is fundamentally aggressive, whenever the ethical collision occurs, the cooperative ethos is destroyed, lending the narratives what Svavar Hrafn Svavarsson calls 'their peculiar poignancy'.[5]

Drawing on Thomas Laqueur's 'one-flesh' model of gender, in which men and women were understood to be two different forms of one sex,[6] Carol Clover has offered a paradigm to clarify the precariousness of manliness in the *Íslendingasögur*, suggesting that rather than operating on a biological binary of physiology, the masculinity that is so vital to the survival of the saga heroes operates on a spectrum of power based 'to an extraordinary extent on winnable and losable attributes'.[7] Far from being a stable trait, maleness, which is correlated with sovereignty and social approbation, can be won and lost. Men (as well as women, to a degree) must, therefore, vie for it:

> The frantic machismo of Norse males, at least as they are portrayed in the literature, would seem on the face of it to suggest a society in which being born male precisely did *not* confer automatic superiority, a society in which distinction had to be acquired, and constantly reacquired, by wresting it away from others ... the fault line runs not between males and females per se, but between able-bodied men (and the exceptional woman) on the one hand and, on the other, a kind of rainbow coalition of everyone else (most women, children, slaves, and old, disabled and otherwise disenfranchised men).[8]

Echoing Judith Butler's assertion that 'gender is a kind of imitation for which there is no original',[9] Clover suggests that by acquiring and reacquiring distinction the men of these sagas must repeatedly *achieve* manhood, which is fragile, in flux and perpetually at risk of loss. The 'economy of the one-sex model' is, in this way, akin to a hostile free market in which masculinity is a finite commodity that is continually sought, bartered for and exchanged.[10] The exchange of manliness, thus, inevitably depends on one character divesting another of it, creating an ongoing antagonistic struggle that renders manhood in the sagas of Icelanders a fragile condition.

The struggle for the attainment of manliness and its impact on male devotion is particularly evident in *Laxdæla saga* over the course of Kjartan and Bolli's relationship. From their first appearance as infants to their departure for Norway on a rite of passage into manhood, the narrative stresses their extraordinary fondness for one another. As soon as the cousins are introduced to the saga, the narrator states that 'The foster-brothers loved one another greatly.'* Subsequently, when, as a young man, Kjartan is about to fall in love with Guðrún Ósvífsdóttir, the author emphasises that 'Kjartan and Bolli loved each other the most. Kjartan never went anywhere where Bolli did not follow him.'† Later, when, on the cusp of manhood, Kjartan travels from the west to the south of Iceland to buy a share of the ship that will take Bolli and him to Norway, it is stressed that 'Bolli went on the journey with him because the foster-brothers were so loving towards one another that neither one was able to endure their not being together.'‡

Yet, alongside the cousins' youthful love for one another, the saga looks forward persistently, even anxiously, to their maturity. As children, the foster-brothers are described primarily in terms of what is *mannvænn* (literally 'man-promising') (p. 76, ch. 28). While Kjartan is portrayed as matchless in every way, in his youth Bolli is portrayed as outstanding but slightly inferior to his cousin (p. 77, ch. 28), creating an early, uneasy prospect of disparity that explains the dubiousness of Bolli's judgement later when he pursues Guðrún despite knowing that she is waiting for Kjartan. In Chapter 33, the saga focuses closely on the cousins' future potential as men in a scene that is unusual in the *Íslendingasögur* for portraying what a modern-day reader might describe as adolescence. Riding together to the Laxá River, the seer, Gestr Oddleifsson, and Kjartan's father, Óláfr Höskuldsson, stop to watch the young men of the district swim:

> The foster-brothers had been swimming all day ... A lot of other young men from other farms were swimming. Kjartan and Bolli ran out of the water as the party rode up. They were nearly fully dressed when Óláfr and Gestr got there. ... And there were many other very promising men there who had got out of the water and sat on the riverbank beside Kjartan and Bolli. ... Then Óláfr said ... 'I want you to tell me which of the young men will surpass the others'. Gestr replied, 'It will be in line with your affection: Kjartan will seem the greatest while he is alive'.§

Most simply, this scene demonstrates the innocence and intimacy of the foster-brothers' existence before the beginning of manhood. Though the youngsters

---

* *Þeir unnusk mikit fóstbrœðr* (p. 77, ch. 28).
† *Þeir Kjartan ok Bolli unnusk mest; fór Kjartan hvergi þess, er eigi fylgði Bolli honum* (p. 112, ch. 39).
‡ *Bolli var í ferð með honum, því at svá var ástúðigt með þeim fóstbrœðrum, at hvárrgi þóttisk nýta mega, at þeir væri eigi ásamt* (p. 114, ch. 40).
§ *Þeir fóstbrœðr hǫfðu verit á sundi um daginn ... Margir váru ungir menn af ǫðrum bœjum á sundi. Þá hljópu þeir Kjartan ok Bolli af sundi, er flokkrinn reið at; váru þá mjǫk klæddir, er þeir Gestr ok Óláfr riðu at. ... en margir váru þar aðrir menn allvænligir, þeir er þá váru af sundi komnir ok sátu á árbakkanum hjá þeim Kjartani. ... Þá mælti Óláfr: ... 'þat vil ek, at þú segir mér, hverr þeira inna ungu manna mun mestr verða fyrir sér'. Gestr svarar: 'Þat mun mjǫk ganga eptir ástríki þínu, at um Kjartan mun þykkja mest vert, meðan hann er uppi* (pp. 91–2, ch. 33).

are competing with one another, perhaps in preparation for their maturity, there is still a leisureliness to this competition that permits the current elders to watch over the latest set of *allvænligir* (all-promising) youths from the neighbouring farms on an unremarkable summer's day, unselfconsciously in states of undress, essentially having fun. However, the older men's discussion of which boys surpass the others also disrupts the apparent innocence of the play, confirming a disparity between Kjartan and Bolli that augurs the impossibility of such ease continuing into adulthood (Gestr goes on to predict that Bolli will one day stand over Kjartan's dead body) (p. 92, ch. 33). Their scrutiny is indicative of a world that, while allowing for harmonious stability between men, nevertheless continually seeks to establish a hierarchy in which one man achieves status at the expense of another. Power relations are so precarious that the established adults thus look to the next generation to monitor who is coming up the ranks, a task which is especially acute (and, thus, of particular interest) when the difference in aptitude between men such as Kjartan and Bolli is slight.

Repeated allusions to the disparity between the foster-brothers, coupled with a tendency in the narrative to look forward to their adulthood with overt intimations of discord (pp. 82–3, ch. 30; pp. 84–5, ch. 31), make the approaching advent of their maturity seem like a Rubicon, the crossing of which will expose their devoted relationship to danger. Thus, it is not wholly surprising that when the cousins reach maturity their relationship immediately begins to break down. Although the two foster-brothers travel together to Norway, soon after their arrival, there is a second swimming scene in the River Nið in which Kjartan invites Bolli to challenge the local champion: 'Then Kjartan asked "I don't think I'd get very far". "I don't know where your competitiveness has gone", said Kjartan, "so I'll do it then".'* A few years have passed since the scene at the Laxá River and the cousins are no longer adolescents. The impression of leisureliness in the earlier passage has disappeared and there is now a quality of overt antagonism in the challenge. In turning it down, Bolli is seen to act for the first time with discrete (and calculating) agency, while Kjartan, disapproving of his cousin's lack of *kapp* (competitiveness), gains an opportunity to demonstrate his peerlessness when he decides to wrestle the local champion (who turns out to be the Norwegian king, Óláfr Tryggvason) himself:

> Kjartan now plunged into the river towards this man who was the best at swimming and pulled him suddenly under and held him below for a time. Kjartan then let him go but as soon as they surfaced then this man caught hold of Kjartan and pulled him down and they were under for what seemed to Kjartan no shorter than a reasonable time. Then they

---

* *Þá spyrr Kjartan Bolla, ef hann vili freista sunds við bæjarmanninn. Bolli svarar: 'Ekki ætla ek þat mitt færi'. 'Eigi veit ek, hvar kapp þitt er nú komit', segir Kjartan, 'ok skal ek þá til'* (p. 117, ch. 40).

came up but they did not exchange any words. A third time they went under and were there for much the longest time. Kjartan was now not sure how it would play out and he thought he had never been in such a tight spot before. At last they came up and swam ashore.*

In this scene Kjartan wrests distinction from Bolli and King Óláfr, quite literally. By physically holding the king underwater, Kjartan wins manliness through the partial emasculation of another: Kjartan's gain is Bolli's (and to an extent King Óláfr's) loss. Kjartan enjoys the highest esteem in Norway thereafter and there is no further mention of the love between the foster-brothers. The sudden lack of overt reference to their mutual devotion, together with the discrepancy between their relative receptions at court, hints at a waning of their closeness. Though inseparable on departing Iceland as youths, they return as men, separately, and with their own distinct ambitions.

The sense that the two men increasingly act as competitors rather than friends is made explicit in the love rivalry that develops over Kjartan's lover Guðrún in Chapters 42 to 54. Bolli returns first to Iceland and, taking advantage of Kjartan's absence, immediately begins to pursue his foster-brother's lover. Bolli tells Guðrún that Kjartan is unlikely to return to Iceland because he has formed a relationship with the king's sister. When Guðrún responds that she will marry nobody but Kjartan, Bolli implies (at best carelessly and at worst maliciously) that Kjartan's affections towards her have waned. Despite her refusing him unequivocally, Bolli continues to pursue Guðrún, informing his foster-father that he would like to marry her now that he considers himself to be *fullkominn at þroska* (fully come into maturity) (pp. 128–9, ch. 43) and ignoring the rejoinder that Kjartan and Guðrún love one another. Pursuing Guðrún with evident determination and probable duplicity, Bolli appears to betray Kjartan at precisely the point that he deems himself to have become a man. Indeed, it is as if his attainment of manhood compels the betrayal. It is implicit that marrying the most renowned woman in the district will enhance Bolli's status and perhaps that making the match that the illustrious Kjartan would otherwise have made will distinguish Bolli even further. Bolli's gain is now Kjartan's loss. When Kjartan returns to Iceland to discover Bolli has recently married Guðrún, the cousins' relationship disintegrates. Although they formally greet one another on meeting, tensions quickly escalate into a succession of insults and reprisals that ultimately leads to Bolli slaying Kjartan, before he is himself slain by Kjartan's kin in vengeance.

---

* *Kjartan fleygir sér nú út á ána ok at þessum manni, er bezt er sundfœrr ok fœrir niðr þegar ok heldr niðri um hríð; lætr Kjartan þenna upp; ok er þeir hafa eigi lengi uppi verit, þá þrífr sá maðr til Kjartans ok keyrir hann niðr, ok eru niðri ekki skemr en Kjartani þótti hóf at; koma enn upp; engi hǫfðusk þeir orð við. It þriðja sinn fara þeir niðr, ok eru þeir þá miklu lengst niðri; þykkisk Kjartan nú eigi skilja, hversu sjá leikr mun fara, ok þykkisk Kjartan aldri komit hafa í jafnrakkan stað fyrr. Þar kemr at lykðum, at þeir koma upp ok leggjask til lands* (p. 117, ch. 40).

In contrast to *Laxdœla saga*, in which it is apparently Bolli's desire to establish himself as a man that first triggers conflict, in *Njáls saga* it is competition between the wives of the loyal friends Gunnarr and Njáll that instigates the initial feud. This feud demonstrates that, in the sagas of Icelanders, perilous external forces may oblige two men to choose between the inviolability of their friendship and upholding manhood through hostility, despite the fact that they possess nothing but devotion for one another. A small slight endured by a man's wife can quickly escalate into severe humiliation, with her appealing to her husband to take vengeance to maintain the household's honour, even when such an action would damage his relationship with his friend. Thus, in these sagas it is not only the highest status men that participate in the economy of masculinity, but all interested parties: wives, male and female relatives, and lesser members of each household all share an interest in the relative status of the chief householder. Where *Laxdœla saga* explores the ethical problems at stake for its male protagonists by portraying the attainment of manhood, *Njáls saga*, therefore, explores the theme by concentrating on its retention. Indeed, Ármann Jakobsson has argued that 'the list of men attacked for not being manly enough' in the saga 'seems almost endless'.[11]

From their introduction as faithful friends in Chapter 21, *Njáls saga* stresses Gunnarr and Njáll's exceptional devotion to one another. Early on Njáll tells Gunnarr: 'Many are the friends to whom I give sound advice, but I will take most pains for you'.* Yet, despite this, the friendship is quickly put under strain when, after a feast held *fyrir vináttu sakir* (on account of their friendship) (p. 90, ch. 35), a feud develops between their wives that results in reciprocal killings. As ever more senior members of each household are killed (edging incrementally closer to Gunnarr and Njáll as the heads of their houses), the husbands arrive at increasingly costly, legally negotiated settlements of reparation in an attempt to stem the tide of vengeance and safeguard their friendship.

When Gunnar's wife Hallgerðr has Njáll's sons' foster-father killed, however, the pressure on the sons to avenge the killing reaches new heights. It is evident that neither family regards coming to settlement to be as manly as taking vengeance (p. 91, ch. 35; p. 102, ch. 38; p. 110, ch. 43), so that, despite Njáll assuring Gunnarr 'I do not want any breach in our friendship because of me',† and requesting the extraordinary sum of two hundred ounces of silver in reparation for the killing,[12] he also reassures his sons that he will permit any further insult to their manhood to be avenged with blood (pp. 110–11, ch. 43). Consequently, after Hallgerðr and her kinsman Sigmundr Lambason verbally emasculate Njáll and his sons in a series of slanders that equate their difficulty in growing facial hair with effeminacy, 'Let's call him "Beardless Man" and

---

* *Margir eru þess vinir mínir makligir, at ek leggja til þat, sem heilt er; en þó ætla leggja mesta stund á við þik*, Einar Ól. Sveinsson, *Brennu-Njáls saga*, 12 (Reykjavík: Hið íslenzka fornritafélag, 1954), pp. 58–9, ch. 21. Further references to this volume are given parenthetically.
† *Vil ek ok eigi, at af mér standi afbrigð okkarrar vináttu* (p. 110, ch. 43).

his sons "Manure-Beardlings", and you, Sigmundr, compose a verse about it',* Njáll gives his eldest son Skarpheðinn tacit approval to take vengeance, despite the strain it will put on his friendship with Gunnarr. On being asked by his father where he is going fully armed that night, Skarpheðinn explains, 'We will catch salmon, father, if we do not find any sheep'† to which Njáll responds pointedly, 'It would be a good thing, if it goes thus, that your catch does not escape'.‡

The vehemence of the men's responses to these insults in Chapters 44 and 45 makes it clear that such slanders are utterly unendurable to their honour (pp. 113–18, chs. 44–5). On hearing them Gunnarr is so furious that he predicts they will have graver consequences than even the killing of the Njálssons' foster-father. Skarpheðinn flushes and begins to sweat (an indication of an extreme emotional reaction in the sagas), and, judging by the response mentioned above, the hitherto diplomatic Njáll appears to consider the ensuing vengeance both acceptable and unavoidable. As Meulengracht Sørensen has shown, the men of the *Íslendingasögur* respond so feverishly to such slurs because they form part of the convention of slander known as *nið* that has at its centre the allegation that a man has been *sorðinn* or *stroðinn* (a word that in Modern English may only satisfactorily be translated as 'fucked') or that he is *ragr* (which implies an innate tendency to enjoy being *sorðinn* by a man or additional acts that medieval Icelanders considered aberrant).[13] Since the associations of any slander that falls within the convention of *nið* are so ruinously emasculating for the men of the sagas, such an insult is akin to a point of no return in the struggle for masculinity, after which vengeance becomes the only course available to the victim to restore his manhood. Thus, Skarpheðinn kills Sigmundr for his slanderous verses and, even though the peace-favouring Gunnarr brings the feud between his and Njáll's households to an end by accepting compensation, he is subsequently drawn into avenging a *nið*-like act of emasculation himself when Otkell Skarfsson accidentally grazes his face with a spur (pp. 136–9, ch. 54). The vengeance that Gunnarr takes for this violation, coupled with the animosity that he causes with yet another chance act of emasculation (the ignominious blow he strikes Þorgeir Starkarðarson at a horse-fight) (pp. 150–1, ch. 59), results in a series of clashes that eventually leads to his death (pp. 189–90, ch. 77). Though Njáll is unwavering in his desire to protect his friend during these later feuds (p. 139, ch. 55; pp. 144–5, ch. 56; pp. 152–3, ch. 60; pp. 164–6, ch. 66; pp. 170–1, ch. 69; pp. 171–3, ch. 70; pp. 180–1, ch. 74), his influence is ultimately insufficient to save him from the chain of vengeance unleashed in the battle to retain manliness. Gunnarr is finally killed by his enemies after he breaks the terms of his settlement, having not heeded Njáll's plea that he leave Iceland (p. 181, ch. 74).

---

* *kǫllum hann nú karl inn skegglausa, en sonu hans taðskegglinga, ok kveð þú um nǫkkut,* Sigmundr (p. 113, ch. 44).
† *Laxa skulu vér veiða, faðir, ef vér rǫtum eigi sauðina* (p. 115, ch. 44).
‡ *Vel væri þat, þó at svá væri, at þá veiði bæri eigi undan* (p. 113, ch. 44).

In both *Laxdæla saga* and *Njáls saga* the portrayal of the struggle for masculinity and its impact on the relationships between Kjartan and Bolli, and Njáll and Gunnarr, permits the thematic exploration of a conflict between an ethos that endorses vengeance on the one hand and one that prefers restraint (and, with it, devotion) on the other. Broadly speaking, the ethos of vengeance encourages reciprocal acts of aggression and the ethos of restraint encourages justice via legal arbitration and settlement. In considering the criticism on this ethical conflict when it appears in the *Íslendingasögur*, Vilhjálmur Árnason has suggested that interpretations have broadly fallen into three categories.[14] Readings that he labels 'romantic' belie a nostalgic admiration for the resolve of the avenging hero, who is considered a 'tragic figure' compelled by 'values and virtues of Nordic heathen origin which were radically opposed to Christian ideals'.[15] Conversely, 'humanist' readings deem the ethical conflict to expose vengeance as 'a cruel criminal act', rendering the sagas 'Christian lessons about the deserving defeat of those who show excessive pride and arrogance' that preach 'peace and moderation in the spirit of medieval Christianity'.[16] By contrast, 'sociological' readings explain the conflict of ethics 'in light of the social structures and political institutions . . . in the Icelandic Free State',[17] suggesting that the sagas demonstrate vengeance to be an outdated, socially inappropriate tradition and its perpetrators 'misplaced Vikings, unable to honour the norms of an agrarian society where peace and order are vital'.[18]

It is notable that in accounting for the ethical dilemma, Norse scholars sometimes employ more than one of these categories at once, occasionally in mutually contradictory ways. Vilhjálmur's own reading draws on both the humanist and sociological perspectives, arguing that the sagas describe 'an ethos in the process of transformation from heathen values to Christian values', while emphasising 'the role of the social need for peace' in which the 'rigid imperative of revenge' is transformed into 'a more deliberative means of handling conflict resolution'.[19] In his reading of *Gísla saga Súrssonar*, David Clark employs all three categories, maintaining that, like 'certain other saga protagonists, Gísli appears to be a glorious hero unfortunately out of time and place', that his behaviour is 'no longer appropriate in a Christian society where one should forgive one's enemies and avoid extramarital sexual acts', and that the ethos of honour and revenge in the saga would have been understood to lead a society 'to a scaled-down Ragnarök'.[20]

Arguments that suggest, however, that those of the *Íslendingasögur* that explore the dilemma portray a bias (either explicitly or implicitly) towards either the ethos of vengeance or the ethos of devotion tend necessarily to overlook the fact that the conflicting forces are frequently presented in such remarkably even counterpoint to one another that it is difficult to argue for an interpretation that cannot be immediately countered with an opposing example. It might be suggested, for instance, that Kjartan's undoubted physical superiority over Bolli means that his decision to choose devotion by laying down his arms rather than fighting his foster-brother should be understood as the superior moral choice. Yet, this is not made explicit by the saga. Guðrún expresses gratitude to Bolli for killing her once beloved Kjartan, blurring the issue of whether Bolli has done right or wrong, and the saga author (or the laconic narratorial voice, at least) in no way aids the process of ethical interpretation for the audience by offering an objective assessment.

One reason that propositions that these sagas clearly endorse one ethos over the other might fall down is that, as Svavar Hrafn Svavarsson has argued, they rely on an ethical world in which 'thin' moral concepts that separate fact and value (such as right, just or good) are commonplace and customarily scrutinised.[21] The didacticism of a humanist reading that espouses devotion over vengeance, for instance, or alternatively the suggestion that the author's silence on the ethical conflict might be 'a deliberate stance . . . to engage his audience and encourage debate'[22] both seem to demand, in Svavar Hrafn's words, 'a reflective ethics that is nowhere to be found in saga culture'.[23] The evenly weighed portrayal of the impulses for vengeance and devotion may demonstrate that this type of discursive examination was not part of either the author's or audience's outlook, which was perhaps governed more fundamentally by 'thick' moral concepts (like coward, lie, brutality and gratitude) that, in uniting fact and value, did not provoke ethical reflection in the same way. For Svavar Hrafn, these sagas 'do not seem to reflect *on* the inadequacy of this culture to deal with internal problems, but rather simply to reflect the thick moral world of the culture'.[24] It would follow from this that sagas such as *Laxdæla saga* and *Njáls saga* use the impulse for vengeance and for devotion in the male condition as a construct to propose baldly the conflict between competitive and cooperative virtues at the heart of saga society without proposing an answer to it.

Readings of *Laxdæla saga* and *Njáls saga* that suggest a didactic inclination towards one ethos or another may assume on some level that sophisticated artistry presupposes the critical faculty of moral thinness. This is not necessarily true. Recognising an insoluble dilemma before perspicaciously portraying its effect on the culture seems as sophisticated as advocating a particular way of life. While the repeated portrayal of the conflict in these sagas may mean that the society that produced them was beginning a process towards a 'thinner' morality in which concepts of right and wrong were more available to be contended, the fact that they portray the effect of the conflicting ethoses of vengeance and male devotion so insightfully, while remaining so reserved on an answer to it, may suggest that, for the time being at least, their authors saw the possibility of resolving the conflict as difficult or even unviable. By repeatedly exposing the fact that the competitive ethos of vengeance is considered more manly than the cooperative ethos of restraint in sagas such as *Laxdæla saga* and *Njáls saga* (and thereby highlighting the miserable dilemma at the heart of the male condition), the authors may well have been consciously stressing the incoherence of what William Ian Miller calls 'the native ideology of justice and revenge' but this does not mean that they were also offering a solution for it.[25] Indeed, that they remained so silent on a solution may suggest that they saw the conflict as inevitable to a degree, perhaps not merely because it stood imbedded within the bounds of their society but because it seemed to them to stand within the bounds of human nature.

NOTES

1. The Íslenzk fornrit editions of *Laxdæla saga and Njáls saga* which I use in this chapter are based principally on the text of the late fourteenth-century *Möðruvallabók* (AM 132 fol.). Though all translations are my own, I have referred to Robert Cook (trans.), *Njal's Saga*, Penguin Classics (London: Penguin, 2001), Magnus Magnusson and Hermann Pálsson (trans.), *Laxdaela Saga* (Harmondsworth: Penguin, 1969) and Keneva Kunz (trans.), *The Saga of the People of Laxardal* (New York: Penguin, 2001). Where relevant I have chosen to render both present and past forms in Old Norse into the simple past in English for consistency.
2. Margaret Clunies Ross, *The Cambridge Introduction to the Old Norse-Icelandic Saga* (Cambridge: Cambridge University Press, 2010), p. 91.
3. Preben Meulengracht Sørensen, *The Unmanly Man: Concepts of Sexual Defamation in Early Northern Society*, The Viking Collection, 1 (Odense: Odense University Press, 1983), pp. 77–8.
4. See, for example, Einar Ól. Sveinsson (ed.), *Laxdæla Saga. Halldórs þættir Snorrasonar. Stúfs þáttr*, Íslenzk Fornrit, 5 (Reykjavík: Hið íslenzka fornritafélag, 1934), p. 75, ch. 27, and Einar Ól. Sveinsson, *Brennu-Njáls saga*, 12 (Reykjavík: Hið íslenzka fornritafélag, 1954), p. 133, ch. 51.
5. Svavar Hrafn Svavarsson, 'Honour and Shame: Comparing Medieval Iceland and Ancient Greece', *Gripla* 20 (2009), pp. 241–56 (p. 249).
6. Thomas Laqueur, *Making Sex: Body and Gender from the Greeks to Freud* (Cambridge, MA: Harvard University Press, 1990), pp. 25–62.
7. Carol J. Clover, 'Regardless of Sex: Men, Women, and Power in Early Northern Europe', *Speculum* 68.2 (1993), pp. 363–87 (p. 379).
8. Ibid. p. 380.
9. Judith Butler, 'Imitation and Gender Insubordination', in Diana Fuss (ed.), *Inside/Out: Lesbian Theories, Gay Theories* (New York; London: Routledge, 1991), pp. 13–31 (p. 21).
10. Clover, 'Regardless of Sex', pp. 379–80.
11. Ármann Jakobsson, 'Masculinity and Politics in *Njáls saga*', *Viator* 38 (2007), pp. 191–215 (p. 209).
12. At twice the sum of full compensation, this is both an indication of how keen the two friends are to secure an effective settlement and how incendiary the slaying of a foster-father is.
13. Meulengracht Sørensen, *Unmanly Man*, pp. 14–32.
14. Vilhjálmur Árnason, 'An Ethos in Transformation: Conflicting Values in the Sagas', *Gripla* 20 (2009), pp. 217–40 (pp. 219–24).
15. Ibid. p. 220.
16. Ibid. p. 223.

17. Ibid.
18. Ibid. p. 224.
19. Ibid. p. 237.
20. David Clark, *Gender, Violence, and the Past in Edda and Saga* (Oxford: Oxford University Press, 2012), p. 115.
21. Svavar Hrafn Svavarsson, 'Honour and Shame', pp. 250–1. Employing the thought of Bernard Williams in his article, Svavar Hrafn recommends Mark P. Jenkins, *Bernard Williams*, Philosophy Now (Chesham: Acumen, 2006), pp. 133–40, as a useful summary of the development of Williams' thought on thick and thin moral concepts.
22. Clark, *Gender, Violence, and the Past*, p. 115.
23. Svavar Hrafn Svavarsson, 'Honour and Shame', p. 252.
24. Ibid.
25. William Ian Miller, *'Why is Your Axe Bloody?': A Reading of* Njáls saga (Oxford: Oxford University Press, 2014), p. 73.

CHAPTER 4

'Now I am Medea': Gender, Identity and the Birth of Revenge in Seneca's *Medea*

Kathrin Winter

At the beginning of Seneca's *Medea* (first century AD), before Medea has formulated her plans of revenge, she responds in a striking way to the Nurse's use of her name:

NUT. *Medea* –
    ME. *Fiam.*
        NUT. *Mater es.*
            ME. *Cui sim, vide.*

NUT. Medea –
    ME. I shall become her.
        NUT. You are a mother.
            ME. You see by whom (171).[1]

When Medea says *fiam*, 'I shall become [Medea]', she evidently considers herself somehow incomplete or insufficient but appears to expect a change in this situation. At the end of the play, Medea refers to this moment when she exclaims triumphantly: 'What great deed could be dared by untrained hands, by the fury of a girl? Now I am Medea: my genius has grown through evils' (908–10).* Shortly before avenging herself on unfaithful Jason by murdering her own children, she indicates that she has completed her development and achieved a state sufficient to be termed 'Medea'. But why is it that Medea must become Medea? And how does she move from the state in which she feels herself to be not-fully entitled to her name to one in which she believes herself to embody it? From one perspective, her words suggest Seneca's – and Medea's – meta-textual awareness; it is as if, as Ulrich von Wilamowitz-Moellendorff has commented, Seneca's Medea has read Euripides' tragedy[2] and knows the

---

* *quid manus poterant rudes / audere magnum, quid puellaris furor? / Medea nunc sum; crevit ingenium malis.*

predetermined aspect of her identity and is self-consciously moving towards a recognisable trajectory of character and plot.[3]

However, there is also a sense in which it is the revenge process itself, and the reconfiguration of her character that this entails, which is crucial to the way that Medea becomes Medea in the final scene. This is evident in Medea's use of birth imagery. When Medea plans her revenge, the process is represented as transformative, enabling her not only to 'give birth' to infanticide but also to create her own identity, an innovative factor in Seneca's representation of Medea. Medea's emergence as an even more terrifying version than the Euripidean figure at the end of the play is thus predicated on her sense of revenge as a generative process, a description which complicates the ways in which she can be seen to appropriate martial, male gender roles. In this chapter, I explore how birth imagery is deployed in a number of different ways in the play and how it contributes to Medea's identity as a female avenger. Frequently returning to metaphors of birth, Medea's revenge is simultaneously configured as an expulsion of the feminine and a quintessentially feminine generative act which gives birth to a new self.

In some respects, it is difficult to see why a transformation of character is necessary for Seneca's Medea to become Medea. While Euripides' Medea ends the play as 'a horrifying incarnation of the worst possible kind of wife ... dangerous, powerful and "manlike" in her outlook',[4] 'a relentless merciless force',[5] a 'victorious goddess of vengeance',[6] Seneca's Medea begins the play already exhibiting many of these characteristics.[7] In Act 1, she appears as an aggressive, vengeful, uncontrollable Fury:[8]

> I pray ... with words of no good omen: Be present now, you goddesses who avenge crime ... your bloody hands grasping a black torch ... Bring death on this new wife, death on the father-in-law and the whole royal stock ... Shall I not attack my enemies? I shall dash the bridal torches from their hands, and the light from heaven. (12–28)*

Unafraid of kings and gods,[9] she repeatedly urges herself to take action, to attack the gods, and to shake the whole world.[10] Preparing herself for violence, she urges herself to: 'Drive out womanish fears, and plant the forbidding Caucasus in your mind ... Arm yourself in anger, prepare to wreak destruction with full rage' (42–52).† Medea dismisses all 'womanish fears' in specifically masculine terms, using vocabulary that is reminiscent of an epic arming scene. She also initially envisages herself as taking revenge with a sword: 'If only he had a brother! He has a wife: let the sword be thrust into

---

* ... *voce non fausta precor. / nunc, nunc adeste sceleris ultrices deae ... / atram cruentis manibus amplexae facem / ... coniugi letum novae / letumque socero et regiae stirpi date ... / non ibo in hostes? manibus excutiam faces / caeloque lucem.*

† ... *pelle femineos metus / et inhospitalem Caucasum mente indue ... / accingere ira teque in exitium para / furore toto.*

her' (125–6).* Medea's language indicates her desire for virtus and honour, in a manner that aligns her with male models of heroic duty and vengeance.[11] Representing herself in such a way, Seneca's Medea conforms to the ancient stereotype of being an utterly transgressive woman.[12] Indeed, Lisl Walsh argues that Medea aims to eradicate her feminine side altogether:

> While she desires femininity to fall away, Medea seems to replace it with an increasingly masculine persona; over the course of the tragedy, Medea habitually uses masculine language to describe her thoughts and actions, and this language increases in frequency as she progresses.[13]

However, while Walsh is right to observe that Medea increasingly adopts a masculine persona as she formulates her revenge, I argue that Medea's use of birth imagery complicates this paradigm. Although I agree with Walsh's view that revenge triggers a realignment in Medea's gender identity (in which her revenge is made possible through an act of self-division in which she others those aspects of herself which are perceived to be maternal and feminine), I do not think this is the whole story. Instead, I argue that Medea's repeated use of birth imagery compels her to retain certain maternal and feminine aspects even while she attempts to expunge these features from her identity. That way, Medea does align herself with the martial and masculine side, but without losing completely the feminine aspect; by doing so, she puts into effect the creative powers associated with birth to wreak revenge and cause death and destruction.

Given the way that Medea constructs her revenge through martial activity and masculine language, her use of birth imagery is particularly striking. Medea first uses this imagery in Act 1: *parta iam, parta ultio est: / peperi*, 'My revenge is born, already born: I have given birth' (24–5). Although Medea uses the verb *parere* here in a figurative sense, suggesting how she is producing or intellectually creating her revenge, the word's literal meaning, 'to give birth, to bear',[14] is also present as she has just mentioned her children.[15] It is the common ground between Medea's children and her abominable deeds, which is ironically appropriate to the vengeance itself because Medea's children are not only the fruit of her womb but also the instruments through which she will achieve her revenge. Medea thus employs imagery typically seen as feminine while simultaneously associating herself with a tradition of heroic masculinity.

The process that Medea undergoes in formulating her revenge is also represented as a birth: although she has a clear idea of the dimension her crimes must have, she does not know from the beginning what form her revenge will take. Rather, it takes her considerable time and labour to find a suitable punishment for Jason, a process that is agonising for her because she is unable to take action while she is desperate to give her fury free rein.[16] Although the

---

* *utinam esset illi frater! est coniunx: in hanc | ferrum exigatur.*

infanticide is already subconsciously present, it only gradually rises to the surface. Accordingly, after her encounters with Creo and Jason in Acts 2 and 3, Medea expresses new and crucial aspects of her future deeds, but does not explicitly insert them into an overall structure: she skilfully secures a day's delay from Creo which she urgently needs in order to wreak a revenge she has not planned. Similarly, she recognises that Jason's love for his children is his greatest weakness, but does not as yet see how she can exploit this to her own advantage.[17]

Only in Act 5 does Medea realise that infanticide provides her with what she believes to be the perfect form of revenge: 'The spirit within me has determined on some brutality, but dare not yet acknowledge it to itself' (917–19).* It is striking how Medea divides herself[18] in this statement between herself and the 'spirit within her', which has planned the revenge, but does not even dare to acknowledge to itself what lies ahead. Eventually, however, she fully conceptualises and describes her plans for revenge:[19] 'This path of punishment is decided on, rightly decided on. My spirit must prepare, I recognise, for its ultimate crime. Children once mine, you must pay the penalty for your father's crimes' (922–5).† At this moment, when Medea formulates the *genus*[20] *poenae* ('path of punishment'), she simultaneously fulfils her initial statement, *ultio parta est, peperi* ('my revenge is born; I have given birth'), using her creative energies to formulate the plan which will destroy her children; or to put it pointedly, she effectively gives birth to infanticide.

The audience's – be it the Neronian audience or any audience thereafter – knowledge that Medea will eventually kill her children infuses her language of birth and words about her children with dark undertones, so that when Medea says in the beginning of the play, *ultio parta est, peperi* ('my revenge is born; I have given birth'), her words ironically anticipate her future actions and imbue the mention of the children with associations of violence. What Deborah Boedeker very aptly comments on the phrase Medea – Fiam ('Medea' – 'I shall become her') is in this way also true for the birth imagery: 'The Neronian audience understands what a threat that is meant to be.'[21] Thus whenever Medea talks about her children the audience also anticipates the 'infanticide' to come.

The birth imagery combines the utterly destructive act of infanticide with the creative and generative energy associated with the term 'birth'. This unresolved tension is evident throughout the play. Shortly after the final formulation of her plan, Medea wonders whether the chosen mode of revenge satisfies her demands: 'If only the throng of the proud Tantalid had issued from my womb, and I had born and mothered twice seven children! I was barren for revenge. Yet I gave birth to two, enough for my brother and my father' (954–7).‡

---

* *nescioquid ferox / decrevit animus intus et nondum sibi / audet fateri.*
† *placuit hoc poenae genus, / meritoque placuit. ultimum agnosco scelus / animo parandum est: liberi quondam mei, / vos pro paternis sceleribus poenas date.*
‡ *utinam superbae turba Tantalidos meo / exisset utero bisque septenos parens / natos tulissem! sterilis in poenas fui – / fratri patrique quod sat est, peperi duos.*

Medea's revenge consists of her repeating her former deeds.[22] Although Jason is her intended victim because he left her for another woman, Medea does not relate her revenge to his infidelity, but to the sacrifices she has made for him. She takes revenge for the loss of her position at Colchis, for the betrayal of her father and for the murder of her brother – in short, for all crimes she committed for Jason's sake.[23] Medea's revenge is thus designed to correlate exactly to, and repay, the crimes she committed before. In line with this, she makes a daughter unintentionally kill her father (once the daughters of Pelias, now her rival Creusa), murders innocent children (once her brother, now her sons), and thrusts the dead children into their father's arms (once Aeetes, now Jason).

The connection between birthing children and creating crimes is evident in the phrase *sterilis in poenas fui* ('I was barren for revenge'). But in contrast to Medea's initial *[ultionem] peperi* ('I have given birth [to revenge]'), the metaphor is used here inversely. Medea recognises the fecund energy within herself that enables her to create her vengeance; but now, she calls herself 'barren' because she considers the revenge she has just devised not grave or destructive enough. She regrets having only two children because if she had fourteen, her bloodbath would be all the more devastating. Medea, however, concludes that two children are sufficient, allowing her to avenge her father and brother. Her choice of words, *exire utero* ('to issue from a womb'), is significant because in comparison to the more obvious *parere* ('to give birth'), the expression is rare[24] and suggests her alienation from both her children and her maternal role: by using it, Medea avoids the impression that such a 'throng' of children would be *her* children, too. The phrase emphasises her reluctance to ascribe any attributes typically associated with an affectionate mother to herself and confirms the impression that she considers her children as mere instruments.[25]

When Medea compares herself to Niobe, she uses the patronymic to simultaneously hint at Tantalus. Niobe is the suitable point of reference because of her many offspring (the reason for her pride as well as her punishment). But she is also a victim who is forced to watch the gods taking revenge on her by killing all her children one after the other.[26] Tantalus, on the other hand, did what Medea is about to do: he killed his son, albeit for another purpose. Medea appears to prefer his role, moving from the role of passive victim to active avenger, while her allusion also calls attention to the fusion of the generative and destructive aspects of their mythologies.

After deciding to commit infanticide, Medea flees to the rooftop with her sons, one already dead, one still alive. Jason pursues her, but stops when he recognises the imminent danger. He pleads in vain for the life of the remaining child when Medea declares: *in matre si quod pignus etiamnunc latet, / scrutabor ense viscera et ferro extraham*, 'If some love pledge is hiding even now in my mothering body, I shall probe my vitals with the sword, drag it out with steel' (1012–13). Medea's maternal and martial sides are divided into the first and second verse respectively. First, Medea's maternal side is expressed in the image of pregnancy: *mater* ('mother') is placed emphatically at the beginning of the sentence, whereas *pignus* ('pledge'), which in a frequent metonymic sense refers to the child and is highly charged with emotion, occupies the place in the centre. The verb *latet* ('hide') not only relates to the vulnerability of the child, but also alludes indirectly to the inclusion and security of a womb.[27] The second verse offers a startling contrast because it depicts the destruction of the *pignus* ('pledge') by means of a martial image: the nouns *ensis* ('sword') and *ferrum* ('steel') – as we have seen, one of the first instruments of revenge that Medea mentions in the play – and in this context *viscera* ('vitals') are also strongly associated with war. Combined with the preceding connotation of the womb, they evoke phallic imagery. This clear-cut dichotomy is underlined by a subtle hint about gender stereotypes: the verb *latet* ('hide') and the phrase *in matre* (lit. 'within the mother') render the description of the maternal side passive because they leave the mother no room for action. In contrast, the two verbs in the next line, *scrutabor* ('probe') and *extraham* ('drag out'), emphasise action and give gruesome details about the process Medea imagines.

However, Medea's promise that if she were pregnant with Jason's child she would perform an abortion upsets any clear-cut division between the maternal and martial, the masculine and feminine, and the active and passive as all parts are attributed simultaneously to the same person, Medea. The structure of the lines seems to indicate that her female, maternal side is expressed only to be destroyed by her martial, masculine aspect. On the one hand, such hyperbolic claims heighten the general impression that Medea becomes more manlike over the course of the play, supporting Lisl Walsh's suggestion that she undergoes three 'metamorphoses', one of which is the 'altering of her gender identity' in which she adopts 'elements of masculinity'.[28] Medea is not only transgressive (as the Euripidean tradition demands) but 'hyper'-transgressive, which, in turn, might be seen as merely affirming the expected stereotype. However, there is another way of understanding how Medea's revenge impacts her sense of self and gender identity.

To understand how Medea's birth imagery contributes to her identity, it is useful to have another look at Euripides' play. In Greek tragedy, the characteristics and traits of a persona are made more comprehensible when the differences to another persona are explored. The dialectic between self and other,[29] between identity and alterity[30] is for example adopted when foreigners or barbarians are introduced to serve as an 'other' for Greek civilisation and culture. Usually, they are not displayed for their own sake, but invented as the Greeks' opposite.[31] In a similar way, women are repeatedly conceptualised as men's 'other' and serve an important place in men's self-definition. As Froma Zeitlin puts it:

> Even when female characters struggle with the conflicts generated by the particularities of their subordinate position, their demands for identity and self-esteem are still designed primarily for exploiting the male project of selfhood in the larger world ... *functionally*, women are never an end in themselves ... Rather, they play the roles of catalysts, agents, instruments, blockers, spoilers, destroyers, and sometimes helpers or sav-

iours for the male characters ... There are other 'others', to be sure, on Athenian stage (e.g. barbarians, servants, enemy antagonists, and even gods), but the dialectic of self and other is consistently and insistently predicated on the distinctions between masculine and feminine ...[32]

As Zeitlin observes, a female character correlates to and serves as 'other' for a male character. That way, the relationship between a man and a woman can be used to reflect on modes of masculine behaviour. In Euripides' *Medea*, for example, manlike, transgressive Medea displays the Homeric-style honour Jason is not able or willing to follow, a behaviour which would be familiar to the male Greek audience.[33] This effect is achieved in part via a dialogical mode of representation in which other characters on stage respond to or interact with Medea. In Euripides' play, all the characters around her (the chorus, Creon, Aegeus and Jason) describe her merely as a normal woman, who is wronged and therefore unfortunate – an underestimation that proves to be fatal.[34] In her final monologue, Medea decides on the infanticide in what can be termed a dialogical structure: her addresses to her children and the chorus indicate how she shifts from sorrowful mother to relentless avenger.[35]

When Seneca's Medea forges her new identity, she employs the same method as explained by Zeitlin: she differentiates herself from somebody else, that is an 'other', in order to define herself. However, two aspects are remarkable here: not only does Medea not function as the 'other' in the play, but she also appropriates this mode of masculine self-definition. The general situation appears reversed because Seneca's Medea does not play the part of anybody's 'other'.[36] Instead, she invokes an 'other' in order to define herself, achieving in the process an identity that seems both independent and self-determined. To do so, she rejects the obvious and appropriate choice of her 'other', namely Jason, but defines herself only by means of her own former self, differentiating her present self from what she was and did before. This is a substantial difference from Euripides' Medea and vital for the characterisation of the 'new' Medea. In line with this, Medea's final monologue, which is comparable to the final monologue in Euripides because Medea finally 'decides' on her vengeance, can, as Chris Gill has shown, appropriately be termed a soliloquy.[37] Medea does not interact with anyone else but focuses exclusively on herself and her former deeds to actively conceptualise herself.

This representation of a self-determined and independent Medea is at loggerheads with the fact that her mythical character and the form of her revenge are predetermined and unchangeable. After all, Medea opens the play as the Fury-like figure that concludes Euripides' drama. This means that Medea not only actively constructs for herself a new identity, as is represented in the play, but also that she is herself the conceptual ground on which this new self is conceptualised and forged. Nevertheless, while she is able to create her own identity independently from all 'others', this new self is, paradoxically, perfectly in line with her well-established mythical characterisation. Although Medea plans her revenge un- or subconsciously, all details she gives birth to during the play mesh together perfectly as if they had been carefully arranged from start. The development is represented as a slow and painful birthing process, in which Medea forges a new identity, which nonetheless fits into a long, established tradition. This is how Medea, who blurs all boundaries in her transgressive nature, is simultaneously 'old' and 'new', becoming anew what she has always been.

This paradox is brought about by means of the birth imagery. The same imagery also shows the – similarly paradoxical – complexity of Medea's gender identity: on the one hand, Medea seems to aim at expunging her female side, an unsurprising move as she is a transgressive woman who crosses from feminine to more masculine and martial realms. But on the other hand, Medea's refusal to construct her identity in relation to somebody else in the play has far-reaching consequences on this stereotypical behaviour: it means that nobody else but Medea can represent her appropriately. As she invents her own identity, her voice has complete authority and is the foremost to be heard. It is striking that Medea, who, as Lisl Walsh puts it, 'endeavour[s] to masculinise herself over the course of the tragedy',[38] refers to herself as a woman and establishes and uses the birth imagery throughout the play.[39] She is in fact the only character in the play to do so while Creo, the Nurse, and Jason usually compare her to a Fury or call her a monster.[40]

In line with this, Medea expresses her progress and shaping of identity at the beginning of the play: *haec virgo feci ... maiora iam me scelera post partus decent*, 'I did all this as a girl ... greater crimes become me now, after giving birth' (49–50). Medea uses female ages, *virgo* ('virgin, girl') and *mater* ('mother'), in order to differentiate her former from her later self and to express her claim on greater crimes.[41] After she has given birth, her revenge must exceed everything she did before: just as Medea's father, Aeetes, had to witness the death of his son, so too does Jason watch as Medea kills his children. But since Medea outdoes her crimes, Jason loses not one son but two. Medea measures the atrocity of her deeds according to her growth as a woman, attributing her ability to commit even greater crimes to the fact that she is now older and a mother. Therefore, she chooses imagery that explicitly refers back to her feminine side. If she intended to exclusively expunge her femininity, this would be a quite surprising mode of expression especially since there would have been other, more masculine or more gruesome possibilities.[42] Instead, Medea uses the essentially feminine imagery of *parere* ('to give birth') to draw the dividing line between her selves (virgin and mother), to signify the thriving, fecund energy within her and to show how the increase or 'newness' in her revenge is achieved.

Again, the ambivalence that characterises Medea's representation throughout the play comes to the fore: although Medea explicitly and repeatedly reminds us of the fact that she is a woman and used to be a *virgo* ('virgin') and *puella* ('girl'),[43] she clearly does not intend to re-humanise herself or to represent herself as a loving mother – this Medea does not try to become a pre-Euripidean *puella* ('girl') again.[44] On the contrary, when she talks about different feminine ages, that is being a girl and being a mother, she is mainly expressing her willingness and her ability to do worse and be even more transgressive than before. As a consequence, it is impossible to consider her just a 'wretched woman' as Jason or the chorus did in Euripides' version, but on the other hand, it is impossible to ignore her feminine side.

Finally, it is the birth imagery which produces the most powerful effect within the issue of identity in Seneca's play, where everything seems to be determinate. It creates ambivalences and renders Medea an even more dangerous character. The feminine side is indeed how the 'new' Medea, the one who confidently states *Medea nunc sum; crevit ingenium malis* ('Now I am Medea; my genius has grown through evils'), outdoes her initial manlike, transgressive self even when she can never become anything else but Medea. In the end, it is not only the infanticide itself or the number of dead children, but also the fecund, creative aspect of the feminine imagery that causes Medea to surpass everything, most of all herself: if the stereotypically manlike, vengeful Medea everybody expects is 'a horrifying incarnation of the worst possible wife',[45] what must this wife be like when she not only adopts masculine and martial aspects to wreak revenge (as Euripides' Medea does), but simultaneously refers back to a feminine and maternal side within her that possesses a creative and generative power which she deploys to surpass her own atrocities? It is the inaccessible but thriving force the feminine imagery conveys that renders the 'victorious goddess of vengeance' even more dangerous.

NOTES

1. The text is taken from Otto Zwierlein, *Senecae Tragoediae* (Oxford: Clarendon Press, 1986) and the translation from John Fitch, *Seneca. Hercules, Trojan Women, Phoenician Women, Medea, Phaedra* (Cambridge, MA: Harvard University Press, 2002); all divergent readings are indicated.
2. Ulrich von Wilamowitz-Moellendorff, *Griechische Tragödien. Band III* (Berlin: Weidmann, 1906), p. 162.
3. Deborah Boedeker, 'Becoming Medea. Assimilation in Euripides', in J. Clauss and S. Iles Johnston (eds), *Medea. Essays on Medea in Myth, Literature, Philosophy, and Art* (Princeton: Princeton University Press, 1997), pp. 127–48, points out that in Euripides' play alternative versions of the plot and the character were still possible (p. 127). Cf. also Bernard Knox, 'The Medea of Euripides', in T. Gould and C. Herington (eds), *Greek Tragedy* (Cambridge: Cambridge University Press, 1977), pp. 193–225 (pp. 194–6).
4. Fiona McHardy, *Revenge in Athenian Culture* (London: Duckworth, 2008), p. 63.
5. Knox, 'The *Medea* of Euripides', p. 225.
6. Boedeker, 'Becoming Medea', pp. 127–8, translating a phrase from Eilhard Schlesinger, 'Euripides' *Medea*', *Hermes* 94 (1966), pp. 26–53 (p. 51).

7. Seneca's play generally follows the Euripidean outline. This does not mean, however, that Euripides' play is the only direct influence or even the strongest influence. The figure of Medea has a complex tradition with many different, even contradictory sides. In the Roman reception of the myth, Medea's portrayal, for example, as powerful sorceress (which can be seen in Ovid's *Metamorphoses*) or as a king's daughter who falls in love with a foreigner and is torn between this love and the loyalty to her own family are also well attested (in Ovid's *Metamorphoses* and *Heroides*, as well as in Valerius Flaccus' later epic version of the Argonauts' myth). These character traits appear to have had an equally strong influence on Seneca's Medea. Since we do not know for certain how the myth was handled in the literature of the Republic, the mode and intensity of influence are difficult to estimate (for an overview, see Anthony Boyle, 'Introduction: Medea in Greece and Rome', *Ramus* 41 (2012), pp. 1–32 and Gesine Manuwald, 'Medea: Transformations of a Greek Figure in Latin Literature', *Greece & Rome* 60 (2013), pp. 114–35).
8. For the representation of the Erinyes and their development through Greek literature and art see Edith Hall's chapter in this volume. Hall lists the characteristics of the Erinyes (citing the 'table of opposites' from Aristotle) as 'plural, female, motile, dark, bad and the cycles of escalating reprisals they symbolise are potentially unlimited' (p. 36). It is striking that Seneca's Medea meets all the criteria apart from one, plurality. However, one could argue that Medea's splitting of herself, which is necessary for the birth of a new self, points towards this missing characteristic.
9. Medea not only reproaches Sol for just watching this calamity happening to her, but also tells him to hand over the reins of his chariot to her so that she can burn down Corinth (*Med.* 29–39). Her contempt and fearlessness towards kings is voiced later in her confrontation with Creo, as well as in her conversation with Jason (*Med.* 192–200, 281–99, 525–9).
10. *Med.* 28–31, 399–414, 424–5, 670–6.
11. Lisl Walsh, 'The Metamorphoses of Seneca's Medea', *Ramus* 41 (2012), pp. 71–93 (p. 82); John Fitch and Siobhan McElduff, 'Construction of the Self in Senecan Drama', *Mnemosyne* 55 (2002), pp. 18–40 (p. 38). On heroic aspects in Euripides' *Medea*, cf. Knox, 'The *Medea* of Euripides', pp. 193–225; Helene Foley, 'Medea's Divided Self', *Classical Antiquity* 8 (1989), pp. 61–85; Elizabeth Bryson Bongie, 'Heroic Elements in the *Medea* of Euripides', *Transactions of the American Philological Association* 107 (1977), pp. 27–56; cf. also McHardy, Revenge, pp. 61–4 and p. 138, n. 111.
12. It is difficult to retrieve information on the social and cultural aspects of revenge from Roman literature because there is a very acute awareness of the literary tradition. Seneca's play is concerned with extreme forms of revenge that were not part of everyday life, but were treated in tragedy; cf. Pat Easterling, 'The Infanticide in Euripides' *Medea*', in T. Gould and C. Herington (eds), *Greek Tragedy* (Cambridge: University Press,

1977), pp. 177–191 (pp. 178–9); on revenge in Attic tragedy and cultural history, cf. also Hans-Joachim Gehrke, 'Die Griechen und die Rache: Ein Versuch in historischer Psychologie', *Saeculum* 38 (1987), pp. 121–49. The Romans, who knew the literary tradition, understood and adopted the Greek treatment of revenge. Although, for example, in Seneca's *Medea*, there is a strong Roman flavour in that a *repudium*, a Roman divorce in which the woman has the right to claim her dowry back, is depicted (cf. Gianni Guastella, '*Virgo, coniunx, mater*: The Wrath of Seneca's Medea', *Classical Antiquity* 20 (2001), pp. 197–219), this fact does not change the general representation of Medea as a transgressive woman.

13. Walsh, 'The Metamorphoses of Seneca's Medea', p. 82. It could be said that this is overall in line with the characterisation in Euripides' play, where Medea shows feminine as well as masculine aspects from the start. As Helen Foley describes, these two sides (or 'selves') of Medea start off as accomplices in pursuing revenge, but then get into tragic conflict with each other until the masculine side (requiring the killing of the children) wins over the feminine (containing maternal love): Foley, 'Medea's Divided Self', pp. 61–85. On particularly feminine ways to pursue revenge in Greek drama cf. McHardy, *Revenge*, pp. 37–42. For a different reading of gender and revenge in the play, see Abbattista in this volume.

14. *Oxford Latin Dictionary*, s.v. pario 4 ('[t]o create [intellectual, artistic or other productions]'), 5 ('[t]o bring into being . . . be the cause of, procure, get') and 1a ('[t]o give birth, to bear').

15. *Med.* 23b–5: *non aliud queam / peius precari, liberos similes patri / similesque matri*, 'I can make no worse prayer – for children resembling their father and resembling their mother'.

16. Cf. Alessandro Schiesaro, *The Passions in Play: Thyestes and the Dynamics of Senecan Drama* (Cambridge: University Press, 2003), p. 17.

17. The gradual but unconscious process of realisation may be linked to the gradual growth of anger in Seneca's de Ira, as observed by Katja Vogt, 'Anger, Present Injustice and Future Revenge in Seneca's De Ira', in K. Volk and G. Williams (eds), *Seeing Seneca Whole: Perspectives on Philosophy, Poetry and Politics* (Leiden: Brill, 2006), pp. 57–74.

18. Cf. Fitch and McElduff, 'Construction of the Self', pp. 18–40; Chris Gill, 'Two Monologues of Self-Division: Euripides, *Medea* 1021–80 and Seneca, *Medea* 893–977', in M. Whitby, P. Hardie and M. Whitby (eds), *Homo Viator. Classical Essays for John Bramble* (Bristol: Bristol Classical Press, 1987), pp. 25–37 (pp. 33–4).

19. In line 923, I follow Fitch's text.

20. The noun *genus* is derived from *gignere* and underlines the genealogical topic. The term *genetrix* is also used once to refer to Medea (*Med.* 144) instead of the much more common *mater*. Similarly, in line 910 (*Medea nunc sum; crevit ingenium malis*, 'Now I am Medea; my genius has grown through evils') we find the terms *ingenium* and *crevit*, which contain an allusion to *genus* and *gignere* and so strengthens the imagery; cf. also

'genius'/*ingenium*, which is a pun on Medea's name in Greek ('the thinking or inventive woman'): Fitch, *Seneca*, p. 423, n. 43.
21. Boedeker, 'Becoming Medea', p. 127.
22. Cf. also Guastella, '*Virgo, coniunx, mater*', pp. 200–3; Walsh, 'The Metamorphoses of Seneca's Medea', pp. 77–81.
23. Medea places much emphasis on the fact that the former crimes were directed against her father and that her future crimes will in a way 'undo' this injustice (cf. Guastella, '*Virgo, coniunx, mater*', p. 203). She describes, for example, the murder of her brother as *funus ingestum patri* ('his death thrust in his father's face', 132) and aligns the death of her own sons to it when she 'thrusts' their dead bodies in their father's face, too (*recipe iam gnatos, parens*, 'Now recover your sons as their parent', 1024). In this respect, Seneca's Medea can be seen as an avenging daughter; on this phenomenon see Marguerite A. Tassi's chapter in this volume.
24. It is extant only once in Plautus, *Truculentus* 511.
25. Medea avoids calling herself a woman, but picks words that express specific functions or positions instead, such as *virgo* or *mater*: cf. Guastella, '*Virgo, coniunx, mater*', pp. 197–219. She also prefers to use the third person singular instead of the first when she talks about herself as *mater*, a phenomenon that is more frequent in Act 5 than before, cf. *Med.* 845, 928, 933, 948, 951, 1012. Strikingly, Medea uses the first person in her confrontation with Creo when she makes a highly emotional appeal to his *pietas*, thereby tricking him into granting her a delay (289): *extrema natis mater infigo oscula*, 'I plant my last kisses on my children as their mother'. It is evident that Medea knows how to exploit emotional ties and structures.
26. This is the version told in Ovid's *Metamorphoses* 6, 146–312.
27. Cf. Alessandro Schiesaro, 'Seneca and the Denial of the Self', in S. Bartsch and D. Wray (eds), *Seneca and the Self* (Cambridge: University Press, 2009), pp. 221–35 (p. 230).
28. Walsh, 'The Metamorphoses of Seneca's Medea', pp. 77, 83–4.
29. Froma Zeitlin, *Playing the Other. Gender and Society in Classical Greek Literature* (Chicago: The University of Chicago Press, 1996), p. 347, n. 13; Monika Fludernik, 'Identity/Alterity', in David Herman (ed.), *The Cambridge Companion to Narrative* (Cambridge: University Press, 2007), pp. 260–73 (p. 261).
30. For a general outline of the concept and its theoretical framework, see Fludernik, 'Identity/Alterity', pp. 260–3.
31. Edith Hall, *Inventing the Barbarian: Greek Self-Definition through Tragedy* (Oxford: Clarendon Press, 1989), pp. 1 and 3. It has to be added, though, that the dialectic of identity and alterity not only aims at differences, but also at similarities: cf. Melanie Möller, 'Subjekt riskiert (sich). Catull, carmen 8', in A. Arweiler and M. Möller (eds), *Vom Selbst-Verständnis in Antike und Neuzeit/Notions of the Self in Antiquity and Beyond* (Berlin: De Gruyter, 2008), pp. 3–20 (pp. 7–9). It seems more

appropriate to presuppose a double purpose in the method of identity and alterity: defining by differences and looking for similarities. This is also evident from women and other 'others' in Greek tragedy: Thebes, for example, is not only the 'other' of Athens, but is partly the same.

32. Zeitlin, *Playing the Other*, p. 347, n. 13.
33. Cf. Melissa Mueller, 'The Language of Reciprocity in Euripides' *Medea*', *American Journal of Philology* 122 (2001), pp. 471–504.
34. Boedeker, 'Becoming Medea', pp. 133–5, shows how all these characters call or describe Medea merely as γυνή ('woman'); cf. also Foley, 'Medea's Divided Self', p. 73. Foley also interprets Medea's pitiable behaviour at the beginning of the play as a deceptive manoeuvre (ibid. p. 76).
35. Gill, 'Two Monologues of Self-Division', pp. 26–30. Foley, 'Medea's Divided Self', pp. 73, 77. See also Abbattista in this volume.
36. Although Medea exposes Creo as an indecisive ruler and Jason as disheartened and craven, this appears to happen rather coincidentally. Medea's opponents are weak figures on whom little focus is placed.
37. Gill, 'Two Monologues of Self-Division', pp. 31–6. Medea's 'otherness' also takes place on a generic level because she inserts what Gill calls 'narrative self-descriptions' into her monologue – parts in which she describes herself in third person as if she were talking about somebody else but without giving the impression of raising two voices instead of one (ibid. 33–4). This stylistic device heightens Medea's solipsism very effectively.
38. Walsh, 'The Metamorphoses of Seneca's Medea', p. 81.
39. Edith Hall in this volume describes the dynamics of how masculine and feminine aspects are attributed to revenge in the development of the representation of the Erinyes.
40. *Med.* 191–2, 266–71, 382–96, 445–6, 674–6. It could be said that, in a way, Wilamowitz is wrong: it is not Medea, but the other characters who have read Euripides.
41. Cf. also *Med.* 55, 130–2, 905–15. This is a noteworthy deviation from Euripides' play, where, as we have seen, the other characters underestimate Medea as an unfortunate and miserable woman.
42. The chorus shows that there are other means of portraying Medea when they illustrate her uncontrollable and dangerous sides by comparing her to dangerous natural forces (*Med.* 579–90). In Euripides' play, similar parallels are used (cf. Boedeker, 'Becoming Medea', pp. 129–33, and Abbattista in this volume).
43. In this respect, it would be interesting to know more about how Medea, the Colchian girl who has to make a life-changing decision, was treated in Roman literary tradition before Seneca. The complexity of the figure is perceptible in Hinds' article on Ovid's version of Medea: Stephen Hinds, 'Medea in Ovid. Scenes from the Life of an Intertextual Heroine', *Materiali e discussioni per l'analisi dei testi classici* 30 (1993), pp. 9–47.
44. Walsh interprets Seneca's Medea differently and stresses that from a

metatheatrical viewpoint Medea 'has powers to rebuild the sympathy we were all so ready to grant her as the love-sick maiden of Colchis' (Walsh, 'The Metamorphoses of Seneca's Medea', p. 90).
45. McHardy, *Revenge*, p. 63.

CHAPTER 5

The Avenging Daughter in *King Lear*

Marguerite A. Tassi

> These injuries the King now bears will be revenged home. (Shakespeare, *King Lear* 3.3.10–11)[1]

Historically, Western literature has featured men, particularly sons, as heroic avengers of wrongful death, dishonour, and moral or bodily injury. When women take revenge, they often appear far from heroic, at least according to patriarchal norms of heroism. In literary representations, avenging women are portrayed as deviants, for they have deviated from the social roles assigned them, roles that carry assumptions about women's morality and nature in patriarchal societies. For a woman to take revenge, she must transgress against all codes of behaviour that govern her domestic roles. Notorious examples from classical antiquity of the terrifying transformations of mothers and wives into savage revengers include Hecuba, Medea and Clytemnestra. In this family of female avengers, however, there is one member who rarely makes an appearance, and that is the daughter. What might explain the absence, or near absence, of avenging daughters? Was the gender exclusivity of the son's role as avenger so ingrained in the social imaginary of older cultures that it was virtually impossible for poets and dramatists to envision the daughter as an agent of vengeance?

In the literature of classical Greece, we find only one representation of a daughter who is prepared to take the part of her father's avenger: Electra. The three extant dramatic depictions of Electra reflect a development over time in the characterisation of her agency as an avenger. In the earliest drama, Aeschylus' *The Libation Bearers*, Electra is represented as a lamenting daughter who subordinates her will to Orestes, the avenging son. Their social and legal functions are clearly demarcated in the play: Electra laments and incites, Orestes avenges. In Sophocles' play, Electra rises above socially prescribed roles and asserts that she alone will avenge her father's death. She is prepared to kill Aegisthus, her father's murderer, and is only prevented from doing so by the arrival of Orestes, who takes the mantle of revenge from his sister. In Euripides' play, the last of the three Electra plays, the brother and sister unite in revenge and together they slay their mother, Clytemnestra, for her murder of their father, Agamemnon. Euripides characterises Electra as fierce, determined, resentful and inclined towards violence. The revenge is represented as horrific and unnatural, yet cruelly fated and just. While Orestes must flee to Athens for judgement and purification, Electra is not required to answer to the gods or the state for spilling her mother's blood. Electra is forced into exile, however, as she is considered polluted, yet she is to have a new life through a second marriage to Orestes' friend, Pylades. A gender distinction is made clear in terms of culpability and legal status, which seems to have been the case historically for societies that practiced revenge. There was no accounting socially or legally for women who took revenge. Daughters in particular were the least likely members of a family and a society to take revenge; thus, the dilemma arises in Euripides' play of what to do with Electra.

Is the avenging daughter, then, a rarity in Western literature, certainly of the ancient period, but also of the medieval and Renaissance periods? Is it possible that avenging daughters are merely invisible, that we have missed seeing them because of our own critical biases? Have our categorisations of genre and our conventional understandings of gender set up expectations of narrative and characterisation that obscure our view of what constitutes a daughter's revenge? In this essay, I would like to consider these questions by starting with two premises: (1) the critical fixation on revenge tragedy as *the* genre of revenge has blinded us to 'the prevalence of revenge across many genres', to echo Linda Woodbridge,[2] and furthermore, critics of Renaissance drama have focused primarily on male characters as agents of revenge, and neglected to notice how female characters exhibit vengefulness and participate in revenge narratives; and (2) subtle forms of gender inversion can be hidden in plain sight, missed by scholars trained to interpret texts along traditional or theoretical lines.[3]

As a case in point, I wish to open up for investigation the dramatic function and gender role of Cordelia in Shakespeare's *King Lear*. For centuries, it has gone virtually unremarked that revenge is an essential motivating force in this tragedy. No one has categorised *King Lear* as a revenge tragedy, and few major critical studies of the play have yielded insight into the complicated revenge dynamics in the play. Careful attention to such dynamics in *King Lear* will repay critics considerably, especially in shedding new light on Cordelia, whose characterisation, function and demise in the tragedy have inspired much critical controversy. If *King Lear* is understood as a revenge play,[4] we can see Cordelia's resemblance to Electra, for Cordelia, too, is a royal daughter who is grieved by injustices done to her father by her own female kin. And, like Sophocles' and Euripides' Electra, she believes that in the absence of a brother, she can assume the masculine role of father's avenger and participate significantly in the action of the tragedy.

Cordelia's enigmatic characterisation and motivation for returning to Britain have inspired conflicting narratives from critics. As Richard Knowles observes, the 'great variety of these narratives reveals a remarkable degree of confusion and disagreement about this crucial action'.[5] Knowles argues that Shakespeare created a 'very carefully calculated' indeterminacy about Cordelia's return to keep audiences from questioning 'the event's verisimilitude while allowing for maximum dramatic effect, particularly in preserving the integrity and intensity of Lear's madness and in propelling the action to its denouement'.[6] I acknowledge Knowles' argument, yet I would argue that there is clarity of interpretation to be gained by re-examining linguistic and structural clues in the play in light of revenge narratives. Indeed, I argue that Shakespeare signalled through language and dramatic structure a narrative so familiar it need not have been articulated fully. In a subtle and indirect way, Cordelia's return to Britain and her war in defence of a wronged father are reminiscent of popular revenge stories Shakespeare's audience would have known from vivid encounters with histories and tragedies in the theatre, as well as literary narratives from antiquity through the Renaissance. *King Lear* is structured as a revenge narrative that enacts the dynamic of reciprocity. The better part of the play displays scenes of horror, cruelty, suffering and political corruption that build a strong desire in the play's characters and the audience for the retribution that follows. Cordelia's sudden reappearance after a long absence from the stage (4.3) fulfils the expectation of revenge in a surprising way, calling attention to King Lear's status as a father without sons to avenge him. Her presence is calculated to heighten emotional responses – wonder at seeing the king's daughter in arms, cathartic relief mingled with fear, the strong rekindling of hope and a palpable yearning to see justice done.

By Shakespeare's time, the quasi-historical tale of an ancient British king, Leir, and his three daughters, two of whom turn against him, and one of whom rescues him and restores his throne, 'had been retold by over fifty writers, historians, and poets' since its first record in Geoffrey of Monmouth's twelfth-century *Historia Regum Britanniae*.[7] Not until the legend was adapted for the stage in 1594, however, did revenge surface as an integral part of the tale. In the anonymous *True Chronicle History of King Leir and his three daughters*, a popular play staged by the Queen's Men and the Earl of Sussex's Men at the Rose playhouse, Leir's eldest daughters and the French king, Gallia, both name revenge as the motive for their actions. When the daughters hear from a courtier of Leir's intention to tie their fortune and marriages to their proclamations of love, they conspire 'To be reveng'd upon [Cordella]' by flattering Leir in the division of the kingdom scene (1.2.74).[8] Gonoril gloatingly says: 'Nay, our revenge we will inflict upon her / Shall be accounted piety in us' (1.2.75–6). Later, Gallia, Cordella's husband, claims the role of Leir's avenging son, ready to pursue 'just revengement of the wronged king' (5.10.47). When Gallia's army is triumphant, he proclaims Leir 'again possessed of your right' (5.11.14). In the final moments of rejoicing, Leir calls Gallia 'my son' and resigns his rule to him: 'For it is yours by right, and none of mine' (5.11.15, 19). In terms of sovereignty and succession, the play performs a political fantasy of patriarchal wish-fulfilment. In the opening speech of the play, the aged King Leir had lamented the lack of a son 'to succeed our crown' and felt compelled, after his wife's death, to marry his daughters to neighbouring royalty; in the end, he has received the desired male heir (1.1.19). The play treats Cordella as pious and passive; her right to rule in Britain is subordinated to his son-in-law's right, and France and Britain are happily united as the end result of a royal son's successful revenge.

Shakespeare's version of the Lear legend differs in many respects from those of his predecessors, particularly in the treatment of Cordelia's character and the way in which it grapples with the nature and consequences of revenge. The play was performed by the King's Men at Whitehall on 26 December 1606 as part of the court's Christmas festivities, and a printed version appeared in 1608, followed later by a revision in the 1623 folio. Shakespeare's *King Lear*, particularly the folio text, recalls the male-like Cordelia of historical chronicles such as Geoffrey's *Historia* and Holinshed's *Chronicles of England, Scotlande, and Irelande* (1577), and poems such as Higgins' *The Mirour for Magistrates* (1574) and Spenser's *The Faerie Queene* (1596). Holinshed, for example, describes Cordelia as 'being a woman of a manlie courage' who 'ruled the land of Britaine right worthilie' after her father's death.[9] Higgins has Cordelia exclaim how she and Lear 'manly fought so long, our enemies venquisht were / By martiall feates, and force by subjects sword and might / The British kings were fayne to yelde our right'.[10] In Shakespeare's folio text, Cordelia returns to Britain to force her sisters to yield their right. Thus, rather than France rising up as Lear's surrogate avenging son, as he did in the anonymous chronicle play, Cordelia takes on that filial role, subverting a narrative tradition dominated by male figures.

Avenging sons appear more than a few times in Shakespeare's tragedies, but only in *King Lear* do we see an active avenging daughter. Cordelia is one of three strong-willed royal daughters in the play who take on roles traditionally inherited by sons. Lear's daughters all become political and military leaders to some extent, but only Cordelia becomes an avenger who exercises her authority as a queen to take up her father's cause through the use of military force. Goneril and Regan, in contrast, pervert law and sovereignty for their own ends and turn against each other in civil war and sexual jealousy. When Goneril asserts to Albany, '[T]he laws are mine, not thine. / Who can arraign me for't?', she strips bare the political reality in Lear's kingdom, that the sovereign's desires may arrest the law and make it his or her own (5.3.148–9). In the critical reception of *King Lear*, Cordelia's public roles as princess, queen, general and avenger have been disregarded or downplayed. Given her minimal stage time, Cordelia's character has been understood as dramatically secondary and interpreted variously as an allegorical figure, a martyr, a sacrifice, an incest victim, a stubborn and prideful daughter, and a political naif. Only recently, in feminist criticism especially, have Cordelia's public identities been examined in terms of politics and gender. The perception of her character as an avenger, however, seems mostly to have eluded critics.[11]

Granted, Cordelia never proclaims herself her father's avenger, as Gallia does in *King Leir*. Bold as her speech is, her rhetoric never reaches the fevered pitch of Sophocles' and Euripides' Electra. Nor does she sound like the Senecan revenger either, as Lear does when his rage consumes him. She does not declare explicitly, as Malcolm, Scotland's heir in *Macbeth*, does, 'Let's make us med'cines of our great revenge' (4.3). And she never speaks with the bloodlust of a Talbot who, driven by the late medieval warrior's sense of honour and valour in Shakespeare's first tetralogy, avenges the death of his comrade-in-arms, the Earl of Salisbury, with a zealous massacre of Frenchmen. Shakespeare builds expectation of her 'great' revenge through small revelations that anticipate her return. Her secret communication with Kent is presented to the audience as one such revelation. When Kent is placed in the stocks, he comforts himself with a letter he has received from Cordelia that promises heroic redress: she 'shall find time / From this enormous state, seeking to give / Losses their remedies' (2.2.153–55). He is thinking of Cordelia in the avenging son's role, bringing metaphoric remedies, or 'med'cines', to use Malcolm's metaphor, to the terrible state of affairs in the kingdom. Or perhaps he is reading from the letter directly, which would mean that Cordelia represents herself as the bringer of remedies, as the revenger. This surprising disclosure builds suspense and hope that a royal daughter, an exiled and disinherited one at that, will be capable of something wondrously heroic, something perceived as the province of men only.

In comparing the quarto with the folio, what becomes clear is how the role of Cordelia has been re-envisioned in the later version. The quarto contains a sentimental scene of reported speech (scene 17) which depicts Cordelia as a passive, grieving daughter and emblem of pity. This scene, wholly unnecessary to the play's action, robs Cordelia of any political identity or ethical force in the public sphere, and radically contradicts her fierce words from Act 1, which appear in both the quarto and folio: 'since what I well intend / I'll do it before I speak' (1.1.214–15, 223–4). The folio revision dispensed with that scene and altered a number of stage directions, which together went some distance toward refashioning Cordelia's character from a pious, impotent figure (bearing some resemblance to the anonymous *Leir*'s Cordelia) into an active, militant female.[12]

In both *King Lear* texts, we hear midway through the drama that 'the army of France is landed' with 'well-armed friends' (3.7.2, 18). In folio 4.3 and quarto 18, the audience finally witnesses onstage the presence of the French army in Britain. Unlike the quarto, the folio's stage direction supports the entrance of Cordelia as a warrior queen: 'Enter with drum and colours, CORDELIA, GENTLEMEN, and soldiers'. The folio's Cordelia ushers onto the stage the masculine world of battle. The dialogue in both quarto and folio scenes is virtually the same, but the introduction of soldiers and war accoutrements in the folio creates a military setting onstage. Cordelia is clearly in command of the French army, and it is she, not her husband or his marshal, as in the quarto text, who lands in Britain ready to defend another monarch's and a father's right to rule.

Cordelia's public identity has shifted considerably from the first scene of the play; by the fourth act she has fulfilled the King of France's proclamation to the

King of Britain: 'Thy dowerless daughter, King, thrown to my chance / Is queen of us, of ours, and of our fair France' (1.1.254–5). Cordelia returns to Britain unexpectedly as 'fair France', long-time enemy of Britain, which yields a sense of irony about the political paradoxes of feminine identity: Cordelia is both English princess *and* French royal consort, an exiled daughter and a foreign wife, an heir-apparent and a disinherited child. That Cordelia is now a French queen returning without the king, her husband, makes starkly evident her loyalty to Britain – the priority of her British blood, if you will – and her function as the fallen king's avenger. Cordelia's 'unhusbanded agency', as Maureen Quilligan calls it,[13] reveals the bold, risky nature of her military venture, as well as her singular status as avenging daughter. Unlike the ancient queen of chronicle history and poetry, Shakespeare's Cordelia is left to fight this battle alone.

Cordelia's invasion of Britain fulfils expectations for revenge that are integral to the plot, and that intensify with each act of injustice and cruelty. Gloucester and Kent look to Cordelia and the French army when they articulate their hope for Lear's rescue and the redemption of Britain from its destructive regime. Lear, too, has cried out for 'revenges' on his eldest daughters, though he cannot imagine what those 'terrors of the earth' might be, much less envision Cordelia as the driving force of revenge (2.2.445, 448). Kent, however, does envision Cordelia as Lear's avenger, as we hear when he reads the letter from Cordelia promising to give 'Losses their remedies' (2.2.154). It was Kent who recognised Cordelia's association with justice in the disastrous first scene, when he said to her, 'The gods to their dear shelter take thee, maid / That justly think'st, and hast most rightly said' (1.1.179–80). Gloucester, too, has received a letter, presumably from Cordelia; he indicates to Edmund that 'These injuries the King now bears will be revenged home. There is part of a power already footed' (3.3.10–11). Gloucester's words point to Cordelia's presumed legitimacy as the retributive force that will avenge the wronged king and restore his 'home'.

'Revenged home' suggests an evocative and troubling metaphor for what characters are driven to do in *King Lear*. The metaphor invites contemplation of 'home', a concept and reality that becomes radically imperilled in Lear's Britain. Lear has initiated the dissolution of home with his division of the kingdom and his failure to retain even one castle as his own. He is then denied a household and dwelling place altogether, and the norms of hospitality are violated thoroughly.[14] Domestic loss is expressed in its most harrowing form through the anti-pastoral experiences of the king and his loyal followers on the heath, but it is also felt through the losses sustained by Cordelia, the exiled heir-apparent. Revenge is intimately bound up with the dissolution of home and the internal conflicts within the royal family. If 'revenging home' is what the audience is made to expect from Cordelia, the metaphor, like an anamorphic perspective, inscribes within it a darker, alternate vision of revenge that is unsparing and destructive of home. The truth about revenge, succinctly conveyed in that metaphor, lies in its double-edged service for destructive and restorative ends.

King Lear acknowledges and activates different kinds of revenge, representing a hierarchy of passions and actions, from the base, vindictive and cruel sort to the politically necessary and morally acceptable kind. The baser kind of revengers are destructive, amoral and mean-spirited; their revenges cast family members out of their dwellings and bring physical harm to others. Edmund follows his goddess Nature in performing unnatural deeds, avenging himself against his brother and father, which results in homelessness for both, and then playing Lear's eldest daughters against each other so that he might rise in power. Goneril and Regan repay their father for presumed insults by strategically withdrawing every 'accommodation' he has reserved for himself after abdicating his kingship, including the most fundamental of human needs, shelter. Goneril's bitter words resemble the revenger's complaint: 'By day and night he wrongs me. Every hour / he flashes into one gross crime or other / That sets us all at odds. I'll not endure it' (1.3.3–5). Goneril later poisons Regan, using a typical woman's weapon of revenge, in a vindictive, jealous ploy to have Edmund to herself.

The more acceptable kinds of revenge are public and aligned with justice. They are undertaken with surprising ethical rigour by the disinherited children of the kingdom. Edgar 'revenges home' by avenging his father, his king and himself in chivalric single combat with Edmund, his traitorous brother. Cordelia attempts to avenge her father by bringing a foreign army to Britain to defeat her sisters and their husbands in battle. These counter-actions follow the demands of the revenge plot, but they also reveal genuinely touching and ethical aspects of character. Both children suffer their father's disinheritance. King Lear's wrathful rejection of Cordelia, which reflected his perversion of nature and the 'form of justice', might rightly be called revenge on his own flesh (3.7.24). His severing of the father–child bond – his making of Cordelia into a 'stranger' to his heart and self – coupled with the disuniting of his kingdom, opened the door to the great destructive force of vindictiveness darkly coiled in the hearts of his eldest daughters, and in Cornwall and Edmund, as well (1.1.113). Cordelia's public revenge represents a counter-force aimed at breaking the cycles of revenge unleashed in the kingdom and reconstituting 'home' in the fullness of its meaning – hospitality, proper guardianship, loving and orderly familial relationships, and a kingdom united under one monarch. Seen in this light, *King Lear* is a profound political and domestic drama of revenge in which the conflicts within the royal family have terrible political and personal consequences.

In the character of Cordelia, the consequences are tragic. Although the Anglo-Saxon derivation for queen (*cwén*) meant king's wife, such is not Cordelia's status or function in the play. She remains steadfastly king's daughter and yet, she becomes the king's avenger through the power granted her as a king's wife. She is both defiant of Lear's abuse of patriarchal power and supportive of patriarchy's authority. One might say, in agreement with Kathleen McLuskie, that 'Cordelia's saving love, so much admired by critics, works in the action ... as an example of patriarchy restored.'[15] Acting as a sovereign power, Cordelia seeks to restore the absolute authority of another sovereign, in adherence with the patriarchal ideology of authoritarian rule by divine right. Though Lear gave away his royal estate – his power, property, revenues and rule – he remains (mystically, as it were) king of Britain to the end, which is signalled in the other characters' continual reference to him as king, even after he has become homeless and mad.

The folio's Cordelia is a representation of a royal daughter assuming the filial avenger role. At the crucial moment before the clash of arms, she clarifies her motives for invasion: 'No blown ambition doth our arms incite, / But love, dear love, and our aged father's right' (4.3.27–8). She has not entirely detached herself from a personal motive, as the tender phrase 'aged father' indicates, but clearly she is not battling for her own lost inheritance. She feels filial love, certainly, and wishes to 'Repair those violent harms' her sisters have done her father, but one might interpret her love as being directed, as well, toward a just political order and authoritarian rule (4.6.25). It is significant that in her touching reconciliation scene with Lear (4.6), she calls him 'King', 'my royal lord', 'majesty' and 'your highness', insists that he must not kneel, and rejects his claim that she has cause to revenge herself upon him, to hate and kill him (4.6.12, 37, 37, 75). In the purity of her reply, 'No cause, no cause' (4.6.68), Cordelia can be perceived as different in kind from common stage revengers whose private wounds produce vindictive passions and sometimes perverse violent behaviour. She is not simply pursuing harm for harm, as her sisters and Cornwall are. Her French forces are in Britain to fight a battle for justice in the hope of restoring the king's 'right'. In her use of the royal pronoun – 'our arms' and 'our aged father's right' – we hear her assertion of both her roles, monarch and daughter (4.3.27, 28).

Shakespeare's catastrophic conclusion to Cordelia's just revenge, however, puts a notorious and memorable signature on his version of the Lear legend. He does not allow Cordelia the heroic triumph she aspired to, nor does he spare her life. Unlike the Cordelia found in former accounts of the Lear legend, she neither wins her war, nor re-establishes her father's rule. As she herself acknowledges with grim stoicism, 'My life will be too short, / And every measure fail me' (4.6.2–3). Her prophetic sense is borne out quickly when she is captured; her final lines convey a wisdom dearly bought:

> We are not the first
> Who with best meaning have incurred the worst
> For thee, oppressed King, I am cast down.
> Myself could else outfrown false fortune's frown.
> Shall we not see these daughters and these sisters? (5.3.3–7)

As a royal daughter, she has acted with 'best meaning', following an unfamiliar path and taking Lear's enemies, her own sisters, as her enemies. She has paid for her revenge, which tragically fails to fulfil Francis Bacon's prescription for public revenges, which he claimed were 'for the most part fortunate'.[16] Her final line expresses the revenger's fierce desire to outface her enemies: 'these daughters and these sisters'. Her double emphasis on kinship relationships lays bare the familial crisis at the heart of the political chaos in the kingdom. It is no wonder that at least one critic was led to call *King Lear* 'an English *Oresteia*', a particularly apt comparison given the tragedy's movement 'from primitive familial cycles of wrath and revenge in legend to the beginning of a more rational era of statehood'.[17]

Cordelia's tragic heroism lies in the limitations and conflicts inherent in her roles and the costs attending her assumption of the son's duty. In the absence of a brother and without the presence of her husband at the head of her army, Cordelia undertakes the terrible obligation of revenge, which for a young woman in a patriarchal culture is courageous, bold and just, even if not socially sanctioned. In this respect, she resembles Sophocles' Electra, who stood alone as her father's avenger, prepared to kill for what she believed was just. That Lear no longer desires his right to rule, that Cordelia does not win the fruit of victory and finally her own reign in Britain, bespeaks a very dark vision of politics and gender at work in Shakespeare's play. The avenging daughter assumes a duty neither her father nor the audience expect of her; yet, revenge is demanded by the very conditions represented in the play – and only Cordelia is in a position to try to fulfil that expectation.

Cordelia's heroic failure intensifies the characters' and audience's harrowing experience of the estrangements, divisions and disunities that have besieged the royal family and kingdom. In the figure of the daughter avenger, Shakespeare found a devastating way to raise and then bitterly defeat expectations for the restoration of Lear's lost kingdom. Edgar, 'godson' of the fallen king (2.1.90) and heir to Britain's throne, speaks the final words in the folio, acknowledging the tragic losses sustained by both filial-avengers who faced overwhelming odds in their respective attempts to restore norms of civilisation to a Britain torn asunder by their corrupt siblings. He laments, 'The weight of this sad time we must obey, / Speak what we feel not what we ought to say / We that are young, / Shall never see so much, nor live so long' (5.3.299–301). His quiet assumption of the royal 'we' points toward future promise in his inheritance of the kingdom of Britain. Yet surely no small part of the 'weight of this sad time' lies in how the avenging daughter has been forced with such senseless violence to concede her place of victory to an avenging son.

NOTES

1. All quotations from Shakespeare's *King Lear* are taken from the 1623 folio text in *The Norton Shakespeare, Based on the Oxford Edition*, ed. Stephen Greenblatt et al. (New York: W. W. Norton and Company, 1997). Quotations from other Shakespeare plays are taken from *The Norton Shakespeare*, as well.

2. Linda Woodbridge, *English Revenge Drama: Money Resistance, Equity* (Cambridge: Cambridge University Press, 2010), p. 5.
3. Careful attention to the ways in which female characters' talk about their motivations for revenge can bring into focus the different social roles they play. Kathrin Winter argues in her chapter in this volume that Seneca's Medea can be understood not only as an avenging wife, but also as an avenging daughter. In Seneca's text, Medea discloses her motives for revenge in a subtly intricate way by claiming that she is taking revenge for all of the crimes she committed for Jason's sake, crimes that were, in effect, a betrayal of her father. In this respect, she will undertake future crimes as a daughter avenging the wrongs she herself was made to perpetrate against her father.
4. In Marguerite A. Tassi, *Women and Revenge in Shakespeare: Gender, Genre, and Ethics* (Selinsgrove: Susquehanna University Press, 2011), I argue that *King Lear* 'is a profoundly disquieting revenge play, its structure of injury, suffering, and punishment enacting the reflexive nature of revenge' (p. 148).
5. Richard Knowles, 'Cordelia's Return', *Shakespeare Quarterly*, 50.1 (Spring 1999), pp. 33–50 (p. 34).
6. Ibid. p. 50.
7. Tiffany Stern, 'Editor's Introduction', *The True Chronicle of King Leir*, Globe Quartos edition (New York: Theatre Arts Books/Routledge, 2003), p. viii.
8. All quotations from *The True Chronicle of King Leir* are from Stern's Globe Quartos edition.
9. Raphael Holinshed, *The First and Second Volume of Chronicles* (London, 1587), vol. 1, book 2, sig. B1r.
10. John Higgins, *The First Parte of the Mirour for Magistrates* (1574), pp. 178–80.
11. Feminist critics include Barbara Millard, 'Virago with a Soft Voice: Cordelia's Tragic Rebellion in *King Lear*', *Philological Quarterly* 68.2 (Spring 1989), pp. 143–65; Gayle Whittier, 'Cordelia as Prince: Gender and Language in *King Lear*', *Exemplaria* 1.2 (1989), pp. 367–99; Kathleen McLuskie, 'The Patriarchal Bard: Feminist Criticism and Shakespeare: *King Lear* and *Measure for Measure*', in Jonathan Dollimore and Alan Sinfield (eds), *Political Shakespeare: New Essays in Culture Materialism* (Manchester: Manchester University Press, 1985), pp. 88–108; Grace Ioppolo, *Revising Shakespeare* (Cambridge, MA: Harvard University Press, 1991); Lesley Kordecki and Karla Koskinen, *Revisioning Lear's Daughters: Testing Feminist Criticism and Theory* (New York: Palgrave Macmillan, 2010); and Maureen Quilligan, *Incest and Agency in Elizabeth's England* (Philadelphia: University of Pennsylvania Press, 2005). I make a case, the first of its kind, for Cordelia as a figure of the virtuous avenger, based on Aristotelian-Thomistic principles. See Chapter 5, '"Revenging Home": Cordelia and the Virtue of Vengeance',

in Tassi, *Women and Revenge*, pp. 148–69. In his sentimental Christian reading of Cordelia's character, Geoffrey Bush observes in *Shakespeare and the Natural Condition* (Cambridge: Harvard University Press, 1956) that 'Hamlet is a revenger, and to some degree Cordelia is as well; they both bring a measure of restoration to sickened and divided nature. The restorations that they bring about seem sometimes to be almost more than natural' (p. 110). He does not address explicitly the implications in his tantalising insight into Cordelia as revenger, but rather focuses on her quasi-religious function, which is to remind us of 'another setting' and 'a further meaning' (p. 118), which are expressive of 'religious continuance' (p. 120). In Kordecki and Koskinen's *Revisioning Lear's Daughters*, a number of descriptive references to Cordelia as avenger crop up, but none of them is developed.

12. In the Arden edition of *King Lear* (Walton-on-Thames: Thomas Nelson and Sons, Ltd, 1997), R. A. Foakes has argued that Cordelia's character in the folio is stronger and more war-like than in the quarto. Gary Taylor, 'The War in *King Lear*', *Shakespeare Survey* 33 (1980), pp. 27–34, recognises Cordelia as the head of an army in the folio and argues that the folio 'produces a more benevolent impression' of the war, 'one more clearly personified by Cordelia herself, as the sole representative of that apocalyptic counter-movement . . .' (pp. 30, 32). See Ioppolo, *Revising Shakespeare*, for an opposing view.

13. Quilligan, *Incest and Agency*, pp. 226–8. Quilligan, however, argues that Cordelia's 'unhusanded agency' signals her vulnerability to the incestuous claims Lear makes on her.

14. Heather Dubrow, *King Lear. Shakespeare and Domestic Loss: Forms of Deprivation, Mourning, and Recuperation* (Cambridge: Cambridge University Press, 1999), pp. 104–20, offers a penetrating analysis of the historical tensions expressed through tropes of homelessness, imperiled guardianship and inhospitality.

15. McLuskie, 'Patriarchal Bard', p. 99.

16. Sir Francis Bacon, 'Of Revenge', in *Essays, Advancement of Learning, New Atlantis, and Other Pieces*, ed. Richard Foster Jones (New York: The Odyssey Press, Inc., 1937), p. 14.

17. Meredith Skura, 'Dragon Fathers and Unnatural Children: Warring Generations in *King Lear* and its Sources', *Comparative Drama* 42.2 (Summer 2008), pp. 121–48 (p. 143).

CHAPTER 6

'Brother Unkind': Annabella's Heart in *'Tis Pity She's a Whore*

Sara Eaton

> Annabella: What means this?
> Giovanni: To save thy fame, and kill thee in a kiss.
> *Stabs her*.
> Thus die, and die by me, and by my hand.
> Revenge is mine; honor doth love command.
> Annabella: Oh, brother, by your hand?
> Giovanni: When thou art dead
> I'll give my reasons for't; for to dispute
> With thee (even in thy death) most lovely beauty
> Would make me stagger to perform this act
> Which I most glory in.
> Annabella: Forgive him heaven – and me my sins! Farewell,
> Brother unkind, unkind – mercy; great heaven! – Oh – Oh!
> *Dies*. (5.5.83–93)[1]

I begin this essay with Annabella's murder in *'Tis Pity She's a Whore* to focus on the end result of her incestuous actions with her brother and his 'revenge' as a means to explore the logic of sexual revenge cast in a courtly love scenario. The tragic costs to both of the main characters is great. Lesel Dawson recently has pointed out that inside the ideology of courtly love 'Giovanni's murder of Annabella is a form of psychological suicide; as well as losing his beloved mistress, he has lost his beloved self'.[2] Similarly, Annabella loses her heart and her life. Why does Giovanni become the revenger instead of the wronged husband, Soranzo? How does Annabella's characterisation function within the courtly love strictures to facilitate both her and her brother's tragic end? What happens to her actual body, her seemingly abject physicality?

While Annabella's last words, 'Brother unkind, unkind', are an analytic touchstone for directors and critics of the play, her body's physical response to his attack is not much remarked on. We can imagine her repeated 'ohs' and 'mercy; great heaven' as heightened emotional outbursts natural to a body in pain, but few performances show her resisting her murder, even fighting for her life, choosing instead to emphasise the eroticised – I will argue abject and masochistic – violence inherent in being 'killed with a kiss', a component of courtly love's script. For a vivid example, in a 2006 production of *'Tis Pity* by Shenandoah Shakespeare at the Blackfriars Playhouse, Giovanni 'hid his poinard behind his back, lying on top of his kneeling sister as if to kiss her, but instead thrusting his knife between her legs, simultaneously killing her and her unborn child'.[3] The allusion to Othello's last words is obvious. However, recent productions of *Othello* have depicted Desdemona resisting Othello's smothering of her, adding pathos to the scene and underscoring her lively body as Othello puts out the light. In effect, staging a resisting and suffering Desdemona demonstrates her interiority and her agency, her desire to live. Unlike this, most productions of *'Tis Pity* '[act] out onstage' Annabella's murder 'in a sexually violent way that mirrored their consummation', their vows repeating 'love me, or kill me', thus highlighting her masochistic acquiescence to the incest, acceptance of her punishment and declared wish to die, and her complicity with Giovanni in her own murder (1.2.259).[4]

Why does Giovanni go after her infamous heart? His decision not only to kill Annabella, but also to remove and display her heart is profoundly linked to the characters' language and reflects a Neoplatonic system of signification, in which the heart is figured as embodying the self's essence. In her review of an American Conservatory Theatre production in 2008, Adrienne Eastwood comments how 'the visual prop is needed to fully realize Ford's use of the metaphor' in the play.[5] An omnipresent metaphor from the play's first lines, Michael Neill unpacks this use, noting that 'heart', 'in a strangely over-insistent repetition', is said eleven times in the last two scenes alone; tracing how the play's language and actions link the heart to the period's emblematic and Eucharistic meanings as well as to public executions where the heart was ripped from the body, he demonstrates how 'the private unclasping of the soul and emptying of the heart [in Giovanni and Annabella's frequent "confessions"] anticipate the ferociously public stripping of the self exhibited in the play's catastrophe'.[6] Neill insists that 'for Giovanni in particular the truths of the self are something hidden within the centre, as though the heart of his mystery were something inalienably bound up with the physical sources of life itself' which 'he carries ... to the point of an insane travesty that ends by decisively undermining the very metaphysic of identity [the emblematic heart] means to express'.[7] For most critics, Annabella's heart is finally about Giovanni's.

Giovanni begins the play disputing the Friar's prohibition of incest by reference to the 'emptied' contents of his own heart:

Gentle father,
To you I have unclasped my burdened soul,
Emptied the storehouse of my thoughts and heart,
Made myself poor of secrets; have not left

Another word untold which hath not spoke
All what I ever durst, or think, or know. (1.1.12–17)

Giovanni's confessed thoughts, contained within what Denis Gauer calls his 'tell-tale heart', reflects contemporary and marginally contested philosophical understandings of the organ's function in a Neoplatonic world.⁸ Scott Manning Stevens explains how debates of the primacy of heart or brain were shaped by the Reformation, Rome's responses and anatomical investigations over several centuries; most early modern writers defined the heart's place in the body as Aristotle did:

> While the vital force most like our term *soul* is found throughout the whole body, it emanates from the heart, which is the source of life and heat. Aristotle worked under the premise that the heart was the first organ formed in the embryonic state and the last organ to cease before death.... Cognition most likely emanated from the heart.⁹

It was also 'the vital force and source of human agency'.¹⁰

But Giovanni alludes to more than his own transgressive heart in the play's opening debate on incestuous love. By 'emptying the storehouse of my thoughts and heart', becoming 'poor in secrets' and leaving no 'word untold', he invokes the belief that the heart's 'contents' should be manifested in language, should tell all. As Carla Mazzio has shown, early modern people worried about the organic and symbolic source of speech and writing, the tongue, a body's potentially 'unruly member', because it could be 'estranged ... from its assumed interior counterpart, the heart'.¹¹ John Martin locates this cultural nervousness in a shift from valuing prudence as such to sincerity, starting in the Reformation, changing from 'Aquinas's emphasis ... on the need to bring the appetites and the will into conformity with properly determined ends' to a 'desire to connect speech with feeling'.¹² Martin Luther, for instance, in the 'Preface to the Psalms' declared that the Psalms 'not only tells what they say about their work and conduct, but also lays bare their hearts ... [I]t enables us to see into their hearts and understand the nature of their thoughts.'¹³ Also fond of the Psalms, John Calvin declared reading them 'A rare and surpassing benefit, when, every lurking-place having been explored, the heart is brought into the light cleansed from hypocrisy, that most noisome pest' and stressed 'a concord and harmony of the heart and tongue'.¹⁴ When Giovanni declares that he and Annabella share 'one soul, one flesh, one love, one heart, one all', he claims for himself and her this 'harmony' of thought, tongues, hearts and volition, his argument repeating Philip Melanchthon's – 'And why do we not use the word "heart" instead of "will" [*voluntas*]' – as he aims for her bed (1.1.34, 37).¹⁵

But as Mazzio's arguments show, the more the sincere heart was promoted as a religious and social value, the more concerns were expressed about dissimulation and hypocrisy, sincerity's binary opposite. Far from creating harmony, Mazzio comments that 'Toxic, petulant, all-consuming, the literal and figurative range of the tongue rendered it suitable for the articulation of collapsing distinctions, be they linguistic, socio-politico, geographic, or cosmic' and was 'often linked explicitly to disturbances of social and political order', in short, *'Tis Pity*'s dramatic world.[16] As numerous critics and historians have argued for decades, early modern fears about hypocrisy and 'disturbances' to social order were legion, ranging from post-Reformation life in the court to merchants' upward mobility and peasant revolts. Martin argues that what emerged was:

> the need for the individual to fashion the public self *from within*, to know when it was appropriate to present in one's expressed life a reflection of 'true' feelings ... or 'true' nature ... or when, by contrast, it was more appropriate to project or to wear a mask, to dissemble, – in short to exercise prudence in one's affairs, whether public or private.[17]

That is, to *act* sincere.

If not prudent, presumably Giovanni is sincere in his disputations with the Friar and his subsequent conversations with Annabella, or so I read his declaration of love for her by offering his dagger to her: 'Rip up my bosom; there thou shalt behold / A heart in which is writ the truth I speak' (1.2.210–11). Annabella is harder to fathom. Gillian Woods calls her 'profoundly fluid. Physically, she changes from virginity to pregnancy; socially from maid to wife to whore; and spiritually, from innocent to sinner to redeemed penitent'.[18] Her characterisation stresses her 'heart' but also her deceptive 'mask', to repeat Martin's point, and her tongue. After Giovanni, acting sincere, tells her he has received 'counsel of the holy church' sanctioning their union, Annabella reveals that she has hidden her affection for him: 'What thou hast urged, / My captive heart had long ago resolved' (1.2.241–2, 245–6). Covering her affair with her brother, she dissembles to all. Her rhetorical patterns with Giovanni tend toward restatements of 'What you will' (1.2.266). In 2.1, the scene after 'yielding, [she] hast conquered and inflamed / A heart whose tribute is thy brother's life', as Giovanni says, she states 'And mine is his', an echoing one-liner consistent with her responses throughout the scene (2.1.4–6).

This compliance and near silence is characteristic of when she is with Giovanni. In their last act together, her longest speech (thirty lines), early in the scene, is a warning to Giovanni and she moves into short questions about her brother's 'unkindness'. The scene belongs to him. With others, her tongue is unruly and she is markedly less than silent and obedient. When she rejects the match with Bergetto, his uncle Donado is surprised by her 'plain dealing' (2.6.55). Similarly, after first proclaiming his love, Soranzo realises she laughs at him and tells her 'These scornful taunts / Neither become your modesty or your years' (3.2.38–9). Her response is saucy: 'You are no looking glass, or, if you were, / I'd dress my language by you' (3.2.40–1). In her first confession with the Friar in 3.6, prior to her marriage, her responses are less than convincing, and at least one critic notices that she continues the affair with Giovanni afterwards.[19] As Soranto physically abuses her in 4.3, she taunts him about her deception of him – 'I would have told 'ee in what case I was / But you would needs be doing' – tells him his bastard son will inherit his estate, and then sings as he threatens to kill her (4.3.19–20, 32–3).

The combination of Annabella's compliant and obedient tongue with Giovanni and a potentially 'toxic' one with others creates questions about her virtue, her own sincerity and, consequently, the nature of her interiority. In 5.1, her last, supposedly sincere, confession, she addresses how 'My conscience now stands up against my lust / With depositions charactered in guilt, / And tells me I am lost' (5.1.9–11). Her conscience, punning, has written gilt 'characters' on her heart, leading her to 'confess / Beauty, that clothes the outside of the face, / Is cursed if it be not clothed with grace' (5.1.11–13). While numerous critics and presumably some audience members find Annabella sincerely repentant here, as Susan Wiseman puts it, 'we find in this speech not an opposition of inner and outer', or even a coherent identity which 'fashioned the public self *from within*', to recall Martin's point.[20] Instead, as Wiseman says, the speech is 'a contrast of surfaces in which grace becomes a kind of clothing' still covering her 'gilty' heart.[21] Annabella does not seem sincere enough as a result, fulfilling Yasco Horsman's perception that 'because a confession needs to be perceived as sincere and heartfelt, it has to be supplemented by an ostentatious show of sincerity. A confession, in fact, relies on a '"theatre of sincerity" that forces the confessor to publicize the veracity of his apology'.[22] While Ford has Annabella mime a 'theatre of sincerity', standing on her balcony as the Friar serendipitously appears to accept her letter to Giovanni written in blood and tears, it can be perceived as not revelatory enough. Although her actions certainly seem like an 'ostentatious show of sincerity', she is potentially 'gilted', merely acting in a show of her own making.

Some productions create an arc of development for Annabella, despite her rhetorical slipperiness, and show her developing from an innocent girl to a mature, sexually knowledgeable married woman.[23] This interpretation of her character attempts to explain her, but misses Ford's point about how she is figured in the play and perceived by Giovanni and the audience alike. As Woods argues, neither the characters nor the audience can see a 'real Annabella, whose identity has eluded family, society, and church'.[24] Avoiding the 'real' is her role. Hent de Vries, summarising Stanley Cavell's response to J. L. Austin's work on the performative, describes how 'the possibility of misunderstanding, of "infelicity," "misfiring," or "abuse," belongs to the heart of the matter' when claiming sincerity:

> Cavell speaks of seriousness and sincerity as being, philosophically speaking, *unfathomable*, that is, immeasurable in terms of any worldly, social, or even subjective importance; and irreducible to any cognitive, normative, or existential register whose criteria or rules would leave us no room for doubt. On the contrary, the flipside of seriousness and

sincerity is anxiety about their absence, a horror of posturing and masquerade; and, perhaps, also a terror at their presence, that is, at the claims they lay upon us . . .²⁵

Annabella is *unfathomable* to Giovanni in particular in this sense, leaving room for doubt from the beginning to the end of the play. He is anxious and needs continual 'proof' of her love. She must say 'I'm in earnest' when they pledge to 'Love me, or kill me' (1.2.261, 256, 259). After they consummate their love, he asks 'canst thou dare to swear / That thou wilt live to me and to no other?' even as he insists that 'I shall lose you, sweetheart' (2.1.26–7, 21). Giovanni's response to Bergetto's gift to her is to become jealous (2.6.137). When Soranzo first woos her, Giovanni worries that she'll prove fickle, and when she rejects her suitor, Giovanni declares, 'Why, now I see she loves me' (3.2.11, 56). Even though he knows of Soranzo's plotting against them, his first words to Annabella prior to killing her are 'What, changed so soon? / . . . Or does the fit come on you to prove treacherous' (5.5.1, 4).

Jennifer Low argues that not only Giovanni, but the other characters – with the audience – 'anxiously examine Annabella's motives', looking to discover 'the truth of [her] heart. Her consciousness, her subjectivity become as much of a focus of the play as her body.'²⁶ Not only depicted as unfathomable, she seems *impenetrable*, as Low points out.²⁷ After their consummation, Giovanni asserts that 'this pretty toy called maidenhead / So strange a loss, when, being lost, 'tis nothing, / And you are still the same', invoking a traditional binary opposition and the contradictory nature of his desire for her, that is, a 'sameness' which is also 'nothing' and a potential unhinging of the Neoplatonic paradigm tying outer physical appearances to inner realities (2.1.10–12). Similarly, after her marriage, he

> thought all taste of love would die
> In such a contract; but I find no change
> Of pleasure in this formal law of sports.
> She is still one to me, and every kiss
> As sweet and as delicious as the first
> I reaped when yet the privilege of youth
> Entitled her virgin. (5.3.5–12)

For Giovanni and the other characters (and hence the audience), Annabella's character demonstrates how desire in the courtly love scenario is constructed so that she is 'immeasurable . . . and irreducible to any cognitive, normative, or existential register whose criteria or rules would leave us no room for doubt', to repeat de Vries.

Perversely, Annabella's character thus asks for (re-)penetration, which *'Tis Pity*'s dramatic action acts out. Highlighting Annabella's inscrutability, Lisa Hopkins suggests that Annabella's opening virginal scene on the balcony, conventionally a space for idealisation, her descent into the corrupted play world, and re-ascent to the balcony for her final confession 'riddles the logic' of the early modern conventional uses of stage space since Annabella's 'paradise' has been 'under' Giovanni (2.1.45).[28] In addition, Hopkins quotes Zenón Luis Martínez about the play's scenic progressions:

> [The play's] movement from the street into the house, from the house into the bedroom, from the bedroom into the bed, from the bed into Annabella's bleeding womb, and from the womb to the heart, proposes a topography of incest which compels the gaze to an endless progress toward the profanation of the very limits of privacy.[29]

Jennifer Low comments that 'in these dramatic instances, the penetration of space serves as a complex representation of gaining access to a character's interior self'.[30] Further, 'the staging seems to reflect back on the audience its prurient desire for the unveiled sex scene that the play initially seemed to promise' until their last scene in which Giovanni penetrates her a final time in her bedroom.[31] The audience is made complicit with Giovanni's search for her heart, one frustrated in the last scene by the unrecognisable organ he brandishes.[32] That is, as Low says, 'Annabella's interiority remains a moving target; her characterization is nowhere more ambiguous than at the play's end.'[33]

Ford's depiction of Annabella, her rhetoric, her stage positions, her unfathomability, even her death, is consistent with the representation of a courtly love lady, the seemingly chaste, silent and obedient actor, either a virgin or a whore, appearing regularly in early modern literature and theatre. The characters' – including her own – rhetoric and actions construct her that way, and she is (mis)understood through that ideology, just as Richard McCabe suggests: 'The play's supreme object of desire is also its supreme object of denigration. It is not merely the Cardinal, but Soranzo, the friar, and ultimately, Giovanni himself who judges Annabella to be a whore', an object inviting (re) penetration both initially in her idealised position and her final compromised one.[34] But the virgin/whore construction is a binary that oscillates into its opposites. When Giovanni woos Annabella in Act 1, he creates a clichéd blazon by describing her forehead as:

> exceeding Juno's, stars for eyes, while
> the lily and the rose, most sweetly strange,
> Upon your dimpled cheeks do strive for change.
> Such lips would tempt a saint; such hands as those
> Would make an anchorite lascivious. (1.2.193–203)

He creates another in his description of her to the Friar: 'View well her face, and in that round / You may observe a world of variety', alluding, perhaps, to Shakespeare's Cleopatra (2.5.49ff.). Giovanni's metaphors combine the sacred and profane, tilting the heavenly toward erotic accessibility and potential whoredom, and thus mirroring Annabella's stage positions and the play's scenic progressions. His idealising courtly metaphors are repeated in Act 5 as he readies to kill her: 'Never till now did Nature do her best / To show a matchless beauty to the world, / . . . Go thou, white in thy soul, to fill a throne / Of innocence and sanctity in heaven' (5.5.59–60, 64–5).

Wiseman argues that this rhetoric of courtly love 'actually serve[s] to *conceal* the "truth" of their incest', becoming the 'absent centre in Giovanni's discourse, the hidden precondition of his platonic language' until the end of the play.[35] Facilitating the play's scenic progression, when he comes into the banquet hall declaring 'Here I swear / By all that you call sacred, by the love / I bore my Annabella whilst she lived, / These hands have from her bosom ripped this heart', Giovanni 'makes literal the discourse of courtly love', from Wiseman's view, filling the 'absent centre', at the same time that 'it makes evident the inability of this discourse to contain, explain, or give meaning to incest' (5.6.56–9).[36] But, as I suggested earlier, as a slippery symbol of (in)sincerity at work in the courtly love dynamics, Annabella herself represents the 'absent centre' of the play, creating the conditions for her (re)penetrability.[37] Giovanni still does not 'have' Annabella, although he has accomplished revenge.

Why Giovanni feels the need for revenge has perplexed audiences and critics. Post-Freudian performances tend to portray him as psychologically unbalanced, a twist on Titus Andronicus, 'dig[ging] for food / In a much richer mine than gold or stone' as his sister is rendered the victim of a madman's delusions, especially those which stress a sincerely repentant Annabella who has matured into marriage with Soranzo (5.6.24–5).[38] Revenge, however, is part of courtly love's ideology, according to Slavoj Žižek in his seminal essay, 'Courtly Love, or, Woman as Thing', and Giovanni's expectations for Annabella's behavior follow the outlines of Žižek's dissection of its 'libidinal economy'.[39] Rather than being sadistic towards his sister, luring her into incest and then killing her, Giovanni has all the marks of an abject masochist, as does Annabella, not only because he seeks pleasure in pain and vice versa, given his investment in the courtly love scenario, but also because he can be seen to be 'involved in an elaborate quarrel pitting an objective reality that is suspended and deferred against a preferred subjective reality'.[40] As Žižek explains: 'we are dealing with a strict fictional formula, with a social game of "as if," where a man pretends that his sweetheart is the inaccessible Lady . . . that is, of feigning, of an "as if" that suspends reality'.[41] While Annabella seems to have given her heart, the lovers behave 'as if' incest taboos do not pertain to them and are suspended in their dramatic world.[42] As Giovanni puts it, 'The laws of conscience and of civil use / May justly blame us, yet when they but know / Our loves, that love will wipe away that rigor / Which in other incests be abhorred' (5.5.70–3).

Annabella's rhetorical shifts from the compliant to the unruly also suggest she plays a part, one in which she acquiesces to Giovanni's game of 'as if': as she sings while being beaten by Soranzo, '*Che morte piu dolce che morire per amore*' – 'What death is sweeter than to die for love?' (4.3.59).[43] Giovanni assumes what Žižek calls 'the stance of a stage director, giving precise instructions . . . *without thereby in the least 'destroying the illusion'*, in which he declares himself 'regent' of her unfathomable (re)penetrative powers (3.2.20).[44] As Žižek says,

> Masochism confronts us with the paradox of the symbolic order *qua* the order of 'fictions': there is more truth in the mask we wear, in the game we play, in the 'fiction' we obey and follow, than in what is concealed beneath the mask.[45]

In *'Tis Pity*, the fictive courtly love rhetoric is most 'true' as the language of incest. Giovanni pulls inside out the religious paradox of where Annabella's interiority lies when 'digging for food' in her heart, his one last attempt to penetrate her body and rid himself of the 'flipside of seriousness and sincerity', the 'anxiety about their absence, a horror of posturing and masquerade; and, perhaps, also a terror of their presence', to requote de Vries. As Giovanni says, his 'Revenge is mine / honor doth love command' (5.5.86). The murder maintains the illusion of the game they act in, one 'In a richer mine than gold or stone / Of any value balanced' as Giovanni plays 'a most glorious executioner' (5.6. 25–6, 33).[46]

Again, paradoxically, Giovanni's murder of Annabella allows him to maintain his illusion-ridden position as the desiring subject in courtly love's dynamics, in which he figures himself as love's sacrificial victim in killing her. Neill reminds us that 'Both Giovanni (11.1.4–5, 32; 5.5.56–8) and Soranzo (3.2.23; 4.3.106–8) present themselves as potential martyrs to Annabella's cruel disdain, having surrendered their hearts into her keeping.'[47] Both men simultaneously maintain the Neoplatonic illusion that her heart 'really' reflects their desires (which ironically are potentially also 'nothing'), so that the heart is represented as both the symbol of their enslavement and the means through which they could regain erotic self-mastery. This contradictory vision of the heart helps to explain the lover's psychological oscillations. As Žižek explains it, '*one and the same signifier had to signify enjoyment as well as its loss.* In this way, it becomes possible that the very agency which entices us to search for enjoyment induces us to renounce it.'[48] Indeed, Giovanni's anxiety about losing Annabella necessitates his murder of her while he savors explaining it after her death (5.6.87–8). Again, Žižek's arguments describing courtly love's oscillating signification and its effects on the 'subject' or masochist point toward the potential violence inherent in the masochist's position:

> the violence breaks out precisely when the masochist is hystericized – when the subject refuses the role of an object-instrument of the enjoyment of his Other, when he is horrified at the prospect of being reduced in the eyes of the Other ... in order to escape this deadlock, he resorts to ... the 'irrational' violence aimed at the other.[49]

In Act 5, Giovanni is facing losing Annabella as well as public shaming and denies it, blaming her. He tells her,

What danger's half so great as thy revolt?
Thou art a faithless sister; else, thou know'st
Malice, or any treachery beside,
Would stoop to my bent brows. Why, I hold Fate
Clasped in my fist, and could command the course
Of Time's eternal motion, hadst thou been
One thought more steady than an ebbing sea. (5.5.8–14)

Giovanni's hystericised response to Annabella's confessional letter is to believe it and is based, as Žižek's analysis of courtly love reminds us, on the loss of his masochistic position in his own imagination. Giovanni thinks that Annabella's 'faithlessness' provokes her murder. Moreover, her resolve to 'welcome' death reflects Žižek's insight into masochism:

> what compelled the murderer to act was the experience of having his desire to kill the victim coincide with the victim's death drive ... What we encounter here is a kind of loop in which the (mis)perceived effect of the brutal act upon the victim retroactively legitimizes the act. (5.5.29)[50]

Annabella would seem to be getting what she wants, asking to be (re)penetrated and acquiescing to Giovanni's 'gilting' of the murder as an act capable of darkening the sun (5.5.79ff.).[51]

Also investigating the abject nature of the courtly lover, Catherine Bates, in her discussion of Sidney's Astrophil, could argue that Ford stages an intentionally ironic, hence abortive, act of masculine mastery and recuperation through Giovanni's actions, a move familiar to the sonneteers (and to their readers) and similar to Žižek's analysis of courtly love's economies:

> If the courtly lover is empty-handed, the courtly poet is blessed with plenitude. Indeed, he is praised for making something out of nothing – for his *fiction*. Out of the state of non-possession – not having the lady – the poet creates a work of art.[52]

Giovanni's language and last actions make a courtly lover's claims for 'glorious death' as an art form and 'a potentially castrating symbol of paternal authority'.[53] Ironically, Giovanni's gesture fails; the diners in the banquet hall below don't recognise that Annabella's actual heart measures the distance between the symbolic order, the incest taboo and his illusions. Instead, Giovanni is perceived by the other characters as abject, 'broken', engaged in what Bates calls an exploration of masculinity 'that rehearses ... the alternative roles of debility and ruination' and, she argues, the 'real' meaning of courtly love scenarios.[54] Ford's representation of this kind of irony, as Bates describes it, 'has no inner content, signified, or point of rest. It is all surface, pure signifier ... and it abolishes the idea of knowledge as something that can be possessed, and leaves mastery an imaginary dream.'[55] In fact, it has been Giovanni's image of Annabella's heart all along.

To Giovanni, to the audience, Annabella has embodied the contradictions inherent in the play's use of courtly love rhetoric. Žižek is clear about the difficulties of finding a way outside courtly love's dynamics, arguing that a 'sexual relationship cannot be transposed into a symmetrical relationship between two subjects', in effect that 'a relationship of domination' is all there is, even if, as he and Bates would have it, it is fictive.[56] To return to issues of Annabella's performance of her death scene, where I began this analysis, the conventional staging of her eagerly complying with Giovanni's grotesque and 'unkind' reaffirmation of their ruin emphasises his 'mastery of an imaginary dream'. A resisting Annabella, one which realigns her brother's 'unkindness' to signify this last painful penetration, would underscore the tragic and empty asymmetry of their relationship while giving her back her body.

NOTES

1. John Ford, *'Tis Pity She's A Whore*, in David Bevington, Lars Engle, Katharine Eisaman Maus and Eric Rasmussen (eds), *English Renaissance Drama* (New York and London: W. W. Norton & Company, 2002), 5.5.83–93.
2. Lesel Dawson, *Lovesickness and Gender in Early Modern English Literature* (Oxford: Oxford University Press, 2008), p. 149.
3. Elizabeth Charlebois, '*Romeo and Juliet*, and *'Tis Pity She's a Whore*', *Shakespeare Bulletin* 24.3 (Fall 2006), pp. 92–7 (p. 96). Alan Shepard, 'Performance Review: *Domage Qu'elle Soit Une Putain* ['*Tis Pity She's a Whore*]', *Theatre Journal* 50.2 (1998), pp. 246–8, reviewing a 1997 Paris production, describes how not Annabella but Putana is killed by Vasques in this fashion. Charlebois discusses in her review the difficulty modern audiences have engaging with Giovanni's characterisation throughout the play. According to Kate Wilkinson, 'The Performance History', in Lisa Hopkins (ed.), *'Tis Pity She's a Whore: A Critical Guide* (London: Continuum, 2010), pp. 34–59, the play was rarely performed until the mid-twentieth century: 'It was the 1960s which acted as a watershed for the play, the liberalization of sexual and moral attitudes opening the stage for numerous productions and indeed, the screen for a couple of filmed interpretations' (p. 35). Initially, productions tended to romanticise the incestuous brother and sister, idealising their love in a corrupt and immoral dramatic world. More recent productions have emphasised a psychopathic Giovanni as well as offering feminist interpretations of Annabella's victimage. For discussion of JoAnne Akalaitis' 1992 production, see Cheryl Black, 'Transgressive Female Desire and Subversive Critique in the Seventeenth Century Canon: JoAnne Akalaitis's Staging of *Phedre*, *The Rover*, and *'Tis Pity She's a Whore*', in Sharon Friedman (ed.),

    Feminist Theatrical Revisions of Classic Works: Critical Essays (Jefferson, NC: McFarland, 2009), pp. 135–51. Even more recently, a provocative production by Cheek by Jowl emphasised Giovanni's mental instability, casting him as 'a stalker' endorsed by a patriarchal culture, according to Pascale Aebisher, *Screening Early Modern Drama: Beyond Shakespeare* (Cambridge: Cambridge University Press, 2013), p. 149. The production has an Annabella who resists rather than acquiesces to her murder, a point I will argue potentially exposes the violence inherent in the logic of courtly love.
4. Elizabeth Zeman, *''Tis Pity She's a Whore'*, *Shakespeare Bulletin* 23.3 (2005), pp. 98–100 (p. 98).
5. Adrienne Eastwood, *''Tis Pity She's a Whore'*, *Shakespeare Bulletin* 27.1 (Spring 2009), pp. 179–83 (p. 179). Eastwood is being critical here of this production's substitution of an audible heartbeat instead of Giovanni's traditional entrance with Annabella's heart impaled on his sword. The scene presents challenges. Alan Dessen, *''Tis Pity She's a Whore*: Modern Productions and the Scholar', in Donald K. Anderson (ed.), *Concord and Discord: The Plays of John Ford, 1586–1986* (New York: AMS Press, 1986), pp. 87–108 notes that 'a director, faced with an audience not conversant with the critical literature, must contend with the danger of losing this climactic scene to one or another spectator reaction (shock, laughter)' (p. 89). In 'A Fairy Tale and a Falling Library, a Bloody Ghost, and a Rabbit-Skinning: Shakespeare (and Ford) on Stage in 2009', *Shakespeare Bulletin* 27.4 (Winter 2009), pp. 537–48, Dessen describes a 2009 production in which 'Giovanni entered not with a heart on a dagger ... but with a heart held in his hand dripping blood. Perhaps the shish kabob image a few feet away from seated playgoers was deemed too risky' (p. 537).
6. Michael Neill, '"What Strange Riddle's This?": Deciphering *'Tis Pity She's a Whore'*, in Stevie Simkin (ed.), *Revenge Tragedy* (New York: Palgrave, 2001), pp. 229–54 (pp. 237, 241).
7. Ibid. p. 241. For further discussion of the religious uses of emblems 'and residual cultural forces which complicate the distinctions between subject and object, discourse and body, present and past in the period', see Scott Dudley, 'Conferring with the Dead: Necrophilia and Nostalgia in the Seventeenth Century', *ELH* 66.2 (1999), pp. 277–94 (p. 278). Pointing out that Giovanni and Annabella's father dies of a heart attack after seeing his daughter's heart, Mark Houlahan, 'New Directions: The Deconstructing *'Tis Pity*: Derrida, Barthes, and Ford', in Hopkins (ed.), *'Tis Pity She's a Whore*, pp. 136–51, investigates the play's exploration of the heart metaphors.
8. Denis Gauer, 'Heart and Blood: Nature and Culture in *'Tis Pity She's a Whore'*, *Cahiers Elisabethans* 31 (1983), pp. 46–56 (p. 51).
9. Scott Manning Stevens, 'Sacred Heart and Secular Brain', in David Hillman and Carla Mazzio (eds), *The Body in Parts: Fantasies of Corporeality in Early Modern Europe* (New York: Routledge, 1997), pp. 263–82 (p. 266).

10. Ibid. p. 265.
11. Carla Mazzio, 'Sins of the Tongue in Early Modern England', *Modern Language Studies* 28.3/4 (1998), pp. 93–124 (p. 96). David Cressy, *Dangerous Talk: Scandalous, Seditious, and Treasonable Speech in Pre-Modern England* (Oxford: Oxford, University Press, 2010), also documents the increased concerns about the tongue and speech, quoting William Perkins, *A Direction for the Government of the Tongue According to God's Word* (1593; 1638 edition): 'It would make a man's heart to bleed ... to hear and consider how swearing, blaspheming, cursed speaking, railing, slandering, chiding, quarreling, contending, jesting, mocking, flattering, lying, dissembling, vain and idle talking, overflow in all places' (p. 2).
12. John Martin, 'Inventing Sincerity, Refashioning Prudence: The Discovery of the Individual in Renaissance Europe', *American Historical Review* (1997), pp. 1309–42 (p. 1326).
13. Martin Luther, 'Preface to the Psalms' (1528); quoted in Martin, 'Inventing Sincerity, Refashioning Prudence', p. 1330.
14. John Calvin, *A Commentary on the Psalms*, Arthur Golding, trans. [1571]; quoted in Martin, 'Inventing Sincerity, Refashioning Prudence', pp. 1331, 1332.
15. Philip Melanchthon, *Loci communes theologici* (1521); quoted in Martin, 'Inventing Sincerity, Refashioning Prudence', p. 1332. Whether Ford had Catholic sympathies is a matter of debate, but it is interesting that reformed religious views are voiced by Giovanni. Gillian Woods, 'New Directions: The Confessional Identities of *'Tis Pity She's a Whore*', in Hopkins (ed.), *'Tis Pity She's a Whore*, pp. 114-35, points out that 'Ford engages anti-Catholic ideas ... but also questions the possibility of a Catholic dynamic' (p. 119). See also Dudley, 'Conferring with the Dead', for the tensions around residual Catholic relics and powers.
16. Mazzio, 'Sins of the Tongue', p. 99. Corinne Abate, 'New Directions: Identifying the Real Whore of Parma', in Hopkins (ed.), *'Tis Pity She's a Whore*, pp. 94–113, discusses the levels of corruption in the play and critical responses to it. Her focus is on Putana's role.
17. Martin, 'Inventing Sincerity, Refashioning Prudence', pp. 1337–8 (italics his). Jane Taylor, '"Why Do you Tear Me from Myself?": Torture, Truth, and the Arts of the Counter-Reformation', in Ernst van Alphen, Mieke Bal and Carel Smith (eds), *The Rhetoric of Sincerity* (Stanford: Stanford, University Press, 2009), pp. 19–43, concurs, arguing that '"sincerity" emerges by the complex negotiation in the shifting terrain between religious devotion, Roman authority, royal prerogative, and Protestant ambitions' (p. 25). See also Sarah Beckwith, *Shakespeare and the Grammar of Forgiveness* (Ithaca: Cornell University Press, 2011), for a discussion of the same, quoting the Protestant John Baxter, *A Toil for Two-Legged Foxes* (1600): 'When Jupiter had made man ... Momus commended the proposition' and said, 'I like not well; that thou hast forgotten to place a

window in his breast through which we might behold whether his tongue and his heart did accord' (p. 23).
18. Woods, 'New Directions', p. 125.
19. Ibid. p. 126.
20. Susan Wiseman, *'Tis Pity She's a Whore*: Representing the Incestuous Body', in Stevie Simkin (ed.), *Revenge Tragedy* (New York: Palgrave, 2001), pp. 208–28 (p. 220). Woods, 'New Directions', finds Annabella sincerely repentant, arguing that Annabella 'achieves a level of repentant confidence unbound by confessional conventions' (p. 129).
21. Wiseman, 'Representing the Incestuous Body', p. 220.
22. Yasco Horsman, 'Like a Dog: Narrative and Confession in J.M. Coetzee's *Disgrace* and *The Lives of Animals*', in Ernst van Alphen, Mieke Bal and Carel Smith (eds), *The Rhetoric of Sincerity* (Stanford: Stanford, University Press, 2009), pp. 144–56 (p. 146).
23. See Wilkinson, 'Performance History'.
24. Woods, 'New Directions', p. 132.
25. Hent de Vries, 'Must We (NOT) Mean What We Say: Seriousness and Sincerity in the Work of J.L. Austin and Stanley Cavell', in Ernst van Alphen, Mieke Bal and Carel Smith (eds), *The Rhetoric of Sincerity* (Stanford: Stanford, University Press, 2009), pp. 90–118 (pp. 91–2).
26. Jennifer Low, '"Bodied Forth": Spectator, Stage, and Actor in the Early Modern Theatre', *Comparative Drama* 39.1 (Spring 2005), pp. 1–29 (p. 11). Low comments, 'If *'Tis Pity* does offer the audience a role, it is that of the onlooker, the peeping Tom whose desires have been legitimized because commodified' (p. 15).
27. Low, 'Bodied Forth', defines penetration carefully, tracing its etymological source in 'the phallic *penile*' and '*penninsula*', meaning 'to make or find its (or one's) way into the interior of ... And even by Shakespeare's time, the word had developed its figurative meaning: to pierce the ear, heart, or feelings of; to affect deeply, to "touch"' (p. 6). I am indebted to Low's argument about dramatic structure in what follows.
28. Hopkins, *''Tis Pity She's a Whore* and the Space of the Stage', in Hopkins (ed.), *'Tis Pity She's a Whore*, p. 159.
29. Zenón Luis Martínez, *In Words and Deeds: The Spectacle of Incest in English Renaissance Tragedy* (Amsterdam: Rodopi, 2002), p. 196.
30. Low 'Bodied Forth', maintains 'the symbolic framework of such stagings, in which the stage space represents the self of a character in either physical or psychological terms, was by no means an innovation' (p. 5).
31. Ibid. p. 12.
32. Ibid. p. 6. Low notes that for anti-theatrical pamphleteers, such as Phillip Stubbes, *The Anatomie of Abuses* (1583), Ford's dramatic structure invokes the fear that what is seen can 'pearce further, and printe deeper in our harts and minds, than that thing which is hard [sic] onely with the ears' (quoted by Low, 'Bodied Forth', p. 16).
33. Ibid. p. 15.

34. Richard McCabe, '*'Tis Pity She's a Whore* and Incest', in Garrett A. Sullivan, Patrick Cheney and Andrew Hadfield (eds), *Early Modern English Drama* (New York: Oxford, University Press, 2006), pp. 309–19 (p. 316).
35. Wiseman, 'Representing the Incestuous Body', pp. 214, 215.
36. Ibid. p. 220.
37. Slavoj Žižek, 'Courtly Love, or, Woman as Thing', in Vincent B. Leitch (gen. ed.), *The Norton Anthology of Theory and Criticism*, 2nd edition (New York: Norton, 2010), pp. 2402–27, comments that 'the Object is attainable only by way of an incessant postponement, as its absent point of reference' (p. 2413).
38. See Wilkinson, 'Performance History', for a discussion of performance history, and Sandra Clark, 'The State of the Art', in Hopkins (ed.), *'Tis Pity She's a Whore*, pp. 60–76, for a comprehensive discussion of critical reactions to the play in the last century.
39. Žižek, 'Courtly Love', p. 2407. Feminist critical work on 'how the feminine object is emptied of all substance' in the Courtly Love scenario is well established. Jacques Lacan, *The Ethics of Psychoanalysis* (New York: Routledge, 1992); quoted by Žižek. Žižek concentrates on the masculine psyche in his analysis, and hence his value to my argument.
40. Victor E. Taylor, 'Contracting Masochism: Pain, Pleasure, and the Language of Power', in Michael C. Finke and Carl Niekerk (eds), *One Hundred Years of Masochism: Literary Texts, Social and Cultural Contexts* (Amsterdam: Rodopi, 2000), pp. 53–70 (p. 63).
41. Žižek, 'Courtly Love', p. 2409.
42. It was exactly this defiance of conventions that endeared *'Tis Pity* to Romantic readers, especially Mary Shelley (Lisa Hopkins, 'The Critical Back Story', in Hopkins (ed.), *'Tis Pity She's a Whore*, pp. 14–33).
43. Translation by Bevington, Engle, Eisaman Maus and Rasmussen (eds), *English Renaissance Drama*, footnote 3 (p. 1951); the phrase is attributed to the Italian phrase book by John Florio, *Florio His First Fruits* (1578).
44. Žižek, 'Courtly Love', p. 2410.
45. Ibid. p. 2410.
46. Wiseman, 'Representing the Incestuous Body', says 'The bodies of the incestuous couple have been represented by the lovers themselves (particularly Giovanni) in the languages of courtly love and Platonism' (p. 223).
47. Neill, 'What Strange Riddle's This?', p. 247.
48. Žižek, 'Courtly Love', p. 2415.
49. Ibid. pp. 2410–11. I am omitting from this quote Žižek's insertion of Lacan's language of the 'Real' and *object a* in the reduction of the subject's perceived significance in the eyes of the Other. Žižek's point is clear enough.
50. Ibid. p. 2411.
51. Žižek's comments here are in reference to a BBC production of P. D. James' novel, *A Taste for Death* (1986).

52. Catherine Bates, 'Astrophil and the Manic Wit of the Abject Male', *SEL Studies in English Literature 1500–1900* 41.1 (2001), pp. 1–24 (p. 6).
53. Neill, 'What Strange Riddle's This?', p. 246.
54. Bates, 'Astrophil', p. 9.
55. Ibid. p. 10.
56. Žižek, 'Courtly Love', p. 2426.

PART III

WOMEN'S WEAPONS

CHAPTER 7

Cursing-Prayers and Female Vengeance in the Ancient Greek World[1]

Lydia Matthews and Irene Salvo

In the ancient Greek world, from the archaic period to late antiquity, cursing was a common way for individuals to express anger and to obtain justice.[2] For women, in particular, who did not have access to legal forms of retribution, cursing provided a means to achieve revenge within socially acceptable roles and practices. Ancient curses can be divided into two types: verbal curses (personal utterances wishing evil to someone without any reference to divine intervention) and cursing-prayers (requests to divine powers). Curses of both sorts functioned as performative utterances, in that the individual 'is *doing* something rather than merely *saying* something'.[3] In the case of the former, the very fact that one states 'I curse the thief who stole my belongings' is enough to render the thief as cursed. Cursing-prayers, while less explicit than verbal curses as performative utterances, were also perceived to effect real change. Although when a woman says 'I hand over the thief who stole my belongings to the goddess so that she may punish him', this utterance does not punish the thief in and of itself, it nonetheless enlists the goddess to punish the thief for his or her crime.[4] However, in order for a curse-prayer to 'work' certain criteria need to be fulfilled: the speaker must utter the curse in the proper way, be in the right setting, and be recognised as possessing the proper authority to make the curse.[5]

The fact that both verbal curses and cursing-prayers are themselves perceived as actions made them especially useful tools for women and those individuals who did not have access to physical or legal forms of revenge. As literary examples and ancient cursing tablets make clear, in certain contexts ancient Greek women used cursing-prayers as their main means of achieving revenge. Scholars have extensively explored Greek and Roman curses and their relationship with prayer,[6] and have tried to highlight the differences between cursing practices attested in inscriptions and papyri versus literary examples.[7] Taking both kinds of documents into account, this chapter explores the relationship between curses and gender in ancient literary texts tablets, demonstrating the ways in which they could provide women with an empowering means of achieving vengeance.

EXAMPLES OF CURSING IN ANCIENT GREEK LITERARY TEXTS: CHRYSES, OEDIPUS AND ALTHAEA

One of the earliest curses in Greek literature is preserved in the first book of Homer's *Iliad*. The story recounts how the Trojan priest Chryses, whose daughter has been captured and made a slave, curses the Achaeans when they refuse to return her. Appealing to the god Apollo, Chryses prays that divine arrows will be sent to attack the Greek army in repayment for his tears (Hom. *Il.* 1.34–52). Chryses' prayer is successful and Apollo sends a plague to the Greeks as punishment. Chryses' actions typify prayer-curses in two ways: no other ways of solving the problem are available, and it involves the divinity that is most suitable to the specific task.[8] It also shows how men invoked the help of those gods to whom they had long been tied in a bond of friendship and mutual support.[9] This pattern can be seen in another famous Greek literary curse, when king Oedipus curses his sons, Eteocles and Polynices, asking that they might kill one other: 'I pray that you die by a related hand' (Soph. *OC.* 1387–8). Oedipus also says that his heart had already previously made the curses that he is now making again out loud (Soph. *OC.* 1375–6).* The intervention of supernatural agents serves to underpin Oedipus' moral condemnation.[10]

Parental reproach and divine punishment fall within the remit of the Erinys, goddess of ancestral curses. The Erinys was an ally in the first example of a woman achieving revenge with a curse-prayer: Althaea, the mother of the hero Meleager. Like Oedipus, Althaea uses a curse-prayer to kill her own child. Her story is worth exploring more in detail. After the Calydonian boar hunt, a quarrel breaks out over the spoils in which Meleager kills his maternal uncle. Althaea, horrified by her son's actions, immediately curses him. Althaea's choice to achieve vengeance for her brother, by killing her own son, suggests a strong tie with her natal kinsfolk, the group which provided a woman with the only help in potential clashes with her affines.[11] Her natal family could also extend this protection to her children. This close bond influenced the nature of kinship and children's fosterage, that is their education and upbringing outside the paternal home. The maternal uncle could play a key role in the education of his sister's son: acting as a role model during the boy's youth, assisting in his transition into adulthood, and accompanying him into war, or on hunts. Indeed, in the Calydonian boar hunt, Meleager was helped by his maternal rather than paternal uncles.[12] Given the intensity of this fraternal bond, Althaea's wish for revenge appears more comprehensible.[13]

---

* τοιάσδ' ἀρὰς σφῶν πρόσθε τ' ἐξανῆκ' ἐγὼ νῦν τ' ἀνακαλοῦμαι ξυμμάχους ἐλθεῖν ἐμοί. ('Such curses as my heart before now sent up against you both, I now invoke to fight for me'.)

The Homeric passage (*Il.* 9.565–72) describes Althaea's cursing-prayer in detail:[14]

> [Meleager] lay nursing his bitter anger, enraged because of his mother's curses, which [Althaea] called down from the gods upon him in deep grief for the murder of her brother. Many times lying prostrate upon the ground, her bosom wet with tears, beating on the bountiful earth with her hands she called on Hades and on dread Persephone to give death to her son. Erinys, the darkness-walking, she of the implacable heart, heard her from Erebus.*

Althaea beats the ground to create contact with the underworld gods, Hades and Persephone.[15] However, it is the Erinys – called an 'aider of justice' by Heraclitus[16] – who responds to her prayer.[17] The perceived effectiveness of Althaea's cursing-prayer is testified by the vigour of Meleager's reaction. Meleager, fighting for the Aetolians in the war that has broken out over the spoils of the boar, abandons the battlefield. Although the Homeric text does not say explicitly what happened next, her prayer must have been clearly heard as Meleager later dies.[18] Her prayer is efficacious and operates like a curse.[19]

Althaea thus achieves vengeance by praying to the gods of the underworld for her son's death. While the rules of vengeance in Homeric epic required that the victims of murder be avenged by their kinsfolk (especially on the battlefield where the closest male relatives were required to take up arms against the culprit),[20] Althaea's cursing-prayer allows her to fulfil this male duty using feminine weapons.[21] Compared with Medea, for example, one notices that Althaea causes the death of her son from a distance, without slaying him with her own hands.[22] She does not pursue conventional blood vengeance, but rather uses a ritual tool that allows her to express her anger, grief and vengeful feelings. Despite Althaea's use of indirect means, the desired effect is still achieved: the wrongdoer is punished, and Althaea's negative emotions are resolved. However, she is said to have committed suicide after the death of Meleager.[23]

It is worth noting that the most famous maternal curses in Greek mythology, those of Clytemnestra, Eriphyle and Epicasta, were cast on the point of death, by women killed either by or because of their sons, in a post-mortem extension of their agency.[24] Perhaps the closest parallel to Althaea is Timoleon's mother, who cursed him when he killed his brother Timophranes, as Plutarch (*Tim.* 5) tells us.[25] Another case of mother's curses, although only feared and not accomplished, are those from Penelope: in the *Odyssey* (2.135), Telemachus feared his mother's curse should he force her to marry one of the suitors. Plato

---

* τῇ ὅ γε παρκατέλεκτο χόλον θυμαλγέα πέσσων / ἐξ ἀρέων μητρὸς κεχολωμένος, ἥ ῥα θεοῖσι / πόλλ᾽ ἀχέους᾽ ἠρᾶτο κασιγνήτοιο φόνοιο, / πολλὰ δὲ καὶ γαῖαν πολυφόρβην χερσὶν ἀλοία / κικλήσκους᾽ Ἀΐδην καὶ ἐπαινὴν Περσεφόνειαν, / πρόχνυ καθεζομένη, δεύοντο δὲ δάκρυσι κόλποι, / παιδὶ δόμεν θάνατον· τῆς δ᾽ ἠεροφοῖτις Ἐρινὺς / ἔκλυεν ἐξ Ἐρέβεσφιν ἀμείλιχον ἦτορ ἔχουσα.

(*Leg.* 11.934e–935a) stigmatised women's propensity to cast curses. Cursing women were seen as a threat to the male order of society, as is clear in the case of Althaea, who cursed and doomed to death the city's defender, its strongest warrior.[26] Without κράτος (strength) and βία (violence), typical male values, women could count on other effective means: deception or divine help.[27]

GENDERED REVENGE PRACTICES IN EPIGRAPHIC DOCUMENTS

It is not only in male-authored literary works that we find women as vengeful cursers. Greek inscriptions provide invaluable evidence for how cursing-prayers were used to exact revenge and to give vent to vengeful feelings. An extraordinary category of documents called 'prayers for justice' or 'prayers for revenge' throws light on this phenomenon. They are particularly valuable because they give voice to non-elite members of society (especially women) whose perspectives are so frequently missing from literary texts authored by elite men. Typically, prayers for justice contained appeals to a god or gods to punish someone who had done wrong by the author.[28] The most common injustices were theft, slander and magical spells. These cursing-prayers co-opted the gods as agents of vengeance. The measures that the gods took in fulfilment of this role were justified by the authors' claims of having suffered injustice. To help win the divine powers over to their side, petitioners could heap flattering titles upon the gods to whom they appealed, while humbling themselves and supplicating to the god. The frequency with which terms concerning legalistic justice and punishment occur suggest that the petitioner expected that the gods would undertake a type of investigative action and carry out a penal sentence.

'Prayers for justice' can thus be seen to have an important psychological and social function, providing a legitimate outlet for potentially disruptive feelings through an established ritual that was recognised as meaningful by the civic community. This rite soothed social tensions. The authors of these texts could be consoled that they had taken a form of revenge against their opponents, and that the perpetrators could now be punished by the gods. 'Prayers for justice' could thus be seen to satisfy vengeful feelings in a manner that is comparable to bringing a lawsuit, and they might offer a similar sense of satisfaction that justice had been achieved.[29] 'Prayers for justice' are found throughout the ancient Mediterranean from the fourth century BC until Late Antiquity and are inscribed on many different materials such as *ostraka*, stone *stelae*, lead tablets or papyri. A special and highly instructive case study comes from Knidos (Caria, modern Turkey).

*

During the excavations at Knidos in South Western Turkey in 1857–9, the Victorian archaeologist Charles Newton discovered thirteen lead tablets dating to between the late second and early first century BC.[30] The thin sheets of lead had been folded over and then deposited at the bases of statues in the sanctuary of Demeter. Inscribed on these tablets were a series of prayers for justice written exclusively by women. Although some are so fragmentary that we can only identify a few words and phrases, the surviving cursing-prayers are all very similar in their structure and wording. One of these, made by a woman named Artemis, can be used to provide a sense of their general shape and phrasing (*I. Knidos* 148):[31]

> [Side A] Artemis dedicates to Demeter, Kore, and all the gods with Demeter, the person who did not return the articles of clothing, the mantle and the short cloak, that I left behind, even though I have asked for them back. Let he himself bring them back to Demeter even if it is another who has my things, let him be burned with fever and let him publicly confess. But may I enjoy divine favour and be free [Side B] even if I eat and drink with him and am under the same roof. For I have been wronged, mistress Demeter.*

In making this cursing-prayer Artemis handed over an unknown thief to Demeter, her daughter Kore (also known as Persephone) and the other gods of the underworld so that they could inflict vengeance on him on her behalf. Artemis prays that Demeter inflict a burning fever on the thief, which will only be alleviated when he makes a public confession of his crime. The culprit is also to hand over the items that he has stolen to Demeter because, by making this prayer, Artemis had transferred ownership of her property to the goddess, so making the thief's crime the goddess' problem. Artemis, on the other hand, should be protected from this divine punishment inadvertently affecting her in any way. Common additions to this basic structure include asking the goddesses to show no mercy to the culprit, the author of the curse protesting her innocence, and requests for the goddesses to also punish the offender's family.[32]

The source of such uniformity is not immediately clear since it seems that would-be petitioners did not have the option of reading for themselves how other women had addressed the goddesses. Newton says that he found the tablets folded up, something we can see for ourselves from Newton's drawings which clearly show the fold marks and breaks.[33] Although one tablet has what appears to be a nail-hole at the top-middle (*I. Knidos* 148), we should not imagine that the text was displayed: apart from the fact that most of the texts show signs of being folded over, many also continue onto their reverse side, so that even an unfolded prayer, if nailed up, would not be fully legible.[34] We need to look instead to the social context of this act of cursing. Christopher

---

* [Side A] ἀνιεροῖ Ἄρτε/μεις Δάματρι, / Κούρα[ι, θεο]ῖς πα/ρὰ Δάματρι πᾶ/σι· ὅστις τὰ ὑπ' ἐμοῦ / καταλιφθέντα ἱ/μάτια καὶ ἔνδυ/μα καὶ ἀνάκω[λ]/ον, ἐμοῦ ἀπαιτ[η]/<σά>σας, οὐκ ἀπέδ[ωκέ] / μοι, ἀνενέγκα[ι] / αὐτὸς παρὰ Δ[ά]/[μ]ατρα, καὶ εἴ τι[ς] / [ἄλλος] τἀμὰ ἔ<χ>[ει], / [πεπρη]μένος ἐξ[α]/[γορεύ]ων· ἐμο[ὶ] / [δὲ ὅσια κ]αὶ ἐλεύ/[θερα [Side B] καὶ συμπιεῖν καὶ / συμφαγεῖν καὶ / ἐπ[ὶ τὸ α]ὐτὸ στέ/γος ἐ[λθ]εῖν· ἀδί/κημαι γάρ, δέσπο[ι]/να Δάματερ.

Faraone has argued that the prayers were made as part of an annual festival of Demeter and Kore called the Thesmophoria.[35] In such a setting, women would be granted the religious authority to make an efficacious speech act: they would be able to make it in the correct setting and be taught the right way of phrasing it. This festival, celebrated throughout the Greek world, took place over a number of days, during which time the women of the polis secluded themselves in the local sanctuary of Demeter. The Thesmophoria would have provided the perfect environment for women to share tales of wrongs done to them, to instruct one another on how to phrase their prayers for justice, and to consult the priestesses of Demeter, who could also act as scribes when the time came to inscribe the prayers.[36]

As Angelos Chaniotis has noted, the similarity of language is so great that we must assume a very high level of interaction amongst the women in the sanctuary.[37] Indeed, as part of the process of making the prayer, these texts were probably read aloud, so that the assembled audience of women could share in the author's anger.[38] As such, the rhetoric of the prayers had to appeal to both divine and mortal, forging commonality between the goddesses and the women who worshipped them. The entire process of making one of these prayers for justice was both extremely social and highly gendered: as part of a religious festival celebrated only by women, female worshippers talked with one another and with the priestesses, and, having shared their grievances, they advised one another on how best to enlist the goddesses in their cause. The prayers were then performed, and the anger of these women physically acted out for the crowd of female worshippers when the prayer had a nail driven through it.

The contents of the surviving prayers bear many similarities with prayers for justice from other parts of the ancient Mediterranean and are concerned with four broad types of injustice: (1) the woman or someone close to her has been the victim of a property crime, either theft or being cheated in a business transaction; (2) the husband of the dedicant has absconded with another woman and/or her domestic affairs have been disrupted; (3) she has been the victim of false accusations, gossip or slander, especially regarding her alleged use of magic or poison; (4) finally, in one prayer we see revenge being sought for an assault that occurred after a false accusation was made.[39]

Only a few of these offences were crimes that were punishable under law. Even in these cases a woman might have found it difficult or impossible to obtain legal retribution, either because the perpetrator's identity was unknown (as is the case in many other prayers for justice) and/or because, as a woman, she did not have direct access to the courts. Ancient Greek courts were male dominated spaces into which women could not independently bring their own accusations.[40] A woman's access to the law was mediated through her *kyrios* (guardian), a man (often her father, brother or husband) who represented her economic and legal interests.[41] This meant that female access to the kind of compensation the state could provide was curtailed. Indeed, polis law failed to provide for female interests on a more fundamental level. Many of the wrongs that these women suffered were not 'crimes' in any legal sense. For example, although Greek law

protected men from adultery this protection was not extended to women.⁴²
While a man might be allowed to kill the seducer of his wife, no such retribution was available to a woman whose domestic affairs had been disrupted.

Like members of other marginal groups such as slaves or foreigners who did not enjoy the rights of citizen men, the Knidian women had to employ a different set of tools to acquire the vengeance that they desired. Members of such groups depended on a variety of self-help strategies including petitioning divine or secular authorities and using magic or gossip.⁴³ The Knidian women can be seen to employ a combination of these in their prayers for justice: their prayers take the form of petitions, but they also share many characteristics with *defixiones*, and they rely on social tools, especially gossip, to help ensure that the requested vengeance is enacted.⁴⁴ These strategies require the careful management of social relationships. To show how this worked we will first examine how the Knidian women cultivated relationships with the goddesses and with the other women present in the sanctuary, before addressing the ways in which they could use gossip to exploit this network of women to obtain vengeance.

The Knidian women relied on their ability to form relationships with the goddesses and with the other worshippers, and to manage public opinion.⁴⁵ The primary relationship is that between goddess and supplicant. Like other petitioners in the ancient world who addressed themselves to government officials, these women could help to ensure that they won divine aid by creating a relationship between themselves and Demeter. For example, a petitioner could use flattering language as Artemis does in *I. Knidos* 148 when she calls Demeter 'Mistress' (δέσποινα), or she could insist on her innocence as a victim of violence in *I. Knidos* 159 does.⁴⁶ A woman named Prosodion, the dedicant of *I. Knidos* 151, managed to create an even more personal bond with Demeter. Prosodion both attacks the woman who has taken away her husband, Anakon, and also aims two subsidiary curses at those who side with Anakon and his mistress:⁴⁷

> Prosodion dedicates to Demeter and Kore and the gods with Demeter, whoever takes away the husband of Prosodion, Anakon, from their children. May Demeter not be merciful nor the gods with Demeter. [Prosodion dedicates] whoever is given hospitality by Anakon to the detriment of Prosodion, but let Prosodion and her children enjoy divine favour in all respects. [Prosodion dedicates] whoever gives hospitality to Anakon to the detriment of Prosodion. Let neither Demeter, nor the gods with Demeter, be merciful. But let Prosodion and her children enjoy divine favour in all respects.*

---

* ἀνιεροῖ Προσόδιο]ν Δάματρι καὶ Κόραι / [καὶ θεοῖς το]ῖς παρὰ Δάματρι, τίς τὸν Προσο/[δίου ἄνδρα {τὸ]ν Προσοδίου ἄνδρα} περιαιρῖται / [Ἀνάκωνα πα]ρὰ τῶν παιδίων· μὴ τύχοι εὐιλά/[του] μὴ Δάμα{μα}τρος {Δάματρος} μὴ θεῶν τῶν παρὰ Δάματρι / [εἴ τίς π]αρ' Ἀνάκωνος ὑποδέχεται ἐπὶ πονηρίαι τᾶι / [Προσοδ]ίου, Προσοδίοι δὲ ὅσια καὶ αὐτᾶι καὶ τοῖς παιδίοις / [κατὰ πᾶ]ν μέρος· καὶ τίς ἄλ<λα> Ἀνάκωνα τὸν Προσοδίου / [ἄνδρα] ὑποδέχεται ἐπὶ πονηρίαι τᾶι Προσοδίο[υ], / μὴ τύχοι εὐιλάτου μὴ Δάματρος μὴ θεῶν [τῶν] / πὰ Δάματρι· Προσοδίοι δὲ ὅσια / καὶ τοῖς τέκνοις/ κατὰ πᾶν μέρος.

As in the other Knidian tablets Prosodion emphasises her own innocence and that of her children and the wrong done to them as part of a rhetorical strategy designed to win over Demeter and to make the threat of Demeter's revenge unattractive enough to discourage support for Anakon and his mistress. Her children are key to this and Prosodion names them as the injured party in her prayer, placing the phrase 'and her children' (καὶ τοῖς τέκνοις) in a centred, visually emphatic position at the bottom of tablet. It is interesting how Prosodion's appeal differs from that of the other female petitioners. While most of the women mention Kore as often as they mention Demeter, some petitioners like Prosodion focus their appeals on Demeter, naming Kore only once.[48] This serves to flatter the chief goddess of the sanctuary, drawing her attention to Prosodion's plight, but even more importantly it forges a relationship between the goddess and worshipper. Demeter is a mother who can empathise with the plight of another mother: in the *Homeric Hymn to Demeter*, she famously travelled the earth in deep mourning searching for her daughter Persephone after she had been abducted by Hades. Prosodion shows that she too is a caring mother, concerned for the plight of her children.

Prosodion's skilful assimilation of her situation to that of Demeter has a second audience: the women in the sanctuary, some of whom might have known Anakon and his mistress. Prosodion's desertion by Anakon has created far-reaching social problems for her that she attempts to remedy with this prayer. She is not only concerned with her unfaithful husband and the woman who has 'taken' him, but also with the broader social network in which her family exists, especially the members of her community who might take Anakon's side, or who might offer him hospitality. To prevent the social isolation of herself and her children, and in revenge for the emotional, and probably financial, suffering that they have undergone, Prosodion makes a public declaration effectively stating that any person who associates with her husband will be punished by the gods.

The secondary audience of female worshippers played a crucial role in helping to ensure that this speech act had very real social consequences. The petitioners asked the goddesses to ensure that the culprit was burned with fever (πεπρημένος) and driven to make a public confession, often together with their whole family.[49] To achieve this, the petitioners relied on the network of women to which the Thesmophoria gave them access. In this context, the prayers functioned as a kind of advertisement, a wanted-notice. The female worshippers, and through them the community at large, knew that they should be on the lookout for anyone who displayed symptoms of fever, a signal of their guilt and of the goddesses' revenge. This gossip also alerted the guilty parties to the fact that they had been cursed, encouraging them to return the property and make a public confession. The form that these punishments took meant that their main impact was on the social standing of the suspected perpetrator: if they confessed they suffered loss of face; if they did not confess they might face social exclusion by members of the community who were afraid of becoming casualties of the goddess' vengeance; in either case they were subject to gossip and surveillance.⁵⁰ A woman who made such a prayer, although unable to plead her case in a court, was nevertheless able to exert a degree of social power through her access to a network of female gossip, and in so doing bring about a very real form of vengeance.

These prayers are not only used to inflict loss of face on others, but also as a way for some petitioners to undo the damage done to their own reputations. This is especially true in cases where women prayed for revenge after being slandered. By far the most common defamatory charge against which they have to defend themselves is that of using poison/magic. Whatever the actual demographics of ancient magical practice might have been, it seems that women were imagined to be its primary practitioners and that they used it against their husbands.⁵¹ For example, in roughly the same period as these prayers were made, a Greek woman named Thais living in Egypt vowed in her marriage contract not to use φάρμακα (both love potions and poisons) against her new husband, not to put these into his food or drink, and not to collude with anyone else to bring him harm.⁵² An accusation that a woman had used magic against her husband or her enemies was therefore at once highly plausible to an ancient audience and yet often completely unverifiable, since magic is, by its nature, a secretive and hidden affair.

The secrecy of magic and poisoning is contrasted with the public nature of the prayers for justice.⁵³ In *I. Knidos* 147, a woman named Antigone is able to respond to whispered gossip that she had poisoned a man called Asklepiadas with a very public declaration of her innocence.⁵⁴

> [Side A] Antigone dedicates to Demeter, Kore, Pluto, all the gods and goddesses with Demeter if I have given poison/spells to Asklapiadas or contemplated in my soul doing any evil to him, or if I have summoned a woman to the temple, offering her a mina and a half⁵⁵ to remove him from the living, may Antigone, having been struck by fever, go up to Demeter and publicly confess, and may she not find Demeter merciful, but rather be tormented with great suffering. If anyone has spoken to Asklapiadas against me, or brought forward the woman by offering her copper coins ... [Side B] May I enjoy divine favour even if I am at the same bath, under the same roof, or at the same table.*

Part of Antigone's strategy was to use a 'conditional self-curse': if the goddess finds that she is in fact guilty of the rumoured crimes, then the goddess should

---

* [Side A] ἀνιεροῖ Ἀντιγό/νη Δάματρι, Κού/ραι, Πλούτωνι, θε/οῖς τοῖς παρὰ Δά/ματρι ἅπασι καὶ / πάσαις· εἰ μὲν ἐ/γὼ φάρμακον Ἀ/σκλαπιάδαι ἢ ἔ/δω[κ]α ἢ ἐνεθυ/μήθην κατὰ ψ/υχὴν κακόν τι / [α]ὐτῷ ποῖσαι ἢ ἐ/κάλεσα γυναῖκ/α ἐπὶ τὸ ἱερόν, / τρία ἡμιμναῖ/α διδοῦσα ἵνα / {ι}αὐτὸν ἐκ τῶν / ζώτων {ζώντων} ἄρη, / ἀναβαῖ Ἀντιγό/νη πὰ Δάμα/τρα πεπρημέ/να ἐξομολ<ογ>ουμ[ένα], / καὶ μὴ γένοιτο / εὐειλάτ[ου] τυ/χεῖν Δάματρο[ς], / ἀλλὰ μεγάλα/ς βασάνους βασ/ανιζομένα· εἰ δ' ε<ἴ>/[πέ] τις κατ' ἐμοῦ π/ρὸς Ἀσκλαπίδα<ν> / εἰ κ/[α]τ' ἐμοῦ καὶ παριστ/άνετα[ι] γυναῖκα / χαλκοῦς δο<ῦ>σα / ΙΑΝ δ' ἐμοῦ ΤΑ [Side B] ἐμοὶ δ' ὅσια καὶ / εἰς βαλανεῖον / καὶ ὑπὸ ταὐτὸ / στέγος εἰσελ/θεῖν καὶ ἐπὶ τὰ/ν αὐτὰν τρ<ά>π/εζαν.

punish her.⁵⁶ All the women in the sanctuary knew that she had made this prayer, and she was therefore able to rely on gossip to work in her favour this time. Proof of her innocence could then be observed by all members of the community when she failed to suffer punishment. Just as social surveillance for the signs of guilt was used to solve crimes of theft, so too could it be used to demonstrate Antigone's innocence.⁵⁷ So, although Antigone could not publicly proclaim her innocence in a court of law, as citizen men could when they successfully defended themselves against charges that were brought against them or when they prosecuted another men for defamation, she could use a prayer for justice to defend her reputation. Conversely, having to confess, being forced to diminish their social capital, is the primary punishment that the Knidian women ask that the Demeter and Kore inflict on their enemies.

While it was not only women who prayed to the gods for justice or revenge, this ritual was a privileged path for wronged women seeking satisfaction. The sorts of injustices for which women sought vengeance and the tools that they used to achieve it were shaped by their marginal position vis-à-vis the legal institutions of the polis. While other groups that included men also shared this marginal status, women exploited their socially approved roles to achieve the vengeance that was otherwise denied to them. Women emphasised their roles as mothers and wives and used religion, one of the few arenas of polis life in which they exercised authority, in order to acquire the power for vengeance. Indeed, the efficacy of their cursing-prayers relied in part on stereotyped fears of feminine anger and vengefulness (both divine and mortal) and this helped to ensure that culprits took the threat of Demeter's punishment seriously.⁵⁸ It is important to stress that prayers for justice challenge the idea that emotional women were irrational and mad (as they were commonly portrayed in tragedy).⁵⁹ The ritual performance of these cursing-prayers was a rational tool of justice, approved by the male order of society. This power was not the same as that which was available to citizen men through the courts or through more direct violent forms of vengeance, but was dependent on their manipulation of social relationships through gossip. Through the very act of making a cursing-prayer and with the help of divine and mortal women, Greek women were able to defend their own reputations and punish their enemies with social surveillance, loss of face and social exclusion.

NOTES

1. Both authors contributed equally to this chapter, although Salvo is mainly responsible for 'Examples of Cursing in Ancient Greek Literary Texts: Chryses, Oedipus and Althaea' and Matthews for 'Gendered Revenge Practices in Epigraphic Documents'. Irene Salvo thanks the Gerda Henkel Stiftung for the support for her research. We would like to thank Henk Versnel for his comments on an early draft.
2. As literary, papyrological, epigraphic and archaeological sources make

clear, curses could be employed in a variety of ways; they could be used, for example, to protect a tombstone from desecration or they could be inserted in oaths as a conditional clause of self-cursing. On Greek curses see, among others, Esther Eidinow, *Oracles, Curses, and Risk among the Ancient Greeks*, 2nd edition (Oxford: Oxford University Press, 2013).

3. John L. Austin, *Philosophical Papers* (Oxford: Oxford University Press, 1961), p. 223. See John L. Austin, *How to Do Things with Words* (Oxford: Clarendon Press, 1962); John Ma, 'Seleukids and Speech-Act Theory: Performative Utterances, Legitimacy and Negotiations in the World of the Maccabees', *Scripta Classica Isrealica* 19 (2000), pp. 71–112 (esp. pp. 75–85); Manuela Giordano, 'Women's Voice and Religious Utterances in Ancient Greece', *Religions* 2 (2011), pp. 729–43 (esp. 731–2), for the definition of curses as 'performative utterances'. It should be noted, however, that we disagree with the sharp opposition between 'curse' (that operates mainly on a human level) and 'prayer' (that works thanks to a communication with divine agents) made by Giordano, 'Women's Voice'.

4. On ancient cursing as a speech act see Christopher A. Faraone, 'The Agonistic Context of Early Greek Binding Spells', in C. Faraone and D. Obbink (eds), *Magika Hiera: Ancient Greek Magic and Religion* (Oxford: Oxford University Press, 1991), pp. 3–32; Amina Kropp, 'How does Magical Language Work? The Spells and *Formulae* of the Latin *defixionum tabellae*', in R. L. Gordon and F. Marco Simón (eds), *Magical Practice in the Latin West* (Leiden: Brill 2010), pp. 357–80.

5. So, for example, the statement 'I now pronounce you man and wife' is only 'felicitous' (i.e. efficacious) if performed by a priest in a church, during a wedding. See Ma, 'Seleukids and Speech-Act Theory', p. 76.

6. See most recently: Henk Versnel, 'Prayer and Curse', in E. Eidinow and J. Kindt (eds), *The Oxford Handbook of Ancient Greek Religion* (Oxford: Oxford University Press, 2015), pp. 447–61, and bibliography.

7. An overview on curse poetry, especially in the Hellenistic and Roman periods, is offered by Lindsay Watson, *Arae. The Curse Poetry of Antiquity* (Leeds: Francis Cairns, 1991).

8. See Watson, *Arae*, p. 63.

9. Jennifer Larson, *Understanding Greek Religion. A Cognitive Approach* (Abingdon/New York: Routledge, 2016), pp. 41–2.

10. See Larson, *Understanding Greek Religion*, p. 132, for a cognitive interpretation of the relationship between morality and supernatural beings.

11. Jan N. Bremmer, 'The Importance of the Maternal Uncle and Grandfather in Archaic and Classical Greece and Early Byzantium', *Zeitschrift für Papyrologie und Epigraphik* 50 (1983), pp. 173–86 (esp. p. 183). Danièle Aubriot-Sévin, *Prière et conceptions religieuses en Grèce ancienne jusqu'à la fin du Ve siècle av. J.-C.* (Lyon: Maison de l'Orient Méditerranéen, 1992), p. 365, compares Althaea with the Sophoclean Antigone, both inspired by the same principle of protecting a deceased member of their original home. See Richard Seaford, 'The Structural Problems of Marriage in Euripides',

in A. Powell (ed.), *Euripides, Women, and Sexuality* (London: Routledge, 1990), pp. 151–76 (esp. pp. 166–8), for other women in Attic tragedy and comedy who, through loyalty to their natal families, damage their families by marriage.

12. In the *Odyssey* (19.429–31), the scar by which Odysseus was recognised upon his return was gained when he was hunting with his maternal uncles in his youth. See Bremmer, 'The Importance of the Maternal Uncle' for further mythical and historical examples of matrilineal fosterage in Archaic and Classical Greece. Jan N. Bremmer, 'La plasticité du mythe. Méléagre dans la poésie homérique', in C. Calame (ed.), *Métamorphoses du mythe en Grèce antique* (Genève: Labor et Fides, 1988), pp. 37–56 (esp. p. 48–9), notes that the killing of his uncles during the hunt symbolises Meleager's initiation into adulthood, away from his mother. The special bond between a mother's brother and his sister's son, known by social-anthropologists as the institution of the avunculate, has frequently been observed in Indo-European and non-literate societies. In early anthropological studies, this institution was interpreted as a vestige of matriarchal and matrilineal systems. In a seminal study Alfred Radcliffe-Brown, *Structure and Function in Primitive Society* (Glencoe, IL: The Free Press, 1952), showed how common the avunculate is in patrilineal societies. Claude Lévi-Strauss, *Structural Anthropology*, trans. C. Jacobson and B. Grundfest Schoepf (New York: Basic Books, 1963), stressed that the avunculate relationship is 'the most elementary form of kinship'. Building on these and further discussions, Jan N. Bremmer, 'Avunculate and Fosterage', *Journal of Indo-European Studies* 4 (1976), pp. 65–78, notes that among the Indo-Europeans the affectionate relationship between the mother's brother (MB) and sister's son (ZS) contrasts with the austere relationship between father and son: without the burden of the *patria postestas*, the MB can develop a loving and caring relationship with the ZS. Thus, Bremmer discards explanations that postulate a previous matriarchal system.

13. For a comprehensive analysis of Meleager's myth in Greek and Roman literature see Peter Grossardt, *Die Erzählung von Meleagros. Zur literarischen Entwicklung der kalydonischen Kultlegende* (Leiden: Brill, 2001). In another well-known mythological variant (preferred by lyric and tragic poets) Meleager's life was linked to a magical brand. When Althaea cast this onto the fire Meleager died (Bacch. 5.127–54; Phryn. *TrGF* 1, 3 F 6; Soph. *TrGF* 4 F 401–6; Eur. *Meleag.* Frr. 515–39 N.). The curse variant is rarer and often the other sources depend on the *Iliad* (Ovid. *Epist.* 3.92–7; Diod. 4.34.5; Ps.-Apollod. *Bibl.* 1.8.3; Paus. 10.31.3). See Grossardt, *Die Erzählung von Meleagros*, pp. 285–90; Onofrio Vox, 'Le maledizioni di Althaia', *Rudiae* 20–1 (2008–9), pp. 357–71 (esp. p. 360). As noted by commentators on the Homeric passage, for example Bryan Hainsworth (ed.), *The Iliad: A Commentary. Volume III: Books 9–12* (Cambridge: Cambridge University Press, 1993), p. 130; Christopher H. Wilson, *Homer, Iliad: Books VIII & IX* (Warminster: Aris & Phillips, 1996),

p. 244; Richmond Lattimore, *The Iliad of Homer*. New Introduction and Notes by Richard Martin; first published 1951 (Chicago: The University of Chicago Press, 2011), p. 542, Meleager's anger brings his story closer to that of Achilles. This is compounded by the fact that Phoenix does not recount the death of Meleager. On the question of whether the magical brand is part of an ancient folk-tale tradition that is adapted by Homer or is a post-Homeric invention, see Bremmer, *La plasticité du mythe*, and Fiona McHardy, 'From Treacherous Wives to Murderous Mothers: Filicide in Tragic Fragments', in F. McHardy, J. Robson and F. D. Harvey (eds), *Lost Dramas of Classical Athens* (Exeter: University of Exeter Press, 2005), pp. 129–50 (p. 146).

14. English translation slightly adapted from Lattimore, *The Iliad*.
15. Parallels for Althaea's gestures are given by Vox, 'Le maledizioni di Althaia', pp. 361–6. On the Erinys' agency see Louis Gernet, *Antropologia della Grecia antica* (Milano: Mondadori, 1983), p. 195, n. 263; Vox, 'Le maledizioni di Althaia', p. 367, nn. 34–5. On the link between funerary lament and revenge in this passage, see Hall in this volume.
16. Heracl. fr. B94 DK on Erinyes: Δίκης ἐπίκουροι.
17. Conversely, Amyntor, king of Ormenium, when cursing his son Phoenix invoked the Erinys, but the gods of the underworld accomplished the curse (Hom. *Il.* 9.454–7).
18. On the death of Meleager in the Homeric account, Bernard Eck, *La Mort Rouge. Homicide, guerre et souillure en Grèce ancienne* (Paris: Les Belles Lettres, 2012), p. 42, is more cautious and argues that, since the Homeric passage does not give further information, we should ignore the effect of Althaea's curses. However, at the mythical level, her curses provoked Meleager's death. As noted by Hainsworth, *The Iliad*, p. 138, the curse was heard by the Erinys, and 'since the action of such a being cannot be ineffective, the death of Meleager is implied'. Also, as William Sax, *God of Justice: Ritual Healing and Social Justice in the Central Himalayas* (Oxford: Oxford University Press, 2009), p. 219, notes, in the Central Himalayas a mother's curse is believed to cause illnesses, misfortunes and certain death. For another example of a woman's curse that brings death and powerful revenge, see Michalopoulos in this volume on Oenone and Paris in Ovid's *Heroides*.
19. See Aubriot-Sévin, *Prière et conceptions religieuses*, p. 328. Althaea herself was believed to have magical powers, and was invoked as divine agent responsible for the curse in a tablet that has elements typical of 'prayers for justice': *DT* 41, Megara, I–II AD; there is a dedication of the cursed persons to Althaea, Kore, Hecate and Selene, and the author of the text requests punishment, retaliation and revenge; see Henk Versnel, 'Beyond Cursing: The Appeal to Justice in Judicial Prayers', in C. A. Faraone and D. Obbink (eds), *Magika Hiera. Ancient Greek Magic and Religion* (Oxford: Oxford University Press, 1991), pp. 60–106 (p. 65); Vox, 'Le maledizioni di Althaia', pp. 367–8.

20. On the theme of revenge and compensation in Homer, see most recently Douglas Cairns, 'Honour and Shame: Modern Controversies and Ancient Values', *Critical Quarterly* 53 (2011), pp. 23–41.
21. On the relationship between revenge and female gender, see Fiona McHardy, 'Women's Influence on Revenge in Ancient Greece', in F. McHardy and E. Marshall (eds), *Women's Influence on Classical Civilization* (London: Routledge, 2004), pp. 92–114; Fiona McHardy, *Revenge in Ancient Greek Culture* (London: Duckworth, 2008), pp. 37–42; Hall in this volume.
22. On filicide in Greek literature, and on Althaea in particular, see McHardy, 'From Treacherous Wives to Murderous Mothers', pp. 145–8. Althaea's actions became deliberate rather than accidental in the representations on the Athenian tragic stage.
23. For the suicide of Althaea, see Ps.-Apollod. *Bibl.* 1.8.3; Ovid. *Met.* 8.560–2. Jean-Michel Renaud, *Le mythe de Meleagre. Essais d'interpretation* (Liège: Renaud, 1993), p. 121, thinks that, because she did not respect the boundaries between male and female roles, through exercising too great a level of agency and too much control over her son, a deadly fate befell her also; he interprets Meleager's destructive destiny as a failed initiation into adulthood.
24. Clytemnestra: Aesch. *Cho.* 912; Eriphyle: Thuc. 2.102.5–6; Epicasta: Hom. *Od.* 11.279f. Aubriot-Sévin, *Prière et conceptions religieuses*, p. 364, downplays gender, and stresses that parents – both mothers and fathers – had the right of life and death over their children.
25. Another case of maternal curses is that of Era against Ares because he helped the Trojans. However, given the immortality of the protagonists, this curse did not result in death, but instead caused his defeat by Athena on the battlefield (Hom. *Il.* 21.410–14).
26. McHardy, 'From Treacherous Wives to Murderous Mothers', p. 101. A mother's curse was more dreadful than a father's curse. Eck, *La Mort Rouge*, p. 40, n. 164, notes that the rancour was proportional to the difficulty involved in finding an avenger: a father could rely on all his consanguines to take revenge, but upon marriage, a mother broke with her natal kin and could only expect to be avenged by her children. The tie between brother and sister outlined here shows that this pattern did not always hold in ancient Greece. A further mythical example can be found in the story of Castor and Pollux, who devastated Attica to avenge their sister Helen after she had been raped by Theseus (Diod. 4.63.1–3; Plut. *Thes.* 29.3). For sisters avenging brothers in stories told in modern Greek funeral laments, see Gail Holst-Warhaft, *Dangerous Voices: Women's Laments and Greek Literature* (London: Routledge, 1992), pp. 69–71.
27. See Françoise Frontisi-Ducrox, *Dédale. Mythologie de l'artisan en Grèce ancienne* (Paris: Maspéro, 1975), p. 189, who notes that, according to the misogynistic Greek stereotype, the victory of a woman could only be due to cunning tricks and deception (the best example for this behaviour is Clytemnestra).

28. For the definition of these documents and for what follows see Versnel, 'Beyond Cursing', p. 68, and Henk Versnel, 'Prayers for Justice, East and West. New Finds and Publications since 1990', in R. L. Gordon and F. Marco Simón (eds), *Magical Practice in the Latin West* (Leiden: Brill, 2010), pp. 275–354 (pp. 278–9), and bibliography. 'Prayers for justice' can be considered as a sub-group within the category of *defixiones*, inscriptions aimed to curse an opponent, generally in an athletic, legal or amatory context, binding his/her freedom of thought or action. Versnel's distinction between prayers for justice or revenge and other curses has not gone uncontested, see Martin Dreher, 'Gerichtsverfahren vor den Göttern? – "Judicial Prayers" und die Kategorisierung der *defixionum tabellae*', in G. Thür (ed.), *Symposion 2009. Vorträge zur griechischen und hellenistischen Rechtsgeschichte* (Wien: ÖAW, 2010), pp. 301–35, and Dreher, '"Prayers for Justice" and the Categorization of Curse Tablets', in M. Piranomonte and F. M. Simón (eds), *Contextos Mágicos – Contesti Magici* (Roma: De Luca, 2012), pp. 29–32.

29. Legal historians might take issue with the comparison of the motivations behind these texts and those behind a lawsuit. Versnel, 'Beyond Cursing', p. 81, highlighted that the authors of the texts trusted that they had brought their case before a 'divine court of arbitration'. Dreher, 'Prayers for Justice' and Julie Vélissaropoulos-Karakostas, 'Gebete um Gerechtigkeit. Réponse à Martin Dreher', in G. Thür (ed.), *Symposion 2009. Vorträge zur griechischen und hellenistischen Rechtsgeschichte* (Wien: ÖAW, 2010), pp. 337–48, criticised the idea of a divine tribunal as well as the stress that has been laid on the judicial aspects of these documents. Henk Versnel, 'Response to a Critique', in M. Piranomonte and F. M. Simón (eds), *Contextos Mágicos - Contesti Magici* (Roma: De Luca, 2012), pp. 33–46, replied that evoking legal contexts and labelling the language of these 'prayers for justice' as 'judicial' or 'legal' is useful for understanding the mentality of these ordinary people, what their needs were, and what they expected from this ritual.

30. Charles T. Newton, *A History of Discoveries at Halicarnassus, Cnidus, and Branchidae* (London: Day & Son, 1863), vol. 2.2, p. 382 (discovery), pp. 719–45 (texts). The most recent edition and the one used here is that of Wolfgang Blümel, *Die Inschriften von Knidos, I* (Bonn: Dr. Rudolf Habelt GmbH, 1992), abbreviated as *I. Knidos*. On these prayers see recently Angelos Chaniotis, 'From Woman to Woman: Female Voices and Emotions in Dedications to Goddesses', in C. Prêtre (ed.), *Le donateur, l'offrande et la déesse. Systèmes votifs dans les sanctuaires de déesses du monde grec* (Liège: Université de Liège, 2009), pp. 51–68; Versnel, 'Beyond Cursing'; Versnel, 'ΠΕΠΡΗΜΕΝΟΣ. The Cnidian Curse Tablets and Ordeal by Fire', in R. Hägg (ed.), *Ancient Greek Cult Practice from the Epigraphical Evidence* (Stockholm: Svenska Institutet i Athen, 1994), pp. 145–54; Versnel, 'Writing Mortals and Reading Gods. Appeal to the Gods as Dual Strategy in Social Control', in D. J. Cohen and

E. Müller-Luckner (eds), *Demokratie, Recht und soziale Kontrolle im klassischen Athen* (München: Oldenbourg, 2002), pp. 37–76; Versnel, 'Prayers for Justice, East and West'; Eidinow, *Oracles, Curses, and Risk*, pp. 387–90; Eidinow, 'Patterns of Persecution: "Witchcraft" Trials in Classical Athens', *Past and Present* 208 (2011), pp. 9–35; Christopher Faraone, 'Curses, Crime Detection, and Conflict Resolution at the Festival of Demeter Thesmophoros', *Journal of Hellenic Studies* 131 (2011), pp. 25–44; Irene Salvo, 'Sweet Revenge. Emotional Factors in "Prayers for Justice"', in A. Chaniotis (ed.), *Unveiling Emotions: Sources and Methods for the Study of Emotions in the Greek World* (Stuttgart: Franz Steiner Verlag, 2012), pp. 235–66. See John J. Gager, *Curse Tablets and Binding Spells from the Ancient World* (Oxford: Oxford University Press, 1992), pp. 188–90 and Chapter 5 for other prayers of this sort. Newton, *A History of Discoveries*, pp. 734–8, counted *I. Knidos* 149 (Newton's Nr. 83 and 84) and *I. Knidos* 150 (Newton's Nr. 85 and 86) as four separate tablets. On this count, he believed that he had discovered not thirteen, but fifteen tablets.

31. See Versnel, 'Beyond Cursing', p. 72 (translation). On πεπρημένος as 'burnt with fever' see Versnel, 'ΠΕΠΡΗΜΕΝΟΣ' and n. 48 below. On the adjective ὅσια see Jean Rudhardt, *Notions Fondamentales de la Pensée Religieuse et Actes Constitutifs du Culte dans la Grèce Classique* (Genève: Droz, 1958), pp. 30–6; Ghislaine Jay-Robert, *Le Sacré et la Loi: Essai sur la Notion d'Hosion d'Homère à Aristote* (Paris: Kimé, 2009); Andreas Willi, 'νόσος and ὁσίη: Etymological and Sociocultural Observations on the Concepts of Disease and Divine (Dis)favour in Ancient Greece', *Journal of Hellenic Studies* 128 (2010), pp. 153–71 (p. 166).
32. See for example *I. Knidos* 147, where the dedicant asks the goddess to be merciless and torture a person who has slandered her; *I. Knidos* 159 where a woman who has been abused after false allegations were made against her protests her innocence; and *I. Knidos* 152, where a woman who has had an item of clothing stolen asks that, if the thief does not bring it to Demeter, he and his family should be punished by the goddesses.
33. See, for example, the illustration of *I. Knidos* 150 in Newton, *A History of Discoveries*, Plate 7.
34. Cf. Versnel, 'Beyond Cursing', p. 80, for previous discussions on the presentation of the tablets.
35. Faraone, 'Curses, Crime Detection'. On the Thesmophoria see also Henk Versnel, 'The Festival for the Bona Dea and the Thesmophoria', *Greece and Rome* 39 (1992), pp. 31–55; Lucia Nixon, 'The Cults of Demeter and Kore', in R. Hawley and B. M. Levick (eds), *Women in Antiquity: New Assessments* (London/New York: 1995), pp. 75–96; Eva M. Stehle, 'Thesmophoria and Eleusinian Mysteries: The Fascination of Women's Secret Ritual', in M. G. Parca and A. Tzanetou (eds), *Finding Persephone: Women's Rituals in the Ancient Mediterranean* (Bloomington: Indiana University Press, 2007), pp. 165–85.

36. Some tablets show evidence of a hand practiced at inscribing on lead, most notably the scribe does not lift the stylus after each stroke, on which see Alexander Dale and Aneurin Ellis-Evans, 'A Cypriot Curser at Mytilene', *Zeitschrift für Papyrologie und Epigraphik* 179 (2011), pp. 189–98 (p. 194). In other cases, most notably *I. Knidos* 153, the scribe seems less practiced at writing on this material. The dittographic errors in *I. Knidos* 151 do not suggest a scribe used to writing texts of this sort. From these examples, it would seem that while some less literate dedicants chose to enlist the help of more experienced scribes (perhaps one of the priestesses), others might inscribe the texts themselves.
37. Chaniotis, 'From Woman to Woman', p. 64.
38. See Salvo, 'Sweet Revenge', on the way that these prayers could be used to satisfy vengeful feelings.
39. (1) *I. Knidos* 148, 149, 150 Side B, 152, 157, 158; (2) *I. Knidos* 150 side B, 151, 156; (3) *I. Knidos* 147, 150 Side A; (4) *I. Knidos* 159. The texts of *I. Knidos* 153, 154 and 155 are too fragmentary to reconstruct satisfactorily. *I. Knidos* 153 seems to deal either with love rivalry or with defamation, while the mention of a man and children in 154 suggests a prayer of Type 2. It is worth noting that this prayer is also an accusation: the dedicant uses it to accuse another woman of employing magic/poison.
40. Only a very few women of exceptional status, like the priestess of Athena Polias in Athens, could independently bring charges. See Stella Georgoudi, 'Lysimaché la prêtresse', in N. Loraux, *La Grèce au féminin* (Paris: Les Belles Lettres, 2003), pp. 167–214 (p. 208).
41. For the role of the *kyrios*, see David M. Schaps, *Economic Rights of Women in Ancient Greece* (Edinburgh: Edinburgh University Press, 1979), p. 48. For women's legal status in Classical Athens, see Sue Blundell, *Women in Ancient Greece* (London: Harvard University Press, 1995), Chapter 11.
42. See David J. Cohen, *Law, Sexuality, and Society: The Enforcement of Morals in Classical Athens* (Cambridge: Cambridge University Press, 1991), Chapter 5, on Athenian adultery laws.
43. See Dale and Ellis-Evans, 'A Cypriot Curser at Mytilene', for cursing as a strategy employed by foreigners. For gossip as a feminine tool, see Eidinow, 'Patterns of Persecution' and McHardy in this volume. For the persuasion strategies in petitions, see Chrysi Kotsifou, 'A Glimpse into the World of Petitions: The Case of Aurelia Artemis and her Orphaned Children', in A. Chaniotis (ed.), *Unveiling Emotions: Sources and Methods for the Study of Emotions in the Greek World* (Stuttgart: Franz Steiner Verlag, 2012), pp. 316–27.
44. See n. 28 above for the distinction between prayers for justice and *defixiones*.
45. For prayers for justice as a form of social control, see Versnel, 'Writing Mortals and Reading Gods'.

46. For these strategies in prayers for justice, see Versnel, 'Prayers for Justice, East and West', pp. 279–80.
47. *I. Knidos* 151 reconstructs the beginning of line 6 as 'εἰ τοὺς...', but Eidinow, *Oracles, Curses, and Risk*, p. 215, n. 50, more plausibly suggests 'εἰ τίς...'. See also Eidinow, *Oracles, Curses, and Risk*, pp. 215ff., 389 (with uncorrected text and translation); Chaniotis, 'From Woman to Woman', p. 65.
48. Compare for example *I. Knidos* 150 (esp. side B) where Kore is mentioned almost as frequently as Demeter.
49. On πεπρημένος see Versnel, 'ΠΕΠΡΗΜΕΝΟΣ' and Angelos Chaniotis, 'Under the Watchful Eyes of the Gods: Divine Justice in Hellenistic and Roman Asia Minor', in S. Colvin (ed.), *The Greco-Roman East* (Cambridge: Cambridge University Press, 2004), pp. 1–43 (p. 7, n. 19). Salvo, 'Sweet Revenge', pp. 255–6, interprets πεπρημένος as referencing both an emotional and physical state of 'burning' (shame and fever): the author sought to provoke suffering equal to that which she had experienced.
50. This speaks to a community in which illness is interpreted as a sign of the gods' displeasure (see Angelos Chaniotis, 'Illness and Cures in the Greek Propitiatory Inscriptions and Dedications of Lydia and Phrygia', *Clio Medica* 28 (1995), pp. 323–44) especially in an environment such as Knidos, in which coming down with a malarial fever can hardly have been rare. On the importance of reputation, see Cairns, 'Honour and Shame', for discussion of trends in scholarship on Greek honour and shame. See Maryline Parca, 'Violence by and against Women in Documentary Papyri from Ptolemaic and Roman Egypt', in *Studia Hellenistica* 37 (2002), pp. 283–96 (p. 291) for the importance of retribution to reputation of the victims of injustice.
51. On the demographics of ancient magic and gender stereotypes, see Christopher Faraone, *Ancient Greek Love Magic* (Cambridge, MA: Harvard University Press, 1999), pp. 146ff.; Matthew W. Dickie, 'Who Practised LoveMagic in Classical Antiquity and in the Late Roman World?', *Classical Quarterly* 50 (2000), pp. 563–83; Kimberley B. Stratton, *Naming the Witch: Magic, Ideology, and Stereotype in the Ancient World* (New York: Columbia University Press, 2007), Chapter 3.
52. *PSI* 1.64 on which see Jane Rowlandson, *Women and Society in Greek and Roman Egypt* (Cambridge: Cambridge University Press, 1998), p. 255.
53. Indeed, the willingness of the petitioners to be named is one of the characteristics of these prayers that distinguishes them from *defixiones*. See Versnel, 'Beyond Cursing', p. 68.
54. Gager, *Curse Tablets*, pp. 189–90; Eidinow, *Oracles, Curses, and Risk*, p. 237, pp. 387–8 (text and translation); Eidinow, 'Patterns of Persecution', p. 22.
55. A substantial sum, equivalent to one hundred and fifty drachmae.
56. Versnel, 'Beyond Cursing', p. 99, n. 62.

57. Conversely, author of *I. Knidos* 154 uses her prayer to suggest that another woman was guilty of using poison/magic against her.
58. For goddesses as especially vindictive, see Chaniotis, 'From Woman to Woman'.
59. See McHardy, 'From Treacherous Wives to Murderous Mothers', on maddened mothers killing their children as an act of revenge.

CHAPTER 8

'The Power of Our Mouths': Gossip as a Female Mode of Revenge[1]

Fiona McHardy

In the Greek popular imagination, vengeance was enacted by mighty heroes such as Achilles killing his enemy Hector in revenge for the death of Patroclus (*Il.* 22.271–2; Aeschines 1.145), by enraged husbands such as Odysseus slaughtering the suitors trying to seduce his wife (*Od.* 22.61–4), or by noble sons such as Orestes avenging the murder of his father (*Od.* 1.296–302; 3.193–200). Classical Athenians depicted themselves emulating these heroes in attempting revenge through the law courts (e.g. Antiphon 1). These examples demonstrate that a variety of methods were thought to be available to men to achieve vengeance, including the use of superior physical force, of disguises and trickery, and of the institutions of the state. Women, though, were more limited in their options. While literary evidence suggests that women, such as Hecuba (*Il.* 24.194–216), were closely associated with bloodthirstiness and a desire for revenge,[2] they were generally deemed too weak to kill a grown man on their own using physical force. Even those women who reached the highest positions in the social hierarchy in places other than Athens are generally represented as too weak to act against men without the aid of other men: their power is restricted to the power of speech by which they can incite, persuade or deceive. Women who wish to achieve revenge are usually shown soliciting help from others, especially male kin, to achieve their ends. Alternatively, women were thought capable of prevailing if they employed deception, used poison or set a trap.[3] Women are also depicted using curses in an attempt to achieve revenge.[4] In Athens, women's powers to achieve legal revenge were very limited as they could not take cases to court themselves, but had to persuade men to act for them.[5]

In this chapter, I explore the potential for women to achieve revenge through the use of another speech mode: gossip.[6] In the first part of the chapter, I examine how gossip is depicted in Greek literature, with a particular focus on Attic oratory. Members of society, regardless of gender or status are able to hear and pass on gossip, and despite its lack of reliability, its strength is such that unsubstantiated rumours are sufficient to discredit or destroy the person involved. Gossip is seen as having a key role to play in judging the powerful through attacks on their reputation as Hunter has demonstrated in her analysis of the use of gossip in the Athenian law courts.[7] Gossip also features prominently in stories concerning sexual fidelity, including speculation about the legitimacy of rulers whose mothers are said to be promiscuous. The ability of gossip to impact on the lives of even the most powerful in society makes it a useful recourse for those who have little influence through official political and legal channels, such as women.

In the second part of the chapter, I examine the role of gossip in literary plotlines, building upon the work of McClure on women's speech in tragedy,[8] to trace how gossip can be used to facilitate revenge. I consider the role of the crowd and of slaves as conduits for rumours and the way in which they can be manipulated to achieve the desires of the protagonists, as Roisman has suggested in her analysis of Euripides' plays about Hippolytus.[9] As Hall has noted, the plotlines reflect a social anxiety concerning the behaviour of women whose husbands are absent.[10] Stories also reflect that hearing gossip about the sexual infidelities of women could provoke angry and violent reactions in their husbands and male relatives.[11] In some of these cases, gossip is depicted being used as a 'weapon' to exact revenge against an enemy.[12]

In the final part of the chapter, I turn to an evaluation of the role of gossip in a particular oration.[13] Porter has argued that the story of Lysias 1, *On the Murder of Eratosthenes*, has been influenced by comic plotlines regarding adultery.[14] I want to develop this argument further by suggesting that there are also tragic resonances in the storyline of this oration, in particular in the depiction of the minor female characters. As well as drawing on the 'adulterer's tale', the speech also alludes to a common revenge plot involving indirect action. Contemporary fears about feminine anger and revenge driven by sexual jealousy, as displayed in Attic drama and other Greek literature, lie at the heart of the narrative in this oration. A close reading of the speech indicates the possibilities for revenge which existed outside the official channels.

GOSSIP, POWER AND SEXUAL JEALOUSY

In Greek sources gossip is characterised as swift (Plut. *Mor.* 507C–F), spreading someone's private business in an uncontrolled way through the city (Aeschines 1.127). Gossipers are both men and women, slave and free.[15] Commentators have noted that gossip is unreliable,[16] and can be based on expectations rather than fact.[17] Examples from oratory suggest that men might make use of gossip networks in shops and marketplaces to spread false information, favourable to themselves (Dem. 24.15; Isoc. 18.9), or disparaging to their enemies (Dem. 21.104).[18] As such, gossip can be used manipulatively to enhance someone's status or to detract from their status.[19] Women too might use their own networks of acquaintances to raise complaints about others and attack their behaviour publicly.[20] The speaker of *Against Aristogeiton 1* cites as one example of his opponent's bad character, an incident which involved Aristogeiton's violent and ungrateful treatment of a metic woman named Zobia who had helped him when he was in trouble. The speaker makes clear that Aristogeiton felt that he was in a position of strength in maltreating Zobia because she was a woman and a metic and, therefore, unable to prosecute him herself through official channels.[21] But despite her gender and lowly status, the woman's use of gossip to complain about how she was treated means that the alleged ill-treatment becomes widely known, not just among low-status women, but also, apparently, among the male elite, including the speaker and, ultimately, the members of the jury. Her complaints are then used to generate an impression of the character of Aristogeiton which is relied on in court to paint his character negatively (Dem. 25.57). The example demonstrates that once shared broadly in public, this woman's complaint could affect how people, both men and women, of high and low status, viewed Aristogeiton, and Zobia's words could be used in an official channel to attack the man who had violently beaten her.[22] Once news of this type has spread, it can be hard to make people forget it as Hesiod observes (*Op.* 760–4). Further, as Larran has pointed out, the line between gaining a high reputation and fame by being talked about positively, and being denigrated by being talked about negatively is a thin one in Greek thinking.[23]

While the intentions of gossipers might be unclear, the emotions felt by some gossipers can be connected to emotions such as anger, envy or hatred, which are similar to the emotions felt by those desiring revenge, and malicious intent towards the victim of the gossip can underlie the urge to gossip (cf. Dem 25.52). As Spacks has written:

> It [gossip] plays with reputations, circulating truths and half-truths and falsehoods about the activities, sometimes about the motives and feelings, of others. Often it serves serious (possibly unconscious) purposes for the gossipers, whose manipulations of reputation can further political or social ambitions by damaging competitors or enemies, gratify envy and rage by diminishing another, generate an immediately satisfying sense of power, although the talkers acknowledge no such intent.[24]

The link to reputation made here by Spacks is picked up by Hunter in her article on the way that rumour and gossip can be used to political advantage by men seeking to better rivals in the law court.[25] She suggests that attacks on reputation in the political arena can be very damaging,[26] and that the possibility to make use of gossip in attacking the character of a rival in court opened up a possibility for it to be used vengefully and destructively at Athens.

Men are not the only targets of rumours and gossip in the Athenian law courts. Gossip about women can be used to attack their male relatives, or to challenge the validity of a will or the legitimacy of a woman's offspring.[27] In Isaeus 3, *On the Estate of Pyrrhus*, as Hunter has shown,[28] the speaker makes use of lurid gossip to discredit his opponents and to further his own case in the eyes of the jury. He presents evidence in the form of gossip by neighbours and acquaintances about her mother's wild behaviour at parties and allegations that her mother was 'at the disposal of anyone' and a courtesan (ἑταίρα) rather than a wife (γυνή) (3.11–16) to suggest that Phile was not a legitimate child, and therefore could not inherit Pyrrhus' estate. The case is one of false witnesses in which the speaker prosecutes Nicodemus for claiming that he had given his daughter, Phile's mother, in legal marriage to Pyrrhus, and it follows on from another case in which the speaker had successfully prosecuted Xenocles, the husband of Phile, for false witnesses using the same gossip-ridden depositions from the neighbours. The speech suggests that this evidence was compelling in ensuring that Phile's claim to be the closest heir of Pyrrhus was rejected, and that the speaker's mother, Pyrrhus' sister, was recognised as the closest heir. At the same time, the attack would have had a profound effect on Phile's perceived status in the city, and on the status of her children, as citizen children could only be born to a citizen woman married to a citizen man.[29] However, as the speaker concedes, it is possible that his uncle actually was legally married to Phile's mother (3.16–17).

In this example 'the power of gossip to create an atmosphere of accusation', as Eidinow describes it,[30] is clearly demonstrated. Although the gossip reported in the speech may not fully reflect the true situation, it hints at an unacceptable level of sexual freedom for a citizen woman which would have been frowned upon by Athenian citizens at the time, and would generate hostility towards the woman involved. As Hunter has argued: 'both directly and indirectly, gossip served as a potent weapon in ensuring the conformity of Athenian women to community standards'.[31]

The connection of gossip to inappropriate sexual relationships is commonplace in Greek texts. Fear of such gossip makes unmarried women think carefully about being connected publicly to strange men. Nausicaa says she will not walk with Odysseus for fear of the scandal it will cause (*Od.* 6.275ff), while Medea contemplates the gossip which will occur if she yields to her love for Jason (Apollonius Rhodius *Argonautica* 3.790ff). In these examples fear of gossip inhibits the women's behaviour and they are keen to avoid any connection to ideas of illicit sexual behaviour. At Athens, there were ideals relating to the seclusion of women, although in reality they would not have been sequestered at home.[32] Playing on this ideal, the speaker of Lysias 3 maintains that his female relatives were ashamed to be seen even by their kinsmen (3.6).[33]

Underlying these concerns is the fear of female power over pregnancy and the potential for women to foist illegitimate children on unsuspecting husbands.[34] In Hyperides 1, *On the Defence of Lycophron*, Lycophron defends himself against an accusation of being the father of such a child by the sister of Dioxippus with whom his opponents claim he has been having an adulterous affair.[35] The significance of this claim is that the estate which passed to the child on the death of its father, would pass to other relatives if the child were shown to be illegitimate.[36] We are told that after her husband died, the woman was remarried. According to the prosecution, Lycophron tried to persuade her not to consummate her new marriage during her wedding procession (1.3). The speaker argues that he would not have been able to speak in this way to the bride because she was surrounded by people who would have overheard his words. He then queries whether her relatives, who could not have failed to overhear if he had spoken to the bride in this way, would have been likely to listen to such things without killing him (1.6). Here he indicates that public attempts at enticing a woman were thought likely to lead to violence on the part of her relatives.

Dramatic characters also discuss the expectation of violence against a man acting inappropriately towards female relatives. In Euripides' *Hippolytus*, Theseus believes that his son Hippolytus has been attacked by a jealous husband who caught him seducing his wife (1164–5). Similarly, in Menander's *Samia*, Niceratus is depicted shouting violent threats against the young man who has seduced his daughter and against the child of this extramarital union (553–6). He also asserts that were his concubine to be unfaithful, he would treat both her and her lover harshly (510–13). The role of gossip in generating such attacks is spelt out by Diogenes Laertius (*Life of Periander* 1.7) when he describes how Periander, tyrant of Corinth, violently attacked his pregnant wife Melissa because he had heard and was ready to believe malicious stories about her spread by his concubines.[37] This tale portrays a husband who is so sensitive to suggestions of infidelity by his wife that he attacks his wife and unborn child violently and kills them. At the same time, it is possible to hypothesise that the concubines in the story are thought to gossip in this way out of sexual jealousy towards Melissa their love rival, and out of envy concerning her pregnancy.

In Attic tragedy attention is given to women's sexual jealousy when confronted with a rival in love. In Sophocles' *Trachiniae*, Deianira is told by the messenger, who reports to her based on what he heard Lichas telling people in the marketplace, that her husband Hercules is in love with Iole and that he has killed Iole's father in order to take her as his concubine (351–74). Deianira's decision to attempt to win back her husband's love by using what she believes to be a love potion, but is actually a poison, is motivated by her jealousy and fear that she will lose the love of her husband to her younger rival, and by envy of Iole's youth and beauty (536–87).[38] The devastating results of this decision are played out in the drama.[39]

A closely comparable tale appears in Antiphon 1 *On the Poisoning by the Stepmother*, an Athenian court case in which a son accuses his stepmother of deliberately murdering his father using poison, while his stepmother apparently claimed it was supposed to act as a love potion. This case also features a concubine who administered the potion to the speaker's father and to her own lover Philoneus. The speaker claims that his stepmother played on the concubine's fears of losing her lover's affections in order to persuade her to give the potion to the two men (1.14–15). This speech hints that Athenian men thought the jealous, gossip-driven, threatening behaviour of women depicted in tragic myth was more than just a fantasy. At the same time, as Apostolakis has shown, in constructing his argument, the speaker clearly plays on the associations that jurors might make with female behaviour in tragic plots by likening the stepmother to Clytemnestra, the most renowned tragic husband-killer (1.17).[40] Although the evidence presented in the case is not full enough to substantiate the idea, this comparison implies that his stepmother acted deliberately and maliciously. The fear generated in the jurors by the power of this image could have been enough to sway their votes.

Another play featuring related themes is Euripides' *Andromache* in which women's gossip is pivotal in egging on a wife to attack her perceived rival (930–5). In the play, Hermione accuses her husband's concubine Andromache of using magic to make her barren and undesirable to her husband. The effect of the gossip is to make Hermione angry and volatile, attempting to have her rival thrown out of her husband's house (31–5, 156–8).[41] Again in this play, women's gossip is depicted as a threat to the household, precipitating a jealous attack by a wife on her husband's concubine.[42]

In Euripides' *Bacchae* (26–42), the household is also brought to destruction following the fierce reaction of the god Dionysus to his aunts' gossip. At the beginning of the play he explains that he has come to seek revenge against his mother's sisters. They are said to have spread a false story claiming that Semele had lied about her liaison with Zeus in order to mask a sexual relationship with a mortal.[43] The key emotion underpinning the sisters' gossip in this example is apparently envy of Semele's fortune in having a son by Zeus. In another example, Pindar makes clear that envy is the underlying motivation for gossip concerning Clytemnestra's affair with Aegisthus when her husband is absent fighting in the Trojan War. He maintains that a young bride who is seduced by a man other than her husband cannot hope to keep it secret, and says that people tend towards malicious talk (κακολόγοι), which is generated by their envy (φθόνος) of the prosperity of others (Pindar *Pythian* 11.25–9). As Eidinow explains: 'For those feeling envy of another's good fortune, gossip may provide both a release of strong feelings, and, more vindictively, a tool for undermining that good fortune.'[44] Here Eidinow suggests that gossip often has no perceived goal, but is cathartic for the gossipers. However, it can also be used maliciously. Sanders notes that feelings of envy drive the envious person to try to deprive the envied person of what they have and this 'begrudging envy' can make the envious person act destructively to achieve their goal.[45] In this respect, he suggests, gossip can be used intentionally to damage or destroy the reputation of the envied person.[46] Further, because of the power of gossip to stir emotions, in particular feelings of anger and sexual jealousy, if used manipulatively gossip can become a weapon which generates revenge.

GOSSIP AND REVENGE IN GREEK LITERATURE

Greek tragic dramatists make use of gossip and rumour as part of their revenge plots, as Ogle has noted. One example cited by Ogle of effective use of gossip to achieve a violent revenge occurs in Euripides' *Andromache* (1090–5), where Orestes spreads a rumour at Delphi that his rival Neoptolemus is coming to loot the temple there.[47] This false report infuriates the local people, who ambush and kill Neoptolemus (1117–60). Orestes' motives for attacking are a combination of anger at the insults delivered to him by Neoptolemus and sexual possessiveness over Hermione whom he had expected to marry, but who was given as a bride to Neoptolemus instead because of his contribution to winning the Trojan War. This example demonstrates the potential for use of manipulative gossip, designed to cause an angry and violent reaction in those who hear it. The messenger who brings the news of Neoptolemus' death to his grandfather makes clear that Orestes carefully contrived everything that happened (1115–16).[48] Instead of taking on the dangerous warrior Neoptolemus himself,[49] Orestes ensures Neoptolemus' death by rallying a mob against him through clever use of malicious gossip. This use of gossip to achieve revenge is characteristic of Orestes' wily nature as he is typically depicted in tragedy.[50] At the same time, he is a dangerous murderer associated with underhand killings in all of the plays in which he appears.[51]

Orestes and his sister Electra are associated with use of false messages and rumours to overcome powerful enemies and achieve deadly revenge in the other tragedies in which they appear too. In Sophocles' *Electra* and Aeschylus' *Choephori*, Orestes pretends to be a messenger bringing news of his own death in order to deceive his mother and gain access to her to kill her. In Euripides' *Electra*, Electra concocts a false story about how she has given birth to lure her mother to her house where the siblings plan to kill her (651–8).[52] Electra is aware that this plan will work because of her mother's keen concern about public gossip about her family (643).[53] To enact her plan, she sends the old man who brought her up (488) and is loyal to her to give this false message to her mother.[54] In this play, the role of a messenger in delivering a manipulative message helps the protagonists to achieve revenge by playing on the curiosity and fears of the receiver of the message. The ability of the dispossessed to overcome the powerful elite through use of a method that employs someone of low social status is an expression of the potential of rumour and gossip to be employed by even the weakest in society as a weapon in exacting revenge.

In Aeschylus' play, the false message which enables revenge is transmitted by a group of women from the lowest social stratum: the chorus of foreign female slaves. The chorus first play a crucial role in generating anger in Orestes and encouraging him to take revenge for his father's death through their great lament.[55] They are then keen to help further, asking how they might use the power of their mouths (στομάτων ... ἰσχὺν) to aid Orestes (720–1). They take their opportunity after the nurse enters, sent by Clytemnestra to instruct Aegisthus to come attended by his retinue (765–9) to hear the news of Orestes' death from the two 'messengers' (actually Orestes and Pylades in disguise). The chorus persuade the nurse to pass on a different message, asking Aegisthus to come alone to hear the news (770–2), hinting that there is something they are aware of that the nurse does not know and encouraging her through their gossipy insinuations (775–8). In order to be helpful to this group of women, though not fully understanding the implications of her message because she believes that Orestes is dead (776), the nurse proceeds to tell Aegisthus to come alone (781). The chorus, though, understand that their false message will help Orestes to achieve vengeance more easily and comment on the ability of their words to achieve justice (διὰ δίκας πᾶν ἔπος / ἔλακον, 787–8).

When Aegisthus enters, he is doubtful about the message he has received, questioning if the news he has heard is true or false. He points to the tendency of women to spread inaccurate gossip (ἢ πρὸς γυναικῶν δειματούμενοι λόγοι / πεδάρσιοι θρῴσκουσι, θνῄσκοντες μάτην; 845–6).[56] Notably, his suspicions that the news is not true are correct, but he is unable to recognise that another aspect of the message he has received (the need to bring his guards with him) has been altered in its passage from speaker (Clytemnestra), through slave (nurse), via chorus, to him. In this example, the messenger listens to the gossip of a group of women who are friendly towards her[57] and as a result, changes the message she has been asked to deliver by her mistress, unwittingly enabling violent revenge to occur. The chorus, though, are aware of the power of their words, and strikingly in this play, intervene through use of gossip and persuasion to enable Orestes to take revenge.[58]

The tendency for slaves to go against the wishes of their masters occurs in plotlines where slaves share information they have been asked to keep private. In Euripides' *Alcestis* (763–4), Admetus tells his servants not to mourn their dead mistress in front of Hercules, but to look after him as a guest. However, one servant reveals the truth initially through his mournful countenance (773–5), then by stating that Admetus' wife is dead (821). In this case, Admetus asks his household to keep quiet in order to be hospitable to Hercules, but the servant who reveals the truth is angered by Hercules' behaviour as a guest and goes against his master's wishes. Aristophanes makes fun of this ability of servants to reveal confidences in a speech where women complain about how they cannot rely on slaves to keep their affairs secret from their husbands or to deliver their messages faithfully (*Thes.* 340–2).

The potential of unsolicited messages by slaves to lead to violence is at the heart of the plot of Euripides' *Hippolytus*. In this play, Phaedra reveals to her nurse the passion she feels for her stepson Hippolytus (350–2). The goddess Aphrodite has inflicted this desire on Phaedra in order to destroy Hippolytus because of his lack of respect for her cult (21–8). The nurse decides to tell Hippolytus in the hopes of curing her mistress of her lovesickness. However, her message only infuriates Hippolytus who blames slaves for facilitating the evil plots of their mistresses (645–50). On hearing the reaction of Hippolytus, Phaedra decides upon suicide to preserve her reputation. Before dying she pens a letter to her husband accusing her stepson of raping her, which causes her husband Theseus to call down a death curse on his son (877–90).[59] In this play, Phaedra's secret is revealed by her nurse (as the chorus comment, τὰ κρυπτὰ γὰρ πέφηνε, 594), leading to the chain of destructive events within the play.[60]

As Hall has pointed out, in tragic plots, 'when slaves act independently as moral agents the results can be catastrophic'.[61] She suggests that this aspect of the play would have resonated with its male audience because of anxiety they felt about the susceptibility of women to manipulation by slaves when their husbands were absent (as Theseus is in this play).[62] Roisman, on the other hand, has interpreted the play differently suggesting that it is possible to see Phaedra as the character who is manipulative, deceptively convincing the slow-witted nurse to approach Hippolytus.[63] Roisman believes it is plausible that some of the audience would have viewed Phaedra as the manipulator in the scenario because of their fears about the loyalty of their wives.[64] At the same time, the silence of the local women who form the chorus concerning Phaedra's true feelings (710–14) generates an impression of a network of women who protect and aid one another in conducting illicit sexual affairs, about which their husbands remain ignorant.[65]

Further evidence of Phaedra's manipulative approach is found in her decision to accuse Hippolytus of raping her in her note to Theseus, thereby simultaneously protecting her own reputation and that of her sons, and avenging herself on Hippolytus for rejecting her advances.[66] Phaedra apparently predicts the furious reaction of her husband, which emanates out of sexual jealousy and possessiveness,[67] when she says that someone else too will suffer following her death, alluding to Hippolytus (728–31).

This tragic situation is picked up and 'echoed' as Scourfield has argued, in Chariton's novel *Chaereas and Callirhoe*.[68] He suggests that the furious reaction of Theseus who curses his son based on receiving false information about his son's sexual relationship with his wife is referenced in the scene in Chariton's novel in which Chaereas furiously attacks his wife based on false information he has heard about her sexual conduct.[69] In the novel, though, the false information about his wife's sexual conduct comes to Chaereas in the form of malicious gossip which is used intentionally by a group of male love rivals to generate anger and jealousy in a husband who is made to believe that his wife is committing adultery.

Towards the beginning of the novel, Callirhoe's father is persuaded by the people in the assembly to give his daughter in marriage to Chaereas because the young man is suffering so badly from lovesickness after encountering the beautiful Callirhoe in the street on his way home from the gymnasium (1.1). However, this decision enrages the many suitors who wished to marry Callirhoe themselves and they come together to formulate an attack on Chaereas (1.2). They are persuaded that they need to employ a subtle method to achieve their revenge so as not to upset Callirhoe's powerful father and they determine upon rousing the young man's suspicions and making him jealous in order to destroy his marriage to Callirhoe (1.2). The rivals achieve this goal by sending a man to tell him that his wife has been seduced. This man suggests that Callirhoe's affair is the talk of the town and declares that he can provide proof (1.4). In fact, he shows Chaereas a man who is having an affair with one of the maids entering the house, but Chaereas is only too ready to believe what he has been told and rushes in to attack the man. In his anger, he attacks Callirhoe so violently that she collapses and is thought to be dead (1.5). He is charged with murder and taken to court, although he is acquitted when his father-in-law speaks up for him (1.6).

In this story, Chaereas' jealous reaction is anticipated by those who plot against him as a natural reaction and it is understood that young men with beautiful brides are readily full of suspicion about their wives. The story makes clear the way that gossip can be used as a weapon by those who cannot attack openly, and demonstrates the way in which gossip can enrage men leading to a devastating violent reaction.

These examples demonstrate that in literary plotlines gossip was used by a variety of characters and in a variety of ways in order to achieve revenge successfully against an enemy. The use of a slave or messenger is a prominent feature of this kind of attack, and their awareness of their role in carrying a message which will lead to revenge is not always clear. While both men and women are depicted making use of gossip to attack their enemies, the examples suggest this use of gossip is most closely associated with those who do not have the power to act openly, making it a good form of attack for women and people of low social status.

Some of the common elements that appear in these texts have led commentators to make comparisons between them and to speculate on the extent to which the similarities are intentional intertextual references or reflections of typical story patterns which recur because of common perceptions about human behaviour. Another text which has been discussed in a similar way is Lysias 1 *On the Murder of Eratosthenes*.

GOSSIP AND REVENGE IN LYSIAS 1

Lysias' *On the Murder of Eratosthenes* is a speech in which an Athenian man named Euphiletus defends himself saying that he justifiably killed a man named Eratosthenes when he caught him in adultery with his wife. In the speech, Euphiletus answers the allegations of those prosecuting him that he plotted the murder, perhaps for reasons other than adultery (1.4, 1.27, 1.43).[70] The absence of the prosecutors' speech is frustrating as there is a lack of detail about their allegations, but it appears they suggested that Eratosthenes was dragged off the street by a mob and killed rather than being caught in the act of adultery.[71] Euphiletus refutes this suggestion claiming that he had with him many witnesses, whom he had gathered from the neighbourhood, when he entered the bedroom and caught Eratosthenes with his wife (1.23–4).

While the witnesses are useful for his defence, Euphiletus' gathering of them implies a level of planning and calculation rather than the hot-blooded attack on an adulterer which we might expect, and for which the law was presumably designed. In addition to this, Euphiletus mentions that he knew in advance about the affair between his wife and Eratosthenes as he claims that he had exacted the truth about his wife's affair from their maidservant (1.18–22) after he had been informed about it by an old woman acting for a former lover of Eratosthenes (1.15–17).

> I was then accosted by a certain old female, who was secretly sent by a woman with whom that man was having an intrigue, as I heard later. This woman was angry with him and felt herself wronged, because he no longer visited her so regularly, and she was keeping a watch on him until she should discover what was the cause. So the old creature accosted me where she was on the look-out, near my house, and said, – 'Euphiletus, do not think it is from any meddlesomeness that I have approached you; for the man who is working both your and your wife's dishonor happens to be our enemy. If, therefore, you take the servant-girl who goes to market and waits on you, and torture her, you will learn all. It is,' she said, 'Eratosthenes of Oe who is doing this; he has debauched not only your wife, but many others besides; he makes an art of it.' With these words, sirs, she took herself off; I was at once perturbed; all that had happened came into my mind, and I was filled with suspicion. (Lysias 1.15–17)[72]

In this extract, Euphiletus brings before the jurors a piece of gossip about Eratosthenes in the form of reported speech by an old woman. The gossip acts on several different levels. It operates as a spur to action which shows the jurors how Euphiletus became aware of Eratosthenes' seduction of his wife and how he proceeded from that point.[73] Porter has suggested that this element is present as it is the way that adultery plotlines standardly work.[74] On another level, the gossip is used by the orator Lysias to paint the character of Euphiletus as naïve, since he has suspected nothing until being informed by this woman,[75] while Eratosthenes is shown to be a serial troublemaker who has seduced at least one other woman. Carey notes that this piece of information helps to reduce the possibility of sympathy for the dead man,[76] while Gagarin points out that Lysias needs to focus the anger of the jurors on Eratosthenes rather than Euphiletus' wife or the maid.[77] At the same time, the introduction of a network of women with knowledge about what is happening behind the backs of unsuspecting husbands creates an anxiety that Lysias is able to play upon in the minds of the jurors and a sense of sympathy for Euphiletus.[78]

However, it is not possible to ascertain whether Euphiletus is being truthful about his encounter with this old woman, and he does not provide any firm evidence that Eratosthenes had committed adultery before.[79] Instead he relies on gossip to suggest that Eratosthenes was a problem not just for himself, but for the whole city. Dover has commented on the difficulties of deciding whether the written versions of speeches which we have are faithful versions of what was delivered in court, since it is possible that elements might have been added for publication, or that orators circulated written versions of speeches which were never delivered.[80] Porter, remarking on the prominence of literary stereotypes in Lysias 1, goes so far as to suggest that this particular speech was composed as an exercise and was never a real trial.[81] While the view that this speech was created by Lysias as a set-piece to sell his rhetorical and artistic skills is seen by commentators as extreme,[82] there has been general acceptance of Porter's view that the speech makes use of the motifs of the stereotypical comic adultery tale to create sympathy for Euphiletus.[83]

Gagarin has shown how Athenian legal speeches regularly feature literary resonances in order to tell a compelling story to the jurors,[84] while Carey notes the likelihood that the characters depicted by Lysias are 'dramatic creations' rather than faithful depictions of the participants' true characters.[85] As seen above, the speaker of Antiphon 1 seeks to characterise his stepmother's behaviour as murderous by use of a mythical allusion. Similarly, as Rosenbloom has shown, the speaker of Demosthenes 25 makes use of comic stereotypes to create a negative impression of Aristogeiton in the minds of the jurors.[86] In Lysias 1, too, Porter outlines the way in which the plotline follows a typical comic 'adulterer's tale' and notes that the rejected former mistress is a comic character who appears in Aristophanes' *Wealth* (Ar. *Plut.* 959–1096). I have previously argued that Lysias drew on ideals depicted in epic poetry to suggest that Euphiletus' actions in killing Eratosthenes were like the heroic and noble revenge of Odysseus.[87] Here I draw on literary parallels to argue that the rejected former mistress and her servant who passes on gossip to Euphiletus also resemble tragic characters involved in revenge plotlines.

According to Euphiletus' version of events, the old woman who approaches him acts as a go-between passing on gossip about his wife's behaviour. Commentators have noted her similarity to the nurse character in tragic plots who also acts as go-between, as discussed above.[88] She claims to speak for her mistress and maintains that she is not being a busybody, but that passing on this information is appropriate because of the relationship between her mistress and Eratosthenes which has turned to enmity. This use of terminology provides a strong indication that the love rival's decision to send a messenger to tell Euphiletus about this affair is vengeful in nature, at least in the way Lysias depicts it.[89] Euphiletus also explains that the woman was angry with Eratosthenes and felt herself wronged (αὕτη δὲ ὀργιζομένη καὶ ἀδικεῖσθαι νομίζουσα) because he no longer visited her so regularly. The vocabulary of anger and justice used here is also suggestive of vengeful feelings in Greek thinking.[90]

After hearing the gossip Euphiletus says that he was immediately perturbed and suspicious. This is a typical dynamic in literary plotlines where a man hears that his wife is involved sexually with another man. In Chariton's novel, the plotters make deliberate use of false gossip in order to generate anger in Chaereas when they have filled his head with suspicions about his wife's behaviour.[91] Likewise in Euripides' *Hippolytus*, Theseus is overwhelmed by anger concerning the false tale his wife leaves for him concerning the behaviour of Hippolytus towards her. In both cases, the motivation behind passing on the information is to generate excessive anger in a jealous husband to create a violent response and bring about the destruction of an enemy. By comparison to Chaereas and Theseus, we can also predict a jealous reaction from Euphiletus on hearing his young wife was unfaithful to him. Hence the motivation of the love rival in Lysias 1 can be seen to be aimed at infuriating Euphiletus so that he attacks Eratosthenes. While killing in cases of adultery was not common at Athens, there were other forms of attack that Euphiletus could have employed including prosecution, extraction of compensation or humiliation against Eratosthenes. So, it is not necessary to suppose that Eratosthenes' former mistress (if she existed) wanted him to be killed. But it is also possible that Euphiletus' character is not as described by himself in his speech, and that in targeting Euphiletus to pass on this gossip, there was a calculation that he would turn to violence.

As discussed above, at Athens a woman would not have been able to achieve revenge in the courts without male help, but would have needed a man to act for her. In the story told in Lysias 1, the angry former mistress would not have been able to appeal to male relatives to help her because it would have involved disclosing an illicit affair. But the tale as it appears in Lysias 1 suggests that this woman was able to find an indirect route to secure revenge through gossip. She goes a step further than Zobia in Demosthenes 25, who makes use of gossip in a general way to reveal the behaviour of Aristogeiton towards her. The wronged woman in Lysias 1 apparently targets a specific man with gossipy information with the hope of generating his angry response against her 'enemy'. As Johnstone has noted, this speech, if presented from the viewpoint of the women involved, could be seen as the outcome of discord between Eratosthenes and his former lover.[92]

This picture of the former lover maps onto Roisman's manipulative Phaedra who, in her interpretation, manages to make the gullible nurse act on her behalf and who uses lying words to make her husband kill his own son because she is angry at his rejection of her advances. At the same time, the image of a network of women supported by their slaves, acting inappropriately in the absence of their husbands, as discussed by Hall, mirrors tragic plots. These underlying images which Lysias hints at go some way towards deflecting the blame from Euphiletus and onto the women in the background – the alleged former lover and her servant – who by implication take the blame for the violent actions of a man. The suggestion, through the allusion to tragedies, that the responsibility for the death of Eratosthenes ultimately lies with these woman, simultaneously implies the lack of culpability of Euphiletus.

CONCLUSION

In this chapter, I have argued that gossip can be used as a mode of revenge and that the typical motivations behind such attacks are envy and sexual jealousy. While men and women can use gossip to achieve revenge, it is a particularly suitable approach for unsupported women at Athens who are unable to use official legal channels. In literary plotlines, women's clever use of words and their ability to spread gossip through networks of other women and slaves can generate successful revenge outcomes, even where the messengers involved do not understand the implication of their words. Hints which are given in legal texts from Athens suggest that orators made use of these literary ideas to play upon the jurors' fears and paint a picture of the guilt of their opponents or of their own innocence. Analysis of Lysias 1 *On the Murder of Eratosthenes* shows a way in which a woman at Athens could have made use of rumours to create suspicion and generate a violent reaction in order to achieve revenge against an 'enemy'. At the same time, Lysias' use of a common revenge story pattern as part of the subtext of his oration allows his client Euphiletus to deflect any thoughts that he might have been unduly full of angry and vengeful feelings onto a woman. A close study of ancient literary texts thus reveals the potential power of women and female networks to exploit gossip for their own ends, while also demonstrating the tendency for men to eschew responsibility for their violent actions by blaming the incendiary power of women's malicious speech.

NOTES

1. Aesch. *Cho.* 720–1. I would like to thank Judith Mossman and Mike Edwards for their helpful comments.
2. Fiona McHardy, *Revenge in Athenian Culture* (London: Duckworth, 2008), pp. 37–42. See Hall in this volume.
3. Fiona McHardy 'Women's Influence on Revenge in Ancient Greece', in F. McHardy and E. Marshall (eds), *Women's Influence on Classical Civilization* (London: Routledge, 2004), pp. 92–114; cf. Anne P. Burnett, *Revenge in Attic and Later Tragedy* (Berkeley: University of California Press, 1998), p. 143.
4. See Matthews and Salvo in this volume on the power of curses in taking revenge.
5. Cf. Stephen C. Todd, *The Shape of Athenian Law* (Oxford: Oxford University Press, 1993), p. 201; Danielle Allen, *The World of Prometheus: the Politics of Punishing in Democratic Athens* (Princeton: Princeton University Press, 2000), p. 99.
6. For the range of terms used to denote gossip in Greek, see Francis Larran, 'De *kleos* à *phèmè*. Approche historique de la rumeur et de la renommée dans la littérature grecque ancienne, d'Homère à Polybe', *Anabases* 11 (2010), pp. 232–7.

7. Virginia Hunter, 'Gossip and the Politics of Reputation in Classical Athens', *Phoenix* 44 (1990), pp. 299–325.
8. Laura K. McClure, *Spoken like a Woman: Speech and Gender in Athenian Drama* (Princeton: Princeton University Press, 1999).
9. Hanna M. Roisman, *Nothing is as it Seems: The Tragedy of the Implicit in Euripides* Hippolytus (Lanham, MD: Rowman and Littlefield, 1999).
10. Edith Hall, 'The Sociology of Athenian Tragedy', in P. E. Easterling (ed.), *Cambridge Companion to Greek Tragedy* (Cambridge: Cambridge University Press, 1997), pp. 91–126 (p. 116).
11. Susan Deacy, and Fiona McHardy, 'Uxoricide in Pregnancy: Ancient Greek Domestic Violence in Evolutionary Perspective', *Evolutionary Psychology Journal* 11.5 (2013), pp. 994–1010.
12. See Esther Eidinow 'Patterns of Persecution: Witchcraft Trials in Classical Athens', *Past and Present* 208 (2010), pp. 9–35 (p. 24) on gossip as a weapon and (pp. 29–30) on how it might be used vindictively. Edith B. Gelles 'Gossip: An Eighteenth-Century Case', *Journal of Social History* 22 (1989), pp. 667–83 (p. 667) refers to the 'malicious use of gossip as a weapon' in a discussion of courtship in the eighteenth century and comments on how gossip could be used in attempting revenge (p. 675).
13. The use of female speech is limited in the Attic orations. For discussion of nine instances where it occurs, see Michael Gagarin, 'Women's Voices in Attic Oratory', in A. Lardinois and L. McClure (eds), *Making Silence Speak* (Princeton: Princeton University Press, 2001), pp. 161–76.
14. John R. Porter, 'Adultery by the Book: Lysias I (On the Murder of Eratosthenes) and Comic Diegesis', in E. Carawan (ed.), *Oxford Readings in Attic Orators* (Oxford: Oxford University Press, 2007), pp. 60–88, updated version of John R. Porter, 'Adultery by the Book: Lysias I (On the Murder of Eratosthenes) and Comic Diegesis', *Échos du monde classique* 16 (1997), pp. 421–53.
15. Chris Wickham, 'Gossip and Resistance among the Medieval Peasantry', *Past and Present* 160 (1998), pp. 3–24 (p. 15) notes that gossiping is not gendered. See Hunter, 'Gossip and the Politics of Reputation', for examples of male and female gossip at Athens. Josiah Ober, *Mass and Elite* (Princeton: Princeton University Press, 1989), p. 149, suggests that slaves and prostitutes acted as a conduit for gossip. See Dem. 50.48; Plut. *On Curiosity* 9. McClure, *Spoken like a Woman*, p. 58, discusses slaves as conduits for gossip in drama.
16. Sophie Gotteland, 'La rumeur chez les orateurs attiques: vérité ou vraisemblance', *L'Antiquité Classique* 66 (1997), pp. 89–119; Larran, 'De *kleos* à *phèmè*', p. 232; Eidinow, 'Patterns of Persecution', p. 24.
17. Max Gluckman, 'Papers in Honor of Melville J. Herskovits: Gossip and Scandal', *Current Anthropology* 4 (1963), pp. 307–16 (p. 307); Patricia M. Spacks, *Gossip* (New York: Knopf, 1985), p. 14.
18. For examples which depict a 'network' of male gossipers see Hunter, 'Gossip and the Politics of Reputation', p. 302; cf. Richard Buxton,

Imaginary Greece (Cambridge: Cambridge University Press, 1994), pp. 11–12.
19. Gelles, 'Gossip', p. 667. On competitive use of gossip, see also R. Paine, 'What is Gossip About? An Alternative Hypothesis', *Man* 2 (1967), pp. 278–85.
20. Andrew Wolpert, 'Lysias 1 and the Politics of the οἶκος', *Classical Journal* 96 (2000–1), pp. 415–24 (pp. 415–17). Cf. David Cohen, *Law, Sexuality and Society* (Cambridge: Cambridge University Press, 1991), pp. 154, 161; Peter Walcot, 'Separatism and the Alleged Conversation of Women', *Classica et mediaevalia* 45 (1994), pp. 27–50.
21. On the precarious legal situation of metic women in Athens, see Rebecca F. Kennedy, *Immigrant Women in Athens: Gender, Ethnicity, and Citizenship in the Classical City* (New York and London: Routledge, 2014). Cf. Deborah Kamen, *Status in Classical Athens* (Princeton: Princeton University Press, 2013), pp. 43–54.
22. Aristotle (*Politics* 1313b) notes women's ability to spread complaints about men in democracies. Cf. McClure, *Spoken like a Woman*, p. 29, on the potential for gossip to be 'subversive of social hierarchy'.
23. Larran, 'De *kleos* à *phèmè*', cf. Kenneth J. Dover, 'Anecdotes, Gossip and Scandal', in *The Greeks and their Legacy. Collected papers*, II (Oxford: Blackwell, 1988), pp. 45–52 (p. 51). Cf. Aristotle *Nicomachean Ethics* 4.3.31
24. Spacks, *Gossip*, p. 4.
25. Hunter, 'Gossip and the Politics of Reputation'. Cf. Cheryl A. Cox, 'Incest, Inheritance and the Political Forum in Fifth-Century Athens', *Classical Journal* 8 (1989), pp. 534–46; Kenneth. J. Dover, *Greek Popular Morality* (Oxford: Oxford University Press, 1974), pp. 30–3; Gotteland 'La rumeur chez les orateurs attiques'; Larran 'De *kleos* à *phèmè*'. Philip Harding, 'All Pigs are Animals, But Are All Animals Pigs?', *Ancient History Bulletin* 5 (1991), pp. 145–8, has argued that many of Hunter's examples are political invective and not 'gossip'.
26. Hunter, 'Gossip and the Politics of Reputation', p. 310, notes that the suit against Timarchus uses gossip to attack his citizenship rights; cf. Umberto Bultrighini, 'Eschine e la phéme in giudizio', *Rivista di cultura classica e medioevale* 56 (2014), pp. 317–30.
27. Hunter, 'Gossip and the Politics of Reputation', pp. 316–21; cf. Eidinow, 'Patterns of Persecution', p. 15. Cf. Dem. 59.110–11.
28. Hunter, 'Gossip and the Politics of Reputation', p. 319.
29. *Ath. Pol.* 26.4. See Cynthia B. Patterson, *Pericles' Citizenship Law of 451/0 BC* (New York: Arno Press, 1981); cf. Hunter, 'Gossip and the Politics of Reputation', p. 320; Todd, *Shape of Athenian Law*, pp. 177–9. The anger and insecurity generated by such gossip is portrayed vividly in Herodotus' account of Demaratus deposed King of Sparta (Hdt. 6.68–9) and Sophocles' play about Oedipus (*OT* 779–86).
30. Eidinow, 'Patterns of Persecution', p. 23.

31. Hunter, 'Gossip and the Politics of Reputation', p. 321. Cf. Cohen, *Law, Sexuality and Society*, p. 161. See Gluckman, 'Gossip and Scandal', on the ways a community preserves its values through gossip.
32. David Cohen, 'Seclusion, Separation, and the Status of Women in Classical Athens', *Greece and Rome* 36 (1989), pp. 3–15.
33. For discussion of this and other examples, see Cohen, *Law, Sexuality and Society*, p. 148.
34. See for example Jane F. Gardner, 'Aristophanes and Male Anxiety, the Defense of the Oikos', *Greece and Rome* 36 (1989), pp. 51–62; David Konstan, 'Premarital Sex, Illegitimacy, and Male Anxiety in Menander and Athens', in A. L. Boegehold and A. C. Scafuro (eds), *Athenian Identity and Civic Ideology* (Baltimore: Johns Hopkins University Press, 1993), pp. 217–35; McHardy, *Revenge*, p. 47; Deacy and McHardy, 'Uxoricide in Pregnancy'.
35. Craig Cooper, 'Hyperides', in I. Worthington, C. Cooper and E. Harris (eds), *Dinarchus, Hyperides, and Lycurgus* (Austin: University of Texas Press, 2001), p. 70.
36. Here, as in Demosthenes 25 discussed above, relatives play on gossip about a woman's sexual fidelity in order to try to gain financial advantage.
37. Herodotus (3.50) states that Periander killed his wife, but does not give any further details. See Deacy and McHardy, 'Uxoricide in Pregnancy', for discussion of this and other similar examples.
38. See Ed Sanders, *Envy and Jealousy in Classical Athens* (Oxford: Oxford University Press, 2014), pp. 143–7, on Deianira's emotions in this play.
39. M. B. Ogle 'Dame Gossip's Rôle in Epic and Drama', *Transactions of the American Philological Association* 55 (1924), pp. 90–119, notes that the events of this play come about because of gossip.
40. Kostas Apostolakis, 'Tragic Patterns in Forensic Speeches: Antiphon 1 against the Stepmother', *Classica et mediaevalia* 58 (2007), pp. 179–92. Cf. Michael Gagarin, 'Telling Stories in Athenian Law', *Transactions of the American Philological Association* 133 (2003), pp. 197–207. On the similarity to Sophocles' tragic heroine Deianira, see Victoria J. Wohl, 'A Tragic Case of Poisoning: Intention between Tragedy and the Law', *Transactions of the American Philological Association* 140 (2010), pp. 33–70; cf. Sanders, *Envy and Jealousy*, pp. 156–8.
41. Sanders, *Envy and Jealousy*, p. 153.
42. Cf. McClure, *Spoken like a Woman*, pp. 160–2.
43. Ogle, 'Dame Gossip's Rôle', p. 103, has pointed out that gossip is the main motivating factor for the plot of this play.
44. Eidinow, 'Patterns of Persecution', pp. 29–30.
45. Sanders, *Envy and Jealousy*, p. 16.
46. Ibid. p. 16. See also p. 57.
47. Ogle, 'Dame Gossip's Rôle', p. 103.
48. For discussion of the messenger's speech, see Irène J. F. de Jong, 'Three Off-Stage Characters in Euripides', *Mnemosyne* 43 (1990), pp. 1–21

(pp. 11–13). Cf. also *Andr.* 993–1008, where Orestes mentions his plan to Hermione without explaining how he will accomplish Neoptolemus' death.

49. On allusions to Achilles in the description of Neoptolemus' military prowess and haughty behaviour, see Susanna Phillippo, 'Family Ties: Significant Patronymics in Euripides' *Andromache*', *Classical Quarterly* 45 (1995), pp. 355–71 (p. 364). Cf. also Judith M. Mossman, 'Waiting for Neoptolemus: the Unity of Euripides' *Andromache*', *Greece and Rome* 43 (1996), pp. 143–56 (pp. 152–3).
50. Mossman, 'Waiting for Neoptolemus', p. 152 describes Orestes as 'ignobly cautious' (cf. also p. 147 on Orestes' caution). For comparison of Orestes to wily Odysseus, see Filippomaria Pontani, 'Shocks, Lies, and Matricide: Thoughts on Aeschylus' *Choephori* 653–718', *Harvard Studies in Classical Philology* 103 (2007), pp. 203–33.
51. For the connection between Orestes' murder of his mother and his attack on Neoptolemus, see Phillippo, 'Family Ties', pp. 363, 366.
52. Cf. Ogle, 'Dame Gossip's Rôle', p. 100.
53. Judith M. Mossman, 'Women's Speech in Greek Tragedy: The Case of Electra and Clytemnestra in Euripides' *Electra*', *Classical Quarterly* 51 (2001), pp. 374–84 (p. 377).
54. In her discussion of gossip in tragedy, McClure, *Spoken like a Woman*, p. 58, notes that the nurse is a stock figure who carries messages, but here Euripides depicts an old man as the servant who acts as go-between.
55. Burnett, *Revenge*, 107–8. For detailed discussion on the role of the chorus in the *kommos*, see Desmond J. Conacher, 'Interaction between Chorus and Characters in the *Oresteia*', *American Journal of Philology* 95 (1974), pp. 323–43, who argues that the chorus both invoke the spirit of Agamemnon and urge on Orestes to vengeance (p. 339). Notably, Conacher does not discuss the interaction of the chorus with the nurse.
56. See McClure, *Spoken like a Woman*, p. 100, on the unreliability of female speech in *Choephori*.
57. On the trust the chorus show towards the nurse, see Joseph S. Margon, 'The Nurse's View of Clytemnestra's Grief for Orestes. *Choephori* 737–40', *Classical World* 76 (1983), pp. 286–97.
58. See Pollard in this volume for discussion of the usual inactivity of the Greek tragic chorus, esp. her note 88 where Oliver Taplin, 'Comedy and the Tragic', in M. S. Silk (ed.), *Tragedy and the Tragic: Greek Theatre and Beyond* (Oxford: Oxford University Press, 1996), pp. 188–202, suggests that 'Women and weak old men seem to be favoured for choruses partly because of their ineffectuality in action' (p. 193).
59. Barbara Goff, *The Noose of Words* (Cambridge: Cambridge University Press, 1990), p. 70, comments on the way words are used in retaliation by men, women and gods in the *Hippolytus*.
60. The nurse achieves the plan of Aphrodite through her actions. See Helen P. Karydas, *Eurykleia and her Successors: Female Figures of Authority in*

Greek Poetics, Lanham, MD: Rowman and Littlefield, 1998), p. 117. Cf. W. S. Barrett, *Euripides,* Hippolytos (Oxford: Clarendon Press, 1964), on lines 170–266.
61. Hall, 'Sociology of Athenian Tragedy', p. 117.
62. Ibid. p. 116.
63. Roisman, *Nothing is as it Seems*, esp. Ch. 3. See also Hanna M. Roisman, 'Women in Senecan Tragedy', *Scholia* 14 (2005), pp. 72–88 (pp. 74–5, 79). Cf. G. J. Fitzgerald, 'Misconception, Hypocrisy, and the Structure of Euripides' *Hippolytus*', *Ramus* 2 (1973), pp. 20–40 (pp. 23–5). Sophie Mills, *Euripides:* Hippolytus (London: Duckworth, 2002), p. 56, argues that Phaedra does not know the nurse is going to betray her.
64. Roisman, 'Women in Senecan Tragedy', p. 87. See Roisman, *Nothing is as it Seems*, p. xiv, on her reading being just one possible interpretation by the ancient audience.
65. See Hall, 'Sociology of Athenian Tragedy', p. 108. See further below on Lysias 1.
66. Roisman, *Nothing is as it Seems*, p. 116.
67. See Deacy and McHardy, 'Uxoricide in Pregnancy', on angry, violent reactions to sexual threats made by men towards female relatives, especially their wives.
68. John H. D. Scourfield, 'Chaereas, Hippolytus, Theseus: Tragic Echoes, Tragic Potential in Chariton', *Phoenix* 64 (2010), pp. 291–313 (p. 293). Maarit Kaimio, 'How to Enjoy a Greek Novel: Chariton Guiding his Audience', *Arctos* 30 (1996), pp. 49–73, argues that where references to tragedy appear in this novel, it reinforces the seriousness of the episode (p. 57). For discussion of references to other genres in this scene, see Richard Hunter, 'History and Historicity in the Romance of Chariton', *Aufstieg und Niedergang der römischen Welt* 2.34.2 (1994), pp. 1055–86 (p. 1082).
69. Scourfield, 'Chaereas, Hippolytus, Theseus', esp. pp. 295, 306.
70. Cf. Allen, *World of Prometheus*, pp. 38, 126–7; Christopher Carey (ed.), *Lysias: Selected Speeches* (Cambridge: Cambridge University Press, 1989), pp. 60–1; David Cohen, *Law, Violence and Community in Classical Athens* (Cambridge: Cambridge University Press, 1995), p. 71. Cf. Christopher Pelling, *Literary Texts and the Greek Historian* (London: Routledge, 2000), p. 222.
71. According to the prosecution the slave girl is used to trick Eratosthenes (1.37). Carey, *Lysias*, p. 82, remarks that the fact that Euphiletus does not deny that he sent her, but says it would have been reasonable to have sent her, is suggestive. Ruth Scodel, 'Meditations on Lysias 1 and Athenian Adultery', *Electronic Antiquity* 1.2 (1993), suggests Euphiletus' could have sent a note from his wife to get Eratosthenes to the house.
72. Translation by W. R. M. Lamb.
73. Wolpert, 'Lysias 1', pp. 415–17, notes that women play an active part in causing events to happen in this speech.

74. John R. Porter, 'Chariton and Lysias 1: Further Considerations', *Hermes* 131 (2003), pp. 433–40. See further below.
75. Wolpert, 'Lysias 1', p. 418 notes: 'This portrayal reveals not so much the actual response of Euphiletus at the moment of discovery; rather it reveals how the defendant retroactively frames his actions as conforming to Athenian law and how he narrates the sequence of events so that he can depict himself in court as a law-abiding citizen.'
76. Carey, *Lysias*, p. 62.
77. Gagarin, 'Telling Stories', p. 204.
78. For discussion of the role played by a network of women in passing the message, see Lin Foxhall, 'The Law and the Lady: Women and Legal Proceedings in Classical Athens', in L. Foxhall and A. D. E. Lewis (eds), *Greek Law in its Political Setting* (Oxford: Oxford University Press, 1996), pp. 133–52 (p. 151); cf. Hall, 'Sociology of Athenian Tragedy', p. 117; McClure, *Spoken like a Woman*, p. 58; Ober, *Mass and Elite*, p. 149; Wolpert, 'Lysias 1', p. 421.
79. Carey, *Lysias*, pp. 62–3; cf. Michael J. Edwards, 'Lysias', in I. De Jong, R. Nünlist and A. Bowie (eds), *Narrators, Narratees, and Narratives in Ancient Greek Literature* (Leiden: Brill, 2004), pp. 333–6, who notes it was probably not legally possible to introduce these women as witnesses (p. 335).
80. Kenneth J. Dover, *Lysias and the Corpus Lysiacum* (Berkeley: University of California Press, 1968), pp. 172, 194–5. Marius Levency, *Aspects de la logographie judiciaire attique* (Louvain: Nauwelaerts, 1964), pp. 183–94, argues that the published version of a speech would have been close to the original. If it had been effective, the orator would have wanted to publish it as it was. If it was not effective, then he would not have wanted to publish it.
81. Porter, 'Adultery by the Book', p. 82.
82. Stephen Usher, 'Lysias for Pleasure?' in D. L. Cairns and R. A. Knox (eds) *Law, Rhetoric, and Comedy in Classical Athens* (Swansea: Classical Press of Wales, 2004), pp. 113–21 (p. 118); cf. Michael J. Edwards (ed.), *Lysias: Five Speeches* (London: Bristol Classical Press, 1999), p. 62. Wolpert, 'Lysias 1', p. 420, n. 15. See also John Bateman, 'Lysias and the Law', *Transactions of the American Philological Association* 89 (1958), pp. 276–85 (p. 277); Carey, *Lysias*, p. 64.
83. Porter, 'Adultery by the Book', p. 61; cf. Porter, 'Chariton and Lysias 1', p. 433. Carey, *Lysias*, comments: 'He falls neatly into the role of the gullible cuckold found in popular tales' (p. 61).
84. Gagarin, 'Telling Stories in Athenian Law', p. 198. Cf. Edwards, 'Lysias', pp. 333–6. See above on the use of mythical allusions in Antiphon 1.
85. Carey, *Lysias*, p. 10. Gagarin, 'Women's Voices in Attic Oratory', p. 162, compares female characters in oratory to those in drama in that they are written and performed by men.
86. David S. Rosenbloom, 'Aristogeiton Son of Cydimachus and the

Scoundrel's Drama', in J. Davidson and A. J. Pomeroy (eds), *Theatres of Action* (Auckland: Polygraphia, 2003), pp. 88–117. See above on this speech.
87. McHardy, *Revenge*, pp. 55–6; cf. Matthew R. Christ, 'Legal Self-Help on Private Property in Classical Athens', *American Journal of Philology* 119 (1998), pp. 521–45.
88. Hall, 'Sociology of Athenian Tragedy', p. 117, n. 59; Porter, 'Adultery by the Book', p. 61.
89. Cf. Wolpert, 'Lysias 1', p. 421.
90. On terminology associated with revenge in Greek texts, see McHardy, *Revenge*, pp. 3–5. Carey, *Lysias*, p. 71, notes that *adikeisthai* is frequently used of those thwarted in love.
91. Konstantinos A. Kapparis, 'Has Chariton Read Lysias 1 "On the Murder of Eratosthenes"?', *Hermes* 128 (2000), pp. 380–3 (p. 381), argues that the novel takes on the story of Lysias 1. Porter, 'Chariton and Lysias', p. 433, maintains both texts share common literary parallels.
92. Steven Johnstone, 'Cracking the Code of Silence: Athenian Legal Oratory and the Histories of Slaves and Women', in S. Joshel and S. Murnaghan (eds), *Women and Slaves in Greco-Roman Culture* (London: Routledge, 1998), pp. 221–35 (p. 227).

CHAPTER 9

'Women's Weapons': Education and Female Revenge on the Early Modern Stage

Chloe Kathleen Preedy

'My tables! Meet it is I set it down', exclaims the most famous revenger of the early modern theatre, as he employs the study methods he has acquired at university to record a ghost's lesson of murder and retribution.[1] While initially promising that 'thy commandment all alone shall live / Within the book and volume of my brain' (1.5.102–3), Hamlet will later rely on his prior learning to test the truth of his uncle's guilt, composing 'a speech of some dozen lines' that, inserted into *The Murder of Gonzago*, enables him to try the king and 'tent him to the quick' (2.2.477, 532). This association between words and violent action, the humanist education system and the pursuit of revenge, became even more emphatic in Jacobean drama, when the figure of the malcontent – often depicted as a socially ambitious scholar whose prospects for advancement have been blocked by entrenched aristocratic privilege – gained in popularity.[2] From De Flores in *The Changeling* and Bosola in *The Duchess of Malfi*, to Vindice in *The Revenger's Tragedy* and the eponymous protagonist of *Antonio's Revenge*, Jacobean revengers invite audiences to reflect on the relationship between humanist learning, with its emphasis on proper governance and moral education, and the violent retribution that they enact upon corrupt rulers and unjust societies. Hinting at early modern doubts about whether humanism would be able to live up to its ideals in practice,[3] such characters are credited with the ability to 'manipulate a fluid and contingent world with a dramatist's inventiveness and authority'; as John Kerrigan has shown, the early modern revenger becomes a 'surrogate artist', 'transmuting creative ambition into narrative and stage action'.[4] The educational heritage that these fictional characters share with their creators is especially significant. Early modern playwrights and their metatheatrical protagonists both drew inspiration from classical models: the Roman author Seneca's influence on Elizabethan and Jacobean revenge drama has long been recognised by critics, while Tanya Pollard's chapter in this collection demonstrates how early modern authors responded to and reworked the legacy of ancient Greek tragedy.⁵ Yet the significance of the associations between humanist education and revenge action for the female avengers of sixteenth- and seventeenth-century drama have not yet been fully addressed. Examining the revenge plots of Shakespeare's *Titus Andronicus*, Kyd's *The Spanish Tragedy* and Chapman's *The Revenge of Bussy D'Ambois*, this chapter argues that women's literacy and classical knowledge play a crucial role in scripting vengeance, enabling educated women to participate actively in the process of revenge rather than being banished to the margins.⁶

If the consequences of humanist learning concerned some sixteenth- and seventeenth-century writers, women's education was an especially controversial topic. Although some humanist commentators suggested that education would aid a female pupil's moral development, others argued that there was something 'intrinsically indecorous' about a woman who violated the 'social code of modest silence'.⁷ The educated woman was often ambiguously portrayed in humanist texts, popular pamphlets, and plays as a potentially unruly figure: 'a threat in the social and sexual sphere'.⁸ Various authors cited the female revengers of ancient Greek and Roman tragedy to condemn women who resisted contemporary expectations: punitive depictions of a weakened Medea were used 'to caution or instruct the reader or audience member', while Thomas Nashe's *Pierce Penilesse* and Christopher Fetherstone's *A dialogue agaynst light, lewde, and lasciuious dauncing* associate promiscuity with the murderous 'strumpet' Clytemnestra.⁹ Those arguing in defence of women were equally aware of such classical precedents. Thus 'Ester Sowernam', responding to Joseph Swetnam's 1615 *Arraignment of Lewd, Idle, Froward, and Unconstant Women*, mockingly suggests that Swetnam should have quoted Euripides to strengthen his argument, since women are vilified in his drama as being without value and 'most hurtfull to men'; she names the '*Gracians, Euripides, Menander, Simonides, Sophocles,* with the like, amongst Latine writers *Invenall, Plautus,* &c' as 'vehement and profest enemies against our sexe'.¹⁰ 'Constantia Munda', another respondent to Swetnam's tract, adds that 'Twas spoken of *Euripides*, that he hated women in *choro*'.¹¹ These comments suggest a shared interest in Euripides' portrayal of female revengers, such as Hecuba and Medea; Sowernam's attribution of the verse fragment she quotes to his tragedy *Medea* strengthens this assumption. Munda is also concerned about the related representation of female characters on the early modern stage, warning that every 'fantasticke Poetaster [who] ... can but patch a hobling verse together, will striue to represent vnseemely figments imputed to our sex, (as a pleasing theme to the vulgar) on the publique Theatre'.¹²

While Munda's text does not specifically attack the depiction of women in Elizabethan and Jacobean revenge drama, the concerns expressed by these seventeenth-century authors about the classical legacy of the female avenger anticipate the conclusions reached by many recent critics. Marguerite A. Tassi, while highlighting the active contribution that female characters make to the revenge plots of Shakespeare's comedies, demonstrates that, for Shakespeare and his contemporaries, avenging women call to mind 'unruly' images of the

Hyrcanian tiger, Amazon and virago: tropes that signify a transformation from a conventionally gendered female into a beast or unnatural creature, as discussed elsewhere in this collection.[13] Janet Clare, evaluating Sir Francis Bacon's claim that 'vindictive persons live the life of witches', suggests that this analogy complements and reinforces the widely held view that the female avenger was an aberration against nature; her chapter in this collection concludes that 'there was little space on the early modern stage for a more positive icon of female revenge, biblical or classical'.[14] Alison Findlay agrees that most contemporary discourses vilified female avengers, but ascribes this tendency to fundamental fears about female agency and maternal power; like Tassi and Deborah Willis, she highlights that women in early modern drama are shown to actively instigate, and even perform, acts of vengeance.[15]

These critics rightly emphasise that the female revenger is typically characterised by early modern authors as unruly and aberrant, just as a number of sixteenth- and seventeenth-century writers expressed concerns about the moral and societal implications of educating women. At the same time, a humanist education enabled female writers to draw upon the authorising power of these classical works in their own writing, as Swetnam's seventeenth-century opponents recognised. Within *Ester hath hang'd Haman* (1617), Sowernam's citation of Euripides is part of her strategy to discredit *The Arraignment of Women* by belittling the author's writing style, his intellect, and the extent of his classical and Biblical learning. Rejecting any scriptural basis for Swetnam's accusation that 'God calleth women *necessary euils*', Sowernam suggests that his false claim must have been 'faigned and framed out of his owne idle, giddie, furious, and franticke imaginations', since Swetnam is unfamiliar with those 'Pagan' sources that he might otherwise have imitated; invention, in this context, is the despised consequence of Swetnam's ignorance. Her second allusion to Euripides enables her to reiterate the charge, as she concludes that this 'seely man' discusses 'nothing but what he hath stolne out of English writers'.[16] Similarly, Sowernam's predecessor Rachel Speght criticised *The Arraignment of Women* as 'altogether without methode, irregular, without Grammaticall Concordance, and a promiscuous mingle mangle',[17] while Munda denounced Swetnam's 'sottish lies' and his 'bald and ribald lines, / Patcht out of English writers'.[18]

The efforts that these women writers make to establish their classical and Christian credentials – Sowernam, for example, claims to defend 'diuine Maiestie, in the worke of his Creation' – recall Eileen Allman's argument that, in some early modern revenge tragedies, avenging heroines are positively associated with a forceful moral authority that is often religious in nature.[19] Swetnam's opponents, too, characterise their words as the weapons of righteous avengers. Sowernam claims that, as a woman first invented the sword, so a woman first invented letters, and promises to arraign Swetnam in the court of public opinion; Munda argues that 'words make worse wounds then swords' and, likening Swetnam to the notorious tyrant Phalaris, threatens to 'beate thee at thine owne weapon'; while Speght, although referring Swetnam's punishment to God, 'who hath appropriated vengeance vnto himselfe', is compared in a dedicatory verse to David, defeating Goliath.[20] Thus, although these early seventeenth-century polemical works have no direct connection with early modern revenge drama, the manner in which their female authors utilise humanist learning as a 'weapon' against their persecutors illuminates how the fictional female protagonists of revenge tragedy seek to assert their own mastery of classical sources. Like their real-life counterparts, the educated women of early modern revenge drama seek to manipulate, contest or take advantage of the very precedents that have been used against them, drawing upon classical and humanist examples in order to script their own narratives of revenge against the men who have wronged them.

Within a number of early modern plays, including *The Spanish Tragedy* and *The Revenge of Bussy D'Ambois*, the narrative authority acquired through learning is further extended when female avengers exchange their pens for the bladed weapons conventionally associated with active masculinity. Coming naturally to the hand of the early modern boy actor, the sword or knife requires direct participation in an attack; physical pressure must be applied to thrust the blade into the victim's body, creating a continuum between hand and weapon. The potential phallic significance of such penetration was recognised by contemporary writers: in Beaumont and Fletcher's *Love's Cure*, the cross-dressed and sword-wielding Clara is warned that 'nature hath given you a sheath only, to signifie women are to put up mens weapons, not to draw them' (2.2).[21] Elizabethan sumptuary laws also limited the carrying of arms to gentlemen. The female character who stabs her victim thus violates social and sexual decorum, while at the same time advertising her affinity with the classical tradition of women's vengeance: in Ovid's *Metamorphoses*, for instance, Medea bathes her 'wicked knife' in her children's blood and Procne slits her son Itys' throat with a knife, while Euripides' Hecuba stabs her enemy Polymestor's eyes out.[22] More centrally, the female character who masters the use of pen and sword can potentially lay claim to the same quasi-authorial power that is often attributed to male revengers.[23] Prior learning can assist female characters in their pursuit of vengeance: while the power possessed by women agents is usually more circumscribed than that of their male counterparts, the female revenger who is knowledgeable about classical sources or possesses eloquence in disputation can intervene in and shape the plot of her tragedy, albeit with varying degrees of success. Thus, from Shakespeare's Lavinia and Kyd's Bel-Imperia to Chapman's Tamyra, female characters draw on their learning and literary skills to script their own revenge plots, as women's learning becomes a weapon of revenge: the silenced tongue supplanted by the martial pen.

LEARNING OVID'S LESSON: *TITUS ANDRONICUS*

Lavinia might seem an unlikely candidate to introduce a discussion of female vengeance. Although *Titus Andronicus* owes much to the classical myth of Philomel, Shakespeare's narrative displaces her sister Procne's vengeful role onto a male agent, Titus. In addition, as Deborah Willis notes, critical interest in the play's spectacular display of the female body, written on by violence, has too often reduced Lavinia's role to that of passive victim: Lisa Jardine, for example, describes Lavinia as 'a visible symbol of patient suffering, a silent, mutilated emblem'.[24] Yet such characterisations of Lavinia underestimate the theatrical potency of her 'lively' onstage presence (3.1.105);[25] as Titus will regularly remind the audience, the actor's body continues to communicate through a language of gestures, sighs and tears. This physical expressiveness complements the verbal assertiveness that Lavinia demonstrates when she first meets Tamora in the forest, as the two women compete for interpretative control over the myth of Diana and Actaeon, with Lavinia seconded by her new husband Bassianus.[26] Although Tamora here gains the upper hand by discursively revising the forest space into the *locus horridus* of classical tradition (2.3.91–111), inspiring her sons to take revenge against Bassianus, it is Lavinia who will eventually, and tragically, learn most from their encounter. After being forced to play the role of Philomel, Lavinia becomes more skilled in manipulating Ovidian precedents to her advantage; her brutal silencing at the hands of Chiron and Demetrius paradoxically enhances the familial and communal value of female literacy, when she communicates the truth that 'womanhood denies my tongue to tell' (2.3.174) by glossing a culturally prestigious text that featured prominently in the humanist curricula of Tudor England's grammar schools.[27]

While Tamora and Lavinia represent different types of the female revenger, Aaron possesses the most authorial power over the events of Act 2. As Willis remarks, it is Aaron who redirects Tamora's thoughts towards vengeance prior to Lavinia's rape, when the adulterous couple become collaborators in an improvisational theatre of revenge,[28] and it is Aaron who determines that Ovid's myth of Philomel, not Actaeon, will provide the model for their revenge action (2.3.43–5). Tamora follows this lead in her description of the forest setting, which recalls the 'woods forgrown' of Ovid's *Metamorphoses* (6.664), and when she allows her sons to rape Lavinia rather than stabbing her opponent to death (2.3.120–1). If the phallic nature of Tamora's threat still broadly suggested the Ovidian precedent, it is Aaron's 'counsel' (2.1.132) that directly guides her sons' actions. Equally, it is Aaron's interpretative power that Lavinia contests through her subsequent use of Ovidian marginalia. In fact, Lavinia's reassertion of narrative control against considerable odds contrasts with Tamora's unwitting submission to Aaron's script in Act 2 as well as her subsequent failure to manipulate Titus: Tamora, who disguises herself as a female Revenge and believes she can use rhetorical eloquence to control Titus (4.4.96–9), represents the dangers of limited education for the typically vilified female revenger. Her sons' deaths might even be characterised as a judgement on a woman who pretends to greater learning than she possesses: Coppélia Kahn aptly identifies Tamora as the anti-muse to Titus' vengeance since, as Heather James and Liberty Stanavage have shown, Shakespeare's male avenger rewrites her schemes to his own ends.[29]

Like the seventeenth-century polemicists Speght, Sowernam and Munda, Lavinia inherits a tainted classical precedent that she must shape to her own ends. After Aaron encourages Chiron and Demetrius to pattern their assault on Tereus' rape of Philomel (2.1.128–30), the Goth brothers self-consciously celebrate their brutal editorial power by cutting off Lavinia's hands as well as her tongue, seeking to distort Ovid's Roman narrative as they mutilate their victim's Roman body.[30] Yet their crude handiwork retains a recognisable affinity with its literary source: Titus' brother Marcus, viewing his niece, concludes that 'some Tereus hath deflowered thee' (2.4.26). He even notes that Lavinia has suffered worse than Philomela 'Fair Philomela, why she but lost her tongue / And in a tedious sampler sewed her mind; / But, lovely niece, that mean is cut from thee. / A craftier Tereus, cousin, hast thou met' (2.4.38–41). The traumatised Marcus seems unable to apply his learning, however; having drawn this comparison, he reduces it to a rhetorical device that decorates his lament. While Chiron and Demetrius are poor readers who evade their interpretative responsibilities, believing they can 'lop' their classical source into an abridged form stripped of its deadly ending, Marcus conversely suffers from an excess of education: trapped within the Ovidian framework of this episode, his only response is to versify.

As the men around her retreat to the extremes of the educational spectrum, Lavinia asserts her independent authority over the text that has been her downfall, and appropriates it as an inspiration to joint action. Thus, when her father fails to interpret her 'martyred signs' correctly (3.2.35–44), her learning provides the solution: at the start of Act 4, she uses the text of Ovid's *Metamorphoses* to communicate with her family. Her active proffering of this volume is crucial, and a striking moment in performance. While critics such as James and Kahn minimise Lavinia's agency, characterising her mutilated body as a co-opted text or the scene's Latin passages as oppressively patriarchal, such readings insufficiently appreciate her literary stature.[31] Rather than her body acting as a passive vehicle for exchange between the male Goths and the male Andronici, Lavinia assumes the role of active communicant, repudiating the gestural alphabet of her father's devising for the written Latin that, to an English audience, advertises her comparatively elite education. Shakespeare's reliance on the *Metamorphoses* affirms Lavinia's textual independence, substituting Ovid's counter-epic for the Virgilian narrative within which 'Lavinia' would signify in exclusively bodily and reproductive terms:[32] as the female-voiced epistles of *Heroides* suggest, Ovid's verse offered a potential corrective to the traditional silencing of women in epic. His text is one that Lavinia can interpret authoritatively, substituting a tale of female vengeance for the mourning rituals of her male relatives.

Lavinia recalls the ideal humanist model of an educated woman, responsible for teaching the children (and now the adults) of her family. As Marcus reminds her nephew, 'Cornelia never with more care / Read to her sons than she hath read to thee / Sweet poetry and Tully's *Orator*' (4.1.12–5); Titus confirms that Lavinia is 'deeper read and better skilled'. Although at first he mistakenly assumes that she is using Ovid's epyllion to 'beguile thy sorrow, till the heavens / Reveal the damned contriver of this deed' (4.1.30–6), Lavinia perseveres, turning the leaves until her father realises (with Marcus' prompting) that she is quoting the pages:

> Lavinia, wert thou thus surprised, sweet girl?
> Ravished and wronged, as Philomela was,
> Forced in the ruthless, vast, and gloomy woods?
> See, see. Ay, such a place there is where we did hunt –
> O, had we never, never hunted there –
> Patterned by that the poet here describes,
> By nature made for murders and for rapes. (4.1.51–7)

Although Lavinia cannot embroider a sampler, Marcus' prayer brings the inspiration that she might write in the sand: a solution perhaps inspired by Lavinia's chosen text, in which Io traces her tale of rape in the dust (*Metamorphoses*, 1.642–67). Lavinia guides the staff she uses as a pen to carve out three simple but powerful words: '*Stuprum* – Chiron – Demetrius' (4.1.77).

Lavinia reveals her attackers through her literary agency. Female learning provides a substitute for Philomel's embroidery, just as Renaissance pedagogic texts compared the pursuit of education by aristocratic women to the activities of spinning and embroidery.[33] Critics sometimes characterise this substitution as a lessening of Lavinia's power: Kahn argues that Lavinia is forced to rely on the same male-authored texts that authorise patriarchal values, while Mary Laughlin Fawcett concludes that when Lavinia writes in Latin 'she uses the language of the fathers, the cultural dominators'.[34] But Ovid is a more subversive cultural 'father' than these readings suggest, while Lavinia's public authoring of a Latin verb and two Greek names becomes a striking advertisement for her educated power to communicate, in a riposte to Chiron's earlier mocking directive that she learn to 'play the scribe' (2.4.4).[35] In reality, Lavinia is more than a scribe, and she carefully distinguishes her own experience from that of Ovid's Philomel. Not only does she substitute the names of her own attackers for that of Tereus, but, as Bethany Packard points out, she inscribes the term *stuprum* rather than *raptus*: *stuprum*, which is not used in *Metamorphoses*, does not carry the same connotations of abduction and theft, of women as the property of husbands or fathers, as *raptus* does.[36] Lavinia's narrative control is further evidenced by the fact that, in this scene, she plays the role of tutor and gives her male relatives a 'lesson' in Ovid's text (4.1.105). In fact, by drawing her father's attention to Procne's tale at the very moment she reveals the identity of her rapists, Lavinia hints at how the action of his vengeance should unfold as well as revealing the cause of her own suffering. Titus may even take on the role of Lavinia's amanuensis, transforming her silently communicated scheme into a written plan of action: he announces that he 'will go get a leaf of brass, / And with a gad of steel will write' (4.1.101–2).[37]

Titus later emerges from his study to confirm that the planned vengeance is set down 'in bloody lines', 'and what is written shall be executed' (5.2.13–5). As the pun on 'execute' hints, this process is repeated when Titus carves the bloody lines that silence Chiron and Demetrius, cutting their throats with a steel gad or blade. Seizing the Ovidian precedent distorted by Aaron and passively reflected by Marcus, Lavinia has conveyed her own version of its 'lesson' to her avenging father; although not the agent of revenge, she provides the classical precedent for Titus' scheme. Her authority in this instance closely replicates Aaron's role at the start of the play, as he advised Chiron and Demetrius in their assault. If anyone in Shakespeare's tragedy scripts a direct response to the latter's mutilation of Ovid's narrative, it is Lavinia, who incites revenge through the careful conjunction of her fragmented words with the complete book of the *Metamorphoses*, re-joining its foretold outcome to the catalytic act of rape. From her carving of their names in the sand, through Titus' steel engraving, to the dagger that slices Chiron's and Demetrius' flesh, Lavinia guides her father's knife along with her uncle's staff, scripting the 'bloody lines' of their mutual vengeance. As Titus tells the doomed Chiron and Demetrius, 'worse than Philomel you used my daughter, / And worse than Procne I will be revenged' (5.2.193–4).

Lavinia's agency is circumscribed in *Titus Andronicus*. Without hands, she cannot directly wield the knife that cuts the rapists' throats, and must instead perform the more passive role of holding a basin to receive their blood. Her ceremonial participation in this execution may even arguably require her to re-experience her rape: the flowing of Chiron's and Demetrius' lifeblood into the vessel she carries echoes their earlier penetration of Lavinia's womb, symbolised onstage by the 'blood-drinking hole' – although, as Willis suggests, the eventual reduction of her attackers to drained corpses, butchered animals at the end of the hunt, allows the Andronici to reassert control over the hunting analogies that Aaron, Tamora and her sons employed in their assault on Lavinia.[38] Titus' subsequent killing of his daughter is even more problematic; with Lavinia silenced, uncertainty arises about whether or not she is complicit in this particular appropriation of classical precedent.[39] Nonetheless, Shakespeare's tragedy suggests an emerging alignment between female education and the ability of the female revenger to script her own vengeance, without being vilified as a cruel or unnatural monster: thus Lavinia, recognising that Philomela's tale was the model for her rape, appropriates this classical allusion to initiate a revenge action that takes Procne as its 'precedent, and lively warrant' (5.2.43). Although she lacks hands to stab, her revenge is realised through the literate actions of reading and writing; female education takes the place of embroidery, in this narrative as in the manuals of humanist educators.

SCRIPTING VENGEANCE IN *THE SPANISH TRAGEDY*

Around the time that Shakespeare wrote *Titus Andronicus*, Thomas Kyd penned *The Spanish Tragedy*. Like his Mediterranean drama *Soliman and Perseda*, Kyd's tragedy features an educated female character whose learning facilitates her vengeance. Indeed, Bel-Imperia is explicitly cast in the role of avenger: a personified Revenge reassures the ghost of the murdered Andrea that he will 'see the author of thy death, / Don Balthazar the prince of Portingale, / Deprived of life by Bel-imperia' (1.1.87–9).[40] Thus, as in *Titus Andronicus*, the 'authoring' aggressor is opposed by a female revenger who is able to script his ending. Moreover, the quasi-directorial authority that Revenge possesses over the events that unfold provides another instance of authoring female revenge: Andrea's plea for vengeance is granted by the goddess Persephone, patron of the play's action, while the drama's self-consciously classical framework suggests that Revenge may also have been played as female.[41]

Bel-Imperia's literary skills are evident within *The Spanish Tragedy*. She is adept in wordplay and classical allusion, which she uses to keep Prince Balthazar at a distance while courting an alliance with Andrea's friend Horatio. Balthazar characterises her as a sharp critic, reporting how his love letters 'work her no delight': their lines 'are but harsh and ill, / Such as do drop from Pan and Marsyas' quill' (2.1.14–16). For the reader of Ovid, the threat of violent retribution haunts his words. In contrast, Bel-Imperia's letters to Horatio are eloquent, 'fraught with lines and arguments of love' (2.1.84–6), and she integrates classical precedents smoothly into their conversation: 'If I be Venus thou must needs be Mars, / And where Mars reigneth there must needs be wars' (2.4.34–5). Although this latter reference unintentionally foreshadows the conclusion to their meeting, when they are surprised by Bel-Imperia's murderous male relatives, it also prophetically anticipates the play's second revenge cycle, which provides the necessary framework for her success.

Deprived of her intended ally, Bel-Imperia recognises Horatio's father Hieronimo as a new partner. However, Hieronimo is not simply her male proxy. Instead, Kyd unites two related but disparate actions of vengeance: Bel-Imperia avenges Andrea, while Hieronimo acts on Horatio's behalf. Although Hieronimo provides the literal script for their joint vengeance, it is Bel-Imperia who first writes herself into his plot. Her letter, which appears in apparently providential response to Hieronimo's plea to the heavens for some means to avenge his son (3.2.22–5), is penned, like Titus' revenge plot, in the author's blood. Since the imprisoned Bel-Imperia cannot pursue her campaign, she urges Hieronimo to act:

For want of ink, receive this bloody writ.
Me hath my hapless brother hid from thee;
Revenge thyself on Balthazar and him,
For these were they that murderèd thy son.

> Hieronimo, revenge Horatio's death,
> And better fare than Bel-Imperia doth. (3.2.26–31)

The legal term 'writ' may hint at Bel-Imperia's awareness of Hieronimo's preoccupations, and outlines a formal partnership. Yet Hieronimo, now appointed her representative, still fails to act. Suspecting the letter is a forgery, he waits on events while Bel-Imperia laments his emasculating passivity: 'Hieronimo, why ... art thou so slack in thy revenge?' (3.9.7–8).

As Hieronimo weighs the morality of vengeance, Lorenzo releases Bel-Imperia from captivity. Her learning plays its part in her escape. Recognising that Lorenzo wishes to persuade her with his oration, she feigns acquiescence (3.10.83–6), before bandying a series of Latin tags with her brother: Lorenzo responds, 'Nay, an you argue things so cunningly, / We'll go continue this discourse at court' (3.10.104–5). Bel-Imperia's carefully managed return then spurs Hieronimo into action; she is 'instrumental' in transforming Hieronimo into an active revenger, of the type she herself personifies.[42] While her catalytic role is arguably problematic, given the controversial morality of private vengeance, Hieronimo at least regards her arrival as a sign from above: 'Why then, I see that heaven applies our drift, / And all the saints do sit soliciting / For vengeance on those cursèd murderers' (4.1.30-4). Here, Bel-Imperia may anticipate the female heroines of Jacobean revenge tragedies such as *The Maid's Tragedy* and *The Second Maiden's Tragedy*, who Allman believes are celebrated for their opposition to tyranny and assumption of moral authority.[43]

Hieronimo characterises Bel-Imperia as a roughly equal partner, entreating her to play an active role in the execution of his revenge. Janet Clare stresses the remarkable nature of this performative collaboration, noting that Hieronimo's exclamation, 'For what's a play without a woman in it' (4.1.97), draws attention to the fact that he has included Bel-Imperia in the cast despite the all-male acting convention of early modern drama; although his play is being staged at court, it is not a masque, and would not typically involve female performers.[44] Hieronimo also acknowledges that Bel-Imperia's involvement is the direct result of her education, which must rival that of the 'gentlemen and scholars' for whom this university drama was originally written (4.1.98–103). Indeed, he emphasises the intellectual requirements of his plot, stating that 'because I know / That Bel-imperia hath practisèd the French, / In courtly French shall all her phrases be'. Bel-Imperia's response suggests that she too regards herself as an independent agent: she takes on the metatheatrical authority of the revenger, joking that 'You mean to try my cunning then, Hieronimo' (4.1.176-9). During the subsequent performance, she appropriates this power for real when she stabs Balthazar, becoming the author of his death in accordance with Revenge's prediction. The fact that she wielded the weapon herself is reiterated several times by the watching courtiers, while her independence is further illustrated by the alteration she makes to Hieronimo's script: he intended her to feign suicide, but she continues along her self-determined trajectory. As interpreted for Kyd's audience by Hieronimo, this decision owes nothing to performative confusion but is rather attributable to her learning; Bel-Imperia knew the precedent for this staged narrative well enough to edit the ending:

> For, though the story saith she should have died,
> Yet I of kindness and of care to her
> Did otherwise determine of her end;
> But love of him whom they did hate too much
> Did urge her resolution to be such. (4.4.141–5)

Hieronimo correctly identifies himself as the main 'author and actor in this tragedy', but Kyd's Bel-Imperia is both his ally and an independent agent who pursues her own objectives. Moreover, though her collaboration in and revision of the male protagonist's revenge scheme significantly exceeds the usual parameters of the female avenger's role, as she concludes a separate revenge action on Andrea's behalf, there is no indication that Kyd's drama condemns her unusually active contribution to the play's narrative of vengeance.

BLOODY LINES AND LETTERS: *THE REVENGE OF BUSSY D'AMBOIS*

In *The Spanish Tragedy*, Bel-Imperia's actions inspire the hesitant Hieronimo, and he credits her intervention to divine inspiration. While George Chapman's *The Revenge of Bussy D'Ambois* continues and extends Kyd's interest in the morality of revenge, however, the female revengers of this Jacobean drama are not as well received by their male counterparts. Of the play's three avenging women, Bussy's sister Charlotte and his former lover Tamyra are both rebuked by male relatives for the actions that they take to avenge him; the Countess, who moves quickly from threats of vengeance to tears after Bussy's brother Clermont is betrayed, suffers for being 'so passionate' (4.3.102) when she weeps her eyes to blindness.[45] The criticisms directed against Tamyra and Charlotte equally draw attention to their passionate behaviour; unlike Kyd's Bel-Imperia, who mourns Andrea and Horatio with restraint, Chapman's female revengers are associated with violent outbursts of grief and anger.[46] Charlotte and Tamyra's highly wrought behaviour is significantly at odds with the Stoic values endorsed by Chapman's protagonist, Clermont; they invoke mythological exemplars of vengeance while Clermont cites classical philosophers to advocate moderation.[47] One possibility is that Chapman, influenced like Kyd by Seneca, contrasts disordered passion with moral constancy in order to drive home his play's didactic message of 'excitation to virtue, and deflection from her contrary',[48] juxtaposing two rival modes of humanist argument in the process. Yet further investigation suggests that the distinction is not so straightforward. Geoffrey Miles points out that even in Seneca's drama, Stoicism is problematised since amoral characters such as Medea are often more constant than their virtuous counterparts, while Richard Ide (discussing

Clermont and Charlotte's Act 3 debate over the morality of revenge) argues that Chapman shows Clermont's Stoic perspective to be as 'partial, limited, and inadequate' as his sister Charlotte's opposing view; Ide concludes that, in *The Revenge of Bussy D'Ambois*, too rigid an adherence to Stoic principles becomes almost as undesirable as an excessively passionate response.[49]

The idea that neither Clermont nor his female counterparts offer an entirely positive model, but rather provoke Chapman's spectators and readers to moral reflection, is persuasive. Both post-Reformation Protestantism and Stoic philosophy promoted a tradition of rigorous self-examination,[50] and Joel Altman has shown that Chapman's prequel *Bussy D'Ambois* is itself structured in accordance with the humanist model of arguing *in utramque partem*; Altman considers that Chapman's drama adopts a 'neutral, interrogative stance'.[51] Thus Charlotte and Tamyra's interventions contribute significantly to Clermont's personal and narrative development, by prompting him to analyse his own actions and values. This argument may also explain why the play's female revengers differ in their methods. Whereas Kyd's Bel-Imperia combined clever plotting and violent action to pursue her vengeance, Chapman's Jacobean play goes further than Shakespeare's *Titus Andronicus* in distinguishing between discrete modes of female retribution: thus Tamyra collaborates with Clermont to script a joint revenge, but it is Charlotte who is most ready with a weapon.[52] Tamyra's contribution to the play's revenge action is especially noteworthy, although often undervalued by critics,[53] since her active contribution is framed and facilitated by her prior learning.

Tamyra, whose love affair with Bussy precipitated her husband Montsurry's violent revenge against the eponymous protagonist of Chapman's prequel, is quickly identified as an important ally in Clermont's quest to avenge his murdered brother (1.1.101–5). In comparison with Bel-Imperia, Tamyra assists her male proxy more than she leads the action; yet her role is not insignificant, since it is only with her cooperation that Clermont can pursue the 'noblest and most manly course' (1.1.90) of retribution against Montsurry. Tamyra's independent plans for vengeance predate her alliance with Clermont, and are informed by a longstanding tradition of female revenge: in her first appearance, she draws upon her classical knowledge to invoke a personified 'Revenge, that ever red sitt'st in the eyes / Of injur'd ladies' (1.2.1–10). Such learning also helps her to refute Montsurry's subsequent attack on her relationship with Bussy. Rather than being shamed by his accusations of 'witchlike' deeds (1.2.31), she counters eloquently, with reference to geometry (1.2.53–7), martial precedent (1.2.63–71) and a classical fable (1.2.79–88). Tamyra demonstrates much greater familiarity with these tenets of humanist education than her husband, and it may even be through her 'design' that Clermont is able to challenge Montsurry in the first place (1.2.106): certainly, as a literate woman, she is shown to actively support Clermont's delivery of a written challenge (1.2.139).

When Montsurry fails to accept Clermont's challenge, Tamyra is instrumental in forcing her husband into the duel that will kill him. Although she and Clermont's ally Renel apparently devise their plan in collaboration – Renel reports that 'The complot / Is now laid sure betwixt us' (4.5.85–6) – it is through Tamyra's letter that Clermont learns the details: her use of written communication is intriguing, since it underlines her authorial contribution to the scene that follows, and would be emphasised in performance by the physical delivery of the letter. Moreover, the fact that Tamyra arranges her husband's betrayal by letter highlights the mimetic nature of the play's revenge action. In *Bussy D'Ambois*, Montsurry tortured Tamyra into sending a message that led Bussy into an ambush, and so her letter writing now implicitly wrests textual control back from her husband in a motif of active, and literate, female reprisal.

The process whereby Tamyra metaphorically transforms her pen into a sword by arranging Clermont's duel with her husband acts as the preface to the play's final scene, in which she will literally wield a blade against Montsurry. When the latter initially refuses to fight despite the revengers' successful ambush, Clermont hands his duelling dagger to Tamyra:

> Revenge your wounds now, madam; I resign him
> Up to your full will, since he will not fight.
> First you shall torture him (as he did you,
> And justice wills) and then pay I my vow.
> Here, take this poniard. (5.5.49–53)

Tamyra, it seems, obliges, writing her revenge onto her husband's body until he hastily agrees to the duel.[54] Since Tamyra had previously written to Bussy in her own blood, the lines she now carves into Montsurry's flesh simultaneously reinforce the significance of writing, both in this play and as used by Shakespeare and Kyd's educated female revengers. While in one sense the female revenger is vilified, as Clermont encourages Tamyra to take retribution in a manner that he considers too ignoble to perform himself, Chapman's protagonist still explicitly defends Tamyra's actions to Montsurry (5.5.56–7). The threat of mimetic retribution may be more in line with his sister Charlotte's ambition to be 'equal' by revenging 'a villainy with villainy' (3.2.96–7), than with Clermont's commitment to the 'noblest and most manly course' (1.1.90), but it is only through introducing the threat of his sister's script that Clermont can pursue his preferred course of action: a course that in turn brings Montsurry the possibility of redemption, when at the end of the duel he repents for his treatment of Bussy and Tamyra (5.5.109–12).

Female revenge is certainly not an unquestioned positive in *The Revenge of Bussy D'Ambois*. Charlotte's attempts to enact violent retribution personally are condemned by numerous commentators, including her own brother, who advises her dismissively to 'Take other ladies' care; practice your face' (3.2.128). Even after she disguises herself as a man in the hope of taking Clermont's place in the duel, her annoyance at Clermont's failure to kill an unarmed man is problematic, while it is Clermont's final refusal to let her fight Montsurry in his stead that seems to inspire the latter's dying plea for forgiveness: as Bussy's Ghost demands, perhaps somewhat anxiously, it is Clermont who 'must author this just tragedy' (5.3.46) – even if Tamyra has scripted their encounter. Moreover, Tamyra's membership of a female community of revengers is inverted in the play's final moments, when she identifies herself unfavourably with the Furies: 'Hide, hide thy snaky head! To cloisters fly, / In penance pine! Too easy 'tis to die' (5.5.208–9). Nonetheless, as in *The Spanish Tragedy* and *Titus Andronicus*, the partnership between an educated female partner and the male avenger is crucial to the successful attainment of revenge for a murdered relative. Women's vengeance may be 'bloody' (4.2.36), but, even in Chapman's more cautious depiction, it is simultaneously associated with learning and the revenger's metatheatrical ability to script the action. Charlotte's ability to dispute the nature of revenge eloquently with her brother, challenging the Ghost's exclusively masculine and patriarchal definition,[55] may help Clermont to appreciate Tamyra's desire for vengeance; he, in turn, allies his honour code to the disturbing power of female fury by handing his poniard to Tamyra so that she may write in bloody lines on her husband's body. Montsurry, who began the play fearful that 'the Furies haunt me' (1.2.102), does indeed suffer at the hands of Revenge's female agents, as they collaborate in his downfall.

CONCLUSION: WOMEN WRITING REVENGE

Charlotte, Tamyra and Bel-Imperia are not the only female avengers to take up the sword in early modern tragedy: Lesel Dawson and Janet Clare have for instance demonstrated how Aspatia and Evadne script the revenge actions of Beaumont and Fletcher's *The Maid's Tragedy*, while Alison Findlay's essay in this collection explores the continued depiction of female-authored retribution in later seventeenth-century drama.[56] Yet *Titus Andronicus*, *The Spanish Tragedy* and *The Revenge of Bussy D'Ambois* illustrate particularly well an apparent association between female learning and active participation in vengeance. The connection between the educated status of these female characters and their aristocratic rank may be a factor in their ability to exert control over the actions of others,[57] within the hierarchically conscious world of early modern drama. At the same time, the narrative importance of classical precedents within Elizabethan and Jacobean revenge plays and the metatheatrical authority often attributed to the revenger suggest a deeper significance: when an educated woman wields the pen, such authoring power in turn facilitates her vengeance. Uniting the persuasive power of female eloquence with the literal penetration of the murdered male body, pen and sword together become 'women's weapons'. Thus, as an aptly named tract from the seventeenth-century women's pamphlet war put it, these female avengers take *Women's Sharp Revenge* on the male characters who have wronged them.

The extent to which the active pursuit of revenge by female characters within these plays is depicted positively remains a more challenging question, however. Lavinia learns to assert interpretative control over the Philomel narrative of Ovid's *Metamorphoses*, rivalling Aaron's authorial power and schooling her male relatives in the revenge script that they will follow, yet she acquires this ability at a terrible personal cost; after her father emerges from his study to appropriate Tamora's masque of a female Revenge to his own purposes, Lavinia returns to a supporting role, and is arguably cast again in the role of victim during the play's final scene. Similarly, in *The Revenge of Bussy D'Ambois*, Charlotte's words eventually influence her brother Clermont's understanding of revenge and prompt him to give Tamyra an authoring role in his vengeance against Montsurry, but the Stoic moral code that informs Chapman's play qualifies the power that Tamyra acquires by bringing the honour of her actions into question. If Clermont's alliance with Tamyra suggests that Chapman's drama attempts to partially reconcile Stoic values with an honour code based on passionate emotion, the play nonetheless ends in gendered fragmentation: the masque establishes a closed male circle of victims and murderers, while the women withdraw to a convent to mourn.[58] Kyd's Bel-Imperia is, conversely, able to appropriate Hieronimo's masque design to her own ends, after she becomes his acknowledged partner in the revenge action of *The Spanish Tragedy* and an avenger in her own right. Her initial involvement and eventual success are, however, dependent upon physical sacrifice, as she first writes a letter to Hieronimo in her own blood and then revises the masque's ending through an act of suicide. Thus, while classical learning and the ability to read, write and dispute successfully enable educated female avengers to play an active role in *Titus Andronicus*, *The Revenge of Bussy D'Ambois* and *The Spanish Tragedy*, wielding authorial power and even physical weapons in their own right, such agency still requires a continuous, often competitive, process of negotiation in order to accommodate the revenge agendas of these female avengers to those of their male relatives and allies. It is perhaps unsurprising that the collaboration between Hieronimo and Bel-Imperia comes closest to an equal partnership, since their prior relationship is furthest removed from the controlling structure of the patriarchal family – yet, in all three plays, the active involvement of women in the dramatic revenge action remains inseparable from physical suffering, bodily weakness and personal sacrifice. A humanist education might present the female avengers of early modern drama with an opportunity to actively perform vengeance, but any authorial revisions to the play's revenge narrative must be written in their own blood.

NOTES

1. William Shakespeare, *Hamlet*, ed. Ann Thompson and Neil Taylor (London: Arden Shakespeare, 2006), 1.5.107.
2. See for example Mark Thornton Burnett, 'Staging the Malcontent in Early Modern England', in Arthur F. Kinney (ed.), *Companion to Renaissance Drama* (Oxford and Malden, MA: Blackwell Publishers,

2002), pp. 336–52; Frank Whigham, 'Sexual and Social Mobility in *The Duchess of Malfi*', *PMLA* 100 (1985), pp. 167–86; Larry S. Champion, '*The Malcontent* and the Shape of Elizabethan-Jacobean Comedy', *Studies in English Literature, 1500–1900* 25.2 (1985), pp. 361–79.

3. Cathy Shrank discussed such concerns in her Tucker-Cruse Lecture, 'Rewriting Robert the Devil: Thomas Lodge and Medieval Romance', delivered at the University of Bristol, May 2013; I am grateful to her for sharing the script of this lecture with me. See also Burnett, 'Staging the Malcontent', pp. 336–52.
4. John Kerrigan, *Revenge Tragedy: Aeschylus to Armageddon* (Oxford: Clarendon, 1996), p. 18.
5. See Gordon Braden, *Renaissance Tragedy and the Senecan Tradition: Anger's Privilege* (New Haven: Yale University Press, 1985); Jessica Winston, 'Seneca in Early Elizabethan England', *Renaissance Quarterly* 59 (2006), pp. 29–59; Tanya Pollard, 'What's Hecuba to Shakespeare?', in this collection; also Katherine Heavey, *The Early Modern Medea: Medea in English Literature, 1558–1688* (Houndsmills: Palgrave MacMillan, 2015), pp. 84–113.
6. The extent to which the traditional revenge narrative marginalises women, who appear as either idealised figures of chastity or 'vulnerable vessels', is discussed by Edward Muir in *Mad Blood Stirring: Vendetta & Factions in Friuli during the Renaissance* (Baltimore and London: Johns Hopkins University Press, 1993), esp. p. xxviii; see also Deborah Willis, '"The Gnawing Vulture": Revenge, Trauma Theory, and *Titus Andronicus*', *Shakespeare Quarterly* 53 (2002), pp. 21–52 (p. 24).
7. Juliet Dusinberre, *Shakespeare and the Nature of Women*, 3rd edition (Basingstoke and New York: Palgrave Macmillan, 2003), p. 2; Lisa Jardine, *Reading Shakespeare Historically* (London and New York: Routledge, 1996), p. 50.
8. Jardine, *Reading Shakespeare Historically*, p. 7; Sara Eaton, 'A Woman of Letters: Lavinia in *Titus Andronicus*', in Shirley Nelson Garner and Madelon Sprengnether (eds) *Shakespearean Tragedy and Gender* (Bloomington: Indiana University Press, 1996), pp. 54–74 (p. 62).
9. Heavey, *Early Modern Medea*, pp. 18, 84–118; Thomas Nashe, *Pierce Penilesse his supplication to the diuell* (London: printed by Abell Jeffes, for J. B[usby], 1592), G1r; Christopher Fetherstone, *A dialogue agaynst light, lewde, and lasciuious daucing* (London: Thomas Dawson, 1582), C8v.
10. Ester Sowernam [pseud.], *Ester hath hang'd Haman* (London: printed [by Thomas Snodham] for Nicholas Bourne, 1617), C2r, E4v; Joseph Swetnam, *Arraignment of Lewd, Idle, Froward, and Unconstant Women* (London: Printed by George Purslowe, 1615).
11. Constantia Munda [pseud.], *The worming of a mad dogge* (London: printed [by George Purslowe] for Laurence Hayes, 1617), C4r–C4v.
12. Ibid. B3r.

13. Marguerite A. Tassi, *Women and Revenge in Shakespeare: Gender, Genre, and Ethics* (Selinsgrove: Susquehanna University Press, 2011), p. 117; Alessandra Abbattista, 'The Vengeful Lioness', in this collection.
14. Sir Francis Bacon, 'Of Revenge', in Brian Vickers (ed.), *The Major Works*, Oxford World's Classics (Oxford: Oxford University Press, 1996), p. 348; Janet Clare (ed.) *Four Revenge Tragedies* (London: Methuen Drama, 2014), pp. xviii–xix; Janet Clare, '"She's Turned Fury": Women Transmogrified in Revenge Plays', in this collection, p. 227.
15. Alison Findlay, *A Feminist Perspective on Renaissance Drama* (Oxford: Blackwell Publishers, 1998), p. 50. See also Willis, 'Gnawing Vulture', pp. 22–4.
16. Sowernam, *Ester hath hang'd Haman*, C2r, E4v.
17. Rachel Speght, *A Mouzell for Melastomus* (London: printed by Nicholas Okes for Thomas Archer, 1616), F1r.
18. Munda, *The worming of a mad dogge*, A4r.
19. Sowernam, *Ester hath hang'd Haman*, B1r; Eileen Allman, *Jacobean Revenge Tragedy and the Politics of Virtue* (London: Associated University Presses, 1999), p. 18.
20. Sowernam, *Ester hath hang'd Haman*, D1r-D1v, E2r; Munda, *The worming of a mad dogge*, B4r, D1v; Rachel Speght, *A Mouzell for Melastomus* (London: Printed by Nicholas Okes, 1616), B3v.
21. Cited by Dusinberre, *Shakespeare and the Nature of Women*, p. 242.
22. Ovid, *XV Bookes Entytuled Metamorphosis* (1567), trans. Arthur Golding (Amsterdam: Theatrum Orbis Terrarum, 1977), 7.503; Euripides, *Hecuba*, in James Morwood (ed.), *The Trojan Woman and Other Plays* (Oxford: Oxford University Press, 2001).
23. Tassi, *Women and Revenge*, p. 23, has demonstrated that female authorship and revenge converge in the drama of Shakespeare and his contemporaries more often than many critics have recognised, arguing that avenging women become amateur dramatists in plays such as *The Merry Wives of Windsor* and *Twelfth Night*. See also Alison Findlay, 'Re-marking Revenge', in this collection, esp. p. 60.
24. Willis, 'Gnawing Vulture', p. 22; Jardine, *Reading Shakespeare Historically*, p. 186.
25. William Shakespeare, *Titus Andronicus*, ed. Sonia Massai (London: Penguin, 2005).
26. See Bethany Packard, 'Lavinia as Coauthor of Shakespeare's *Titus Andronicus*', *Studies in English Literature, 1500–1900*, 50.2 (2010), pp. 281–300 (pp. 286–7).
27. T. W. Baldwin, *William Shakspere's Small Latine & Lesse Greeke*, 2 vols (Urbana: University of Illinois Press, 1944), vol. 2, p. 418.
28. Willis, 'Gnawing Vulture', p. 39.
29. Coppélia Kahn, *Roman Shakespeare: Warriors, Wounds, and Women* (London: Routledge, 1997), p. 69; Liberty Stanavage, '"Welcome, Dread Fury, to my Woeful House": The Female Revenger as Masculine Escape

Fantasy in *Titus Andronicus* and *The Spanish Tragedy*', paper presented at Revenge and Gender conference, University of Bristol, 6 September 2012; Heather James, *Shakespeare's Troy: Drama, Politics, and the Translation of Empire* (Cambridge: Cambridge University Press, 1997), p. 73.
30. James, *Shakespeare's Troy*, pp. 63–8, identifies the attack on Lavinia as an assault on the textual legacy of Virgil's *Aeneid*. Crucially, however, it is the ignorant Goth brothers (who later misinterpret a Horatian ode [4.2.19–28]) who engage with an incomplete version of Rome's literary heritage. While Shrank rightly notes that Aaron's lesson is suggestive of early modern concerns about the failure of education, or literature, to guarantee its moral efficaciousness, Chiron and Demetrius' partial knowledge of their source suggests that the fault lies in their reading practices.
31. James, *Shakespeare's Troy*, pp. 77–8; Kahn, *Roman Shakespeare*, pp. 61–2.
32. See James, *Shakespeare's Troy*, p. 77; Packard, 'Lavinia as Coauthor', pp. 282, 292.
33. Jardine, *Reading Shakespeare Historically*, p. 52.
34. Kahn, *Roman Shakespeare*, pp. 61–2; Mary Laughlin Fawcett, 'Arms/Words/Tears: Language and the Body in *Titus Andronicus*', *English Literary History* 50 (1983), p. 269.
35. Eaton, 'Woman of Letters', p. 57.
36. Packard, 'Lavinia as Coauthor', p. 293.
37. Caroline Bicks, 'Incited Minds: Rethinking Early Modern Girls', *Shakespeare Studies* 44 (2016), pp. 180–202, explores how various early modern authors depicted acts of joint artistic creation by father and daughter, sometimes crediting the latter's inventive powers after the classical model of Dibutades and his daughter. I am grateful to her for sharing the manuscript of this article.
38. Willis, 'Gnawing Vulture', p. 48. Katherine Rowe 'Dismembering and Forgetting in *Titus Andronicus*', *Shakespeare Quarterly* 45 (1995), pp. 279–303, also argues that Lavinia, by receiving her persecutors' blood, transforms herself from 'a figure of dismemberment into a figure of agency' (p. 300). Cf. Findlay, *Feminist Perspective*, p. 65.
39. See James, *Shakespeare's Troy*, pp. 78–9. In recent productions of the play, the depiction of Lavinia's response to Titus' words has varied substantially, although live performance provides the opportunity to offer an interpretation of her complicity with or resistance to her father's act.
40. Thomas Kyd, *The Spanish Tragedy*, ed. David Bevington (Manchester and New York: Manchester University Press, 1996).
41. Tassi, *Women and Revenge*, p. 145. Edith Hall's finding that the Erinyes, or female Furies, are often shown sleeping in ancient Greek iconography may support this identification, since Kyd's play draws attention to Revenge's sleepiness (3.15). See Hall, 'Why are the Erinyes Female?', p. 49.
42. Findlay, *Feminist Perspective*, p. 57.
43. Allman, *Jacobean Revenge Tragedy*, p. 19.

44. Clare, *Four Revenge Tragedies*, p. xix.
45. George Chapman, *The Revenge of Bussy D'Ambois*, in Katherine Eisaman Maus (ed.), *Four Revenge Tragedies* (Oxford and New York: Oxford University Press, 1995), pp. 175–248.
46. For a full account of how female mourning is represented by early modern authors, see Lesel Dawson, *Lovesickness and Gender in Early Modern English Literature* (Oxford: Oxford University Press, 2008), esp. pp. 92–127.
47. See for example Fred M. Fetrow, 'Chapman's Stoic Hero in *The Revenge of Bussy D'Ambois*', *Studies in English Literature, 1500–1900* 19.2 (1979), pp. 229–37.
48. George Chapman, 'To the right virtuous and truly noble knight, Sir Thomas Howard', in Katherine Eisaman Maus (ed.), *Four Revenge Tragedies* (Oxford and New York: Oxford University Press, 1995), p. 176.
49. Geoffrey Miles, *Shakespeare and the Constant Romans* (Oxford: Clarendon Press, 1996), pp. 58–62; Richard S. Ide, 'Exploiting the Tradition: The Elizabethan Revenger as Chapman's "Complete Man"', *Medieval & Renaissance Drama in England* 1 (1984), pp. 159–72 (p. 165).
50. See for example Book 3 of Marcus Aurelius' *Meditations*, ed. and trans. C. R. Haines (Cambridge, MA: Harvard University Press, 2014), pp. 44–65.
51. Joel B. Altman, *The Tudor Play of Mind: Rhetorical Inquiry and the Development of Elizabethan Drama* (Berkeley and London: University of California Press, 1978), p. 305.
52. Findlay, *Feminist Perspective*, p. 68, characterises Charlotte as 'vengeance personified'.
53. Maus, *Four Revenge Tragedies*, p. xxvi, for instance, suggests that 'women become virtually irrelevant' in this play, describing Tamyra's contribution as 'peripheral'.
54. Maus' edition does not provide a stage direction for this action, but Clermont's imperatives and Montsurry's subsequent exclamation suggest a performance signal for the actors in accordance with standard early modern practice.
55. Findlay, *Feminist Perspective*, p. 70.
56. Dawson, *Lovesickness and Gender*, pp. 91–126; Janet Clare, 'She's Turned Fury', pp. 00; Alison Findlay, 'Re-marking Revenge'.
57. Cf. Dawson, *Lovesickness and Gender*, pp. 96–7.
58. Findlay, *Feminist Perspective*, p. 72.

PART IV

WOMEN TRANSMOGRIFIED

CHAPTER 10

The Vengeful Lioness in Greek Tragedy: A Posthumanist Perspective[1]

Alessandra Abbattista

The characterisation of female avengers in ancient Greek tragedy has received a substantial amount of attention in classical scholarship. However, a consensus has not been reached on how the fifth-century Athenian audience would have reacted to the tragic representation of female acts of vengeance. Whilst Burnett has hypothesised that revenge in tragic plays would have been perceived as unproblematic, because 'among early Greeks revenge was not a problem, but a solution',[2] others have argued that it would have recalled archaic tyranny rather than classical democracy, and therefore would have been viewed negatively.[3] The question remains unsolved mainly due to the complicated way in which tragic heroines are gendered in revenge plots. Depicted committing vengeance within and against their own family, female characters do not play the natural and social role that the democratic polis would have expected. Their transgressive behaviour has been generally interpreted as either an inversion[4] or a perversion[5] of gender roles in tragic characterisation, typical of and suitable for the festival of Dionysus at which the tragedies were originally performed. Given that the ritual context of dramatic festivals encouraged the representation of female acts of vengeance, it is necessary to clarify how and why this could trigger a tragic effect on the ancient audience.

I propose a new methodological approach to the reading and interpretation of the contradictory gendered identity of female avengers in ancient Greek tragedy. Through the application of a posthumanist perspective as suggested by Braidotti,[6] I explore the dramatic significance of lioness imagery in the depiction of tragic heroines who are empowered in intra-familial vengeful conflicts. My textual analysis of the specific tragic passages from the *Agamemnon* and the *Medea* where the lioness metaphorically occurs reveals the human contradictions of the agency of the two most transgressive female avengers performing on the Attic stage. When the Aeschylean Clytemnestra and the Euripidean Medea are compared to vengeful lionesses, they are attributed what Braidotti calls the 'protean quality' of being 'complicitous with genocides and crimes on the one hand, and supportive of enormous hopes and aspiration to freedom on the other'.[7] Building on this idea, I demonstrate that the metamorphic identity of the tragic heroines could provoke an effect of pathos on the ancient audience. Their tragic humanity consists in embodying the transformative change that fifth-century Athens undertook to develop its democracy. This change was celebrated at the festival of Dionysus through plays depicting the self-destruction of the household[8] as announced by the image of the lioness in the tragic depiction of female avengers.

THE VENGEFUL AGENCY OF THE TRAGIC LIONESS

I start exploring the dramatic significance of lioness imagery in the characterisation of female avengers by looking at linguistic and gendered considerations. The term λέαινα, which indicates the 'lioness' in ancient Greek, is a derivative noun. Just as in the formation of other feminine nouns, the suffix -αινα is added to the masculine noun λέων, 'lion'. However, judging by extant ancient Greek literary texts, it seems that the term λέαινα was introduced only in the fifth century BC.[9] Whereas in the Homeric tradition the lion, which is denoted by the term λέων and its epic form λίς, is metaphorically employed in comparison with both male and female characters, on the Attic stage it is linguistically distinguished from the lioness. In extant ancient Greek tragedies, the masculine noun λέων is mainly related to male characters,[10] but it is also used in the description of real lions and mythological monsters, such as the Nemaean lion, and the god Dionysus.[11] Despite the masculine form, the goddess Cybele and the Erinyes are also associated with the lion figure. When it comes to the feminine noun λέαινα, it is always used of female characters,[12] but it is also evoked in the description of a hunting scene, mythological monsters, such as the Chimaera, and the divine metamorphoses of Callisto and Merops, and Io.[13] In addition, the cub of the lion and the lioness is defined with the masculine noun σκύμνος in both the Homeric and tragic traditions. Other tragic references consist of the feminine noun δρόσος, which literally means 'dew', but metaphorically indicates the 'young of animals', and the masculine/feminine noun ἶνις, 'son, daughter', plus the genitive form of the lion and/or the lioness. The term σκύμνος, like the other expressions indicating the lion cub, is used to refer to both male and female characters.[14]

The tragic introduction of the term λέαινα is significant, when considering the Dionysiac empowerment of female characters in intra-family vengeful conflicts.[15] However, the majority of classical scholars have overlooked the gendered distinctions within the lion family in ancient Greek tragedy. Extensive work has been undertaken on the lion similes in Homer, specifically on male characterisation.[16] Among the few scholars who have noticed the absence of the lioness in the Homeric tradition,[17] Foley discusses the case of Penelope, who is compared to a male lion, after realising the murderous intentions of the suitors against her son Telemachus (Hom. *Od.* 4.791).[18] In Foley's words, this is a 'reverse simile', since it implies a metaphorical inversion of gender roles between Penelope and Odysseus. In the absence of her husband, Penelope becomes a strong and resolute woman, despite her bewildered and helpless position. As the result of a gender reversal, she defends her household against the attack of her suitors through the feminine art of weaving. Other studies have focused on the use of the lion image in the depiction of tragic heroes, such as Aegisthus and Paris.[19] Through comparison with the Homeric tradition, Wolff interprets the image of the paired lions in connection to Neoptolemus and Philoctetes (Soph. *Phil.* 1436).[20] He argues that whereas in Homer the lion represents the courage, power, strength and violence of the heroes, it is mainly associated with vengeance in ancient Greek tragedy. He does not deny the vengeful nature of the lion in Homer, but he points out that it is a symbol of inhumanity rather than of heroism in tragic characterisation. In contrast, Sommerstein, commenting on the lion image in the representation of the Erinyes (Aesch. *Eum.* 193), argues that the lion is 'an ambivalent symbol throughout the trilogy, as a beast of nobility and fierce power, on the one hand, and as a murderous creature revelling in blood-shed, on the other'.[21] This reading explains the similarities between the Homeric and the tragic use of the lion metaphor. In the same way as Achilles is compared to a vengeful lion when he kills Hector and mutilates his body (Hom. *Il.* 24.41), tragic heroes are represented as powerful and violent lions in committing acts of vengeance.

Given the association of the Homeric and tragic lion with vengeance, I turn now to the metaphorical employment of the lioness in the depiction of female avengers. Previous classical scholars have tended to read the tragic image of the lioness in terms of an opposition between the animal and the human worlds. The lioness has been interpreted, for example, as 'the emblem of a savage woman',[22] 'the expression of non-humanity'[23] and the reflection of 'perverted motherhood'.[24] Through comparison with the epic tradition, Konstantinou identifies the bestial, wild and aggressive connotations of the lioness in ancient Greek tragedy.[25] In order to interpret the tragic image of the lioness and reconstruct its development, she defines the gendered identity of the Homeric lion. As she explains, in Homeric similes the lion shows its masculinity through 'strength, agility, swiftness of attack and persistence'.[26] However, it can also assume a more vulnerable and protective role, like a lion(ess) in defence of its cubs. For example, Menelaus is compared to the lion, because of his mourning role on the battlefield (Hom. *Il.* 17.109). Split between suffering and anger for the loss of Patroclus, he urges Ajax to fight against the Trojans. Like a lion(ess) that defends its cubs from the attack of the hunters, Ajax protects the corpse of his companion with his shield (Hom. *Il.* 17.132–7). Another similar image is the description of Achilles mourning the death of Patroclus (Hom. *Il.* 18.316–22). The bereaved hero raises a γόος, 'lament', to express his grief, just like a lion realising that its cubs have been captured (Hom. *Il.* 18.318–19). As Konstantinou comments on this Homeric image, 'the lion goes in search of its lost children, with a feeling of anguish mixed with anger, growing to potential ferocity out of the failure to be protective'.[27] From her perspective, the female traits of the Homeric lion are emphasised in the tragic image of the lioness to express the savagery of emotions and the transgressive behaviour of female avengers. Whereas the lion assumes 'positive connotations' in comparison with Homeric heroes, the lioness acquires a 'negative tone' in the characterisation of tragic heroines like Clytemnestra and Medea.[28]

I agree with Konstantinou on several points: first, there is a strong literary connection between the Homeric lion and the tragic lioness; second, the Homeric lion is attributed both male and female traits on the battlefield; third, the tragic lioness is employed to empower female characters in revenge plots. However, the relationship between the Homeric lion and the tragic lioness should not be read in terms of opposition. Attic dramatists do not compare tragic heroines like Clytemnestra and Medea with the lioness simply to denounce 'the inappropriateness of power', as Konstantinou argues.[29] Through the application of a posthumanist perspective, I argue that adapted from the Homeric tradition the lioness–woman metaphor expresses the tragic humanity of these acts of vengeance. As I explain in the next section, the theory of the posthuman postulated by Braidotti leads towards an empathic understanding of the metaphorical employment of lioness imagery in the depiction of female avengers. By merging both the male and female traits of the Homeric lion in the image of the vengeful lioness, Aeschylus and Euripides could provoke an effect of pathos for their audience. Through the combination of power, strength and violence, on the one hand, and protection, danger and bereavement, on the other, they stage the Dionysiac self-destruction of the household. The difference from the epic use of the lion image consists in fact in the reasons and implications of the vengeful agency of the tragic lioness. Female vengeance is not committed against the enemies of the lion family to preserve power and defend the cubs. It is caused by intra-familial tensions and brings about loss and suffering. By relocating vengeance from the battlefield to the household, Attic dramatists metaphorically transform female characters into tragic lionesses.

THE METAPHORICAL METAMORPHOSES OF FEMALE AVENGERS

My reading and interpretation of lioness imagery in the tragic depiction of female avengers is informed and influenced by the theory of the posthuman postulated by Braidotti. By combining poststructuralism, postfeminism and animal studies, her theory explains and justifies the metaphorical comparison of tragic heroines with the vengeful lioness. The posthuman condition 'introduces a qualitative shift in our thinking about what exactly is the basic unit of common reference for our species', as Braidotti states.[30] In contrast to humanist and anthropocentric views, she does not equate humanity with consciousness and rationality. Instead she takes into account the interaction with the non-human world to define the complex nature of human identity. The traditional human divisions between nature and culture, animality and humanity, masculinity and femininity, mind and body, organic and technology, self and other blur in the posthumanist worldview. Therefore, Braidotti rejects the traditional definition of difference, through which Humanism has constantly justified the supremacy and centrality of man in the world. By embracing a non-dualistic understanding of human identity, she advocates the possibility of decentring wo/man and rethinking his/her relationship with the non-human. From her perspective, being human should not spell the inferiority of animals and women as 'naturalised and sexualised others', but rather give expression to these multiple voices which 'remerge with vengeance' in postmodernity.[31]

Posthumanism sheds fresh light on the contradictory identity of tragic women who are metaphorically transformed into vengeful lionesses. Through the rejection of a dichotomic structure of the world, Braidotti looks at the human in its transformative nature. She asserts that human identity cannot be seen in its unity and fixity, because of its transitional tendency to move from one place to another. It is through a metamorphosis that the wo/man can be decentred and seen in her/his active, dynamic and composite nature. In Braidotti's words, metamorphosis is a 'form of figuration that expresses the hybrid nature we are in the process of becoming'.[32] Among the possibilities of metamorphosis, she specifically analyses the process of 'becoming-animal'. In this posthuman condition, the human and the animal worlds are not in a hierarchical opposition. Posthumanism implies a world of '*zoe*-centred egalitarianism', where animals and wo/men share a common ground.[33] The posthuman condition is marked by the return of the non-human, which generates a materialist and immanent transformation. From her perspective, it is the process of becoming-animal that exposes the 'shared ties of vulnerability' and produces 'new forms of posthuman community and compassion'.[34] Therefore, Braidotti argues that an empathic turn is necessary to reconsider the relationship between the human and the animal world, to identify emotions, and not reason, as the expression of humanity, and to read violence as an evolutionary tool.

The theory of the posthuman postulated by Braidotti is valuable for, and applicable to, my dramatic analysis of the lioness–woman metaphor in revenge plots. Although there are other possibilities for analysis,[35] I have chosen to focus on the metaphorical employment of the lioness in comparison with the Aeschylean Clytemnestra and the Euripidean Medea because of their controversial vengeful identity. By framing my study in relation to the posthumanist discourse of Braidotti, I restructure the dichotomies of humanity and animality, masculinity and femininity, hunting and childbirth that blur in their tragic characterisation. As I show in the following textual analysis, these dichotomies are mediated by the image of the lioness to capture the tragic heroines in the dramaturgical passage from suffering to vengeance. In what I define as the 'metaphorical metamorphoses' of female avengers, the lioness image expresses the emotional contradictions of their tragic empowerment. Split between grief and anger, the tragic heroines enact an astonishing transformation into vengeful lionesses turning against the members of their own family. Through the reconstruction of the metaphorical metamorphoses of Clytemnestra and Medea, I demonstrate that the vengeful agency of the tragic lioness could trigger an effect of pathos in the theatre of Dionysus. In response to the injuries suffered, the tragic heroines become powerful, dangerous and violent lionesses, but the result of their vengeance is nothing but the destruction of the lion's house.

The Aeschylean Clytemnestra

Clytemnestra enacts a metaphorical metamorphosis into a vengeful lioness in the *Agamemnon*. Unlike in the epic tradition (Hom. *Od.* 11.385–434), she is represented as responsible not only for planning, but also for committing vengeance against her husband. The negative implications of the violent subversion of male power in her tragic depiction have been widely discussed in classical scholarship. Within the play, Clytemnestra is specifically defined ἀνδρόβουλος, 'man-minded' (Aesch. *Ag.* 11) by the Watcher, and as ἄρσενος φονεύς, 'man-slayer' (1231) by Cassandra. With particular reference to her masculine connotations, Winnington-Ingram states that the vengeful act committed by Clytemnestra brings about the destruction of Agamemnon because she is jealous of him as a ruling man.[36] Goldhill also offers a negative reading of the vengeful role of Clytemnestra, commenting upon her man-like behaviour as a 'monstrous reversal of the female role'.[37] Despite her masculine connections, Clytemnestra has been recently rehabilitated as a mother and her vengeance read as a female reaction to patriarchal oppression and violence. As Hall says, she 'dominates the Aeschylean play named after her husband', not only as 'a murderer, an androgyne, a liar, an orator, and executor of a palace coup', but also as 'an avenging mother'.[38] McHardy identifies multiple reasons behind the decision of Clytemnestra to kill Agamemnon. She argues that although Clytemnestra manifestly declares herself to have taken vengeance for the sacrifice of Iphigenia, she does so to hide her intention of gaining political and economic power in Argos. Whereas in the Homeric tradition she is depicted as an unfaithful wife led astray by Aegisthus, on the Attic stage she becomes a powerful leader and instigator of vengeance.[39]

I apply the posthumanist perspective as suggested by Braidotti to go beyond either positive or negative, male or female interpretations of Clytemnestra's vengeful identity. Through the reconstruction of her metaphorical metamorphosis into a lioness, I show the human contradictions of her active avenging role in the *Agamemnon*. Aeschylus merges both the masculine and the feminine traits of the Homeric lion in order to empower Clytemnestra to commit vengeance within and against her own household. Reflecting her metamorphic nature, the vengeful lioness signals the dramaturgical passage from the sacrifice of Iphigenia to the death of Agamemnon. All the members of Clytemnestra's family, namely Iphigenia (141), Orestes (717), Agamemnon (141, 827, 1259) and Aegisthus (1224), are compared to tragic lions. According to Thomson, the lion, which is common on Lydian coins and still extant on the ancient gates of Mycenae, was probably the emblem of the dynasty of Pelops.[40] Knox adds that it is through the lion metaphor that Aeschylus connects royal blood and the vengeful temper of the descendants of Pelops in his tragedy.[41] I argue that the *Agamemnon* evokes all the members of the lion family to unfold the tragic action towards Clytemnestra's vengeance. By actively involving the lioness in the conflicts of the House of Atreus, Aeschylus stages the tragic death of the lion. With these words, the chorus of the Argive men remind the audience of the vengeful conflict between Clytemnestra and Agamemnon in the *parodos* (140–4): 'So kindly is the goddess / to the helpless young of ravening lions, / and delightful to the suckling young / of all the hunting beasts of the wild; / she asks that these omens will be fulfilled.' In their celebration of the Greek expedition to Troy, the chorus define Iphigenia, the sacrificial victim of Artemis, as the cub of μαλερῶν λεόντων, 'ravening lions' (141). The Atreides had committed an impious act by hunting a mother hare with young in the womb. Despite Zeus' plan, Artemis, the goddess of childbirth and the patron of the hunters, interfered in the departure of the Greeks and demanded compensation. Because of the abortive attempts to sail to Troy, Agamemnon was therefore constrained to kill his daughter Iphigenia.[42] The adjective μαλερός, ά, όν, 'ravening', in reference to the lions, not only denounces the violent act committed by Agamemnon, but it also anticipates the vengeance of Clytemnestra. The term, which is used in Homer as an epithet of fire,[43] assumes the emotional connotation of 'terrible, violent, fierce' in ancient Greek tragedy. By invoking the healing god Apollo, brother of Artemis, the chorus enter on stage to sing the original cause of Clytemnestra's vengeance. It is the death of Iphigenia by Agamemnon's hands that has caused her μῆνις, 'wrath' (155). The term, which can generally indicate the wrath of the gods,[44] of the dead worshipped as heroes[45] and of suppliants,[46] and specifically opens the epic on the wrath of Achilles,[47] is used here of injured parents. Connoted with the adjective τεκνόποινος, 'child-avenging' (155), it emphasises the tragic bond between Agamemnon and Clytemnestra. Iphigenia is the female cub that was killed by the former and will be avenged by the latter. As the daughter of the violent male and female lions, she represents one of the causes of the intra-familial conflicts in the House of Atreus.

By creating a confusion between the human hunter and the hunted animal,[48] Aeschylus forecasts the tragic realisation of Clytemnestra's vengeance. In the fourth episode, Cassandra evokes the ἄρκυς, 'the hunting's net' (1116) of Hades through which Clytemnestra will kill her husband. With this metaphorical image, she provides the audience with the first hint of the avenging nature of the tragic lioness. Attributed the strength, power and violence of the Homeric lion, Clytemnestra deceitfully captures and slaughters her prey. When she refuses to take responsibility for the murder of Agamemnon, the chorus say: 'who hunts is caught, who kills pays' (1562). Displayed by the lion metaphor, the aspect of treachery in Clytemnestra's vengeance is connected to the hunting skills of Agamemnon during the Trojan War. In the third episode, the king arrives on the chariot, followed by his concubine Cassandra, to the palace of Argos. With these words, he describes the most treacherous act of the Greeks to destroy Troy (821–8):

> For this to the gods very mindful thanks should
> be paid, since an arrogant seizure
> we punished and it was for a woman that
> Troy was utterly destroyed by the Argives' beast,
> the offspring of the horse, an army of shield-bearers,
> launching their bound at the Pleiades' sunset.
> By assaulting the tower, the ravening lion
> licked up its fill of royal blood.

In his speech, Agamemnon evokes the image of the ὠμηστὴς λέων, 'ravening lion' (827) to boast the superiority of the Greeks on the battlefield. The adjectival noun ὠμηστής, which literally means 'eating raw flesh' in reference to animals,[49] metaphorically conveys the concepts of savagery and brutality. In this passage, it refers to the treachery, violence and impiety of Agamemnon against the Trojans. The metaphorical reference to the savage lion specifically depicts the Greek army sacking Troy at the end of the war. To capture this triumphant moment, Aeschylus describes the jumping of the Greek soldiers from the stomach–uterus of the Trojan Horse. Thanking the gods, Agamemnon justifies the leonine attack of the Greeks on Troy. In reaction to the ἁρπαγή, 'seizure' (822) of Helen, the Greeks took vengeance against Paris by assaulting Troy. This metaphorical image intensifies the link between the hunting skills of Agamemnon during the Trojan War and the vengeful plan of Clytemnestra. By weaving a terrible net in the house of the lion, Clytemnestra assumes the strength, power and violence of her husband. Unlike Penelope, who becomes a lion to defend her house from the suitors, Clytemnestra captures the lion with the net and directly attacks him with the sword.

Aeschylus involves another member of the lion family to disclose the vengeful identity of the murderer of Agamemnon. Because of his passive role in Clytemnestra's plan of vengeance, Aegisthus is compared by Cassandra to an ἄναλκις λέων, 'cowardly lion' (1224). The adjective ἄναλκις not only contradicts the epic description of the lion equipped with strength, violence and power, but also confirms the vengeful agency of the tragic lioness. Taking advantage of the absence of Agamemnon, Aegisthus does nothing but roam in the marriage-bed of the λέων εὐγενής, 'noble lion' (1259).[50] This metaphorical comparison reveals the gendered identity of the actual ῥαφεύς, 'stitcher' (1604) of Agamemnon's murder. However, the chorus have not grasped the hints suggested by Cassandra in tracking the moves of the female avenger. Despite the consistency of her prophecy, they do not even suspect that the misdeed will be committed by a woman. In fact, they ask Cassandra to reveal τίνος πρὸς ἀνδρός, 'by which man' (1251) the destruction of the house will be caused. With these words, Cassandra anticipates her own death and that of Agamemnon (1258–63):

This two-footed lioness, bedding
the wolf in the absence of the noble lion,
will kill me, miserable that I am; as if preparing a drug,
she will mix in her wrath my requital;
she vows, after sharpening her sword against her husband,
to take murderous vengeance for bringing me here.

Aeschylus involves the lioness actively in the conflict between the lion and the wolf,[51] with the aim of revealing the complexity of Clytemnestra's vengeance. She is compared to a lioness by Cassandra in the light of her marital relationship with the powerful, noble and strong lion Agamemnon. Because of her sexual intercourse with the wolf Aegisthus, Clytemnestra is also depicted as a treacherous, impious and adulterous wife. In addition to her political and erotic desires, she shows her κότος, 'wrath' (1261)[52] as the protective mother of the female cub Iphigenia. The noun, which can generally mean 'grudge, rancour, ill-will',[53] is frequent in the Aeschylean *lexis* to define the divine demand for vengeance.[54] In this passage, the term refers to the vengeful response of Clytemnestra to the homecoming of Agamemnon. She prepares a lethal potion, where she blends her anger for the sacrifice of her daughter with her jealousy for the arrival of the concubine of her husband. By dislocating vengeance from the Trojan War to the House of Atreus, Aeschylus empowers Clytemnestra to stage the death of Agamemnon.

The triumphant position of the lioness in Cassandra's prophecy signals the imminent accomplishment of the vengeful act of Clytemnestra. According to Fraenkel, the expression δίπους λέαινα, 'the two-footed lioness' (1258), can be read as a poetic device used in riddles and oracles.[55] Konstantinou argues that the position of Clytemnestra has a connection with the ancient Greek iconographic representation of the lion in 'the moment of overpowering another animal, usually a bull'.[56] From a posthumanist perspective, I argue that the two-footed position of the lioness does not de-humanise, but rather humanises the vengeful attack of Clytemnestra against Agamemnon. By giving a human posture to the lioness, Aeschylus reveals the tragic implications of her empowerment in the conflicts of the House of Atreus. As sung by the chorus in the second *stasimon* (717–36), the lion cub, reared distant from his/her mother, will return home to exact vengeance. The verb τρέφω, 'I rear' (717), which introduces the parable of the cub, is also employed in the desperate words of Clytemnestra after the realisation of her vengeance. In the *Choephori*, she tries to persuade Orestes not to commit matricide, by uncovering her breast and claiming to have 'reared' (908) him. Therefore, I argue that the metaphorical metamorphosis of Clytemnestra into a vengeful lioness would have provoked an effect of pathos for the fifth-century Athenian audience. By blurring the boundaries between humanity and animality, masculinity and femininity, and hunting and childbirth, the lioness foreshadows the tragic result of Clytemnestra's vengeance: the self-destruction of the lion family.

The Euripidean Medea

Medea enacts a metaphorical metamorphosis into a vengeful lioness in response to the betrayal of her husband. Empowered in her conflict with Jason, she commits the most controversial act of vengeance staged in the fifth-century Athenian theatre. Previous classical scholars have hotly debated the gendered contradictions of the vengeful agency of Medea to either justify or condemn her act of infanticide.[57] Through comparison with Sophoclean heroes, Knox argues that Euripides does not build up the character of Medea as a passive sufferer, but rather as a heroic figure.[58] Attributed masculine traits, such as firmness, resistance and temper, Medea plans and commits vengeance within and against her own household. Classical scholars have also questioned the psychological status of Medea between rationality and irrationality in committing the vengeful act of infanticide.[59] After clarifying her motivation, namely the introduction of a second wife in her house, Medea deliberatively exacts vengeance to defend her honour. According to McHardy, the vengeful reaction of Medea to Jason's decision of marrying another woman needs to be interpreted as the tragic result of a gender inversion.[60] Medea acts violently in order to give her husband a punishment equal to her suffering and humiliation. Her act of infanticide cannot be read, though, as 'quintessentially masculine'.[61] Although Medea presents masculine traits, such as sexual jealousy and the heroic defence of honour, she employs female instruments of vengeance, such as deceit, treachery and sorcery.

Through the application of a posthumanist perspective as suggested by my reading of Braidotti, I redefine the vengeful identity of Medea. I reconstruct her metaphorical metamorphosis into a lioness in order to show the human contradictions of her tragic act of vengeance. Euripides merges both the masculine and feminine traits of the Homeric lion in the image of the lioness to empower Medea to commit infanticide. By giving expression to her tragic humanity, the lioness captures Medea from her first intentions to kill her sons to their final burial. Unlike in the *Agamemnon*, where all the members of Clytemnestra's family are compared with the lion/ess, in the *Medea* the tragic heroine alone is lioness-like. After Jason's decision to marry the daughter of the King of Corinth, Medea manifests both her suffering and anger in animal terms. Still offstage, she is heard invoking Themis and Artemis to witness the injustice she has to suffer and to demand vengeance (160). With these words, the Nurse describes the tragic status of her mistress to the chorus (187–9): 'And indeed, like a bull she casts / the fierce glance of a lioness with cubs towards the slaves, / whenever someone approaches to utter a word to her.' By perceiving the world surrounding her as a threat, Medea refuses to be helped and reacts to suffering with violence. She is captured in her vengeful response to Jason's betrayal, through the hybrid image of the lioness and the bull.[62] The Nurse has already used the metaphor ὄμμα ταυρουμένη, the 'bull's gaze' (92), in the prologue, to describe the how Medea looks at her sons, anticipating that she will turn her anger against them. Concerned about the possible implications of the χόλος, 'wrath' (172) of her mistress, she predicts her infanticidal act. The chorus also see Medea's ὀργή, 'rage' (176) as a constraint to alleviate her grief and avoid violence. As Konstantinou suggests, the double image of the bull and the lioness displays the psychological conflicted identity of Medea as 'aggressor and victim, hunter and hunted'.[63] By playing the roles of both the lioness and the bull, Medea reveals anger, strength and power, on the one hand, and suffering, loss and vulnerability, on the other, in her conflict with Jason. Therefore, I argue that Euripides does not metaphorically compare Medea to a lioness, with the aim of dehumanising her, but rather in order to express the tragic humanity behind her vengeful intentions. Unlike in the Homeric tradition, the lioness does not protect its cubs from the potential attack of hunters. The danger is inverted, since Medea will turn her wrath, violence and fury against her own sons.

Split between suffering and anger, Medea commits the vengeful act of filicide offstage. The fifth *stasimon* (1271–81), which is the song that accompanies the tragic action, is composed of the lyric words of the Corinthian women and the cries of the children. According to Hall, Euripides 'certainly created a shocking (and probably new) effect with the offstage death cries of children interrupting a choral lyric in *Medea*'.[64] She suggests that the Euripidean innovation consists in the substitution of the death cries of a tragic character with 'the screams of a labouring woman'. I would add that to stage the infanticide, the initial cries of Medea lying down like a lioness after delivery are being recalled (187–9). Just as in the *parodos*, the chorus listen to a βοή, 'loud cry' (1273), which comes from inside, without intervening. The Corinthian women not only raise a vain lament to dissuade Medea, but they appear hesitant to save her sons from the ἀρκύων ξίφους, 'the net of the sword' (1278). Like the Aeschylean Clytemnestra, she weaves a murderous net to capture and kill her prey. However, the tragic effect is enhanced by her heroism, courage, fury and power in killing with the sword her sons, instead of her husband. Her transgressive behaviour is denounced by Jason after the realisation of her act of infanticide. Thus, the deprived father reacts to Medea's vengeance (1339–43):

> For the sake of sex and the marriage-bed you killed them.
> There is no Greek woman who would ever have
> dared to do this, instead of whom I thought it worthy
> to marry you, a hateful and destructive union for me,
> a lioness not a woman with
> a more savage nature than Thyrsenian Scylla.

In this passage, the lioness–woman metaphor assumes a negative connotation from Jason's perspective. Without admitting any responsibility for the infanticide, he denounces the bestiality of Medea. He calls her μῖσος (1323), a neuter noun indicating a 'hateful creature'. By showing resentment and disgust, Jason regrets having married Medea and brought her from a barbarian land to Greece. In his insulting words, he specifically mentions the Thyrsenian

Scylla (1343), the multi-headed sea-beast that was said to threaten the sailors, probably in the Strait of Messina.[65] However, just as in the depiction of the Aeschylean Clytemnestra,[66] the mythological reference does not simply connote the savagery of Medea. It rather reveals the powerlessness, failure and inferiority of Jason when confronted by a dangerous woman. It is indeed the heroism of Medea that made his journey to Corinth successful. As a result of her transgression, Medea is connoted with the term θράσος (1345). The noun is a *vox media*: in positive terms, it assumes the meaning of 'courage',[67] especially in war contexts, and in negative terms it can mean 'over-boldness'.[68] It is the same term that Medea uses in the beginning of the tragedy (469) to reproach Jason with ingratitude, cowardice and insolence. The ambiguity of the term emphasises here the tragic heroism, courage, power and violence of Medea in committing the infanticidal act.

The deliberative act of infanticide is confirmed by the reference to the lioness (1359) spoken by Medea in the last episode of the tragedy. As Mossman argues in relation to the following passage, the speech of Medea is denoted by effectiveness and brevity, which implies a refusal to prolong the discussion with Jason.[69] With these words, Medea admits and accepts her psychological metamorphosis into a vengeful lioness to defend her cause (1358–60): 'Call me even a lioness in the face of this if you want / [and Scylla who dwelt in the Tyrsenian plain] / for I have got back at your heart as was necessary.' Medea does not react to Jason's insults, but rather accepts the comparison to a lioness (1359). As a result of the way he has broken their marriage oaths and dishonoured her bed, she has willingly killed her sons to make the initial fears of Jason real (569–75). She has condemned him to live instead of dying, since getting old without children is even worse than death (1396). Defined by Jason as παιδολέτειραν, 'child-slaying' (849), Medea does not simply manifest the disruption of her maternal bond with her sons: she claims an even more possessive sense of motherhood. In Jason's words τεκοῦσα κἄμ᾽ ἄπαιδ᾽ ἀπώλεσας (1326), the antithetical verbs referring to the actions of 'giving birth' and 'destroying' intensify the internal object 'childless'. By being able to procreate and kill, Medea has made not only her husband but also herself a bereaved parent. With these words, Jason expresses his suffering and anger in response to Medea's defence (1405–14):

> Zeus, do you hear this, how I am driven away
> and what I have suffered from this loathsome
> and child-killing lioness?
> Until in fact I can and I am able,
> I mourn these things and invoke with imprecations
> the gods to witness that you
> killed my children and are preventing me
> from touching them with my hands and burying their bodies.
> Would I had never generated them,
> to have to see them killed by you.

As the last expression of his hatred towards Medea, Jason calls her παιδοφόνου λεαίνης, 'child-killing lioness' (1407). The adjective παιδοφόνος, ον evidences the intertextual relationship between the tragic lioness and the Homeric image of the lion, where it is used by Priam to define Achilles as 'the slayer of his children' (Hom. Il. 24.506).[70] In reference to Medea, the adjective expresses the tragic humanity of her vengeful reaction to the betrayal of Jason. By specifically referring to the lion-like depiction of Achilles,[71] Euripides gives emphasis to the human contradictions of Medea's act of infanticide. Through a reversal in the last mourning scene, violence is not committed after loss, but rather causes bereavement. Whereas Achilles after the funeral mourning for Patroclus kills and dismembers the corpse of Hector, Medea buries her children after killing them. The image of the lioness anticipates in fact the entrance of the *deus ex machina* through which she will fly away. Medea will drive the chariot of her grandfather Sun towards Athens to bury her sons on the acropolis of Corinth (1379). By blurring the boundaries between humanity and non-humanity, masculinity and femininity, hunting and childbirth, Medea enacts a metaphorical metamorphosis into a vengeful lioness to deprive her husband, and inevitably herself, of their sons.

CONCLUSION

My analysis of the lioness–woman metaphor has provided a new reading and interpretation of the contradictory gendered identity of the Aeschylean Clytemnestra and the Euripidean Medea. By moving beyond either positive or negative views of their transgressive nature, I have reconstructed the metaphorical metamorphoses enacted by the tragic heroines into avenging lionesses in the *Agamemnon* and the *Medea*. As I have shown, adapted from the Homeric image of the lion, the lioness does not simply denounce the bestiality, cruelty and irrationality of the acts of vengeance committed by Clytemnestra and Medea. Aeschylus and Euripides merge both the masculine and the feminine traits of the Homeric lion to rather reveal the human contradictions of their active avenging role in intra-family conflicts. The concepts of power and strength, on the one hand, and the protectiveness following childbirth, on the other, are interwoven in the image of the lioness to stage the self-destruction of the lion's house.

The application of a posthuman perspective as suggested by Braidotti has given insight into the metaphorical employment of the vengeful lioness in the tragic depiction of Clytemnestra and Medea. I have specifically considered her non-dualistic understanding of human dichotomies, her positive reading of the differences between the human and the non-human worlds, and her concept of metamorphosis in the definition of human identity to determine the tragic effect that Aeschylus and Euripides would have triggered through the lioness–woman metaphor. As a result of the combination of women's studies and animal studies, the posthuman discourse of Braidotti has led towards an empathic understanding of the metamorphic identity of Clytemnestra and Medea. Captured in their metaphorical metamorphoses into avenging lionesses, the tragic heroines claim compensation for the injuries suffered within their own household but provoke nothing but loss and suffering. This reading shows the tragic humanity of the acts of vengeance committed by the lioness-like Clytemnestra and Medea and the potential for this approach to be applied to other tragedies.

NOTES

1. I would like to thank the organisers of the Conference *Bestiarium*: Human-Animal Representations (University of Verona, September 2016), and the delegates of the Humanities Research Seminar (Roehampton University, June 2015) for the feedback received on an earlier version of this paper. In particular, I would like to thank Fiona McHardy and Susan Deacy for their extremely helpful comments and suggestions on the final draft of this paper.
2. A. P. Burnett, *Revenge in Attic and Later Tragedy* (Oxford: University of California Press, 1998), p. xvi.
3. M. W. Blundell, *Helping Friends and Harming Enemies* (Cambridge: Cambridge University Press, 1989); R. Seaford, *Reciprocity and Ritual: Homer and Tragedy in the Developing City-State* (Oxford: Clarendon Press, 1994); E. Belfiore, *Murder among Friends: Violation of Philia in Greek Tragedy* (New York: University Press, 2000); F. McHardy, *Revenge in Athenian Culture* (London: Duckworth, 2008); A. Tzanetou, 'Citizen-Mothers on the Tragic Stage', in L. Hackwork Peterson and P. Salzman-Mitchell (eds), *Mothering and Motherhood in Ancient Greece and Rome* (Austin: University of Texas Press, 2012), pp. 97–120.
4. F. I. Zeitlin, *Playing the Other: Gender and Society in Classical Greek Literature* (Chicago: The University of Chicago Press, 1996); Burnett, *Revenge*; H. P. Foley, *Female Acts in Greek Tragedy* (Princeton: Princeton University Press, 2001); McHardy, *Revenge*.
5. R. Seaford, 'The Tragic Wedding', *The Journal of Hellenic Studies* 107 (1987), pp. 106–30; S. Goldhill, 'The Language of Tragedy: Rhetoric and Communication', in P. E. Easterling (ed.), *The Cambridge Companion to Greek Tragedy* (Cambridge: Cambridge University Press, 1997), pp. 127–50; M. Wright, 'The Joy of Sophocles' *Electra*', *Greece & Rome* 52 (2005), pp. 172–94.
6. R. Braidotti, *The Posthuman* (Cambridge: Polity Press, 2013).
7. Ibid. p. 16.
8. For a definition of the self-destruction of the household in relation to the Dionysiac context of tragic plays see Seaford, *Reciprocity*, pp. 344–62.
9. As confirmed by A. Konstantinou, 'The Lioness Imagery in Greek tragedy', *Quaderni Urbinati di Cultura Classica* 101 (2012), pp. 125–40, the

first occurrences of the feminine noun λέαινα are in Aesch. *Ag.* 1258 and Hdt. 3.108, 12. Aeschylus employs the lioness image to describe his tragic heroine Clytemnestra and Herodotus reports the anecdote according to which the lioness is the animal that most suffers in giving birth.

10. The tragic characters metaphorically associated to the lion are: Agamemnon (Aesch. *Ag.* 141, 827, 1259), Adrastus (Aesch. *Sept.* 53), Aegisthus (Aesch. *Ag.* 1224), Eteocles (Eur. *Phoen.* 1573), Hector (Eur. *Rhes.* 57), Heracles (Eur. *HF* 1211, *Heracl.* 1006), Neoptolemus and Philoctetes (Soph. *Phil.* 1436), Orestes (Aesch. *Cho.* 938; Eur. *IT* 297, *Or.* 1402, 1555), Pentheus (Eur. *Bacch.* 1142, 1196, 1215, 1278, 1283), Pylades (Aesch. *Cho.* 938; Eur. *Or.* 1401, 1555), Polynices (Eur. *Supp.* 140, *Phoen.* 411, 1573) and Tydeus (Eur. *Phoen.* 1120).

11. The masculine noun λέων is used to denote real lions (Eur. *Andr.* 720, *Ion* 1162, *Alc.* 580, *Heracl.* 950, *Cyc.* 248), the Nemean lion (Soph. *Trach.* 1093; Eur. *HF* 360, 466, 579, 1271), the god Dionysus (Eur. *Bacch.* 1019), the goddess Cybele (Soph. *Phil.* 401) and the Erinyes (Aesch. *Eum.* 193). The other animals depicted in the divine metamorphoses of Dionysus are the snake and the bull (Eur. *Bacch.* 100-1, 1017-19).

12. The tragic characters metaphorically associated to the lioness are: Clytemnestra (Aesch. *Ag.* 141, 1258; Eur. *El.* 1163), Tecmessa (Soph. *Aj.* 987), Medea (Eur. *Med.* 187, 1342, 1358, 1407) and Agave (Eur. *Bacch.* 990).

13. The feminine noun λέαινα is used to denote real lionesses (Aesch. fr. 660,3 Mette), the Chimaera (Eur. *El.* 473) and divine metamorphoses (Eur. *Hel.* 379; Soph. fr. 269a,42 Radt). There are two specific references of mythological metamorphoses into lionesses: in the monodic song of the Euripidean Helen, the tragic heroine says to be different from Callisto, the 'blessed virgin' (375) who 'left the bed of Zeus on four paws' (376), and Merops who Artemis banished from her dances, by transforming her into a hind with golden horns (384). In the fragmentary Sophoclean *Inachos*, Io is captured in a multi-faceted metamorphosis: she becomes cow, lioness and bull.

14. The tragic characters metaphorically compared to the lion cub are: Iphigenia (Aesch. *Ag.* 141), Orestes (Aesch. *Ag.* 717), Eurysace (Soph. *Aj.* 987), Pentheus (Eur. *Bacch.* 1174), Diomede (Eur. *Supp.* 1223), Neoptolemus (Eur. *Andr.* 1170), Hermione (Eur. *Or.* 1213, 1493) and Helen (Eur. *Or.* 1387).

15. F. I. Zeitlin, 'Playing the Other: Theatre, Theatricality and the Feminine in Greek Drama', in J. Winkler, and F. I. Zeitlin (eds), *Nothing to Do with Dionysos?* (Princeton: Princeton University Press, 1992), pp. 63–96; Burnett, *Revenge*, pp. 142-4; Tzanetou, 'Citizen-Mothers'.

16. A. Schnapp-Gourbeillon, *Lions, Héros, Masques* (Paris: Maspero, 1981); A. Schnapp-Gourbeillon, 'Le lion et le loup. Diomédie et Dolonie dans l'*Iliade*', *Quaderni di Storia* 8 (1982), pp. 47–55; W. T. Magrath, 'The Progression of the Lion Simile in the *Odyssey*', *Classical Journal* 77 (1982),

pp. 205–12; G. E. Markoe, 'The Lion Attack in Archaic Greek Art: Heroic Triumph', *Classical Antiquity* 8 (1989), pp. 86–115; M. Clarke, 'Between Lions and Men: Images of the Hero in the *Iliad*', *Greek, Roman and Byzantine Studies* 36 (1995), pp. 137–59; J. Glenn, 'Odysseus Confronts Nausicaa: The Lion Simile of *Odyssey* 6, 130–6', *Classical World* 92 (1998), pp. 107–16; M. Curti, 'Leoni, aquile e cani: Odisseo e i suoi doppi nel mondo animale', *Materiali e discussioni per l'analisi dei testi classici* 50 (2003), pp. 9–54; M. Alden, 'Lions in Paradise: Lion Similes in the *Iliad* and the Lion Cubs of *Il*. XVIII 318–22', *Classical Quarterly* 55 (2005), pp. 335–42; McHardy, *Revenge*, pp. 29–33.

17. S. H. Lonsdale, *Creatures of Speech: Lion, Herding and Hunting Similes* (Stuttgart: Teubner, 1990); Konstantinou, 'Lioness Imagery', pp. 125–40.
18. H. P. Foley, 'Reverse Similes and Sex Roles in the *Odyssey*', in J. Peradotto and J. P. Sullivan (eds), *Women in the Ancient World* (Albany: State University of New York Press, 1984), pp. 59–78.
19. D. A. Miller, 'A Note on Aegisthus as "Hero"', *Arethusa* 10 (1977), pp. 259–65; C. Nappa, '*Agamemnon* 717–36: The Parable of the Lion Cub', *Mnemosyne* 47 (1994), pp. 82–7; A. Coppola, 'Eschilo e il leone', *Athaeneum* 85 (1997), pp. 227–33; C. Battistella, 'Egisto imbelle leone', *Quaderni di Storia* 54 (2005), pp. 179–84; S. West, 'Aegisthus the Cowardly Lion: A Note on Aeschylus *Ag*. 1224', *Mnemosyne* 56 (2003), pp. 480–4.
20. C. Wolff, 'A Note on Lions and Sophocles, *Philoctetes* 1436', in G. W. Bowersock, W. Burkert and M. C. Putnam (eds), *Arktouros: Hellenic Studies Presented to Bernard M. W. Knox on the Occasion of his 65th Birthday* (New York: de Gruyter, 1979), pp. 144–50.
21. A. H. Sommerstein, *Aeschylus: Eumenides* (Cambridge: Cambridge University Press, 1989), p. 116.
22. D. J. Mastronarde, *Euripides: Medea* (Cambridge: Cambridge University Press, 2002), p. 201.
23. V. Di Benedetto, *Euripide: Le Baccanti* (Milano: BUR, 2004), p. 430.
24. D. Susanetti, *Euripide: Le Baccanti* (Roma: Carocci, 2010), p. 258.
25. Konstantinou, 'Lioness Imagery'.
26. Ibid. p. 135.
27. Ibid. p. 128.
28. Ibid. p. 126.
29. Ibid. p. 133.
30. Braidotti, *Posthuman*, p. 1.
31. Ibid. p. 37.
32. R. Braidotti, *Metamorphoses. Towards a Materialist Theory of Becoming* (Cambridge: Polity Press, 2002), pp. 2–3.
33. Braidotti, *Posthuman*, p. 60.
34. Ibid. p. 69.
35. The other tragic heroines metaphorically associated to the lioness are Tecmessa (Soph. *Aj*. 987), Clytemnestra (Eur. *El*. 1163) and Agave (Eur. *Bacch*. 990).

36. R. P. Winnington-Ingram, 'Clytemnestra and the Vote of Athena', *Journal of Hellenic Studies* 48 (1948), pp. 130–47.
37. S. Goldhill, *Aeschylus. The Oresteia* (Cambridge: Cambridge University Press, 1992), p. 40.
38. E. Hall, 'Aeschylus' Clytemnestra and her Senecan Tradition', in F. Macintosh, P. Mikelakis, E. Hall and O. Taplin (eds), *Agamemnon in Performance: 458 BC to AD 2004* (Oxford: Oxford University Press, 2005), pp. 53–76.
39. McHardy, *Revenge*, pp. 103–17.
40. G. Thomson, *The Oresteia of Aeschylus* (Cambridge: Cambridge University Press, 1938), pp. 21–2.
41. B. M. Knox, 'The Lion in the House', *Classical Philology* 67 (1952), pp. 17–25.
42. For an interpretation of the Aeschylean representation of the sacrifice of Iphigenia, see for example, R. Seaford, 'Homeric and Tragic Sacrifice', *Transactions of the American Philological Association* 119 (1989), pp. 87–95; G. Ferrari, 'Figures in the Text: Metaphors and Riddles in the *Agamemnon*', *Classical Philology* 92 (1997), pp. 1–45; J. Grethlein, 'Choral Intertemporality in the *Oresteia*', in R. Gagné, and M. Hopman (eds), *Choral Mediations in Greek Tragedy* (Cambridge: Cambridge University Press, 2013), pp. 78–99.
43. Hom. *Il.* 9.242, 20.316, 21.375.
44. Hom. *Il.* 5.34; Aesch. *Ag.* 701.
45. Hdt. 7.134, cf. 137.
46. Aesch. *Cho.* 294; *Eum.* 234.
47. Hom. *Il.* 1.1.
48. For the relationship between hunting and sacrifice in ancient Greek tragedy, with specific reference to the god Dionysus, see for example, P. Vidal-Naquet, *The Black Hunter: Forms of Thought and Forms of Society in the Greek World*, trans. A. Szegedy-Maszak (Baltimore and London: Johns Hopkins University Press, 1986); P. Vidal-Naquet, 'Hunting and Sacrifice in Aeschylus' *Oresteia*', in J. P. Vernant and P. Vidal-Naquet, *Myth and Tragedy in Ancient Greece*, trans. J. Lloyd (New York: Zone Books, 1988), pp. 141–56; C. Segal, *Dionysiac Poetics and Euripides' Bacchae* (Princeton: Princeton University Press, 1997); C. Thumiger, 'Greek tragedy between Human and Animal', *Leeds International Classical Studies* 7 (2008), pp. 1–21.
49. Hom. *Il.* 11.454, 22.67; Soph. *Ant.* 697.
50. Cf. the depiction of Clytemnestra as a lioness roaming in the bed with Aegisthus in Eur. *El.* 1163.
51. The conflict between the lion and the wolf was proverbial in the classical world (see for example the Aesopic fables 52 and 269 H).
52. I preserve the *lectio* of the cod. T κοτῷ.
53. Hom. *Il.* 1.82, 8.449, 16.449, *Od.* 11.102.
54. Aesch. *Ag.* 635, 1211; *Supp.* 347.

55. E. Fraenkel, *Aeschylus: Agamemnon* (Oxford: Clarendon Press, 1950), p. 581.
56. Konstantinou, 'Lioness Imagery', p. 130.
57. See for example, E. Griffiths, *Medea* (London: Routledge, 2006); C. Luschnig, *Granddaughter of the Sun: A Study of Euripides' Medea* (Leiden: Brill, 2007); R. Buxton, 'How Medea Moves: Versions of a Myth in Apollonius and Elsewhere', in H. Bartel and A. Simon (eds), *Unbinding Medea. Interdisciplinary Approaches to a Classical Myth from Antiquity to the 21st Century* (London: Modern Humanities Research Association and Maney Publishing, 2010), pp. 25–38.
58. B. M. Knox, *Word and Action: Essays on the Ancient Theatre* (Baltimore and London: Johns Hopkins University Press, 1979), pp. 295–322.
59. See for example, F. McHardy, 'From Treacherous Wives to Murderous Mothers: Filicide in Tragic Fragments', in F. McHardy, J. Robson and D. Harvey (eds), *Lost Dramas of Classical Athens: Greek Tragic Fragments* (Exeter: University of Exeter Press, 2005), pp. 129–50; E. Hall, 'Medea and the Mind of the Murderer', in H. Bartel and A. Simon (eds), *Unbinding Medea. Interdisciplinary Approaches to a Classical Myth from Antiquity to the 21st Century* (London: Modern Humanities Research Association and Maney Publishing, 2010), pp. 16–24; M. Mackay and A. L. Allan 'Filicide in Euripides' *Medea*: A Biopoetic Approach', *Helios* 41 (2014), pp. 59–86.
60. McHardy, *Revenge*, pp. 61–3.
61. Ibid. p. 62.
62. For a Dionysiac interpretation of the bull image in the Euripidean depiction of Medea see J. Mossman, *Euripides: Medea* (Oxford: Aris and Phillips, 2011), p. 223.
63. Konstantinou, 'Lioness Imagery', p. 131.
64. E. Hall, *The Theatrical Cast of Athens* (Oxford: Oxford University Press, 2006), p. 70.
65. Hom. *Od.* 12.85–100, 245–59.
66. Cf. the comparison of Clytemnestra to the mythological monster in Aesch. *Ag.* 1233–4.
67. Hom. *Il.* 14.416; Aesch. *Pers.* 394; Pind. *Pyth.* 2.63.
68. Aesch. *Ag.* 169; Eur. *Or.* 1568.
69. Mossman, *Euripides: Medea*, pp. 360–1.
70. Cf. Eur. *HF* 1201, where it connotes 'the blood of slain children'.
71. For the intertextual reference to the Homeric depiction of Achilles in this passage, see, for example, Mastronarde, *Euripides: Medea*, p. 386 and Mossman, *Euripides: Medea*, pp. 368–9.

CHAPTER 11

'She's Turned Fury': Women Transmogrified in Revenge Plays

Janet Clare

The Trojan Hecuba, widow of Priam, enters *Hamlet* – Shakespeare's second revenge tragedy – in the player's rendition of Aeneas' speech to Dido. After Pirrhus' bleeding sword has fallen on Priam, Hecuba, her body, we are told, worn out with childbearing, covered only by a blanket, is distracted with fear and grief at her loss, milking tears from the burning eyes of heaven. The player performs with tears in his eyes and, according to Polonius, manages to 'turn' his own colour to match his performance. The evocation of Hecuba's emotion is too much for Polonius and he asks for 'no more'. Hamlet too is deeply affected and in his ensuing soliloquy he muses on the performance he has witnessed:

> Tears in his eyes, distraction in 's aspect,
> A broken voice, and his whole function suiting
> With forms to his conceit? And all for nothing.
> For Hecuba!
> What's Hecuba to him, or he to Hecuba,
> That he should weep for her? (2.2.557–62)[1]

Hecuba is here the paradigm of the grieving, lamenting woman evoking pity in the actor who recounts her story and in the audience. It is a role that Hecuba assumes in Euripides' tragedy[2] as she asks Agamemnon to pity her, to look at her as at a picture, studying her sufferings, 'homeless, forlorn, of all mankind most wretched' (E. *Hec.* 811).[3] And it is as a figure of pity that Hecuba produces such empathy in player and audience. And, yet, as Hamlet remarks in a brilliantly compacted line, the player and Hecuba have no relationship: 'What's Hecuba to him, or he to Hecuba?' In this chiasmus there is an implicit contrast between a fictive and an actual cause for grief, the player's and Hamlet's. The submerged contrast emerges in the strange 'he to Hecuba' with its suggestion of a deeply personal, familial, relation. What is significant here is the choice of Hecuba as a figure to embody the power of fiction to move actor and audience alike, offering, as Tanya Pollard has stated, 'a distinctive model of tragic impact, one that shadows, complements, and competes with that produced by men'.[4] The player has indeed, as Pollard notes, brought classical tragedy to Elsinore and England, albeit, I would add, in an incomplete performance. At this moment in *Hamlet* neither Hamlet's grief nor Hecuba's has been transformed to revenge. There is, as Marguerite A. Tassi has remarked, far more to Hecuba than appears in the player's recitation.[5]

In a play of multiple revengers – Hamlet, Laertes, Fortinbras, Pirrhus – Hecuba is the only woman referenced, but not as a potential avenger. Her story is arrested, still untransformed from one of loss and pathos, yet to become one of revenge and horror. In Euripides' rendering of her tragedy, and in other classical accounts, suffering and lament evolve into retribution as Hecuba is driven by a similar compulsive moral logic as any male avenger. She experiences one cruel loss after another, of city, home, husband, children and freedom. Her daughter has been ritualistically sacrificed. However, it is only when her trust is betrayed that her thoughts turn to recompense and vengeance. Her son has been murdered by the man who should have been protecting him. We observe Hecuba's dawning recognition that the only way she will get recompense and some kind of solace for this child-murder is by herself enacting vengeance against Polymestor. She appeals to male agency in the figure of Agamemnon: 'lend your avenging hand / To this old woman' (E. *Hec.* 842–3). Agamemnon questions how she will succeed in exacting vengeance: 'Yes, but how? Can a woman of your age / Handle a sword, and kill this savage? / Or poison him? What help can you rely on? / Who'll stand beside you? Where will you find friends?' (876–9). Finally he asks, 'How can women have the strength of men?' (883).

But the play invalidates the criteria of both physique and disposition: Polymestor must pay what he owes her and if Agamemnon will only tacitly aid her she and her Trojan women will themselves do the deed. The women's blinding of Polymestor and the murder of his sons are, as Martha Nussbaum and others have commented, retributive and mimetic.[6] The child-killer must suffer child-killing; the person who destroyed her trust must be destroyed. Polymestor enters the tent of the Trojan women without fear, just as Hecuba had once trustingly accepted his hospitality for her son. In his mad rage, Polymestor recognises no equivalence between his murder of Polydorus and the women's act of revenge. He lashes out, transmogrifying them into 'murderous bitches' (1173), declaring that 'earth and water never spawned their like' (1181–2). His curses of Hecuba extend to all women, which provokes the cautionary intervention of the chorus: 'You go too far. You must not let your troubles / Make you judge all women harshly. / Some are born bad. There are others / hated by the world unjustly' (1183–6). The chorus' admonition as a corrective to Polymestor's curses is evident. It is, though, ambiguous about Hecuba, leaving open which of its statements relates to her legacy, possibly including her amongst those the world hates unjustly.

In the figure of Hecuba are combined, as Pollard and others have commented, 'passionate grief and triumphant revenge',[7] a story well known to early modern readers from Ovid's *Metamorphoses* and from Arthur Golding's English translation. In the latter, Hecuba is presented as 'dumbe for sorrow' when she discovers Polydore's 'carkasse', before her sorrow turns to revenge:

> Anon
> She looked on the face of him that lay before her killd.
> Sometimes his woundes (his wounds I say) she specially behild.
> And therwithall she arm'd herselfe and furnisht her with ire:
> Wherethrough as soone as that her hart was fully set on fire,
> As though shee still had beene a Queene, to vengeance she her bent,
> Enforcing all her wits to finde some kind of punishment:
> And as a Lyon robbed of her whelpes becommeth wood,
> And taking on the footing of her enmie where he stood,
> Purseweth them though out of sight: even so Queene Hecubee
> (Now having meynt her teares with wrath) forgetting quight that shee
> Was old, but not her princely heart, to Polemnestor went
> . . .
> And beeing sore inflam'd with wrath, caught hold upon him, and
> Streight calling out for succour to the wives of Troy at hand,
> Did in the traytors face bestowe her nayles, and scratched out
> His eyes, her anger gave her heart and made her strong and stout.[8]

To undertake an act of vengeance, Hecuba has to remake herself: 'enforcing all her wits' to focus on vengeance, she steels herself for the task, at once suppressing gentler feelings – 'becoming wooden', like a lioness robbed of her cubs – and inflamed with anger impelling her to scratch out Polymestor's eyes.[9] The horror is undermined by Golding's homely idiom. He recognises her courage and nobility, 'forgetting quight that she / Was old, but not her princely heart', and repeats this motif in 'her anger gave her heart' as he renders her transformation from the epitome of female frailty to incensed avenger as a woman 'strong and stout', before her barking announces her final metamorphosis into a dog (a destiny forecast by Polymestor in *Hecuba*).

In alluding in general to Hecuba's fate, John Kerrigan has commented that 'the projected metamorphosis makes concrete the degradation which the queen brings upon herself, through revenge, when she sinks to the level of her enemy, the child-killer Polymestor' and refers to Hecuba's tragedy as one of 'self-reduction'.[10] Such an interpretation is not uncommon, although like all interpretations it is a product of historically affected consciousness. In examining the mainstream of twentieth-century critical readings of the play, Malcolm Heath concludes that almost all see Hecuba's revenge as 'hideously and disproportionately cruel' and her character 'warped and corrupted'.[11] In a broader survey of the post-Euripidean tradition, Judith Mossman has commented that responses to the metamorphosis as the standard end for Hecuba have been divided.[12] Some interpretations rest on a belief that the transformation was an expression of savagery while the majority understood it as a further aspect of Hecuba's unhappiness. Another view of Hecuba's fate was that transformation was better than a life of slavery. Returning to the version of the story probably most familiar to the early modern reader, *Metamorphoses*, Ovid identifies no self-reduction or degradation through revenge, declaring that Hecuba's 'sad fortune touched the Trojans and her Grecian foes and all the gods as well; yes, all ... declared that Hecuba had not deserved such an end'.[13]

Classicists have observed that *Hecuba* was the most translated and imitated Greek play of the sixteenth century.[14] It was translated into Latin by Erasmus, although only as practice before his translation of the New Testament,[15] and was admired by Philip Sidney.[16] But, it should also be borne in mind that, except from Lady Jane Lumley's *Iphigeneia*, in manuscript until 1909, no Greek tragedies were translated into English until the eighteenth century.[17] The avenging *Hecuba*, rather than the more familiar figure of Hecuba as icon of grief, does not have a substantial presence in early modern English culture. Unlike Seneca's plays which underwent translation into English and proved highly influential in the playhouse, there is no known English vernacular *Hecuba* in the period, nor did the play filter down to the commercial stage through popular adaptation. The first English *Hecuba* was Richard West's adaptation, published in 1726. West's version morally reinstates Agamemnon, who acts as judge of the conduct of Hecuba and Polymestor, respectively, naturalising Hecuba's revenge and condemning Polymestor. While Polymestor is banished to the mountains, to howl, wolf-like, in despair and hunger, Hecuba is told to prepare for the funerals of her children with scarcely a hint of future transformation. The play imports pious sentiments from Iphigenia on the wisdom of the gods, leaving little sense of catharsis in the aftermath of terrible revenge. Even with changes to accommodate the tastes of the time, stripping the play of its rawer emotional elements, the play was a commercial failure with only one performance at the Theatre Royal in Drury Lane.[18]

It is the contention of this essay that cultural constraints determined that the paradigmatic role of Hecuba as a tragic heroine and avenger could not be replicated on the early modern stage. The two parts which Hecuba might be seen to embody, that of lamenting mother and figure of pathos and that of revenger armed with ferocious energy, rarely coalesce. Instead, the role tends to bifurcate in English revenge tragedy. The Hecuba of *Hamlet*, the woman overcome by grief at maternal loss, before revenge becomes the only certainty left to her, is mirrored in a number of female roles in early modern revenge tragedies, although these roles are limited in dramatic scope. Such scenes dominated by women could be compared to the compressed feminine 'proto-tragic' narratives in the *Iliad*, described by Edith Hall in this volume.[19] In *The Spanish Tragedy*, for example, Isabella – wife to Hieronimo – goes mad with grief not only at the loss of her son, Horatio, but because neither 'piety nor pity' will move the king to give justice for his murder.[20] She is portrayed as a frustrated and failed avenger. Despairing that Hieronimo will ever take action against their son's murderers, in an act of displaced revenge Isabella cuts down and destroys the bower where Horatio's corpse was discovered, cursing the garden: 'I will not leave a root, a stalk, a tree. / A bough, a branch, a blossom, nor a leaf, / No, not an herb within this garden-plot. / Accursed complot of my misery, / Fruitless for ever may this garden be!' (4.2.10–14).

She later thinks that she sees the ghost of Horatio, and interprets this as a sign of her own failure and ineffectuality: 'revenge on her that should revenge his death',[21] thus implicitly rejecting the female role as non-avenger. Then, anguished and self-castigating, she turns the failed instrument of revenge against herself, employing the knife she used to destroy the garden to end her own life. In a more mannered and less affecting scene, Cornelia in *The White Devil* descends into madness after the murder of her younger son by the elder; her display of grief plainly borrows from Ophelia's acts of madness in *Hamlet* following the death of her father. Neither Cornelia nor Ophelia seeks vengeance, instead conforming with ways of acting or reacting regarded as befitting their gender.

Amongst Shakespeare's plays, two female roles, those of Queen Margaret in the *Henry VI* trilogy and Tamora in *Titus Andronicus*, evoke that of Hecuba. Her role is strangely distorted in the primitive, metamorphic world of *Titus Andronicus* in which a woman and a man, both wronged and outraged by the killing of their children, attempt to outwit each other in vengeance. Emrys Jones has claimed that Euripides' play served as a model for *Titus Andronicus* on the grounds that the two movements of feeling in *Titus Andronicus*, as Titus moves from passionate suffering to purposeful revenge, correspond to the structural divisions of *Hecuba*.[22] For Jones the link between the two plays is not gender and revenge (indeed, Tamora is scarcely mentioned in his account) but the dynamic of grief and revenge. Jones ignores the premise of this revenge play: that it is Titus' ritualistic sacrifice of Tamora's son, Alarbus – effectively revenge against the enemy responsible for his sons' deaths – and his refusals to heed Tamora's pleas for mercy that initiate the chain of events. At this point Hecuba is introduced into the play as the model of the female avenger: Demetrius, one of Tamora's sons, advises his mother that she might enact Hecuba's revenge:

> The selfsame gods that arm'd the Queen of Troy
> With opportunity of sharp revenge
> Upon the Thracian tyrant in his tent
> May favour Tamora, the Queen of Goths –
> When Goths were Goths and Tamora was queen –
> To quit her bloody wrongs upon her foes. (1.1.137–41)

It is not altogether clear what effect Shakespeare or Peele, his possible collaborator, might have been striving for in appropriating Hecuba as a model for Tamora. The parallel between them consists in the experience of the violent death of a child and to that extent Tamora's vengefulness is not without cause. But, when Tamora's opportunity to exact revenge comes, she is 'arm'd' not with her own strength, as Hecuba is against Polymestor, but with the rapine strengths of her sons. Tamora's revenge is altogether different from that of the image of the wronged, suffering and energised old woman of Troy. Tamora's revenge is mediated, not through the demonising voice of a man who has done her harm, but through the voice of her victim, another woman. Tamora is presented as a woman who has de-sexed herself. As her sons prepare to rape and mutilate Lavinia, her incitement to revenge is presented, through Lavinia's unheeded appeals, as the antithesis of the feminine: 'No grace, no womanhood – ah, beastly creature, / The blot and enemy to our general name, / Confusion fall – ' (2.3.182–4). 'Confusion' – the penultimate word that Lavinia will ever speak – communicates a sense of the unnaturalness, the deviancy of Tamora in urging not only revenge, but such a revenge as sexual violation.

In Shakespeare's first tetralogy of history plays – the three parts of *Henry VI* and *Richard III* – the role of Queen Margaret conforms at the end of 3 *Henry VI* to that of the lamenting sorrowing mother. The murder of her son, Edward, by the three sons of the Duke of York, an act which can be seen as retaliation for Margaret's participation in the murder of York, produces a howl of anguish from the queen:

> O Ned, sweet Ned – speak to thy mother, boy.
> Canst thou not speak? O traitors, murderers!
> They that stabbed Caesar shed no blood at all,
> Did not offend, nor were not worthy blame,
> If this foul deed were by to equal it.
> He was a man – this, in respect, a child;
> And men ne'er spend their fury on a child. (5.5.50–6)

Margaret's emphasis on her child gives considerable emotional impact to the speech, although she demonstrated no such remorse as she taunted York with the napkin soaked in the blood of his young son, Rutland. In the crowded stage of Shakespeare's epic dramatisation of the blood feuds that constituted the Wars of the Roses, Margaret's role is one of many, although she does, of course, stand out as a woman. Her taunting, mock crowning and stabbing of York following the Battle of Towton depicts a woman who does not shrink from vengeful killing in a play of serial dynastic violence. Along with another female who enters battle – Joan of Arc, derided by both her compatriots and the English in *I Henry VI* – Margaret is vilified for her nationality and her sex. In the eyes of York, she is a 'She-wolf of France' whose acts are 'ill beseeming of her sex' and in her taunting York with the death of young Rutland 'more inhuman, more inexorable ... than tigers of Hyrcania' (1.4.112–14; 1.4.155–6). For York's son, the future Richard III, Margaret has usurped her gender and 'stol'n the breech from Lancaster' (5.5.24). At the end of *Henry VI* Margaret is banished to France, and then she reappears – unhistorically – in *Richard III* to take up a more passive – and conventional – role as female avenger, the originator of curses.

Marguerite A. Tassi identifies Margaret with Hecuba as a fierce, resourceful, avenging woman for whom justice is at stake and who is far from silent and passive in the fight against injustice.²³ In the context of her discussion, Tassi argues that Margaret, and also Tamora in *Titus Andronicus*, exist within the same bellicose cultures where revenge is the norm and follow the same warlike terms of engagement. This is a valid point and one that I have echoed above, but I would argue that Hecuba's tragic predicament and that of Margaret and Tamora diverge. Hecuba is a victim of war. She has lost a husband, fifty children and is a prisoner in exile. She survives catastrophe after catastrophe and, as noted above, it is only when there is a breakdown of her trust and when Agamemnon fails to act that Hecuba turns implacably to revenge. It is difficult to see in Tamora a legacy of Hecuba, a woman so wronged that she is driven finally to take on a terrible aspect. As a slave, Hecuba acts from a position of weakness; Margaret and Tamora act from positions of dominance and power. Athenian audiences may have wept for Hecuba; it is doubtful that an early modern audience would have been moved to weep for Tamora or Margaret.

That Tamora is no Hecuba – despite her son's evocation of the Trojan queen – suggests, I think, that there was little space on the early modern stage for a more positive icon of female revenge, biblical or classical. Put simply, in a culture that condemned revenge and saw it as a last resort to which only a male should have recourse, revenge was quite definitely not a woman's business. In *The English Gentlewoman*, a female conduct book, Richard Braithwaite cautioned against displays of passion, citing a cautionary tale of a woman who takes revenge against an unfaithful lover. Women should 'allay or abate these passionate furies', 'parley with reason' and 'chastise all such innovating motions as disquiet the inward repose of the mind'.²⁴ The anti-exemplum offered by Braithwaite is Jocasta, Oedipus' mother/wife, not the most representative of avenging females. The gender ideology inherent in Braithwaite's notion of proper female conduct precludes any recognition of what we might view as heroic female action as it was represented in other European cultures and across a variety of art forms in the period.

It is notable, for example, that unlike French and German dramatic culture the English Renaissance stage saw no play about the Apocryphal Judith, the pious widow who saves the Jews of Bethulia from ruination by decapitating the Assyrian General Holofernes. Kathleen Llewellyn has examined the surge of interest in Judith in sixteenth-century France, a fascination with what a woman could become within the strictures of early modern patriarchal society.²⁵ In France during the wars of religion Judith was celebrated by both Huguenots and Catholics as an image of female resistance to tyranny. Judith presents an interesting case as a model for the female avenger. Convinced that she is an agent of God, she tells the Bethulia elders that she has a plan to save the city and persuades them to let her exit the city gates to go to the Assyrian camp. Her murder of the drunken Holofernes in his tent tended to be portrayed as an act of heroic liberation rather than revenge, although in the Apocrypha Judith sees herself as an agent of a vengeful God, proclaiming to the men of

Jerusalem that the Lord had smitten Holofernes 'by the hand of a woman'.[26] In art, painted by Lucas Cranach the Elder, Caravaggio and Artemisia Gentileschi among others, the depiction of Judith's violent act was variously depicted and nuanced: sombre and pious, dispassionate, triumphant and ferocious. In many respects Judith conforms to English Renaissance ideals of female conduct: as a young widow, she is chaste and pious, but in her resolute act of violence, she is the antithesis of womanhood, a potentially subversive figure. As far back as the Old English poem, her agency is muted, as the author exaggerates the heroine's simplicity, eliminates her seductiveness and stresses that her heroism is divinely sanctioned.[27]

Francis Bacon in his essay 'On Revenge'[28] had compared vengeful individuals to the malevolence of witches, equating revenger and transgressive female. Witch and revenger are, or become, liminal subjects. When a woman becomes an avenger, she assumes qualities of the former, out of control and deviant. Indeed, images of female avengers in English Renaissance revenge tragedies are more in the negative mode of Seneca's *Medea* – translated by John Studley in 1581 – than of the more ambiguous Hecuba or a heroic Judith who counter tyranny in its various guises. Medea, especially in the Senecan tradition, embodies two aspects of vengeance: imprecatory powers, the verbal power to invoke calamity or divine vengeance against another, associated with the female, and revenge as excess, far outweighing any original slight or crime. In her opening soliloquy she calls on the Furies, 'hellish hags', to assist her in her revenge against Jason, for his desertion, and his wife and father-in-law: 'What shall not I with vyolence get up agaynst my foes?'[29] Such is Medea's obsession and violent passion towards Jason for his betrayal that she claims that she will find rest only when she has thrown everything she sees 'topsie turvey downe to ruthfull ende with mee'.[30] Cultural opprobrium towards such unfemale-like behaviour is registered in Studley's translation through the voice of the nurse as she protests at Medea's necromancy 'let thy mynde on matters runne that seeme a modest wight'.[31] The chorus at the end of the fourth act, though, sees in Medea's expression of resolve an act which dehumanises and unsexes her, equating her state to that of the male tiger:

> Her chaunging lookes no colour longe can holde,
> Her shifting feete still travasse to and froe.
> Even as the fearce and ravening Tyger olde
> That doth unware his sucking whelpes forgoe,
> Doth rampe, and rage . . .
> Even so Medea sometime wantes her wits
> To rule the rage of her unbrydled ire. (IV, p. 136v)

Medea is abandoning her children as the male tiger abandons his cubs. The contrast here with Hecuba is forceful. Hecuba, too, in Ovid and in Golding's version, is likened to a tiger, but a female tiger, raging because her cubs have been stolen from her. The wild cat imagery conveys a naturalness in Hecuba's motivation for revenge, maternal loss, while that applied to Medea enhances the perversion of her motherhood. As she contemplates the killing of her children as a means of revenge against their father, and wavering for an instant, she personifies herself as 'doting fury'.[32] But to kill she has to be invaded by the furies who control her action. The imagery of the furies appropriated by Medea – and variously used by others with reference to her – contributes further to her dehumanising, a trope which climaxes with her ascending to the heavens in the serpent-drawn chariot of the sun. The final choral ode is entirely concerned with Medea's anger, violence, force and animality.

In plays of the English Renaissance stage women do not generally with violence 'get up' against their foes. Any Medea-like compulsion to revenge is diverted to performative speech acts, cursing, representing a vengeance enacted in thought and word, or goading and inciting men to take action. The curse represents a descriptive, imaginative killing, a surrogate weapon, the obverse in intention to prayer. Cursing-prayers, in which the gods are co-opted as agents of vengeance, are, as Matthew and Salvo have illustrated in this volume, features of the ancient Mediterranean world from the fourth century BC until late Antiquity.[33] It is not surprising, then, that they are found in English history plays which offer a providential interpretation of events. In a scene in *Richard III* dominated by women, the queens conjoin in opposition and curse Richard. Elizabeth and the Duchess of York lament their loss of children and their helplessness against Richard's tyranny. Old Queen Margaret hovers, eavesdropping, and then advances, claiming seniority in suffering. In desperation, Elizabeth wills imprecatory power, appealing to Margaret: 'O thou, well skilled in curses, stay a while, / And teach me how to curse mine enemies' (5.5.116–17). Learning to curse, Margaret replies, involves intensifying feelings of love for that which is lost and of hate towards the murderer: a condition and process that parallels the male avenger's obsessive state of mind. Cursing eases the heart. When Richard enters, his mother – the Duchess of York – summons up all her imprecatory power, willing that in the coming day of battle her 'grievous curse' will tire him more than all the armour he wears while her prayers will 'fight' for the adverse party. The juxtaposition of piety and sorcery precludes any demonisation of the queens as their vengeful curses are aligned with the providential pattern of the play. Even Margaret, so demonised in the *Henry VI* trilogy, is given a different voice in *Richard III*. Her curses are realised as the feminine equivalent of revenge and have the physical force of revenge. Richard's sometime allies come to see, as Hastings has, that Margaret's 'heavy curse' is lighted on their 'wretched' heads (3.4.92–3). In terms of depicting revenge on stage, however, Margaret's curses are contained within the play's historical framework.

Cursing is the limit of female agency in this history play, although, as I have said, it is not ineffectual. In a different scenario, Richard knows that he is on safe ground when he offers his sword to Lady Anne – the woman whose husband and father-in-law he has killed and whom audaciously he is now wooing: 'If thy revengeful heart cannot forgive, / Lo, here I lend thee this sharp-pointed sword, / Which if thou please to hide in this true breast / [. . .] / I lay it naked to the deadly stroke' (1.2.162–5). As he kneels, chest bared, with Anne, sword drawn, standing over him in mock revenger pose, this is another of Richard's comic charades, although there is still the element of the gambler. The audience laughs at the tableau knowing that Anne will not kill. There is a strange reversal of roles in Richard's sadistic goading as he reminds her of the retribution she could take, wants to take, but cannot. The sword is arrested: an image of female impotence.

Female desire for vengeance is more fiercely articulated in early modern plays than it is acted out because it is mostly a frustrated desire, only to be satisfied through a curse or male agency. Deprived of a direct outlet of action, the woman compensates by an imaginary vengeance. In the very secular, scheming, misogynist, decidedly unheroic world of Webster's *The White Devil*, Vittoria Corombona is on trial for the murder of her husband although there is no direct evidence against her. Most of the accusation is founded on her powers of display and her sexual relationship with Bracciano. The castigation of whore is elided into that of murderess: 'You know what whore is', insinuates the cardinal, 'next the Devil, Adultery, / Enters the devil, Murder'.[34] Vittoria repeatedly confounds her accusers, but seeing that what little evidence there is has been weighed against her in a court where judge and jury are the same, she retaliates with images of sexual violation. The climax of this travesty of a trial is Vittoria's angry, frustrated outburst: 'A rape, a rape. . . . Yes, you have ravish'd justice / Forc'd her to do your pleasure'. And she curses the cardinal, predicting that he will choke to death even as he sits on the bench, declaring woman's revenge is poor since it 'dwells but in the tongue' (3.2.274–5, 284). Vittoria's verbal revenge is effective in exposing the hypocrisy of the male prosecution, vehemently denouncing Cardinal Monticelso as having 'ravished justice'. Her voice of resistance strikes home and her male detractors move to contain the threat. To the transgressive roles of whore and murderess is added 'fury'. 'She's turned fury' responds the cardinal, brushing away her impassioned denunciations as the words of a non-human vengeful spirit (3.2.278). The cardinal's demonisation of Vittoria here and elsewhere is not endorsed by a play that exposes deeply ingrained misogyny and double standards: it is Vittoria who is arraigned for murder while her lover casually looks on. Vittoria is demonstrably treated unjustly and her resistance to state corruption gratifyingly rebellious, but the potential threat of her destabilising influence on stage is diminished by the fact that she is guilty: her concerns are selfish and her acts are not justified by the wrongs she has suffered.

When women take the law into their own hands – defying societal norm – a double standard similarly operates both in the courts and on the stage. In her study of the representation of early modern domestic crime, Frances Dolan points out that the possibility that a wife might actually kill her husband was so disturbing that the crime had a special legal status after 1352 when killing one's husband was defined as petty treason, carefully distinguished from other forms of murder, and legally equivalent to high treason. Thus, a wife who killed a husband or a servant a master was to be convicted of treason while a husband who killed a wife or servant was accused of murder, for according to one justice of the peace, 'one is in subjection and oweth obedience, and not the other'.[35] The revengeful wife was a house traitor. The difference between men who kill and women who kill is treated with some irony in Beaumont and Fletcher's *The Maid's Tragedy*, the only play of the period in which a woman avenges her own honour and – significantly – that of her male kin, who are unwilling to take action themselves. In the tone and narrative of the opening scenes of the play, there is little to suggest that this could be a revenge tragedy. We are thrust into the celebration of a court wedding, that of Amintor and Evadne; the dialogue is relaxed and urbane as the courtiers prepare for the performance of the wedding masque. The plot builds slowly towards Evadne's refusal to sleep with Amintor who puts it down to excessive female modesty; Evadne is incredulous at Amintor's naïve view of female sexuality, remarking sardonically: 'A maidenhead, Amintor, at my years?'[36] The line challenges all the conventional assumptions about female chastity, just as Evadne's later role as avenger transgresses notions of woman's passivity. Indeed, the two extremes of conduct are later made to seem concomitant.

Amintor's resolve to kill Evadne's lover is shaken when he learns it is the king. On hearing this, Amintor expresses his loyalty in absolute terms:

O, thou hast named a word that wipes away
All thoughts revengeful; in that sacred name,
'The King' there lies a terror. What frail man
Dares lift his hand against it? Let the gods
Speak to him when they please; till when, let us
Suffer and wait. (2.1.307–12)

Within the hierarchical nexus he is reduced to impotence and ineffectuality. The code confines and restricts him, like a woman. Evadne transgresses two codes: she wields a knife and kills, and in so doing she commits regicide.

The dynamics of the scene of confrontation between Evadne and her brother, Melantius, are pivotal to the play. Melantius incites her to revenge in increasing degrees of severity. At first, he demonstrates a conventional understanding of the female role in exacting revenge by commanding Evadne merely to curse the king, 'till the gods hear and deliver him / To thy just wishes' (4.1.137–8). Then the idea of Evadne's killing the king emerges, apparently from nowhere, resolving the dilemma earlier posed by Amintor ('In that sacred name, / 'The King' there lies a terror. What frail man / Dares lift his hand against it?'). Honour can be restored without imperilling the bodies or souls of her male kin. Evadne herself displays a conflicted sensibility. She is aware that the murder of the king goes against norms of conduct, but she also sees her action as in some way recuperating not only her own honour, but all lost female honour. As she swears to her brother that she will do the deed, she calls on 'spirits of abused ladies' to help in her performance (4.1.169). It is possible to read Melantius' reply, 'Enough', as betraying male anxiety that his sister is contradicting the spirit of this act of revenge in appropriating it in the cause of expressly female protest. By the end of their confrontation, Melantius has succeeded in convincing her of her 'dishonour' and this revelation has in her own eyes transmogrified her into a monster (4.1.183).

Once Evadne's initial response to Melantius' call to regicide – 'all the gods forbid it!' – has been swept aside without any apparent qualm, Evadne displays a resolution and a logic that are rare even amongst male avengers (4.1.144). At the same time, there is an element of bathos in the playful intertextuality of the scene of regicide. Evadne's soliloquy as she approaches the sleeping king is metadramatic. She opens with a mock Senecan line: 'The night growes horrible, and all about me / Like my black purpose'. Then she assumes the exemplary role of the penitent 'lost virgin' before determining on full-blooded revenge:

> I must kill him,
> And I will do't bravely: the mere joy
> Tells me I merit in it. Yet I must not
> Thus tamely do it as he sleeps: that were
> To rocke him to another world; my vengeance
> Shall seize him waking, and then lay before him
> The number of his wrongs and punishments.
> I'll shape his sins like furies till I waken
> His evil angel, his sick conscience,
> And then I'll strike him dead. (5.1.26–35)

The echoes from Hamlet's soliloquy as he determines against killing the praying Claudius are unmistakable and indicative of some theatrical self-consciousness, as is the reference in this urbane court setting to the king's sins being transformed into the furies. This is no more than decorative. Superficially the scene may evoke that of Judith's killing Holofernes in his tent; both the Assyrian general and the king anticipate sex with the woman who is about to kill them. Judith, though, is not defending her honour, she is taking political action; Holofernes has not sought her out to ravish her, she has sought him out to kill him. Judith's 'seduction' of Holofernes is a means to an end on behalf of her countrymen. Evadne is no heroic Judith, the lead-up to the king's murder is not a moment of tragic nemesis but of tragicomic prurience: 'What pretty new device is this Evadne?' he asks as she ties him to the bed (5.1.47). Faced with the image of his lover holding a knife and threatening his life, the king calls her name and Evadne in reply disclaims her sex: 'I am not she, nor bear I in this breast / So much cold spirit to be called a woman: / I am a tiger; I am any thing / That knows not pity' (5.1.65–8). Having rejected the idea of killing the king 'tamely' while he sleeps, Evadne imagines herself as a pitiless tiger hunting its prey, evoking and self-appropriating conventional imagery of the female avenger, applied by men. But she denies her sexual identity – 'I am not she' – seemingly embodying male and female in her revenge. She uses both the dagger, the more traditional male weapon of vengeance, and her tongue, the female weapon: 'If thy hot soul had substance with thy blood / I would kill that too, which, being past my steel, / My tongue shall reach' (5.1.89–91). Killing as both a male and a female, she stabs first for male honour: the first stroke is 'for my lord Amintor, / This for my noble brother', and, as she administers the fatal stab to the king, she reclaims retribution in feminine terms: 'this stroke / For the most wronged of women!' (5.1.111–12). When the regicide is discovered, her act is greeted with incredulity by the male courtiers. The first gentleman fears that he will be accused of treason for 'who can believe / A woman could do this?' (5.1.128–2). In reply to the gentleman's report on 'her woeful act', Cleon emphasises female aberrance: 'Her act! A woman' (5.1.131). In a feminist reading of the revenge genre this could be said to be a heroic moment. Evadne recognises her own exploitation and abasement and kills a man who has repeatedly been denounced as a tyrant but against whom no one but a woman has dared act.

The Maid's Tragedy may be the one play of the period that confronts head-on the gendering of revenge and contests the idea that women cannot kill. The sexually titillating nature of the revenge and the blatant male manipulation of the woman, however, undermines any heroic potential that the action might have. Any female self-assertion is momentary as Evadne turns to Amintor for approval of her deed. The stage direction reads 'her hands bloody, with a knife', a scenario which clashes with her pathetic words as she implores Amintor, 'take me home' (5.3.155). Amintor rejects her for a revenge that her brother has incited her to do. Fending off any thought that she has done something that he should have done himself, and exploiting the conventional view that her act is unfeminine, Amintor condemns her as black and diseased. The more emphatic he is, the more he distances any sense of guilt at his own inaction. In his eyes, her revenge simply confirms that she is a bad woman, even though – or perhaps because – she has done his business. Amintor's rejection of Evadne and her suicide are the logical outcome of this revenge: there is no way that regicide can be sanctioned. Moreover, in killing the king, Evadne has shown herself capable of the same crime as killing a husband: both are acts of treason. In the end, the play is perhaps appealing to different constituencies of audience. Evadne is not made out as the play's heroine. The maid of the tragedy is the pathetic figure of Aspatia – Amintor's rejected lover who has followed him slavishly in male disguise and in a death-wish contrives to be killed by him. Possibly such a rival female, exuding pathos and self-abnegation, may have been perceived as an essential, reassuring counterpoint to Evadne's moment of vengeful self-assertion, an image which, equally possibly, may have thrilled in its audacious transgression of the in-built codes that women should not and cannot kill.

Other essays in this volume have considered the varied roles performed by women as instigators or collaborators in early modern English revenge tragedy. The focus of this essay has been on the divergence between a classical legacy of an empathetic woman avenger, configured in Hecuba, and early modern culture in which female revenge was deemed both abhorrent and aberrant. The Hecuba of the player's speech, with its exclusive emphasis on pathos, captures the aspect of her role which was culturally acceptable. In the one popular theatre play of the period, *Titus Andronicus*, in which Hecuba is appropriated as a paradigm of the female avenger, she seems disturbingly misappropriated. There is no female figure on the early modern stage representing what in Euripides is presented as understandable revenge; loss, grief and revenge are not conjoined positively in any female tragic heroine. The women who variously seek revenge in early modern drama lack Hecuba's cause or are less of a threat than a woman who takes the law into her own hands in a time of war. Their acts are subject to male control and manipulation. I would suggest that to be moved by Hecuba was perceived as a dangerous emotion; conceivably, this is another reason why Polonius tells the player to stop his performance. Here is a woman, disenfranchised, enslaved, robbed of everything she values, representative, we might say, of any socially marginalised figure, whose personal desire for revenge is manifestly tangled up with her political status. *Hecuba* does not end with her death. She is not 'punished' within the framework of the play for wreaking revenge: her transformation and death are prophesised but not depicted. To stage a Hecuba would be to stage rebellion.

NOTES

1. William Shakespeare, *Hamlet*, in *The Oxford Shakespeare: The Complete Works*, ed. Stanley Wells and Gary Taylor, 2nd edition (Oxford: Oxford University Press, 2006), p. 696. Unless otherwise stated, quotations from the works of Shakespeare are taken from this edition. Polonius' line, 'Look whe'er he has not turned his colour and has / tears in's eyes', is at 2.2.522–3.
2. There are two Euripides plays about Hecuba and we do not know to which, if either, Hamlet is referring. *Hecuba* (c. 425 bc) is a revenge tragedy, whereas *Trojan Women* from c.10 years later reduces revenge to a curse, however prescient.
3. Trans. Peter D. Arnott, Euripides, *Plays: II*, Introduced by J. Michael Walton (London: Methuen, 1991). All quotations are from this version.
4. Tanya Pollard, 'What's Hecuba to Shakespeare?', *Renaissance Quarterly* 65.4 (2012), pp. 1060–93 (p. 1062).
5. Marguerite A. Tassi, *Women and Revenge in Shakespeare: Gender, Genre, and Ethics* (Selinsgrove: Susquehanna University Press, 2011), p. 97.
6. Martha C. Nussbaum, *The Fragility of Goodness: Luck and Ethics in Greek Tragedy and Philosophy* (Cambridge: Cambridge University Press, 1986), p. 410.
7. Pollard, 'What's Hecuba to Shakespeare?', in this volume.

8. Ovid 'The thirteenth Booke of Ovids Metamorphosis', *The XV Bookes of P. Ovidius Naso, entytuled Metamorphosis, translated oute of Latin into English meeter by Arthur Golding* (London, 1567), Y3r–Y3v. Golding uses the anglicised form 'Polydore' rather than the latinised 'Polydorus'.
9. For lion imagery in Greek tragedy and its relationship to how the female revengers are gendered, see Alessandra Abbattista, 'The Vengeful Lioness in Greek Tragedy', in this volume.
10. John Kerrigan, *Revenge Tragedy: Aeschylus to Armageddon* (Oxford: Clarendon Press, 1996), p. 194.
11. Malcolm Heath, '"Jure Principem locum tenet": Euripides' *Hecuba*', *Bulletin of the Institute of Classical Studies* 34 (1987), pp. 40–68 (p. 63).
12. Judith Mossman, *Wild Justice: A Study of Euripides' Hecuba* (Oxford: Clarendon Press, 1995), p. 199.
13. Ovid, *Metamorphoses*, trans. Frank Justus Miller, 2 vols (Cambridge, MA: Harvard University Press, 1946), vol. 2, p. 269. Golding refers to the Greeks, Trojans and the Gods and repeats that they were all moved 'to ruth' by Hecuba's fate and states that even Juno did deny that Hecuba did 'deserve such end', Golding, y3v.
14. See Mossman, *Wild Justice*, pp. 220–43, and Heath, 'Jure Principem locum tenet', pp. 43–8. See also Pollard, 'What's Hecuba to Shakespeare?', in this volume.
15. See Erika Rummel, *Erasmus as a Translator of the Classics* (Toronto: University of Toronto Press, 1985), pp. 28–9.
16. See Philip Sidney, *Apology for Poetry*, ed. G. Shepherd (London: T. Nelson and Sons, 1965), p. 135.
17. See J. Michael Walton, *Found in Translation: Greek Drama in English* (Cambridge: Cambridge University Press, 2006), pp. 26–42.
18. In the Preface, Richard West, *Hecuba: A Tragedy* (London, 1726), gave his account of the play's failure: 'The Objections to it were, that it was too short, too regular, and conducted with natural Simplicity [. . .] I shall offer but one Reason more, and I presume it will be allow'd a very solid one, why this Tragedy did not succeed; and that is, *It was not heard*. A Rout of Vandals in the Galleries, intimidated the young Actresses, disturb'd the Audience, and prevented all Attention' (pp. iii–iv).
19. Edith Hall, 'Why are the Erinyes Female?', in this volume.
20. Thomas Kyd, *The Spanish Tragedy*, ed. J. R. Mulryne, revised and with a new Introduction by Andrew Gurr (London: Methuen Drama, 2009), 4.2.2.
21. Ibid. 4.2.25.
22. Emrys Jones, *The Origins of Shakespeare* (Oxford: Clarendon Press, 1977), pp. 85–107 (esp. pp. 97–9).
23. Tassi, *Women and Revenge*, p. 121.
24. Richard Braithwaite, *The English Gentlewoman* (London, 1631), p. 36.
25. Kathleen M. Llewellyn, *Representing Judith in Early Modern French Literature* (Farnham: Ashgate, 2014).

26. See 'Judith, 13:15' in *The Apocrypha* (Cambridge: Cambridge University Press, 1984), p. 52.
27. See *Judith*, ed. Mark Griffith (Exeter: University of Exeter Press), pp. 47–61.
28. Francis Bacon, 'Of Revenge', in *The Essays of Lord Bacon* (London: Frederick Warne, 1889).
29. Seneca *Medea*, in *Seneca his Tenne Tragedies, Translated into Englysh* (London, 1581), p. 120r.
30. Ibid. p. 128v.
31. Ibid. p. 130v.
32. Ibid. p. 138r.
33. Matthews and Salvo, 'Cursing-Prayers and Female Vengeance in the Ancient Greek World'.
34. John Webster, *The White Devil*, ed. John Russell Brown (Manchester: Manchester University Press, 1992), 3.2.108–9.
35. Frances E. Dolan, *Dangerous Familiars: Representations of Domestic Crime in England, 1550–1700* (Ithaca and London: Cornell University Press, 1994), pp. 21–2.
36. Beaumont and Fletcher, *The Maid's Tragedy*, ed. T. W. Craik (Manchester: Manchester University Press, 1988), 2.1.194.

PART V

LAMENTATION, GENDER ROLES AND VENGEANCE

CHAPTER 12

A Phrygian Tale of Love and Revenge: *Oenone Paridi* (Ovid *Heroides* 5)

Andreas N. Michalopoulos

> *vindicta nemo magis gaudet quam femina.*
> 'Noone exults in revenge more keenly than a woman.' (Juv. *Sat.* 13.191–2, trans. Rudd)

The *Heroides*[1] is a collection of verse letters, written in elegiac couplets, supposedly sent by mythological heroines (or heroes) to their lovers, who are absent for various reasons. It is the work of the Roman poet Publius Ovidius Naso (43 BC – AD 17), and it comprises two parts: the first part contains fourteen letters – the so-called 'single letters' – written by women,[2] while the second part comprises the correspondence of Paris and Helen (16–17), Leander and Hero (18–19), Acontius and Cydippe (20–1).

The fifth letter of Ovid's *Heroides* is the letter supposedly sent by the Phrygian nymph Oenone to Paris, the son of king Priam.[3] Here is an outline of the story: Oenone, daughter of the river-god Cebren and skilled in the art of medicine,[4] was Paris' first love, while he was still a shepherd on Mount Ida,[5] unaware that he was the Prince of Troy. Paris later left her for Helen, whom he received as a gift from Venus for granting her first prize in the beauty contest against Juno and Minerva. During the ensuing Trojan War Paris was wounded by Philoctetes' arrows. He returned to Oenone and begged her to heal him, but she refused. After Paris died, Oenone killed herself, filled with remorse. Oenone's Ovidian letter is written after Paris' return to Troy with Helen and before the outbreak of the Trojan War.

Before I discuss this letter, let me first underline three important points about the *Heroides*:

1. The letters of the *Heroides* have double senders and double receivers: the senders are Ovid and the heroines, and the receivers are the lovers of the heroines and us, the external readers (as 'super-readers').
2. The general situation of each heroine in the single letters, *mutatis mutandis*,

is similar to that of an elegiac lover: she has been betrayed by a faithless man, who has broken his promises and has abandoned her. The heroine tries to persuade the recipient to act in accordance with her desires, accusing him of cruelty and lamenting her miserable fate. In this way the *Heroides* are perfectly in line with elegy's original function as a genre of lamentation.[6]

3. The letters of these mythological women are imagined to be composed at a specific point in time, often between traumatic events and their consequences. We as readers are required to locate this particular point, in which to place the letters, and to consider the new possibilities arising from their appearance. That being said, the dramatic time in the letters of the *Heroides* is not static. Through a series of flashbacks and veiled flash-forwards Ovid offers an overall picture of each story.

Ovid's choice to treat the myth of Oenone and Paris in the form of a letter sent by the nymph is original. As far as we know from surviving literature, this is the first time that Oenone voices her thoughts and emotions in the first person. Equally original is Ovid's choice to treat the story at this particular point, namely right after Paris' return to Troy with Helen and before the Greeks respond to her abduction. All the other accounts of the story that we know of[7] mainly focus on the final parts of the Paris–Oenone story.[8] This is important for my reading of the letter: Oenone's Ovidian letter antedates the Trojan War and a series of crucial incidents, such as Paris' injury by Philoctetes, his appeal to Oenone to heal him, and her bitter and vindictive refusal.

With the notable exception of Laurel Fulkerson,[9] who picks up the vengeful aspect of this letter, so far scholars, such as Bradley,[10] have read Oenone's letter as a typical example of a letter sent by a betrayed woman to the man who abandoned and replaced her with a new wife. Palmer[11] maintains that Ovid intended to present Oenone as soft and gentle, arguing that this is why he omitted every vengeful feature of her character. Indeed, Oenone's letter shares many features with other letters of the *Heroides* collection written by abandoned women (e.g. Phyllis, Briseis, Dido, Ariadne). Oenone is a betrayed woman in love who complains and laments.

However, I believe that Oenone's letter to Paris can actually be read as a letter of revenge. Ovid has inserted among Oenone's complaints and lamentations certain hints and allusions pointing at her revenge against Paris which awaits in the dramatic future of the letter.[12] Although these are allusions that only the all-knowing external reader, and not the writer or the recipient of the letter, is able to pick up, they are crucial for our understanding of the letter.[13] I will look into the reasons for and behind Oenone's revenge, the targets of her vengeance, and the ways in which she exacts her revenge, trying to determine at the same time how revenge is associated, if at all, with lamentation and gender. On account of its 'vengeful' quality Oenone's letter stands out from the majority of the *Heroides* letters, and in this respect, it can be placed alongside two other letters of the collection that display obvious and readily recognisable features of revenge: the letters by Hypsipyle (*Her.* 6) and Medea (*Her.* 12), both addressed to Jason, who betrayed and abandoned them.

HINTS, THREATS AND CURSES

The threatening and aggressive tone of Oenone's letter, combined with ominous hints scattered throughout, paves the way for the abandoned nymph's revenge. This tone is felt right from the beginning. The notable absence of a traditional epistolary salutation betrays Oenone's rage. Instead of greeting Paris properly, the nymph (assuming that he must be expecting an angry letter from Greece – most probably from Menelaus, Helen's husband or his brother, Agamemnon) ironically asks him not to worry (1–2):* 'Will you read? Or does your new wife forbid it? / Read! This is not a letter created by a Mycenaean hand.'[14] Already from the start of her letter Oenone ominously touches on the issue of Paris' punishment, not yet by herself, but by Helen's insulted husband, Menelaus. Oenone reminds Paris that his actions will have dire consequences and will not/cannot be left unavenged by the Greeks.

Oenone's letter catalogues Paris' mistreatment of her. She complains about her abandonment (4, 7–8) and about Paris' ungratefulness despite her good services to him (9–20). She reminds Paris that she deigned to live with him in the forest as a couple, although he was socially inferior to her, and then tries to exalt herself and to prove that she is worthy of Paris and of his royal family (77ff.). Oenone's complaints not only illustrate Paris' ingratitude, depicting her as morally superior,[15] but they also unfold her reasons for her future decision to take revenge: she has been insulted, hurt, betrayed and abandoned; another woman has taken her place. Oenone's wounded pride will turn into rage and spite. Paris ought to be more careful.

Oenone's despair begins immediately after she sees Helen alongside Paris. She bursts into lamentations and cries, in a manner clearly and ominously reminiscent of a maenad or a Fury (71–4): 'Then truly I tore my clothes, and beat my breast and scratched my wet cheeks with sharp nails, and filled sacred Ida with howls of complaint and I carried my tears there among the rocks.'† Oenone's reaction reveals her wild side and foreshadows her future attitude towards Paris and Helen.[16] For a woman, mourning is a socially accepted means of articulating anger. Lamentation is a typical elegiac feature totally in line with the elegiac identity of the *Heroides*, as noted earlier. Moreover, mourning is also an indirect way that women influence retribution; Oenone's mourning is the first step towards her revenge. I return to this thought in 'Lamentation and Revenge', below.

---

* *perlegis? an coniunx prohibet nova? perlege: non est / ista Mycenaea littera facta manu!*
† *tunc vero rupique sinus et pectora planxi, / et secui madidas ungue rigente genas, / inplevique sacram querulis ululatibus Iden / illuc has lacrimas in mea saxa tuli.*

Paris, however, whom she still loves, is not going to be Oenone's first target; instead, she begins her revenge by cursing Helen,[17] the woman who 'stole' her husband (75–6):[18] 'So may Helen grieve and weep and lose her husband; / let her suffer what she first brought me!'* Positioned at the heart of the letter, Oenone curses Helen asking that she might lose her husband, mourn for him and suffer what Oenone herself has suffered. Cursing is a means through which women can take revenge and it provides a psychological outlet for Oenone.[19] Her curse seems, at a first glance, to be directed at Helen. But when Oenone asks that Helen might lose a husband, what exactly does she have in mind? Does she mean that Helen's husband will leave her or rather that he will die? And which husband is she referring to? Menelaus or Paris? And what would Paris make of this curse? Ovid leaves the matter open. By using the term *coniunx*, 'husband' (75), Oenone appears to have Menelaus in mind;[20] besides, it is better for her to consider Menelaus as Helen's husband or else she would have to acknowledge Paris' wedding to Helen. Perhaps, Paris too is supposed to understand that *coniunx* in Oenone's curse actually refers to Menelaus.

But what if Oenone has Paris in mind, when she writes about Helen's *coniunx*? What would be the meaning of her curse in that case? One should only remember that in the first line of her letter (quoted above) Oenone calls Helen the *coniunx* of Paris; hence one has every reason to assume that Oenone's curse against Helen may actually apply to Paris, not Menelaus. In this case the curse becomes extremely sinister: it foretells Paris' death, in which Oenone will play a decisive part.

At lines 99–106 of the letter there is another pointed, yet covert reference to the future. Oenone warns Paris about Helen's inclination to extramarital affairs; she is certain that Helen will not remain faithful to him, as was the case with Menelaus:

> Don't expect the Spartan to be loyal to you, if you're wise,
> she who fell so quickly into your embrace.
> Like Menelaus who cries out at the desecration of his marriage bed,
> and wounded grieves at this love for a stranger,
> you will also cry. Wounded chastity is restored
> by no art: it remains lost forever.
> She's on fire with your love: just so, she loved Menelaus;
> now, too trusting, he lies there in an empty bed.†

Oenone's words do make sense. Helen will cheat again, as she has cheated before. The well-informed readers of the letter may detect here an Ovidian

---

* sic Helene doleat defectaque coniuge ploret, / quaeque prior nobis intulit, ipsa ferat!

† nec tibi, si sapias, fidam promitte Lacaenam, / quae sit in amplexus tam cito versa tuos. / ut minor Atrides temerati foedera lecti / clamat et externo laesus amore dolet, / tu quoque clamabis. nulla reparabilis arte / laesa pudicitia est; deperit illa semel. / ardet amore tui? sic et Menelaon amavit. / nunc iacet in viduo credulus ille toro.

allusion to Helen's future affair with Corythus,[21] the son of Paris and Oenone, who is not, however, openly mentioned in the letter. Corythus' affair with Helen will be an excellent revenge for Oenone: her son will ruin his father's affair with the woman who ruined his mother's marriage.[22]

Oenone's words at lines 89–92 can also be read as a pointer to another future event in which Corythus will bring about Paris' downfall. While ostensibly Oenone warns Paris that a war is certain to break out because of Helen's abduction, her oblique phrasing can be read as carrying a double meaning: 'Finally, my love is safe. It brings you no war and the sea carries no vengeful ships. The fugitive daughter of Tyndareus is demanded back with enemy weapons: she comes to your chamber with a proud dowry' (89–92).* Oenone's (i.e. Ovid's) reference to ships that will come to take revenge (*ultrices rates*) can be read as an allusion to a certain version of the myth, whereby a vengeful Oenone sent her son, Corythus, to guide the Greek ships to Troy.[23] For Ovid's readers such implicit foreshadowing undermines Oenone's reassurance to Paris that her love is safe (*tutus amor meus est*).[24]

Furthermore, at lines 113–20 Oenone quotes Cassandra's prophecy about the war, destruction and death, which Helen will bring to Troy.[25] Cassandra's prophecy contributes to the dark and ominous tone of the letter, but it is not expected to change Paris' mind. As is well-known, although Cassandra's prophecies were always true, they were doomed to be incomprehensible and not believed by anyone.[26] Although Oenone acknowledges the truth of the prophecy, because it serves her cause, it is certain that Paris will ignore it. Besides, this has happened before. In his letter to Helen while in Menelaus' palace – Ov. *Her.* 16, which antedates Oenone's letter in dramatic time, but was written after that in historical time – Paris conveniently misinterprets Cassandra's prophecy, claiming that the fires she predicted when he was departing for Sparta were indeed the fires of his love for Helen (16.121–4):[27]

'Where are you rushing to? You'll bring fire back with you! / You don't know how great the flames are you seek in those waters!' / The prophetess was right: I found the fires she spoke of, / and savage love blazes in my tender heart.†

APOLLO AND MEDICINE

Just before closing her letter Oenone speaks proudly of her medical skills, which she got from Apollo himself as a compensation for her rape[28] (139–58):[29]

---

* *denique tutus amor meus est tibi. nulla parantur / bella, nec **ultrices** advehit unda **rates**. / Tyndaris infestis fugitiva reposcitur armis; / hac venit in thalamos dote superba tuos.*
† *'quo ruis?' exclamat, 'referes incendia tecum! / quanta per has nescis flamma petatur aquas!' / vera fuit vates; dictos invenimus ignes, / et ferus in molli pectore flagrat amor.*

> Apollo, who built Troy, loved me truly:
> he took the prize of my virginity.
> By a struggle too: all the same, his hair was torn,
> and his face was scratched, by my fingernails.
> I didn't ask gold and gems for the price of my unchastity:
> it's shameful for gifts to buy a free-born body.
> He entrusted me with his arts of medicine, certain I was worthy,
> and allowed my hands to use his gifts.
> I know every useful herb, with power to aid,
> and every healing root, growing in the world.
> Alas for me, that love's not curable with herbs!
> The skill in that art's lacking from my arts.
> What neither the fruitful earth with its herbs, nor a god,
> can create, that help you can bring to me.
> You can and I deserve it. Pity this worthy girl!*

Oenone's relationship with Apollo and the gift of medicine leads the letter to an ominous closure. Firstly, Oenone stresses that she strongly resisted the god's sexual attack: she tore his hair and scratched his face with her fingernails. Her fight against Apollo emphatically shows that she is a very strong and potentially dangerous woman, a considerable opponent even for a god, much more so for a mortal such as Paris. Secondly, Oenone advertises her knowledge of all the herbs of the world, yet she admits she is unable to heal herself from her love for Paris.[30] Only *he* could do this. Oenone asks Paris for help and mercy, but he will turn his back on her. Ten years later the roles will be reversed. An attentive reader may discern here a preview of Oenone's final revenge, when she will refuse to cure Paris from his fatal wound – *nota bene*, 'refuse', not 'will be unable' to cure him.[31] Revenge can be read between the lines. Oenone's appeal to Paris for help could easily be turned into *Paris' future appeal to Oenone* for help. Ovid thus cleverly foreshadows Oenone's revenge and the form it is to take. The external readers need only to replace the word *puellae* with the word *amanti* for Oenone's plea to anticipate that of Paris' (153–5): 'What neither the fruitful earth with its herbs, nor a god, / can create, that help you can bring to me. / You can and I deserve it. Pity your **worthy lover!**'†

---

* *me fide conspicuus Troiae munitor amavit: / ille meae spolium virginitatis habet, / id quoque luctando. rupi tamen ungue capillos, / oraque sunt digitis aspera facta meis. / nec pretium stupri gemmas aurumque poposci: / turpiter ingenuum munera corpus emunt. / ipse ratus dignam medicas mihi tradidit artes / admisitque meas ad sua dona manus. / quaecumque herba potens ad opem radixque medenti / utilis in toto nascitur orbe, mea est. / me miseram, quod amor non est medicabilis herbis! / deficior prudens artis ab arte mea. / quod nec graminibus tellus fecunda creandis / nec deus, auxilium tu mihi ferre potes. / et potes et merui: dignae miserere puellae!*

† *quod nec graminibus tellus fecunda creandis / nec deus, auxilium tu mihi ferre potes. / et potes et merui:* **digna~~e~~o** *miserere* ~~puellae~~ **amanti**!

LAMENTATION AND REVENGE

Other women in the *Heroides* collection, most notably Phyllis (*Her.* 2) and Dido (*Her.* 7), opt for suicide after their abandonment. These women seem to have limited ways to express their anger. Their rage and frustration is redirected at the self, and suicide may be considered the more socially acceptable outlet for their anger. Oenone, on the other hand, does not choose to harm herself. Instead, her initial reaction is to mourn Paris' betrayal and abandonment, using lamentation to express her frustration and anger. This grieving process functions as a form of complaint and as a first, inward stage in the revenge process.[32] In the dramatic future of the letter Oenone will move on to the final stage of her revenge and will refuse to save Paris' life. Although Oenone is initially absolutely sure about her revenge, after Paris dies, she regrets her actions and kills herself. Oenone's deadly revenge against Paris thus eventually proves self-destructive.

Nevertheless, at the moment when Oenone is still writing her letter, revenge against Paris does not seem to be on her mind. Her rage is aimed only at Helen. Oenone clearly states that she longs to remain forever by Paris' side (5.158: *et tua, quod superest temporis, esse precor*), even though this statement sounds ironic to the literate reader, given her future refusal to save Paris.[33] Only the external reader is able to sense the threat that Oenone poses for Paris.[34] The Trojan prince is so carried away by his new-found love that he is blind to the danger and is unable to pick up on the letter's ominous hints. Besides, one does not really know for sure if Paris actually read Oenone's letter at all. Writing and sending a letter does not automatically guarantee its reception and reading.[35]

Oenone's revenge does not entail physical violence, as is the case with Medea and her children. She limits herself to cursing Helen (in her letter) and to denying Paris help (in the letter's future). She is the only letter writer of the *Heroides* collection who eventually faces and punishes the man who has abandoned her. Whereas other heroines try to harm their ex-lovers through a curse from a distance (e.g. Hypsipyle in *Her.* 6), Oenone lets Paris die by refusing to heal him. This is not blood revenge, but it certainly takes courage and strength which surpasses the traditional 'feminine' stereotype dominating the *Heroides*, in which women are typically depicted as wholly dependent upon their lovers or husbands in a male-dominated world.[36] Although Paris' insult to Oenone concerns the domestic sphere, it will eventually have wider consequences. Oenone emerges as one of the agents for the fall of Troy by bringing about the death of an important defender of the city.[37]

There is more gender-related irony in Oenone's revenge on Paris. Oenone has twice fallen victim to male violence and injustice, first by Apollo who raped her and then by Paris who abandoned her. Now she finds herself in a position of power: the medical skills she acquired from her rapist, Apollo, render her the only person who can save Paris, the other man who wronged her. By withholding these skills Oenone gets even with Paris.[38]

Oenone's letter to Paris can thus be read as a revenge letter: it is a letter of a betrayed woman, who exacts a harsh vengeance on the unfaithful man that abandoned her. This revenge takes place in the dramatic future of their relationship and not at the time of the letter's composition. Paris will most probably read the letter unsuspecting and indifferent, since he is infatuated with Helen. In all fairness, it would have been impossible for him to predict Oenone's future revenge; however, the tone of her letter and her menacing allusions should at least make him cautious.

Ovid is the mastermind behind all this. Revenge enables him to enrich the poetics of this letter with a series of references to the dramatic future of the story. The attentive readers can find in the letter a full account of Oenone's reasons for revenge as well as the exact way in which this revenge is going to take place. Ovid offers the past, present and future of a story of erotic betrayal which ends in revenge: Oenone eventually gets even with her unfaithful ex-lover, after first undergoing a phase of lamentation, in which she finds a means of expressing anger and frustration. As a mourner Oenone is a potential revenger and, although initially a victim, she will soon move from lamentation to revenge and make Paris pay for his erotic betrayal.

NOTES

1. At *Ars* 3.345 Ovid refers to his work as *Epistula* (*vel tibi composita cantetur Epistula voce*). Priscian (*Gramm. Lat.* 2.544.4 Keil) calls the collection *Heroides*, which may have been the title Ovid gave to the work (or *Heroidum liber*). In the manuscripts the titles vary between *Liber epistularum* and *Liber heroidum*. On the title see E. J. Kenney, *Ovid Heroides XVI–XXI* (Cambridge: Cambridge University Press, 1996), p. 1; G. Rosati, *P. Ovidii Nasonis Heroidum Epistulae XVIII–XIX Leander Heroni, Hero Leandro* (Florence: Le Monnier, 1996), pp. 29–30.
2. The order of the letters is: (1) Penelope to Odysseus, (2) Phyllis to Demophoon, (3) Briseis to Achilles, (4) Phaedra to Hippolytus, (5) Oenone to Paris, (6) Hypsipyle to Jason, (7) Dido to Aeneas, (8) Hermione to Orestes, (9) Deianira to Hercules, (10) Ariadne to Theseus, (11) Canace to Macareus, (12) Medea to Jason, (13) Laodamia to Protesilaus, (14) Hypermestra to Lynceus. There is also a fifteenth letter, supposedly sent by Sappho, the well-known Greek lyric poetess, to her legendary lover, Phaon. It is generally agreed that this letter is not Ovidian.
3. Oenone writes her letter from a clearly subjective point of view; Paris is nowhere to be heard.
4. According to tradition Oenone was also skilled in prophecy, but Ovid rejects this attribution. See A. Palmer, *P. Ovidi Nasonis Heroides with the Greek Translation of Planudes* (Oxford: Clarendon Press, 1898), on 5.156; P. E. Knox, *Ovid Heroides. Select Epistles* (Cambridge: Cambridge University Press, 1995), p. 141. Cf. H. Jacobson, *Ovid's Heroides*

(Princeton: Princeton University Press, 1974), pp. 175–6; Alessandro Barchiesi, 'Problemi di interpretazione in Ovidio: continuità delle storie, continuazione dei testi', *Materiali e discussioni per l'analisi dei testi classici* 16 (1986), pp. 77–107 (pp. 94ff.); Sergio Casali, 'Enone, Apollo pastore e l'amore immedicabile: giochi ovidiani su di un topos elegiaco', *Materiali e discussioni per l'analisi dei testi classici* 28 (1992), pp. 85–100 (pp. 86–8); Knox, *Ovid Heroides* on 5.39; L. Landolfi, *Scribentis Imago: Eroine Ovidiane e Lamento Epistolare* (Bologna: Pàtron, 2000), pp. 56–62. Casali, 'Enone, Apollo pastore', p. 88, rightly attributes the silencing of Oenone's prophetic ability to the generic peculiarity of the *Heroides* and to the need for ironic prefiguration as opposed to prophetic certainty. For the ironic prefiguration as an inherent element of the *Heroides*, see Barchiesi, 'Problemi di interpretazione' and Alessandro Barchiesi, 'Narratività e convenzione nelle *Heroides*', *Materiali e discussioni per l'analisi dei testi classici* 19 (1987), pp. 63–90.

5. For Oenone's bucolic nature, see Sara H. Lindheim, '*Omnia Vincit Amor*: Or, Why Oenone Should Have Known It Would Never Work out (*Eclogue* 10 and *Heroides* 5)', *Materiali e discussioni per l'analisi dei testi classici* 44 (2000), pp. 83–101; E. Spentzou, *Readers and Writers in Ovid's Heroides. Transgressions of Genre and Gender* (Oxford: Oxford University Press, 2003), pp. 50–1. See also M. D. Ottone, *Epic and Elegy in Ovid's Heroides: Paris, Helen, and Homeric Intertext* (Diss. Duke University, 2003), who reads Oenone not only as a pastoral figure, but also as elegiac (and epic).

6. For the close association of elegy with complaints, lamentation and tears see A. N. Michalopoulos, *Ovid Heroides 16 and 17: Introduction, Text and Commentary* (Cambridge: Cairns, 2006) on Her. 17.11–12.

7. Hellanicus, *FGrH* 4 F 29; Lycoph. *Alex*. 57–68; Bion 15.10; Apollod. *Bibl*. 3.12.6; Conon *Narr*. 23; Parth. IV; Ov. *Rem. Am*. 457; Prop. 2.32.35ff.; Strab. 596; *Anth. Pal*. 2.215–21; Luc. 9.973; Quint. Smyrn. 10.259–489.

8. See Knox, *Ovid Heroides*, p. 141; Lindheim, *Omnia Vincit Amor*, p. 84; Spentzou, *Readers and Writers*, p. 179. For Oenone and the sources of her myth, see also T. C. W. Stinton, *Euripides and the Judgment of Paris* (London: Society for the Promotion of Hellenic Studies, 1965), pp. 40–50; Jacobson, *Ovid's Heroides*, pp. 176–9; Casali, 'Enone, Apollo pastore', p. 85, n. 3; Edward J. Kenney, '"Dear Helen ...": The Pithanotate Prophasis?', *Papers of the Leeds International Latin Seminar* 8 (1995), pp. 187–207 (p. 194 and n. 42); J.-C. Jolivet, *Allusion et fiction épistolaire dans les Heroides. Recherches sur l'intertextualité ovidienne* (Paris: Diff. De Boccard, 2001), Chapter 1; L. Fulkerson, *The Ovidian Heroine as Author: Reading, Writing, and Community in the Heroides* (Cambridge: Cambridge University Press, 2005), p. 56 n. 48. Knox, *Ovid Heroides*, pp. 140–1 assumes the existence of a lost Hellenistic narrative on Oenone and Paris, whereas Purser *ap*. Palmer, *P. Ovidi Nasonis Heroides*, p. xvi claims that Ovid's source appears to have been Parthenius or the *Cypria*.

9. Fulkerson, *The Ovidian Heroine*, pp. 64–5 rightly touches on Oenone's malicious aspect, focusing on her imprecations against Helen (*Her.* 5.75–6, 99–104). Fulkerson further argues that Oenone models her letter to Paris on the letters of Hypsipyle (*Her.* 6) and Medea (*Her.* 12) to Jason, using principles she has gained from these two women (p. 64).
10. Edward M. Bradley, 'Ovid *Heroides* V: Reality and Illusion', *Classical Journal* 64 (1969), pp. 158–62 (pp. 161–2).
11. Palmer, *P. Ovidi Nasonis Heroides* on 5.156.
12. Casali, 'Enone, Apollo pastore', p. 85 and *passim*.
13. On dramatic irony in the *Heroides*, with an emphasis on *Her.* 16-17, see Michalopoulos, *Ovid Heroides 16 and 17*, pp. 25–9.
14. All translations by A. S. Kline (with slight modifications), available at <http://www.poetryintranslation.com/PITBR/Latin/Heroides1-7.htm> (last accessed 25 October 2016). For Oenone's scornful tone see Lucille Haley, 'The Feminine Complex in the *Heroides*', *Classical Journal* 20 (1924), pp. 15–25 (p. 17).
15. Cf. Ov. *Her.* 5.98 (*causa pudenda tua est; iusta vir arma movet*), where Oenone claims that Paris' cause is disgraceful and that Menelaus will conduct a 'just war'. Oenone sides with the righteous Menelaus fighting against the unrighteous Paris and Helen. As a consequence, her revenge will be an act of justice.
16. This reaction is also a prequel to her future reaction, when she will hear of Paris' death, after she refused to heal him.
17. Curses against Paris and especially Helen are frequent. They are cursed, for example, by Eumaeus (Hom. *Od.* 14.68–9), Hecuba (Eur. *Hec.* 440–2), the Trojan women (Hom. *Il.* 3.411–12; Eur. *Hec.* 943–52), Electra (Eur. *Or.* 130–1), Andromache (Eur. *Tro.* 772). Knox, *Ovid Heroides* on 5.75 rightly notes that in this case Oenone reduces this motif to a strictly personal level.
18. For Oenone and Helen as recursive readers and interlocutors in this epistolary exchange see Fulkerson, *The Ovidian Heroine*, Chapter 2. For the relationship between Oenone and Helen, and for Oenone's effort and failure to resemble Helen, see Fulkerson, *The Ovidian Heroine*, p. 61 with n. 61 and p. 62.
19. Cf. Hypsipyle's curses and threats against Medea. See Fulkerson, *The Ovidian Heroine*, p. 65. On the relationship of Oenone's letter with Hypsipyle's and Medea's, see ibid. pp. 55ff. On female vengeance and women as vengeful cursers in ancient Greece, see Matthews and Salvo in this volume.
20. Casali, 'Enone, Apollo pastore', p. 86 is perhaps hasty in taking it for granted that Oenone refers to Menelaus and notes that this curse will not be fulfilled. He then (p. 89) associates this 'wrong' prophecy with the prophecies of the betrayed elegists for their mistresses. According to Casali, Oenone resembles the elegiac poet–lover in two respects: by issuing a warning of future abandonment and heartbreak to her rival

and by taking as her own the very elegiac *topos* of her incurable love (pp. 89–91).

21. Ἐκ δὲ Οἰνώνης καὶ Ἀλεξάνδρου παῖς ἐγένετο Κόρυθος. οὗτος ἐπίκουρος ἀφικόμενος εἰς Ἴλιον Ἑλένης ἠράσθη· καὶ αὐτὸν ἐκείνη μάλα φιλοφρόνως ὑπεδέχετο. ἦν δὲ τὴν ἰδέαν κράτιστος. φωράσας δὲ αὐτὸν ὁ πατὴρ ἀνεῖλεν (Parth. 34.1).

22. See Jolivet, *Allusion et fiction épistolaire*, p. 48 and Fulkerson, *The Ovidian Heroine*, p. 65.

23. Lycoph. *Alex.* 57–60. On Corythus and his role as a guide of the Greeks see Palmer, *P. Ovidi Nasonis Heroides* on 5.156; Casali, 'Enone, Apollo pastore', p. 94; Knox, *Ovid Heroides* on 5.156.

24. See Jolivet, *Allusion et fiction épistolaire*, p. 49 on 5.89. Alessandro Barchiesi, 'Future Reflexive: Two Modes of Allusion and Ovid's *Heroides*', *Harvard Studies in Classical Philology* 95 (1993), pp. 333–65 (pp. 338–9) associates Oenone's assurance to Paris with Dido's similar promise to Aeneas (Verg. *Aen.* 4.425–6) that she does not seek to destroy the Trojans with the Greeks. He notes at p. 339: 'Paris's future is written in reverse in Ovid's Vergilian model'.

25. On Cassandra's prophecies to Oenone about Helen and the forthcoming war, see Jolivet, *Allusion et fiction épistolaire*, pp. 37–40. According to Knox, *Ovid Heroides* on 5.113 this incident may be an Ovidian addition to the story, although *recolo* could signal allusion to a (lost) text.

26. Apollo fell in love with Cassandra and offered her the art of foretelling the future. Nevertheless, after securing the god's gift Cassandra rejected his love. To punish her, Apollo made sure that her prophecies would not be believed by anyone (Aesch. *Ag.* 1203–12, 1269–74; Hyg. *Fab.* 93). Cassandra mourns her useless prophecies in Lycophron's *Alexandra*. On the identification of Cassandra with Alexandra, see A. Erskine, *Troy Between Greece and Rome. Local Tradition and Imperial Power* (Oxford: Oxford University Press, 2001), pp. 114–15. On Cassandra, see J. Davreux, *La légende de la prophétesse Cassandre* (Liège: Université de Liège, 1942); K. Ledergerber, *Kassandra* (Diss. Fribourg, 1950); and the detailed study of S. Mazzoldi, *Cassandra, la vergine e l'indovina: identità di un personaggio da Omero all'Ellenismo* (Pisa: Istituti editoriali e poligrafici internazionali, 2001).

27. See Michalopoulos, *Ovid Heroides 16 and 17* on *Her.* 16.121–2 and 123–4. Paris also misinterprets Cassandra's interpretation of the dream Hecuba saw when she was pregnant with him (16.43–50). See Michalopoulos, *Ovid Heroides 16 and 17* on *Her.* 16.47–8 and 49–50.

28. Knox, *Ovid Heroides* on 5.139–46 notes that the association of Oenone's medical skill with a gift from Apollo or with her rape by him may be an Ovidian innovation based on a familiar model.

29. The authenticity of lines 135–46 is disputed. See Palmer, *P. Ovidi Nasonis Heroides* ad loc. and Sergio Casali, 'The Cambridge *Heroides*', *Classical Journal* 92 (1997), pp. 305–14 (pp. 306–7), who concedes that lines

135–8 may not be excised. Cf. Casali, 'Enone, Apollo pastore', p. 92, n. 18. G. Rosati, *Lettere di eroine* (Milan: Biblioteca universale Rizzoli, 1989) and Knox, *Ovid Heroides*, followed by Lindheim, *Omnia Vincit Amor*, p. 91, n. 27 and 42, consider lines 135–46 as a genuine part of the poem.
30. For an informed reading of this passage as an expression of the elegiac *topos* of *amor immedicabilis* see Casali, 'Enone, Apollo pastore', pp. 91ff.
31. For the ironical prefiguration here, see Casali, 'Enone, Apollo pastore', p. 93.
32. In her book on lovesickness, *Lovesickness and Gender in Early Modern English Literature* (Oxford: Oxford University Press, 2008), pp. 8–10, Lesel Dawson discusses suicide and other kinds of masochistic behaviour as anger turned inward.
33. See Spentzou, *Readers and Writers*, p. 184.
34. Cf. Knox, *Ovid Heroides* on 5.154: 'There is an ironic hint of Paris' fated death when only Oenone could have cured him, but the irony is Ovid's not Oenone's, since Ovid does not follow the tradition that she had the gift of prophecy.'
35. On the precariousness of the letter, see Spentzou, *Readers and Writers*, p. 137, Fulkerson, *The Ovidian Heroine*, p. 57.
36. For revenge as the turning of female grief into manly action, see Yearling in this volume. See also Pollard in this volume on how Euripides' Hecuba uses lament to transform her grief into violence.
37. Although Paris is not the epitome of epic masculinity and military prowess, he is nonetheless the man who caused the war and killed Achilles, the greatest hero of the Greeks, albeit with decisive help from Apollo.
38. For a thorough discussion of femininity's association with revenge and vengeful crimes, and an enquiry into the gender and role of the Erinyes see Hall in this volume.

CHAPTER 13

Lament and Vengeance in the Alliterative *Morte Arthure*

Anne Baden-Daintree

At the opening of the Alliterative *Morte Arthure*, King Arthur's victory celebrations are interrupted by a demand from Rome for tribute. Furious over what he perceives to be an insulting and unjust mandate, Arthur launches his kingdom into a succession of wars. King Arthur's fury over Rome's demand, and the speed with which he moves to revenge the wrong done to his honour, is characteristic of this rendition of King Arthur. Unlike Malory's fifteenth-century prose romance, *Le Morte Darthur*, which draws mainly on courtly French romance for its source material, the less well-known fourteenth-century Alliterative *Morte Arthure* has a narrative based largely on the pseudo-historical accounts of Chronicle texts in Latin, Middle English and Anglo-Norman. Honour and vengeance are both central to the economy of masculinity in this textual tradition; when reputation comes under attack, Arthur's court responds with retaliatory violence. While the Alliterative *Morte Arthure* shares with other Middle English Arthurian texts a celebration of *wirchipe* (honour) and *menske* (reputation), it is less clearly allied to the romance genre than to history or epic, with more of the action taking place on the battlefield than at court. However, within these wider political conflicts, there are moments when the poem slows down to focus on more personal revenge narratives, in which an individual's private grief drives forward the military action.

This chapter focuses on the role of lament in the Alliterative *Morte Arthure*, examining how it fits into the poem's revenge narratives and influences the presentation of Arthur's character and his masculinity. In the first of these, Arthur is called on to end the suffering of his subjects under the cruel terror of the Giant of Mont St Michel. On his way to fight the giant, he encounters a widow, who, grieving over the body of her brutally raped and murdered ward, the Duchess of Brittany, demands that Arthur kill the giant to avenge the young woman's death. In the second example, Arthur mourns the death of Gawain, his most beloved soldier and kinsman, after he is killed in hand-to-hand combat with Mordred. Here, the lamentation is performed by Arthur himself, over Gawain's dead body. While both instances shift the focus away from a wider, political quarrel and towards a more personal injury, the differences between these two laments and their role in the revenge process are significant: whereas the first (performed by the widow) strengthens Arthur's courage and resolve, the second (performed by Arthur) stalls the action and temporarily halts the revenge process. Indeed, Arthur's intense sorrow, viewed by his knights as dangerously emasculating, anticipates and contributes to his eventual downfall and death.

The catalogue of deaths in the *Morte Arthure* is marked out by expressions of grief; these are intimately associated with, and almost always precede, acts of vengeance.[1] However, the only speeches which bear distinct characteristics of the lament tradition are those made by the foster-mother to the Duchess of Brittany, and those made by Arthur on three occasions: on the duchess' death, on Gawain's death and finally anticipating his own death at the end of the text.[2] Despite the many expressions of grief by other knights, it is only King Arthur who adopts the conventionally female role of lamentation, and this clearly invites comparison with the only female character with any significant voice. Lamentation is frequently presented as a female-gendered activity, which has a particular function in the revenge process, similar to that presented in the blood feuds of Icelandic sagas. Although it is unlikely that the Icelandic saga tradition has a direct influence on this text, the parallels are striking in terms of the process of incitement to revenge, and the operation of lament. In the saga tradition, it is the woman's role to mourn a death, through a number of conventional verbal patterns and physical gestures such as wringing hands, weeping and the tearing of clothes and hair. Where there is family honour to defend and a death to avenge, the female family members also incite the men to take revenge. Women are responsible for the *hvǫt* (incitement or whetting), in which the woman encourages the man to take the necessary retaliatory action through a formalised speech, often accompanied by ritualised actions.[3]

The exchange between Flosi and Hildigunnr in *Njáls saga* illustrates this relationship between gender and vengeance in Icelandic sagas.[4] In this scene, Hildigunnr, the widow of Hoskuld, invites her uncle, the chieftain Flosi, to a meal where her words and actions demand retributive action for the death of her husband. The meal is designed to emphasise her husband's absence and the brutal way that he was killed: she leaves an empty chair at her dead husband's place at the head of the table, provides Flosi with a torn and ragged cloth to dry his hands, expresses her grief and loss following Hoskuld's death, and brings out the bloodied cloak in which he was murdered, shaking out the dried blood over Flosi's shoulders. Hildigunnr's words then make clear that, regardless of legal process, Flosi is responsible for taking revenge: while it is necessary for Hildigunnr to initiate the revenge action, Flosi must carry it out. As Carol Clover argues, the scene between Hildigunnr and Flosi also demonstrates how the two female activities of mourning and the *hvǫt* are interrelated. In this episode, a single speech by Hildigunnr performs both functions: Hildigunnr 'whets and laments at the same time and even in the same words. As his lamenter, Hildigunnr is the medium through which Hǫskuldr's wounded corpse demands revenge.'[5] These processes are not confined to the sagas: drawing on Clover's work, David Clark has examined the wider literary context for such associations. His analysis of the processes of mourning and vengeance in the *Poetic Edda* shows that here, too, lament operates as *hvǫt*, and he argues that 'these inextricably linked functions are often seen to be the paradigms for female participation in revenge'.[6]

A similar relationship between lamentation and revenge is evident in King Arthur's interaction with the grieving widow he meets before he fights the Giant of Mont St Michel. This exchange occurs after he has already set out to confront the giant, who has been terrorising the local population. When he encounters this woman, she is mourning the death of her ward, the Duchess of Brittany, who has been raped and murdered. The widow performs what is, in effect, an Icelandic *hvǫt*, first weeping and wringing her hands at the site of a freshly dug grave, before going on to urge Arthur to take revenge (950–2). Her opening words to Arthur warn him of the danger. Even though Arthur's appearance is impressive (he is disguised as one of his own knights), she fears for his safety, implicitly challenging his masculine strength: '*Thou arte frely and faire and in thy fyrste flourez; / Bot thow arte fay, be my faythe*' (You are noble, handsome, in the prime of life – but you are fated to die, by my faith, 970–1).[7] The widow provides an account of the duchess' death – the body being slit to the navel in the process of rape and murder – and then describes her acts of mourning:

> Look, here lies the duchess, dead and buried deep in the earth; she was seized just today and murdered without mercy, before midday was rung – I don't know why. He has raped and defiled her and left her for dead: he clumsily slaughtered her, and slit her to the navel. I have embalmed her body here and buried her. Because of this sorrow beyond remedy, I shall never be happy. Of all the family she had, none attended her except me, her foster-mother [nurse] for fifteen years. I shall never attempt to leave this headland, but shall be found here until I fall to my fate. (974–85)*

Her lament concludes with a statement of her life-long dedication to mourning this death. Just as the duchess was cruelly *fay leuede* (left for dead) by the giant, so too will she be *fay leuede* over the grave of her beloved foster-daughter, a repetition which suggests her identification with the duchess and her sense

---

* Loo, here the duchez dere – todaye was cho takyn – / Depe doluen and dede, dyked in moldez. / He hade morthirede this mylde be middaye war rongen / Withowttyn mercy one molde; I not watte it ment. / He has forsede hir and fylede, and cho es fay leuede: / He slewe her vnslely and slitt hir to þe nauyll,/ And here haue I bawmede hir and beryede þeraftyr. / For bale of þe botelesse blythe be I neuer! / Of alle þe frendez cho hade, þere folowede none aftyre / Bot I, hir foster modyr of fyftene wynter; / To ferke of this farlande fande sall I neuer, / Bot here be foundan on felde till I be fay leuede.

that they will share a common fate. The widow then goes on to enumerate the atrocities inflicted by the giant on the other women and children of the region, including rape, torture and cannibalism. Arthur responds to the widow's account of the duchess' murder with a restatement of his opening address: that he has come, as one of Arthur's boldest knights, to confront the giant and negotiate some kind of truce. The widow is scornful: '*thir words are but waste* [worthless]' (993), she tells him, suggesting that as the giant is so powerful and ruthlessly violent, Arthur's task is hopeless. For several years the giant has demanded the presence in combat of King Arthur himself and seeks his beard as trophy (although as he is disguised the widow does not recognise him as the king). The widow's words, as well as being a statement of despair, are a direct challenge to Arthur's personal strength and political governance. While Arthur was already prepared to act to prevent further atrocities, the widow's words strengthen his determination and clarify for him that the only real choice is to challenge the giant himself.

The widow's words and gestures thus act as an incitement to vengeance, recalling the patterns of lament and *hvǫt* that Clover has identified in the saga tradition. The king's honour depends on an appropriately violent response, as a verbally negotiated truce would be insufficient retribution for the devastation and terror that have been inflicted. Although Arthur demonstrates little of the horror that we might expect, this emotionally charged situation reinforces his resolve in the final moments before his direct confrontation with the giant. Furthermore, from the perspective of the late medieval readership, Arthur would also have had a legal as well as moral responsibility to enact revenge. As Christopher Cannon observes, legal changes in the late thirteenth century that conflated the crimes of rape and 'ravishment' had 'the implicit result of converting rapes from crimes that harmed a woman victim into trespassory wrongs that damaged property' (whereby the duchess is the damaged 'property' who would have been rendered unmarriageable had she survived the attack).[8] So in legal terms, in the absence of any other male guardian, the right of appeal would have been Arthur's: the female guardian laments the duchess' death and commemorates her by building a chapel on the site, while Arthur seeks retribution, responding to the implicit challenge to his masculinity by facing the aggressor alone.[9] The giant, who wears a cloak decorated with the beards of the men he has vanquished, clearly aims not only to kill but also to emasculate the men who challenge him.[10] Resolved not to become another of the giant's trophies, Arthur defeats the giant single-handedly, before continuing on his wider mission to wage war across Europe. The widow's lament clearly plays an important role within this episode, rousing Arthur to engage in combat and prove his masculine strength.

The patterning of this episode, and the way that a formal lament is shown to precede vengeance, anticipates the response to the death of Gawain and the climatic events that lead to Arthur's downfall and death. As in the first instance, when Arthur is already preparing to confront the giant when he encounters the widow, the king is similarly on his way to fight Mordred when he discovers that his nephew, Gawain, has been slain. And, in both examples, the wider atrocities are understood through the death of a specific individual. However, where the widow's words inspire Arthur to fight, in this later scene Arthur's grief overwhelms him, compromising his ability to act. His expression of sorrow is seen by his men as emasculating; the king withdraws from the battle that continues to take place around him, entering a feminised space which enables the articulation of grief.[11] This pause in the narrative is typical of the way in which alliterative set pieces function within this textual tradition, where the text temporarily suspends action to focus on detailed description. But the change of pace is particularly distinctive here, as it is being employed for the expression of emotion, rather than the more typical description of armour, landscape or battle. Nor does Arthur fully leave this feminised space even when reassuming his kingly authority and martial role: he receives wounds which are symbolically castrating, and he eventually performs his own lament.

The closing stages of the narrative of the *Morte Arthure*, which lead up to Gawain's death, are concerned with the revelation of Mordred's betrayal of King Arthur's trust and the civil war that ensues. Arthur declares war on his nephew, Mordred, who, in this version of the Arthurian legend, is Arthur's nephew and not his illegitimate son. Awarded regency while Arthur is engaged in war abroad, Mordred abuses his power taking both Arthur's kingdom and his wife. Mordred's cruel mismanagement of the kingdom is finally revealed to Arthur by a loyal servant the day after he has a prophetic dream about the Wheel of Fortune that foretells his downfall. Having listened to his sage's interpretation of this dream, Arthur sets off alone, deep in thought '*with brethe* [wrath] *at his herte*' (3465). He is greeted by Sir Craddoke, disguised as a pilgrim, who explains how he has been driven from his homeland as a result of Mordred's actions, and outlines for the king the scale of the destruction:

> Sir, your regent is wicked and reckless in his behaviour, for he has wrought evil and horror since you left your land. He has appropriated castles and crowned himself in your place, and collected all the revenues that belong to the Round Table. (3523–6)*

While Sir Craddoke's speech is more a complaint than a lament, it nonetheless has a structural and affective affinity to the lament of the widow in the way that it enumerates crimes and inspires Arthur to retaliatory action. As with the widow's lament, Sir Craddoke begins his speech with an extensive catalogue of atrocities. Mordred has divided the country, handing out land and titles as he pleases and assembling a powerful army of strong warriors from Scotland, Wales and Ireland against the king. Taxes are imposed on the people, and monasteries and convents come under attack. Paupers are held to ransom

---

* *Sir, thi wardane es wikkede and wilde of his dedys, / For he wandreth has wroghte sen þou awaye passede; / He has castells encrochede, and corownde hym seluen, / Kaughte in all þe rentis of þe Rownde Tabill.*

and fierce troops begin to assemble on board ships docked at the south coast ready to fight Arthur's men on their return to England. At the end of this long list of crimes, Craddoke finally discloses what he considers to be the *werste* (worst) news: Mordred has married Guinevere and she has borne his children. This speech, with its series of revelations carefully managed in order to gain the strongest response from Arthur concludes: '*Thus has sir Modrede merrede* [ruined] *vs all!*' (3555). This clearly has the intended effect: 'Then, with anger in his heart, this brave king's countenance changed, because of this grief beyond remedy. "By the Cross", cried the king, "I shall revenge this. He shall fully repent all his wicked deeds!"' (3557–60).* Arthur's change of countenance, the anger and instinctive call for vengeance are typical of the king throughout this text. The catalogue of Mordred's deeds acts (as did the account of the giant) as an incitement to revenge. Arthur withdraws to his tents to gather his men and explain to them Mordred's acts of treason and betrayal, and they begin their long journey back to England. The battle begins at sea, off the coast of Southampton, and when the opposing army has been roundly defeated, Arthur and Gawain turn their attention to the substantial armies that Mordred has gathered on the shore. Gawain rashly disembarks before the ships can properly be landed, and engages in battle with great zeal and success until he meets his death in hand-to-hand combat with Mordred.

The grief that Gawain's death will cause the king is foregrounded by the multiple eulogies that precede Arthur's lament. As Haas has observed, we hear authorial lament (with repetitions of '*thus sir Gawayne es gon* [is gone]'), King Froderike of Fres' praise, and Mordred's eloquent eulogy in which he expresses regret for what he has done; Mordred leaves the site speechless and tearful: '*Whene he thoghte on þis thynge, it thirllede* [pierced] *his herte*' (3890).[12] When Arthur first hears of Gawain's death, he wrings his hands (3920), following the formulaic gestures of extreme emotion.[13] He then picks up the dead body, holding it in his arms and addressing it directly:

> My beloved kinsman, I am left in sorrow, for now my honour has gone and my combat has come to an end. Here lie my hopes of prosperity, my success in battle. My courage and strength rested entirely in him. My counsellor, my comfort who maintained my hopes; king of all the knights who lived under Christ. You were worthy to be king, even though I wore the crown. (3956–62)†

---

* *Than the burliche kynge, for brethe at his herte / And for this botelesse bale, all his ble chaungede. / 'By þe Rode' sais þe roye, 'I sall it revenge! / Hym sall repente full rathe all his rewthe werkes!'*

† *Dere kosyn o kynde, in kare am I leuede, / For nowe my wirchipe es wente and my were endide. / Here es þe hope of my hele, my happynge in armes; / My herte and my hardynes hale one hym lengede – / My concell, my comforthe þat kepide myn herte! / Of all knyghtes þe kynge þat vndir Criste lifede, / Þou was worthy to be kynge, þofe I þe corown bare.*

Arthur's personal grief is compounded by his sense that Gawain's death represents the culmination of all his losses and the end of his military success: his *wirchipe* (honour) is gone and with it his good fortune in battle. Gawain's skilled combat has been central to Arthur's territorial gains: 'All my prosperity and honour in this great world were won through Sir Gawain, and through his prowess alone' (3963–4).* That this lament functions in part as *hvǫt* resides not only in the fact that Gawain's battle prowess is vital to Arthur's reputation as a conqueror, but also that the death of Arthur's legitimate heir threatens the future security of the kingdom.

The king spends time lamenting, embracing Gawain's body so that his beard becomes bloodied, and scooping up some of the blood and gore spilt on the battlefield. He later bears the blood-filled helmet away with the body before he sets forth to avenge the death. Arthur's men are clearly taken aback by Arthur's passionate response. They reproach him for his weeping and the way that he embraces and repeatedly kisses Gawain's body, in terms that suggest such behaviour is emasculating:

'Stop, you stain yourself with blood,' say these brave men. 'This grief is hopeless, it cannot amend anything. Surely there is no honour in the wringing of your hands? To weep like a woman is without reason. Be knightly in your bearing, as befits a king, and for Christ's love of heaven, set aside such clamorous grief!' (3975–80)†

Arthur's lament is perceived by his companions to be pointless and debilitating: rather than rousing him to action, it threatens his royal authority and martial ability. However, despite the men's concerns, Arthur's laments eventually do lead to action, in a similar manner to the whetting scenes found in Icelandic sagas. His speech demanding revenge, accompanied by the staged and symbolic engagement with the spilt blood, has structural affinity to the episode between Flosi and Hildigunnr in *Njáls saga*. Arthur's lament can thus be seen to function as *hvǫt*, but it combines the different gendered roles of men and women in the Icelandic tradition, in a process of 'self-whetting'. Arthur sets out his grief and loss as evidence for the need for vengeance, knowing that he alone bears responsibility for its enactment.

However, Arthur defends his right to mourn as he sees fit, and announces his intent to avenge in the same rash way as Gawain, ignoring advice. Sir Wycharde advises the king to wait until more troops have assembled ('*Sojorne* [stay] *in this ceté* [city] *and semble thi berynes* [gather your men]', 4027), but

---

* *My wele and my wirchipe of all þis werlde riche / Was wonnen thourghe sir Wawayne and thourghe his witt one!*
† *"Blyne," sais thies bolde men, thow blodies þi selfen! / Þis es botles bale, for bettir bees it neuer. / It es no wirchipe, iwysse, to wryng thyn hondes; / To wepe als a woman it es no witt holden. / Be knyghtly of contenaunce, als a kyng scholde, / And leue siche clamoure, for Cristes lufe of heuen!*

Arthur is intent on vengeance and determined to enact it personally:[14] 'I shall never rest soundly or with peace in my heart, in any city or town in this earth, I will neither rest nor sleep, despite my heavy eyes, until he who slew him is slain' (4042–5).* Arthur's rejection of advice is made explicit through his echo of Wycharde's words. His anger is directed specifically towards Mordred, and there is a sense that Gawain's death has somehow unmanned Arthur. This is carried over into their final confrontation, when Arthur is fatally wounded in hand-to-hand combat by his own sword, now in Mordred's hands. As in this text's other instances of genital wounding, Arthur's injuries are indicative of a more symbolic process of emasculation.[15] This particular wound, as Dorsey Armstrong has suggested, also has specific resonance for the relationship between gender and revenge.[16] Armstrong observes that Arthur's handing over the regency of his kingdom to his nephew is complicated by the way in which Mordred abuses his position of power. Not only does he fail to relinquish his control when Arthur returns, but it emerges that his wardship of Guinevere has resulted in his fathering two children (a detail unique to this version of the Arthurian story). This enhanced masculinity, confirming Mordred's virility in the face of Arthur's failure to produce an heir, is then emphasised by Mordred's appropriation of Arthur's sword, Clarent, which had been in Guinevere's personal safekeeping. As Armstrong summarises:

> It is significant as well that when Mordred inflicts the fatal wound upon Arthur with that sword, the blow strikes the king in the *felettes*, the loins – a bodily sign of the emasculation that Mordred has already inflicted on his uncle by conceiving children with the queen.[17]

This sword, once a symbol of Arthur's power, here becomes an emblem and signifier of the betrayal that leads to Arthur's death. Its appearance on the battlefield is the moment when Arthur understands the extent to which he has been betrayed by both his wife and his nephew, intensifying the need for vengeance. But while Arthur succeeds in killing Mordred, he dies in the process.

As he lies dying on the battlefield, Arthur performs his own lament, an act that accentuates his isolation and his alignment with a female gendered role. Drawing attention to his own failures of masculinity, Arthur compares himself to a widow: 'I must take shelter alone on the heath. Like a woeful widow in want of her husband, I shall weep and curse and wring my hands, for my honour and judgement have gone for ever' (4284–7).† Arthur's description of himself as '*a wafull wedowe þat wanttes hir beryn*' (a woeful widow in want of her husband) emphasises the connection between this lament and that of the

---

* *I sall neuer sojourne sounde ne sawghte at myn herte, / In ceté ne in subarbe sett appon erthe / Ne ʒitt slomyre ne slepe with my slawe eyghne, / Till he be slayne þat hym slowghe.*
† *I may helples one hethe house by myn one, / Alls a wafull wedowe þat wanttes hir beryn / I may werye and wepe and wrynge myn handys, / For my wytt and my wirchipe awaye es for euer!*

widow who mourns the Duchess of Brittany. As Hamel points out, none of the sources or analogues describes the foster-mother of the duchess as a widow, so that this detail appears designed to connect Arthur's situation with the grieving woman, drawing attention to their isolation (in that they can be seen as doubly bereft).[18] That there is no one left to lament the king's death contrasts with Gawain's multiple eulogies, increasing the sense of his isolation and failure. No longer seeing himself as the masculine avenging hero, Arthur presents himself as a feminised, solitary mourner. He expresses his loss of patriarchal power in terms which also recall that power:

> King, nobly crowned, I am left in sorrow. All my lordship is now laid low on the field. You who have given me reward, by God's grace, upheld my honour and dignity by the strength of their hands, made me noble in this world and conqueror of this earth. In this troublesome time this injury was brought about – that through a traitor all my faithful lords are destroyed. Here lies the noble blood of the Round Table. (4275–82)*

Arthur's speech here closely echoes his words to his men early in the poem, before the succession of battles that make up the large part of the text. A comparison of the two statements shows just how far he has fallen and how his fate is interwoven with the collective fate of his men. His celebratory speech at the opening of the narrative is intended to rouse his men to further successes: 'You uphold my reputation and manly virtue throughout the earth, all my honour in foreign lands, my prosperity and renown over all this great world; all that rightly belongs to my crown, has been achieved through your knightly valour' (399–402).† This rallying cry to the troops is replayed more than once at times of personal crisis. Arthur's lament for Gawain's death is also expressed in markedly similar terms: '*My wele and my wirchipe of all þis werlde riche / Was wonnen thourghe sir Wawayne*' (My well-being and my honour, through all this great world, were won through Sir Gawain, 3963–4). These instances of repetition emphasise Arthur's failure to fulfil the promises made in his opening address; there is a particular poignancy in the recollection of collective honour as a driving force as Arthur lies dying, alone, on the battlefield.

King Arthur cannot call for his own death to be avenged directly as Mordred is already dead. However, the one specific instruction that might be seen as *huot* has clear resonance for the slight to masculinity occasioned by Mordred's act of cuckoldry. The close association between lament and

---

* *Kyng, comly with crowne, in care am I leuyde! / All my lordchipe lawe in lande es layde vndyre, / That me has gyfen gwerdouns, be grace of Hym seluen, / Mayntenyde my manhede by myghte of theire handes, / Made me manly one molde and mayster in erthe! / In a tenefull tym this torfere was rereryde, / That for a traytoure has tynte all my trewe lordys; / Here rystys the riche blude of the Rownde Table.*

† *My menske and my manhede 3e mayntene in erthe, / Myn honour all vtterly in oþer kyngys landes, / My wele and my wyrchipe of all þis werlde ryche; / 3e haue knyghtly conqueryde þat to my coroun langes.*

vengeance is loosened here as Arthur lies dying, his lament focusing on what has been stripped away, and the suggestion that there is no one left to avenge the destruction of his kingdom. The *hvqt* element of his speech comes almost as an afterthought, occurring once he has been safely removed to Glastonbury, and as well as being incitement, is also a final act of kingly authority. Arthur's last words tie up all loose ends, ensuring his own confession and absolution, then the ongoing governance of his kingdom, the enactment of appropriate funerary rites for his troops and, finally, retribution:

> Call me a confessor, that I may quickly be given the Eucharist, whatever else happens. If Christ allows, my kinsman, Constantine shall inherit the crown, as is fitting to his birth-right. To gain my blessing, take those of my men who have died in battle and ensure their burial. And afterwards see that Mordred's children are secretly slain, and cast into the sea: let no wicked weed grow or flourish on this earth. I caution you, for your honour, to carry out all I command. I forgive all wrongdoing, for Christ's love in Heaven. If Guinevere has fared well, then good fortune be with her. (4314–25)*

Arthur's compromised enactment of retribution is apparent in the closing gesture of transfer of power to Constantine in the absence of a surviving male heir. Mordred's fathering of children on Arthur's wife emphasised the king's lack of successful paternity, and the death of his most apt and worthy heir, Gawain, leaves him isolated, having failed to ensure a familial line of succession. Arthur's final act of revenge against Mordred and Guinevere is the ordering of the murder of their children. Although (as Armstrong points out) these are blood relations and therefore could legitimately be named as heirs, their survival would be a lasting reminder of Arthur's failure to prove his virility through the production of a son.[19] And while much of the poem is couched in terms of male rivalry and combat, at the end of the narrative it is Guinevere who is left alone, childless and presumably stripped of all material security and status. The command is to be carried out as a matter of honour ('*fore thy wirchipe*'), and the sense of honour and justice carries through to the end, where Arthur appears to forgive Guinevere for her role in his downfall, but rather ambiguously neither ensures her safety and well-being, nor wishes ill upon her.

The way in which Arthur is presented at different points in the narrative,

---

* *Doo calle me a confessour with Criste in his armes! / I will be howselde in haste, whate happe so betyddys. / Constantyn, my cosyn, he sall the corown bere / Alls becommys hym of kynde, ʒife Criste will hym thole. / Beryn, fore my benison, thowe berye ʒone lordys / That in baytaille with brondez are broghte owte of lyfe; / And sythen merke manly to Mordrede children, / That they bee sleyghely slayne and slongen in watyrs – / Latt no wykkyde wede waxe ne wrythe one this erthe! / I warne fore thy wirchipe, wirke alls I bydde. / I foregyffe all greffe, for Cristez lufe of heuen; / ʒife Waynor hafe wele wroghte, wele hir betydde.*

and the ways in which an audience might be expected to respond, represent sharp contrasts rather than a linear or gradual character development. Arthur's defeat of the Giant of Mont St Michel represents him in a manner that is distinct from his commanding presence as a leader and successful warrior. His anonymity through disguise, his defence of the vulnerable, his evident compassion, and his determination to avenge the duchess' death, all demonstrate his capacity for empathy and selfless endeavour. The subsequent battle accounts, however, show him to be motivated by personal gain and glory, ruthlessly and often needlessly cruel. But Gawain's death returns the focus to Arthur's positive personal characteristics, in which the call for vengeance is motivated by grief, but also the strategic significance of this death, and the emphasis is on past glories more than future conquests. The tragic shaping of the plot, and the signposting of this final stage through the dream of the Wheel of Fortune, encourages a re-evaluation of Arthur's actions, and the possibility that the final acts of vengeance serve to redeem his character. While the *Morte Arthure* is renowned for its battle accounts and its representation of Arthur as a conquering hero, the poem also employs lament and vengeance as shaping forces, and offers a distinction between the kind of contained grief that leads to military action and the type that overwhelms the griever. It is striking that Arthur mourns Gawain in a manner which recalls 'feminine' mourning behaviour and the laments of the widow: Arthur's men see his behaviour as emasculating, threatening his kingly status and military ability. But the heroic action that follows might be seen to restore his status as a just king, so that his mourning functions as the final pivotal point in the narrative. It marks a return of his honourable conduct, where Arthur's grief-driven military activity is viewed as justified; his mourning behaviours, his military action and his final commands transferring power all serve to reinforce the bonds of male fellowship, while simultaneously restoring governance and social order.

NOTES

1. Renate Haas, 'The Laments for the Dead', in Karl Heinz Göller (ed.), *The Alliterative* Morte Arthure: *A Reassessment of the Poem* (Cambridge: D. S. Brewer, 1981), pp. 117–29, defines most of these as 'lament', and identifies ten in total in this text; these are mainly clustered around the Giant episode, and on Gawain and Arthur at the end of the text.
2. The episodes identified by Haas as lament are 852–76, the Templar informing Arthur of the Giant's actions; 868–75, Arthur's immediate response; 950–1, the widow's lament; 1153–5, Kay's distress at Arthur's apparently fatal injuries; 2678–85, Sir Wicher and Sir Walter's 'anticipatory lament' on Gawain's serious wounds; 2962–8, Gawain's response to the death of his young ward, Childric; 3858–63, 'authorial lament' on Gawain's death; King Fredericke's praise-filled enquiry as to Gawain's identity; 3875–85, Mordred's eulogy; 3956–68, 3981–4008, Arthur's lament for Gawain (in

two stages); and 4275–6, Arthur's 'secular' lament reflecting on both his own death and the many casualties among his men.
3. Carol Clover, 'Hildigunnr's Lament', in John Lindlow, Lars Lönnroth and Gerd Wolfgang Weber (eds), *Structure and Meaning in Old Norse Literature: New Approaches to Textual Analysis and Literary Criticism* (Odense: Odense University Press, 1986), pp. 141–83, explains that the term *hvǫt* is related etymologically to 'whetting' 'in both its literal and figurative meanings'. See also Jóhanna Friðriksdóttir, *Women in Old Norse Literature: Bodies, Words and Power* (Basingstoke: Palgrave Macmillan, 2013), pp. 15–45, for a reconsideration of the scope and nature of the *hvǫt* in a wider range of literature than considered by earlier critics.
4. See Anne Baden-Daintree, 'Kingship and the Intimacy of Grief in the Alliterative *Morte Arthure*', in Frank Brandsma, Carolyne Larrington and Corinne Saunders (eds) *Emotions in Medieval Arthurian Literature: Body, Mind, Voice* (Woodbridge: D. S. Brewer, 2015), pp. 87–104, where I examined the exchange between Flosi and Hildigunnr in *Njáls saga*, in terms of its comparable use of the dead man's blood in the incitement to revenge. Here I examine this episode and its critical heritage in order to explore further the gender implications of the relationship between grief and vengeance.
5. Clover, 'Hildigunnr's Lament', p. 40.
6. David Clark, 'Undermining and En-Gendering Vengeance: Distancing and Anti-Feminism in the *Poetic Edda*', *Scandinavian Studies* 77 (2005), pp. 173–200 (p. 190).
7. Mary Hamel (ed.), *Morte Arthure: A Critical Edition* (New York and London: Garland, 1984).
8. Statutes of 1275 and 1285: Westminster I and II, respectively. See Christopher Cannon, 'The Rights of Medieval English Women: Crime and the Issue of Representation', in Barbara A. Hanawalt and David Wallace (eds), *Medieval Crime and Social Control* (Minneapolis: University of Minnesota Press, 1999), pp. 156–85 (pp. 172–3).
9. While this might be anachronistic to the Arthurian context, much of this text speaks to a fourteenth-century audience, such as the similarly anachronistic significance of the City of Metz, as noted by Arlyn Diamond, 'Heroic Subjects: Women and the Alliterative *Morte Arthure*', in Jocelyn Wogan-Browne, Rosalynn Voaden, Arlyn Diamond, Ann Hutchison, Carol Meale and Lesley Johnson (eds), *Medieval Women: Texts and Contexts in Late Medieval Britain* (Turnhout: Brepols, 2000), pp. 293–308. See also Karl Heinz Göller, 'Reality versus Romance: A Reassessment of the Alliterative *Morte Arthure*', in Karl Heinz Göller (ed.) *The Alliterative* Morte Arthure: *A Reassessment of the Poem* (Cambridge: D.S. Brewer, 1981), pp. 15–29, particularly his discussion of the employment of details derived from concrete events of the fourteenth century (pp. 18–19). The legal definition of women as property also anticipates the way in which Guinevere's betrayal initiates the final conflict which destroys Arthur's reign. Guinevere's

transfer to the protection of Mordred is part of the regency of land and other property which he (reluctantly, he claims) takes on to enable Arthur to engage in the Roman wars. So when Mordred violates the terms of this relationship through usurpation of land and fathering of children by Arthur's wife, it is, again, an injury to property which Arthur is required to avenge.

10. Robert Bartlett, 'Symbolic Meanings of Hair in the Middle Ages', *Transactions of the Royal Historical Society* 4 (1994), pp. 43–60, examines the complexities of interpreting the significance of beards as physical markers of masculinity across different cultures during the Middle Ages. See also Carl Phelpstead, 'Hair Today, Gone Tomorrow: Hair Loss, the Tonsure, and Masculinity in Medieval Iceland', *Scandinavian Studies* 85 (2013), pp. 1–19 (p. 9), for a summary of scholarship on beardlessness and masculinity across various languages and cultures.
11. See Baden-Daintree, 'Kingship and the Intimacy of Grief', p. 88.
12. Haas, 'Laments for the Dead'.
13. See Baden-Daintree, 'Kingship and the Intimacy of Grief', for a detailed account of these words and gestures.
14. See Hamel, *Morte Arthure*, p. 386 (esp. nn. 4034–9).
15. Göller, 'Reality versus Romance', p. 23, provides a summary of this focus on genital wounds.
16. Dorsey Armstrong, 'Rewriting the Chronicle Tradition: The Alliterative *Morte Arthure* and Arthur's Sword of Peace', *Parergon* 25.1 (2008), pp. 81–101. See also Jeff Westover, 'Arthur's End: The King's Emasculation in the Alliterative *Morte Arthure*', *The Chaucer Review* 32 (1998), pp. 310–24.
17. Armstrong, 'Rewriting the Chronicle Tradition', p. 94.
18. Hamel, *Morte Arthure*, suggests that this is 'an idea of thematic importance for the poem' (p. 290, n. 950).
19. Armstrong, 'Rewriting the Chronicle Tradition', p. 99, also notes that this means not only the end of Mordred's lineage, but also Arthur's.

CHAPTER 14

What's Hecuba to Shakespeare?[1]

Tanya Pollard

When Hamlet reflects on the power of tragic performance, he turns to Hecuba: 'What's Hecuba to him, or he to Hecuba, / That he should weep for her?'[2] Of all Shakespeare's characters, Hamlet is the most self-consciously preoccupied with the theatre: he accordingly has a privileged position as a tragic commentator. Yet critics have paid little attention to his fascination with the protagonist of the period's most popular Greek tragedy. Hamlet's metatheatrical reflections have typically been situated in the context of Shakespeare's competition with contemporary playwrights. Shakespeare, we understand, vied for the Senecan legacy of Kyd's *Spanish Tragedy* (1587) and his *Hamlet* (1588–9), while the 'little eyases' of the boys' companies offered a particular catalyst for reconceiving the shape and function of tragedy (*Hamlet*, 2.2.326).[3] Yet this picture of England's dramatic landscape has overshadowed another genealogy of tragedy, pervasive during Shakespeare's time, for which Hecuba served as icon. This genealogy has become almost invisible to critics, who have largely accepted the maxims that 'in tragedy the privileges of the Self are attributed to the masculine hero', and that 'the canon of tragic drama, on the whole, concentrates on the experience of male protagonists'.[4] Although recent criticism has attended more fully to female experience in early modern tragedy, we have not yet acknowledged or understood the significance of the period's engagement with a predominantly female-centred canon of Greek tragedy.[5] If Hamlet has become the icon of tragedy, then tracing his responses to Hecuba illuminates how he came to replace her in this role.

WHAT'S HECUBA TO HAMLET?

When Hamlet meets the players, he asks them for 'a passionate speech', and quickly identifies a particular one: 'Aeneas' tale to Dido, and thereabout of it especially where he speaks of Priam's slaughter'. This apparent invocation of

Virgil, however, obscures an unexpected swerve toward a different literary focus. Although Hamlet refers to Priam, and the player begins with Pyrrhus, the speech meets with a lacklustre response ('This is too long') until Hamlet hurries it towards its true centre: 'Say on; come to Hecuba.' As his eagerness suggests, the scene finds its climactic force in Hecuba's passions:

> But who, O who, had seen the mobled queen . . .
> Run barefoot up and down, threat'ning the flames
> With bisson rheum; a clout upon that head
> Where late the diadem stood, and for a robe,
> About her lank and all o'erteemed loins,
> A blanket, in th'alarm of fear caught up –
> Who this had seen, with tongue in venom steeped
> 'Gainst Fortune's state would treason have pronounced.
> But if the gods themselves did see her then . . .
> The instant burst of clamour that she made –
> Unless things mortal move them not at all –
> Would have made milch the burning eyes of heaven,
> And passion in the gods. (2.2.414, 426–8, 478, 481, 482–98)

Hecuba's wretched state – bereaved, barefoot and clothed only in rags – suggests powerlessness, but paradoxically intensifies her power. Threatening Troy's flames with her 'bisson rheum', she both embodies tears and incites them in others, making 'milch the burning eyes of heaven'. As these examples suggest, the passage's insistently Anglo-Saxon vocabulary implicitly translates Hecuba's foreign and classical origins to an intimate, local setting, just as 'milch' and 'o'erteemed loins' emphasise her maternity. In evoking her, the player brings classical tragedy to Elsinore, to England and to the domestic sphere, with a promise of powerful consequences for audiences. Other moments in the play, such as the ghost's account of how his terrible story would affect 'ears of flesh and blood', also dramatise the affective and physiological consequences of tragic performances on their audiences, evoking the period's discussions about the effects of tragic pathos on audiences (1.5.22).[6] Yet while the ghost warns that his tragedy will freeze and stiffen its audiences, Hecuba's tragedy promises the opposite effect: it will melt, liquefy, even douse flames. The performance of female grief, the player suggests, offers a distinctive model of tragic impact, one that shadows, complements and competes with that produced by men.

Beyond Hecuba's reported effects on her mortal and immortal audiences, her most obvious immediate impact is on the player, whose passionate performance Polonius breaks off in concern: 'Look, whe'er he has not turned his colour, and has tears in's eyes. Prithee no more!' Yet her deeper impact is on Hamlet himself. Disconcerted by the player's tears and broken voice, Hamlet famously condemns his display of grief as 'monstrous': 'And all for nothing! / For Hecuba. / What's Hecuba to him, or he to Hecuba, / That he should weep for her?' (2.2.499–500, 534–7). Although it is the player whose reaction

Hamlet attacks, it is Hecuba who occupies his thoughts. He tries to reduce her to 'nothing', but she proves a substantial presence. He harps insistently on her name, three times in two lines, as he puzzles over her apparently inexplicable effect on a man lacking any direct ties to her. Hecuba is a distant figure, who has neither appeared nor even been given a direct voice. Nonetheless, the mere evocation of her suffering is enough to produce tears in audiences both within and beyond the player's speech.

The moving power of Hecuba's laments directly highlights Hamlet's sense of his own failings. 'Yet I', he complains, 'A dull and muddy-mettled rascal, peak / Like John-a-dreams, unpregnant of my cause, / And can say nothing' (2.2.543–6). Technically he is comparing himself with the player, but Hamlet's curious indictment of himself as 'unpregnant' suggests that it is Hecuba herself against whom he fails to measure up. Although editors and critics have taken pains to distance the word from its maternal connotations, its literal sense was known and used in Shakespeare's time.[7] More compellingly, its appearance here resonates with later passages linking Hamlet with pregnancy: Claudius meditates on 'the hatch and the disclose' of 'something in his soul / O'er which his melancholy sits on brood', and later imagines him as 'the female dove / When that her golden couplets are disclosed' (3.1.163–5, 271–2). The play's insistent interest in Hamlet's potential maternity highlights the player's identification of Hecuba with milk and teeming loins: identified by Euripides as a mother of fifty, she was also a strikingly fertile literary figure, widely cited and imitated. Although her grief most conspicuously indicts Gertrude, the play's other widowed mother, for her failure to mourn, at a deeper level it calls attention to Hamlet's unlikely status as tragic protagonist. Hamlet, in contrast with Hecuba, is incapable of fertility: male rather than female, child rather than parent, belated literary imitator rather than origin.[8] These recurring allusions to female fertility, combined with Hamlet's powerful response to the player's depiction of Hecuba, suggest that there is more than one ghostly parent haunting this play.

HECUBA IN SIXTEENTH-CENTURY EUROPE

Hamlet acquires different meanings if one takes seriously the play's preoccupation with Hecuba as a symbol of the moving power of tragedy. Critics who have discussed the player's speech have not generally commented on Hecuba; when they have, they have typically identified her with Virgil and/or Ovid.[9] Yet in the early modern period, Hecuba was the established icon of Greek tragedy, the literary tradition widely recognised as the genre's origin.[10] Continuing a tradition rooted in late antiquity, Euripides' *Hecuba* was by far the most popular of the Greek plays printed, translated and performed in sixteenth-century Europe. It was the first Greek play to be translated into Latin, by Erasmus, who published it with *Iphigenia in Aulis* in 1506 – only three years after the Greek *editio princeps* was published by Venice's Aldine

Press – in an edition that went on to be frequently reprinted.[11] Beyond its inclusion in complete editions of Euripides, the play appeared in thirty-seven individual or partial editions during the century, far more than the runner-up, *Iphigenia*, with twenty-two, and one of only a few plays to appear in more than four.[12] It was translated into Spanish in 1533; French in 1544; and Italian in 1543, 1550, 1563 and 1592, for a total of seven vernacular editions – again, far more than any other Greek play.[13] It is also the first Greek tragedy with documented postclassical performances, directed by Melanchthon in the Low Countries between 1506 and 1514, and again in 1525 in Wittenberg – where Shakespeare sent Hamlet to study – as well as in numerous adaptations.[14] Gasparus Stiblinus, the translator and editor of the first Greek–Latin volume of Euripides' complete works (1562), pronounced Euripides the prince of tragedy and claimed that *Hecuba* held the first place among the tragedies.[15] Philip Sidney used the play as an example of the power of well-made tragedy, and Joseph Scaliger and Antonio Minturno similarly used it to illustrate proper tragic structure – compact, but with a complex variety of incidents in the plot – in their discussions of the genre.[16]

Scholars have explained *Hecuba*'s remarkable popularity in the Renaissance in a number of ways, including the play's earlier prestige, its violence, its visibility in a standard composition textbook, European fascination with Troy, and Hecuba's familiarity from other sources.[17] Yet each of these suggestions falls short of accounting for the play's extraordinary appeal. In particular, early modern English responses to Hecuba suggest that the play's popularity derived especially from its combination of passionate grief and triumphant revenge, each of which embodied a crucial aspect of what the period's writers found compelling in tragedy.

Later versions of Hecuba consistently emphasise her overwhelming grief. She appears weeping in texts by Ovid, Dante, Boccaccio, Chaucer, Ariosto and Rabelais, among others.[18] In the first English revenge tragedy, Thomas Norton and Thomas Sackville's *Gorboduc* (1561), she is described as 'the wofullest wretch / That euer liued to make a myrour of'.[19] As an epitome of female grief, in particular, Hecuba offers a synecdoche for her genre. The most frequently published and translated Greek tragedies in the sixteenth century all featured female protagonists, suggesting that the genre's attractions were identified especially with the emotional intensity generated by suffering women.[20] After *Hecuba*, the Euripidean plays that appeared most frequently in individual or partial editions during the sixteenth century were *Iphigenia in Aulis*, *Medea*, *Alcestis*, and *The Phoenician Women* (in that order); those with the next largest number of vernacular translations were *The Phoenician Women*, *The Trojan Women*, *Iphigenia in Aulis*, *Medea*, and *Electra*.[21] Similarly, the most frequently printed and translated plays by Sophocles were *Antigone* and *Electra*.[22] Performance records tell a similar story: of the sixteen documented European stagings of plays by Euripides before 1600, thirteen featured female protagonists (and if we see *Hippolytus* as centring on Phaedra, the number rises to fourteen).[23] The canon of preferred plays, and in particular the exceptionally popular pairing of *Hecuba* and *Iphigenia in Aulis*, suggests the period's particular interest in the tragic potential of bereaved mothers and sacrificial daughters, a juxtaposition whose significance for *Hamlet* we will explore later.

Yet as with the similar figure of Clytemnestra, allusions to Hecuba emphasised not only her grief, but also its consequences for her revenge. Unlike Seneca's Hecuba, Euripides' Hecuba uses lament, the ritual voicing of mourning for the dead, to transform her grief into violence that is depicted as both successful and justified. After passionately lamenting, first her sacrificed daughter and then her newly discovered, murdered son, she earns the moral authority to persuade not only her sympathetic chorus, but also the ruler Agamemnon, that she must punish the murderer Polymestor. Ultimately, with the help of her female attendants, she kills Polymestor's children in front of him, and then blinds him. Recent scholarship has called attention to anxiety about female lament in ancient Greece, rooted in the perceived threat of its power to mobilise violence and political upheaval.[24] Christian Billing has argued that 'the verbal expression of female lament constitutes as powerful an act of violence as the deed of vengeance itself', and that *Hecuba* in particular shows it to be 'a powerfully affective force' that catalyses violent action.[25] Although most of the play depicts Hecuba's grief, her final turn to vengeful action – unlike that of Hamlet – is carefully planned, successfully orchestrated and publicly upheld as both triumphant and just.[26] It is even a civic duty: in agreeing that she has the right to carry out her revenge, Agamemnon tells her that 'this is for the common good, for both the individual and the state [polis], that the bad person should be punished and the good one succeed' (902–4).* And despite her widespread association with sorrow, Hecuba takes satisfaction in achieving what she sees as justice: when Polymestor asks her 'Do you take pleasure in insulting me, you evil-doer?', she replies, 'Why should I not take pleasure in taking revenge on you?' (1257–8).†

Although for much of the play Hecuba evokes tragic pathos, here she points to another model of tragedy: the triumph of action, and in particular, of revenge. Her delight in her victim's suffering evokes Euripides' Medea – a figure identified more widely with scheming cruelty than sympathetic grief – and the charismatic monstrosity of Seneca's hero-villains, especially Medea and Atreus, who played a crucial role in mediating Greek tragic material to Renaissance readers and audiences.[27] Perhaps more surprisingly, her blinding of Polymestor, as Froma Zeitlin has noted, echoes Odysseus' blinding of the Cyclops Polyphemus, an action widely identified by Renaissance writers not only with cleverness, but also with the origins of tragicomedy.[28] For some sixteenth-century theorists of tragedy, Hecuba's triumph represented an aesthetic failing, because it jarred with their conceptions of the genre. Despite his

---

* πᾶσι γὰρ κοινὸν τόδε, / ἰδίᾳ θ' ἑκάστῳ καὶ πόλει, τὸν μὲν κακὸν / κακόν τι πάσχειν, τὸν δὲ χρηστὸν εὐτυχεῖν.
† χαίρεις ὑβρίζουσ' εἰς ἔμ', ὦ πανοῦργε σύ. / οὐ γάρ με χαίρειν χρή σε τιμωρουμένην.

praise for the play's structure, Scaliger objected that her revenge provided too upbeat an ending,

> since the issue of tragedy should be unhappy, and *Hecuba* is a tragedy, Hecuba ought to have been made more miserable at the end than at the beginning; this is certainly not done, for the end furnishes some scant relief to her misery.[29]

Yet Seneca's tragedies of atrocity were strikingly popular in the sixteenth century, and other contemporary critics relished the triumphant endings that audiences clearly enjoyed. Cinthio contributed to the rise of tragicomedy when he justified writing 'tragedies with happy endings' by explaining that he found it wrong 'to displease those for whose pleasure the play is put on the stage', and in this he followed not only Castelvetro – who argued that 'poetry was invented for the sole purpose of providing pleasure' – but arguably Aristotle himself.[30] If the tragedy of pathos competed with the tragedy of triumph in the early modern period, Hecuba had the unusual distinction of embodying both. In doing so, she created – crucially, for *Hamlet* – a template for the exceptionally popular genre of revenge drama, which mitigated the grief of loss with the pleasure of retribution.[31]

Yet Hamlet cannot precisely recreate Hecuba's particular pathos or triumph, and not simply because intervening Christian beliefs problematised the idea of pleasurable and justified revenge.[32] Although Judith Mossman has argued that Renaissance audiences admired Hecuba despite her gender, accepting her as 'an honorary man', contemporary responses to other Greek plays suggest that her appeal lay especially in the emotional intensity identified with her femininity.[33] Even her violent efficacy is depicted as having roots in her gender, and especially in her maternity. In the ancient Greek world, mothers were accorded special rights and obligations as mourners: the physiological consequences of their labour pains were understood to give them both a distinctive access to intense grief, and the right to enact this grief publicly.[34] Early modern English translations of Greek drama not only recognised this link, but actively intensified it.[35] In their *Jocasta* (1566), George Gascoigne and Francis Kinwelmersh follow Lodovico Dolce's *Giocasta* (1549), an Italian translation of Euripides' *The Phoenician Women*, in heightening both the centrality of its female protagonist, and the significance of her motherhood.[36] 'There is no love', the play's chorus insists, 'may be comparde to that, / The tender mother beares unto hir chyld: / For even so muche the more it doth encrease, / As their griefe growes, or contentations cease.'[37] This choral passage, which commonplace marks show was singled out as a *sententia*, follows Dolce's translation closely in expanding the two lines of Euripides that it recreates.[38] Euripides' text reads,* 'The children of

---

* δεινὸν γυναιξὶν αἱ δι' ὠδίνων γοναί, / καὶ φιλότεκνόν πως πᾶν γυναικεῖον γένος.

their labor pangs are wondrous and terrible [δεινὸν] to women, and the whole female race is somehow attached to their children' (*Phoenissae* 355–6),³⁹ and the translators' Latin edition renders these lines (also in commonplace marks) as* 'To give birth through pains is a precious thing to women, and the female race is somehow affectionate to their children'.⁴⁰ Intriguingly, and contrary to typical claims, the vernacular versions are closer here to the emotional spirit of the Greek original than is the more academic, and technically correct, Latin. Their suggestion that grief is inherent in maternity acknowledges the ambivalent overtones of the Greek *deinon* – terrible, dangerous, marvellous – in stark contrast to the straightforwardly positive *preciosa* as a modifier for the effects of giving birth. The expansion of these and other lines on motherhood suggests that, to these translators, maternal suffering was central to the tragedy's power, offering a suggestive background for *Hamlet*'s pervasive pregnancy references.

Meditations on the intensity of maternal emotions are similarly pervasive in the other extant early English translation of a Greek play, *Iphigenia in Aulis* (c.1550–3) by Jane, Lady Lumley. Despite the play's apparent focus on a daughter, Euripides gave Clytemnestra almost as many lines (205) as Iphigenia (207), and Lumley amplified the maternal emphasis by giving Clytemnestra 280 lines to Iphigenia's 192. After Clytemnestra learns that Iphigenia will be sacrificed, the chorus laments the suffering that her death will bring. 'Truly', they note, 'it is a verie troblesome thinge to have children: for we are even by nature compelled to be sorie for their mishappes' (831–3).⁴¹ Like Gascoigne and Kinwelmersh, Lumley emphasises the negative aspects of ambiguous Greek terms, and in this respect is closer to Euripides than to Erasmus' translation, which she owned.⁴² Euripides' chorus says 'Giving birth carries a strange and terrible [δεινὸν] spell, and suffering for their children is shared by all women' (Euripides *Iphigenia in Aulis* 917–18).† In the Greek, this line, like the early chorus from *Jocasta*, uses the word *deinon* – strange, terrible, marvellous, dangerous – to frame the emotional impact of maternity as ambivalent, and *hyperkamnein* denotes excessive suffering. Erasmus, on the other hand, omits the metaphor of a drug or spell (φίλτρον) with its implications of powerlessness, and instead emphasises strength: 'It is a powerful thing to have given birth, and it brings the greatest force of love to all women in common, so that they expend the greatest amount of effort for their children.'‡ Erasmus' Latin words *efficax*, *vim* and *adlaborent* suggest power, force and effort, rather than the strange marvels and suffering of the Greek and English versions. And although Lumley's choices are in keeping with other vernacular translators' approaches

---

* *preciosa res mulieribus per dolores fiunt geni / et amans liberorum est quodammodo muliebre genus*: Euripidis ... *Tragoediae XVIII* (Basel, 1541), p. 140.
† δεινὸν τὸ τίκτειν καὶ φέρει φίλτρον μέγα / πᾶσίν τε κοινὸν ὥσθ' ὑπερκάμνειν τέκνων.
‡ *res efficax peperisse, uimque maximam / amoris adfert omnibus communiter, / vti pro suis summe adlaborent liberis*: Εὐριπίδου Τραγῳδίαι ... *Evripidis tragoediae dvae, Hercuba & Iphigenia in Aulide*, trans. Desiderius Erasmus (Basel, 1524), sig. n6ʳ.

to Euripides' plays, in the light of her emphasis it is poignant to note that her own three children all died in infancy.[43]

Whether or not Lumley's interest in Euripides was directly linked to the play's emphasis on maternal experience, Euripides' plays clearly attracted female attention in early modern England. Queen Elizabeth herself translated a play by Euripides – we do not know which – in keeping with women's substantial contributions to translation and closet drama more broadly.[44] In a brief afterword to *Jocasta*, Gascoigne and Kinwelmersh suggest that explanatory notes resulted from a woman's curiosity: 'I did begin these notes at request of a gentlewoman who understode not poetycall words or termes.'[45] These various signs of female interest in Euripides suggest that his works served as a particular magnet for the period's pervasive identification of tragedy with women. Because tragedy was seen as inducing overwhelming emotions, women were often identified as the paradigmatic tragic audience: Plato (*Republic* 605c–e) described surrendering to the emotional intensity of tragedy as a woman's response (ἐκεῖνο δὲ γυναικός), and in 1582 Stephen Gosson similarly complained that 'The beholding of troubles and miserable slaughters that are in tragedies drive us to immoderate sorrow, heaviness, womanish weeping and mourning', anticipating *Hamlet*'s anxieties about the emasculating effects of tears.[46] Tragedy itself was typically personified as female, in a range of texts including *A Warning for Fair Women* (1599) and Heywood's *Apology for Actors* (1612).[47] Hamlet's attention to Hecuba, then, hints not only at the impact of Greek tragedy, but at the centrality of women, and especially maternal lament, in English and European conceptions of the genre.

Women's identification with tragedy reflected the genre's association with vulnerability. Hecuba's status as a fallen queen embodied tragedy's emphasis on the instability of fortune, and gave her a particular cautionary power in an England ruled by a female monarch. Jessica Winston has pointed out that in the first English translation of Seneca's *Troas* (1559), Jasper Heywood added and reassigned lines in order to accentuate Hecuba's status as victim of fortune, and offered the translation to the newly crowned Elizabeth as 'a salutary gift of cautionary advice'.[48] The hints in Heywood's added lines were hardly subtle: 'Hecuba that wayleth now in care, / That was so late, of high estate a queene / A Mirrour is, to teach you what you are / Your wavering welth, O princes, here is seene.'[49] Hecuba may have embodied certain kinds of emotional and political power, but she also represented their fragility.

Yet beyond its consequences for other queens, Hecuba's suffering was also perceived as a potent threat to unjust male rulers. In representing the power of grief and rage to bring about the deserved punishment of wrongdoers, *Hecuba* offered rich material for theories about the power of tragedy to combat tyranny.[50] When Sidney wrote that 'Tragedy maketh kings fear to be tyrants, and tyrants manifest their tyrannical humors', he turned to the figure of Hecuba, albeit indirectly. 'But how much it [tragedy] can move', he wrote,

> Plutarch yieldeth a notable testimony of the abominable tyrant Alexander Pheraeus, from whose eyes a tragedy well made and represented drew abundance of tears, who without all pity had murdered infinite numbers, and some of his own blood: so as he that was not ashamed to make matters for tragedies, yet could not resist the sweet violence of a tragedy. And if it wrought no further good in him, it was that he in despite of himself withdrew himself from hearkening to that which might mollify his hardened heart.[51]

This story – which critics have routinely linked with Hamlet's play-within-the-play – in fact appears twice in Plutarch's writings, in his *Life of Pelopidas* and *On the Fortune or Virtue of Alexander the Great*, both of which mention Hecuba. In *Pelopidas* (29.5), Plutarch refers to the play in question as Euripides' *Trojan Women* – a tragedy of pathos – but in *de Alexandri* (2.1) he points to the revenge drama of Euripides' *Hecuba*.[52] Sidney had access to modern translations of both, but a specific verbal echo points to *de Alexandri* as his source.[53] The phrase 'mollify his hardened heart', which anticipates the melting effect attributed to Hecuba in *Hamlet*, closely resembles 'qu'il l'avoit amolly comme du fer' in Amyot's translation of the *de Alexandri*.[54] This echo suggests that it is *Hecuba*, not *The Trojan Women*, that Sidney highlights as a model for tragedy's impact on tyrants, a conclusion supported by Sidney's earlier citation of *Hecuba* as an example of the well-made play. Given the play's depiction of successful revenge against an unjust male ruler, we might ask whether Pheraeus' mollification – a term that in English could also mean weakening – perhaps indicated not only pity, but also fear: a possibility that resonates with Claudius' reaction to a performance featuring regicide and a grieving widow.[55]

Sidney's account of tragedy's affective power points to the threat for rulers in the violence unleashed by female suffering, suggesting why the player's performance of Hecuba inspires Hamlet with a plan for attacking Claudius. And while Sidney's discussion focuses on the emotional impact of witnessing female grief, it also evokes the importance of the genre's political contexts. In the early modern imagination, tragedy's power over tyranny was firmly identified with its Greek roots. When George Puttenham identifies tragedy with levelling tyranny, he names its origins as 'Euripides and Sophocles with the Greeks, Seneca with the Latins'.[56] The genre's interest in the fall of kings was widely attributed to its close association with the institutions of Athenian democracy.[57] In his commentary on Aristotle's *Poetics*, Castelvetro goes so far as to assert that tragedies and monarchies cannot coexist:

> for a king is very jealous of his royal condition, and is careful about putting before the humble and before individuals examples that may arouse and direct their spirits toward innovations and a change of rulers. On the contrary, because the king knows that the common people delight in and enjoy the evil fortunes of the great, they do not ever have tragedies

produced in public. Tragedies never appear on the stage except among people who are subject to no individual ruler.[58]

According to Castelvetro, the genre is fundamentally inimical to maintaining stable royalty, an idea in keeping with Nicole Loraux's account of the challenges that bereaved mothers pose for civic authority. The female figures whose grief induces sympathetic anger toward rulers' wrongs play a crucial role in undermining tyrannical power. As a synecdoche for Greek tragedy, then, Hecuba shows that the powerful emotions generated by female lament, especially when authorised by maternity, can lead to justified violence against tyranny. Capable of melting audiences and destroying kings, Hecuba offers a model of tragedy with both emotional and political power.

SHAKESPEARE'S HECUBA

This array of Hecuba's early modern meanings offers a useful background from which to revisit this essay's central question: what is Hecuba to Shakespeare? Clearly she was a figure of some fascination: he alludes to her fifteen times by name, and additionally by status ('the queen of Troy'), throughout his works.[59] In *Titus Andronicus* (c.1592), which Emrys Jones has argued uses Euripides' *Hecuba* as a structural model, Tamora's son Demetrius calls upon her as a symbol for his mother's hopes of vengeance – 'The self-same gods that armed the Queen of Troy / With opportunity of sharp revenge / Upon the Thracian tyrant in his tent, / May favor Tamora, the Queen of Goths'– and young Lucius invokes her as a parallel for the maddened Lavinia.[60] In *The Rape of Lucrece* (1594), Lucrece's ekphrastic meditation on 'despairing Hecuba' enables her to see herself as a classical tragic heroine, one who 'shapes her sorrow to the beldame's woes' and transforms it into a plan for taking action against her wrongdoer.[61] In *Coriolanus* (1608–9), Volumnia uses Hecuba's associations with maternal tenderness to chide her daughter-in-law's concern for Coriolanus' safety over his honour: 'The breasts of Hecuba, / When she did suckle Hector looked not lovelier / Than Hector's forehead when it spit forth blood / At Grecian sword.'[62] And in *Cymbeline* (1610–11), upon mistaking Cloten's corpse for that of Posthumus, Imogen invokes her as a kindred spirit of bereaved vindictive fury: 'Pisanio, / All curses madded Hecuba gave the Greeks, / And mine to boot, be darted on thee!'[63] Throughout these examples, Shakespeare's Hecuba represents not the passive suffering we see in Seneca, but active responses to wrongdoers, the possibility of transforming grief into the satisfaction of revenge.[64] She has, in short, Euripides' fingerprints all over her.

Hecuba and the model of tragedy she embodies form as haunting a presence to Shakespeare as the ghost to Hamlet. Strangely, however, critics have failed to see this. Feminist criticism has excavated underexplored female figures in Shakespeare's writings, but Hecuba has also suffered from her Greek literary origins. It is a longstanding critical commonplace that Shakespeare, along with other early modern commercial playwrights, could not have been familiar with Greek tragedy, and recent preferences for situating the plays in contemporary, rather than diachronic, contexts have discouraged challenges to this assumption.[65] Even the recurring wistful musings on Shakespeare's affinity with the Greeks have typically conceded a lack of historic grounding for this apparent kinship.[66] Yet scholars have begun to identify specific links between Shakespeare and Greek plays, and to take seriously the forms of mediation that made both the plays themselves and their subject matter widely accessible in the period.[67] Shakespeare's intimate engagement with Hecuba offers a particularly vivid demonstration of the broad visibility of material drawing on the Greek dramatic tradition in the period.[68] Even if his Greek was not strong enough to read the original without support, Shakespeare could easily have read the bilingual Greek–Latin editions of Euripides' play, especially Erasmus' widely circulating translation, and/or any of the vernacular translations, and his extensive verbal echoes from the play suggest that he almost certainly did.[69] Yet, perhaps more importantly, he did not need to. His exposure to the late classical, medieval and Renaissance texts inspired by Euripides' play, as well as to accounts of the play in contemporary writings, would have ensured his awareness of the play and its reputation, and shaped his engagement with the figure of Hecuba.

In arguing that Hecuba's association with Euripidean tragedy is crucial to understanding her meanings for Shakespeare, this essay does not exclude other depictions of Hecuba from the play's web of literary engagement. Shakespeare's compounding and confounding of literary models have been widely acknowledged, and critics have persuasively demonstrated his engagement with Virgil and Ovid, among other classical sources.[70] Yet identifying Euripides' role in this intertextual web points to Shakespeare's engagement with the power of theatrical performance. As Jones has pointed out, *Hecuba* offered Shakespeare a classical model for a highly successful, publicly performed tragedy, something he could not find elsewhere.[71] For Shakespeare's evocations of Hecuba do not only explore grief: they also, especially in *Hamlet*, explicitly explore the effects of tragedy, and especially of a tragic protagonist, upon audiences. Euripides' play offered Shakespeare not only the generic conventions he exploits in *Hamlet* – a pre-existing crime, ghost, delay, deceit and violence – but also a dramatic model for engaging audiences with tragic affect. In particular, it offered him a tradition of emotionally affecting tragedy that was female-centred, rooted in lament and culminated in triumphant action: a tradition that he translated, in subtle and complex ways, into a new model of tragedy.

HAMLET'S FAILED HECUBAS

In the context of Hecuba's contemporary association with female, and especially maternal, lament, it is not surprising that Shakespeare most frequently evokes Hecuba in the context of suffering women. As noted, Tamora, Lavinia, Lucrece, Virgilia and Imogen are all linked with Hecuba in ways that suggest active responses to tragic grief. Oddly, however, it is Hamlet – male, unmarried, childless – through whom Shakespeare most fully explores Hecuba's dramatic possibilities. At least at first glance, the play's central drama moves its mothers and daughters to the sidelines in order to focus on a son's commemoration of his father, apparently bearing out the critical truism that Shakespeare's tragedies primarily attend to men.[72] Yet Hecuba's name occurs four times in *Hamlet*, more often than in any Shakespeare text beyond *Troilus and Cressida*, in which she has a background (though not speaking) role.[73] The fact that *Hamlet* provides a focal point for Shakespeare's fascination with Hecuba raises questions about how the play responds to the tragic tradition she represents.

As Shakespeare's most self-conscious exploration of tragedy and its effects, *Hamlet* in fact offers an ideal site for rewriting Hecuba's dramatic legacy, and recovering this legacy illuminates the play's challenges to it. Perhaps most conspicuously, evoking Hecuba's model of tragedy directs audiences to expect that Gertrude, a widow and mother, will be the play's primary grieving figure.[74] Despite the prominence of their father–son relationships, the most visible English revenge tragedies before *Hamlet* – *The Spanish Tragedy* and *Titus Andronicus* – had both continued a tradition of dramatising maternal grief as a catalyst to revenge. Shakespeare's decision to withhold this convention in *Hamlet* is striking. As Katharine Goodland has observed, acts of female mourning in the play are consistently dismissed, interrupted or otherwise contained.[75] In particular, whatever mourning Gertrude may have done is blocked from the audience's view. Both she and Ophelia offer versions of Hecuba, but fall short of recreating her role. Perhaps more surprisingly, their failures highlight Hamlet's own inability to match Hecuba, and his resulting evolution into a new model of tragic protagonist. By moving tragic female characters to the margins of the play, and centring our attention on a protagonist who observes and comments on them, Shakespeare self-consciously reflects on a male character's experience of watching traditional – that is, female – tragic protagonists. *Hamlet* constructs, scrutinises and critiques an emerging English model of tragedy, through conversation with its earlier counterpart.

Situating the play in this tragic genealogy sheds a new light on one of Hamlet's most vehement fixations, Gertrude's insufficient mourning. 'Heaven and earth!', he exclaims,

> Must I remember? why, she would hang on him,
> As if increase of appetite had grown
> By what it fed on: and yet, within a month –
> Let me not think on't – Frailty, thy name is woman! –
> A little month, or ere those shoes were old
> With which she follow'd my poor father's body,

> Like Niobe, all tears: why she, even she –
> O God, a beast that wants discourse of reason
> Would have mourned longer! –married with mine uncle. (1.2.142–51)

As this passage suggests, Hamlet has more to say about his mother's failure to grieve than about his own grief. His preoccupation with Gertrude has been widely read as a sign of his misogyny, and his Oedipal fixation on her sexuality.[76] But in the context of Shakespeare's interest in Hecuba, it might be more fruitfully understood as representing a confrontation with the genre's conventions. Although Hamlet depicts Gertrude as passionately attached to his father, and as having mourned him 'like Niobe, all tears', he insists that her grief is not substantial enough to merit its traditional place at the genre's emotional centre. Like Hecuba, with whom Achilles indirectly links her in the *Iliad*, Niobe was primarily known for mourning her numerous children, of whom she was so excessively proud that the gods punished her with their deaths.[77] Yet Niobe is a fallen Hecuba, sporting her tears without either her innocence or her heroic response. The identification both insinuates Gertrude's guilt and underlines her continuing maternal responsibility: unlike Niobe, she has not lost any children. The rapid truncation of her tears, furthermore, suggests that Gertrude cannot match even Niobe's tainted grief.

The comparison with Niobe, who lived for her children, also paints Gertrude as insufficiently maternal, an indictment supported by Gertrude's apparent indifference to Hamlet's grief.[78] But if the implicit corollary to Hamlet's accusation of Gertrude is that his own grief, by contrast, constitutes the rightful heart of the tragedy, he seems to protest too much. For Hamlet's quickness to attack Gertrude masks his own discomfort with confronting his father's death. Whenever he begins to remember his father, he immediately reverts to outrage about his mother and her remarriage. 'Remember thee?', he addresses the ghost, 'Yes, yes, by heaven. / O most pernicious woman!' (1.5.95, 104–5) As his frequent slippage from his father's memory to his mother's marriage shows, it is not only acts of female mourning that are interrupted, pre-empted or otherwise prevented in the play. Hamlet's relationship to his grief is vexed: unlike Hecuba's passionate and lyrical laments, his are fraught with ambivalence, uncertainty and anxiety.

It is not simply that, as has been widely observed, Hamlet cannot bring himself to act – or, at least, act in accordance with the ghost's mandate. More surprisingly, and in contrast to the critical consensus on the play, he cannot actually *speak*: at least not 'to the purpose' of his grief (2.2.271). Hamlet's preoccupation with Gertrude masks his anxiety that he, like she, is no Hecuba. If Hecuba, to early modern readers in general and to Shakespeare in particular, represents the power of passionate lament both as a speech act in itself and as a catalyst to righteous action, Hamlet is striking precisely for his struggle to fulfil these ends. On a broader level, if *Hecuba* embodies both the tragedy of pathos and the tragedy of triumph, *Hamlet* is caught uneasily between the two: it cannot fully provide the cathartic pleasures of unfettered grief, nor the satisfaction of seeing a victim heroically bring down a wrongdoer. Instead, Shakespeare must rewrite *Hecuba*'s model of tragedy to demonstrate an alternative approach to conjuring emotional intensity. In fact, it is precisely through exploring Hamlet's failure to match Hecuba that Shakespeare succeeds in creating his own form of tragic power.

Hamlet confronts this failure most fully in his meditation on the player's reaction to Hecuba. 'O, what a rogue and peasant slave am I!' he castigates himself. Comparing himself with the tragic passion that she has inspired in the player, he asks:

> What would he do
> Had he the motive and the cue for passion
> That I have? He would drown the stage with tears,
> And cleave the general ear with horrid speech,
> Make mad the guilty and appal the free,
> Confound the ignorant, and amaze indeed
> The very faculty of eyes and ears. Yet I,
> The dull and muddy-mettled rascal, peak
> Like John-a-dreams, unpregnant of my cause,
> And can say nothing. (2.2.527, 536–45)

Technically Hamlet compares himself here with the player, and proclaims the superiority of his own 'motive and ... cue for passion'. Yet although he criticises the player's response, he also compares Hecuba's pain to his own, suggesting that the player would conjure even more tragic power if inspired by Hamlet's woes. At the same time, he implicitly competes with Hecuba's performance, which includes drowning the stage with tears, maddening the guilty murderer of her son, and amazing her audiences, both onstage and off. Despite his claim to possess a stronger motive for passion, he sees himself as unable to match either the moving power of a theatrical fiction or Hecuba's ability to speak and act on her passion.

Yet Hamlet revises his indictment of his inability to speak when he considers the even greater problem of his inability to demonstrate filial loyalty through revenge. 'Why, what an ass am I?' he reflects: 'Ay, sure, this is most brave, / That I, the son of the dear murdered, / Prompted to my revenge by heaven and hell, / Must, like a whore, unpack my heart with words / And fall a-cursing like a very drab, / A scullion!' (2.2.560–5). Although Hamlet at first sees himself as insufficiently female to match Hecuba's pregnant capacity for emotion-laden speech, here he worries that his predilection for words over action makes him excessively feminine. He is not alone in this interpretation: critics, directors and the many actresses who have played his role have emphasised what Tony Howard has called 'the issue of Hamlet's "femininity"'.[79] Nor does he see his feminine verbal facility as an asset: his comparisons of himself to a 'whore', a 'very drab' and a 'scullion' suggest that his failure to act makes him both subservient and unfaithful to his father's memory, closer to Gertrude's 'wicked speed ... to incestuous sheets' (*Hamlet*, 1.2.156–7) than to Hecuba's passionate commemoration of her husband and children.

Paradoxically, it is in the act of lamenting his inferiority to Hecuba's emotional power that Hamlet speaks some of his most moving lines. Ultimately, however, he refuses to follow the genre's conventions, modelled on Hecuba, of transforming lament into revenge. Instead, his reflections on Hecuba lead him to unearth and rewrite an alternative role from classical tragedy, predicated more on watching and reflecting than on action. Hamlet is no Hecuba, but the role that he constructs for himself, and in many ways for a generation of English stage revengers, grows directly out of his confrontation and negotiation with her iconic power.

'AS GOOD AS A CHORUS?' STAGING AND WATCHING TRAGEDY IN *HAMLET*

If the player's evocation of Hecuba's tragic power makes Hamlet question his status as a tragic protagonist, it simultaneously inspires him to stage a performance of a tragedy. In confronting an unjust ruler with a theatrical version of Hecuba's story – a newly widowed queen who 'makes passionate action' upon discovering her dead husband – he gestures to the tyrant-melting powers attributed to Euripides' play (s.d. 3.2.122). If he cannot play Hecuba's role himself, he will find another way to exploit her tragic formula for his purposes.

Hamlet's idea of using a play as part of his revenge strategy is hardly original. After its extraordinarily popular debut in *The Spanish Tragedy*, the play-within-the-play became not only a central convention of early modern English revenge tragedy, but the most common vehicle for revenge itself.[80] Yet curiously, despite considerable critical interest in Renaissance metatheatre, no one has asked how the play-within-the-play originated. There are clues in its links with the dumb-show, a device also featured in *The Spanish Tragedy*.[81] The English dumb-show had its roots in neoclassical plays and translations – including *Gorbuduc* and *Jocasta* – and through them, in the *intermedii* that appeared as spectacles staged between the acts in Italian neoclassical plays.[82] In light of this history, and the period's broader engagement with classical models of tragedy, the early modern development of these theatrical devices – *intermedii*, dumb-show, and play-within-the-play – can be seen to respond to the Greek chorus, which they first complement and eventually replace.[83]

*

Hamlet's choric position towards the play he stages offers a model for his role within his own drama. It is not simply that he finds himself unable to embody the traditional figure of lament and revenge represented by Hecuba: he cannot find any way to undertake the action that the ghost has required of him. When Hamlet is served up a chance to play a conventional active role in his own drama, he baulks. Just after the performance, he stumbles upon the opportunity to kill Claudius – 'Now might I do it pat, now he is a-praying, / And now I'll do't' – but stops short of action (3.3.73–4). In considering but refusing to play a part in revenge, he evokes Hecuba's own chorus of Trojan women, who wonder whether they should help Hecuba attack Polymestor, but hold back from taking action.[84] In place of accepting the revenger's role, Hamlet instead reverts to observing and interpreting his mother. 'You go not till I set you up a glass', he tells her upon subsequently finding her in her closet, 'Where you may see the inmost part of you' (3.4.19–20).[85] As in his famous claim that 'the purpose of playing ... is to hold, as 'twere, the mirror up to nature', Hamlet uses the vocabulary of mirroring to describe his metatheatrical reflections on the tragic characters and events that he observes and discusses (3.2.18–22).[86]

Hamlet's choric role establishes parameters for the melancholy malcontent revengers who follow him on the early modern stage, who also frequently step outside the tragic events they contemplate and engineer. Certainly the role offers Hamlet a position from which to reflect on the play he inhabits. Robert Miola has observed that Hamlet's 'To be or not to be' speech echoes a choral ode from Seneca's *Troas*, and suggested that Hamlet follows the Senecan chorus in voicing 'an ancient and profound world-weariness, infusing the choral perspective with anguished awareness of his own situation'.[87] Stepping outside the tragedy's conventional centre also allows Hamlet to reflect on the female characters who represent the more paradigmatic tragic protagonists. His choric status on one hand puts him in a position more typically feminine than theirs – marginal, passive and observing, rather than central, active and defining – and yet paradoxically strengthens him by giving him the leverage of an external vantage point on their drama.[88]

*

As a quasi-choral figure, Hamlet mediates between the audience and the play's female figures, framing and shaping our perspectives on them. One primary focus of his observations is the widowed queen, the play's most obvious counterpart to Hecuba, whom he attacks with a ferocity unwarranted by the play's presentation of her.[89] He is similarly caustic in his assessment of the player queen, when she declares her love for her husband and her refusal to marry a second time. Perhaps more surprisingly, he also implicitly identifies Ophelia with a Greek tragic model. Between Polonius' announcement of the players and their entrance, Hamlet announces, 'O Jephthah, judge of Israel, what a treasure hadst thou!' After some puzzlement, Polonius concedes that 'If you call me Jephthah, my lord, I have a daughter that I love passing well', to which Hamlet in turn cryptically replies with lines of verse (2.2.385–94).

Editors and critics have glossed this exchange through reference to the story of Jephthah, a biblical figure from Judges 11 who vowed to sacrifice the first living thing he met if he returned successfully from war, and subsequently met his daughter coming out of his door.[90] Yet although Hamlet quotes from a ballad about Jephthah, his allusion implicitly links biblical and popular sources with the spectre of Greek tragedy. Jephthah was famous in the period as the subject of neoclassical drama modelled on Euripides: the *Jephthes sive votum tragoedia* (1540–7, published 1554) of George Buchanan, a humanist, poet and translator of Greek plays, and John Christopherson's *Jephthah* (c.1544), the first English play composed in Greek.[91] Both plays self-consciously imitated *Iphigenia in Aulis*, another story of a father sacrificing a daughter for the sake of a war, and the second-most popular Greek play in the period, after *Hecuba*. Buchanan's exceptionally well-received play, which was widely reprinted and translated, and praised by Roger Ascham and Philip Sidney, among others, forged a link between classical drama and the English stage: a Jephthah play was performed at Trinity College, Cambridge in 1566–7, and a commercial play about Jephthah, written by Dekker and Munday, was performed by the Admiral's Men in 1602.[92] With their focus on a sacrificial daughter, moreover, these plays implicitly evoke not only *Iphigenia* but also *Hecuba*, which similarly dramatises a daughter's sacrifice as preamble (though not as direct catalyst) to a mother's revenge.[93]

Between hearing of the players and watching them represent Hecuba, then, Hamlet is already thinking about a female sacrifice linked to classical tragedy: his meditation on Jephthah's daughter implicitly frames the speech he requests a few dozen lines later. The allusion foreshadows that Ophelia – who, like Iphigenia, is sacrificed by her father for matters of state negotiated between men – will both mirror Hamlet and compete with him for the play's tragic centre. Like Hamlet, Ophelia responds to a father's death by staging spectacles – whether intentionally or inadvertently – for audiences. And, like Hecuba, she seems to outdo Hamlet in her ability to produce an emotional impact with her lyrical performances. Just as the player reports that Hecuba's grief would melt her audiences, Claudius says of Ophelia's singing that 'this, / Like to a murd'ring-piece, in many places / Gives me superfluous death'. Laertes identifies her performance as a catalyst to revenge: 'Hadst thou thy wits and didst persuade revenge, / It could not move thus' (4.5.90–2, 167–8). Although Ophelia cannot match Hecuba by directly carrying out revenge, the affective power of both her grief and her death nonetheless threatens to melt and mobilise her audiences as Hecuba did hers.

With her songs of grief, Ophelia is the play's closest approximation to the lyrically lamenting female figures of classical tragedy.[94] Like Hecuba, she both represents and elicits pathos. Yet with limited appearances and even more limited agency, Ophelia cannot fully recreate Greek tragic daughters such as Iphigenia, Polyxena and Antigone, who make active decisions to accept their fated deaths with pride in their honour. Directed by her brother, her father and Hamlet, Ophelia breaks away from their control only to surrender to the equally incapacitating force of madness. Despite her emotional impact, she is not a conventional tragic protagonist; instead, she forges a combination of female grief, madness and sexuality that melds Hecuba and Iphigenia with the passionate performances of Renaissance Italian actresses, through what Eric Nicholson has described as 'the process of transnational *contaminatio*'.[95]

Between them, Gertrude and Ophelia encompass the primary attributes of the period's favourite Greek tragic protagonists: bereaved mother and widow, sacrificed daughter, grief, madness, violence and revenge. Yet Shakespeare implicitly confirms Hamlet's critique of their claims to centrality by giving him the play's title, and its overwhelmingly dominant voice. Presented as audience and mirror to the play's female figures, Hamlet takes the choral role from its characteristic position on the play's margins and moves it to the centre, reversing its relationship with the grieving women to whom it responds. If Hamlet is primarily an observer and critic of tragedy, Shakespeare accordingly refocuses the genre on the experience of the audiences who watch and respond to it.

Hamlet is, of course, not a passive observer, nor does he abide by the restrictions typically imposed on the classical chorus. Along with actively overseeing the staging of a play, he kills Polonius, arranges the deaths of Rosencrantz and Guildenstern, and toward the end of the play announces his readiness to take on a more typically masculine heroic role. 'Why, I will fight with him upon this theme', he says of Laertes, 'Until my eyelids will no longer wag' (5.1.251–2). Yet unlike Hieronimo, Titus or Hecuba, he never actually achieves the satisfaction of a triumphant revenge. Even when he finally succeeds in killing Claudius, the act is almost accidental, and essentially posthumous. The audience, like Hamlet, can neither luxuriate in passionate grief nor revel in the achievement of revenge. Instead, they join Hamlet in watching others' grief and violence, and reflecting on the distinctive affective and ethical challenges of participating vicariously in someone else's experience of tragedy: of weeping for nothing, or rather, for Hecuba.

Male, childless, reticent of passionate speech and action, Hamlet is no Hecuba. Our icon of grief and revenge tragedy struggles both to grieve and to revenge. Yet Shakespeare constructs Hamlet's distinctive innovation to the genre – a new focus on audiences' relationship with the moving spectacles they watch, at a moment when theatres were rapidly rising in prominence – in intimate conversation with paradigmatic elements of Greek tragedy, Hecuba's passionate grief and the reflections of an onlooking chorus. Just as it is in confronting his failure to be Hecuba that Hamlet most forcefully conjures her emotional intensity, it is similarly in Shakespeare's challenges to Greek tragic conventions that he most explicitly engages with them, producing a very different but no less powerful solicitation of audiences' emotions. Although contemporary accounts of the genre have lost sight of it, Hecuba's passionate, mobilising grief was for two millennia the primary prototype for tragic possibilities. Appreciating the literary genealogy she spawned offers a deeper understanding, not only of the nature of Shakespeare's innovations, but of the broader transformation of a Greek genre into one of the most influential legacies of the early modern stage.

NOTES

1. This chapter is a condensed version of an article originally published in *Renaissance Quarterly* 65.4 (Winter 2012), pp. 1060–93. For comments on earlier versions of this essay, I am grateful to Bianca Calabresi, Katharine Craik, Julie Crawford, Natasha Korda, Lucy Munro, Nancy Selleck, William Stenhouse and Oliver Taplin. I am grateful to Melina Moore for help with editing and formatting. Unless otherwise noted, all translations are my own.
2. William Shakespeare, *Hamlet*, in Stephen Greenblatt, Walter Cohen, Jean E. Howard and Katharine Eisaman Maus (eds), *The Norton Shakespeare* (London: W. W. Norton and Company, 1997), 2.2.536–7.
3. See, for instance, David Farley-Hills, *Shakespeare and the Rival Playwrights 1600–1606* (London: Routledge, 1990), esp. pp. 7–40; R. A. Foakes, 'Tragedy at the Children's Theatres after 1600: A Challenge to the Adult Stage', in David Galloway (ed.), *The Elizabethan Theatre II* (Toronto: Macmillan of Canada, 1970), pp. 37–59. On Kyd's probable authorship of the earlier *Hamlet*, and its likely dating, see especially Lukas Erne, *Beyond the Spanish Tragedy: A Study of the Works of Thomas Kyd* (Manchester: Manchester University Press, 2001), pp. 146–56.
4. Linda Bamber, *Comic Women, Tragic Men: A Study of Gender and Genre in Shakespeare* (Stanford: Stanford University Press, 1982), p. 6; Susan Letzler Cole, *The Absent One: Mourning, Ritual, Tragedy, and the Performance of Ambivalence* (University Park: Pennsylvania State University Press, 1985), p. 5.
5. See especially Naomi Conn Liebler (ed.), *The Female Tragic Hero in Renaissance Drama* (New York: Palgrave Macmillian, 2002).
6. On the ghost's account of his story's effects, see Kenneth Gross, *Shakespeare's Noise* (Chicago: The University of Chicago Press, 2001), pp. 10–32; David Hillman, *Shakespeare's Entrails* (Basingstoke: Palgrave Macmillan, 2007), pp. 81–116; Tanya Pollard, *Drugs and Theater in Early Modern England* (Oxford: Oxford University Press, 2005), pp. 123–41.
7. See the *Oxford English Dictionary*'s (*OED*'s) definition for the term. Its sense here has been glossed by Wells and Taylor as 'unapt' (William Shakespeare, *The Complete Works*, ed. Stanley Wells and Gary Taylor [Oxford: Oxford University Press, 1986], p. 1429), by Braunmuller as 'barren of realization' (William Shakespeare, *The Tragical History of Hamlet Prince of Denmark*, ed. A. R. Braunmuller, *The Pelican Shakespeare* [New York: Penguin Classics, 2001], p. 61), and by Swynfen Jervis, *A Dictionary of the Language of Shakespeare* (London: John Russel Smith, 1868), as 'insensible, unmindful, unready' (p. 349); Edwards claims that '"pregnant" is not used by Shakespeare to mean "with child"'; see William Shakespeare, *Hamlet, Prince of Denmark*, ed. Philip Edwards (Cambridge: Cambridge University Press, 2003), p. 153. Mary Thomas Crane, 'Male Pregnancy and Cognitive Permeability in

Measure for Measure', *Shakespeare Quarterly* 49.3 (1998), pp. 269–92, similarly argues that Shakespeare did not use the term to refer to child-bearing, though she notes that Shakespeare would have been aware of this definition (pp. 275–85).

8. Most immediately, though not exclusively, he imitates an earlier *Hamlet*, which itself imitates two European sources. On pregnancy imagery as representing literary fecundity in the period, see Katharine Eisaman Maus, 'A Womb of His Own: Male Renaissance Poets in the Female Body', in James Grantham Turner (ed.), *Sexuality and Gender in Early Modern Europe* (Cambridge: Cambridge University Press, 1993), pp. 266–88.

9. Heather James, *Shakespeare's Troy* (Cambridge: Cambridge University Press, 1997), discusses this episode's Trojan and Virgilian contexts, but dismisses Hecuba's significance: 'Any interest that Shakespeare may have had in Hecuba ... is subordinate to Hamlet's troubled fascination with mimicry and widowed mothers' (p. 40). On the episode's Virgilian roots, see also Robert S. Miola, 'Aeneas and Hamlet', *Classical and Modern Literature* 8 (1988), pp. 281–6; on the influence of Ovid's Hecuba, see Jonathan Bate, *Shakespeare and Ovid* (Oxford: Clarendon Press, 1993), p. 20; Lynn Enterline, *The Rhetoric of the Body from Ovid to Shakespeare* (Cambridge: Cambridge University Press, 2000), pp. 166–7; Mary Jo Kietzman, '"What Is Hecuba to Him or [S]he to Hecuba?" Lucrece's Complaint and Shakespearean Poetic Agency', *Modern Philology* 97.1 (1999), pp. 21–45. Lizette Westney, 'Hecuba in Sixteenth-Century English Literature', *College Language Association Journal* 27.4 (1984), pp. 436–9, surveys the period's allusions to Hecuba. The richest account of Hamlet's uses of Hecuba is that of Katharine Goodland, *Female Mourning in Medieval and Renaissance English Drama* (Aldershot: Ashgate Publishing Ltd, 2006), pp. 71–199. This article is indebted to Goodland's sensitive exploration of Hecuba's associations with female grief and tragedy, though the emphasis here on the reception and adaptation of classical tragedy diverges from her focus on Protestant England's nostalgia for the Virgin Mary.

10. On Hecuba's exceptional status, see Malcolm Heath, '"Jure principem locum tenet": Euripides' *Hecuba*', *Bulletin of the Institute of Classical Studies* 34 (1987), pp. 40–68; Judith Mossman, *Wild Justice: A Study of Euripides' Hecuba* (Oxford: Clarendon Press, 1995).

11. Erasmus' translation was especially influential in England, where he shaped humanist study; he dedicated it to William Warham, the Archbishop of Canterbury. *Hecuba* had also been the subject of the first partial Latin translations of Greek drama: the Calabrian Greek scholar Leontius Pilatus translated the first 146 lines in 1362, followed by similar work by Francesco Filelfo (1398–1481) and Pietro da Montagnana (fl. 1432–78); see Robert Garland, *Surviving Greek Tragedy* (London: Duckworth Publishers, 2004), pp. 96–7.

12. After *Medea*, *Alcestis* and *The Phoenician Women*, which appeared in eighteen, eleven and eight editions respectively, no other Greek play

appeared in more than four individual or partial editions in the sixteenth century. For details on these numbers and the early printing of Greek plays, see Jean Christophe Saladin, 'Euripide Luthérien?', *Mélanges de l'Ecole française de Rome* 108.1 (1996), pp. 155–70 (p. 164); Rudolf Hirsch, 'The Printing Tradition of Aeschylus, Euripides, Sophocles and Aristophanes', *Gutenberg Jahrbuch* 39 (1964), pp. 138–46.

13. See R. R. Bolgar, *The Classical Heritage and its Beneficiaries* (Cambridge: Cambridge University Press, 1954), pp. 512–15. Very few Greek plays were translated into vernacular languages in the sixteenth century: again, *Iphigenia* came second with four, with very little competition.

14. See Heath, 'Jure principem locum tenet', p. 43; Jan Hendrik Waszink, *Erasmi opera omnia*, 10 vols (Amsterdam: North Holland, 1969), vol. 1, p. 207. Adaptations staged in the sixteenth century include Robert Garnier's *La Troade* (France, 1579), *Polyxène* (France, 1584), and three versions of Seneca's *Troas* – one under the title *Hecuba* – staged at Trinity College, Cambridge, in 1551, 1559 and 1560. On these performances, see the APGRD Database, University of Oxford, <http://www.apgrd.ox.ac.uk/database> (last accessed 29 March 2011).

15. Gasparus Stiblinus, 'In Hecabam Euripidis Praefatio', in *Euripides Poeta Tragicorum Princeps* (Basel, 1562), pp. 38–9 (p. 38).

16. Complaining about contemporary approaches to dramatic structure, Philip Sidney, *The Defense of Poesy*, in Tanya Pollard (ed.), *Shakespeare's Theater: A Sourcebook* (Oxford: Wiley-Blackwell, 2004), describes the plot of *Hecuba* and asks 'Where now would one of our tragedy writers begin, but with the delivery of the child? Then should he sail over into Thrace, and so spend I know not how many years, and travel numbers of places. But where doth Euripides? Even with the finding of the body, the rest leaving to be told by the spirit of Polydorus. This needs no further to be enlarged; the dullest wit may conceive it' (p. 160 [sig. K2r]). See also J. C. Scaliger, *Select Translations from Scaliger's Poetics*, ed. and trans. Frederick Morgan Padelford (New York: Henry Holt and Company, 1905), p. 60; Antonio Minturno, *L'Arte Poetica* (Venice: per Gio. Andrea Valvassori, 1564), pp. 85–8. On Renaissance interest in the play's structure, see Emrys Jones, *The Origins of Shakespeare* (Oxford: Oxford University Press, 1977), p. 95.

17. On the play's status as first in the Byzantine triad of Euripides' plays established around AD 500, which both reflected and furthered its visibility, see Heath, 'Jure principem locum tenet', p. 43. On violence, see F. L. Lucas, *Euripides and His Influence* (New York: Cooper Square Publishers, Inc., 1963), p. 93; Judith Weil, 'Visible Hecubas', in *The Female Tragic Hero*, pp. 51–69, although the latter does not discuss routes of reception or specific references to the figure of Hecuba. On Hecuba in Aphthonius' *Progymnasmata*, see Charles Osborne McDonald, *The Rhetoric of Tragedy* (Amherst: University of Massachusetts Press, 1966), p. 107; on fascination with Troy, see Jones, *Origins of Shakespeare*, p. 94.

18. On this catalogue of examples, see Mossman, *Wild Justice*, pp. 226–9; Mossman argues that Euripides deliberately solicited such imitations by presenting Hecuba as an archetype (pp. 219–20).
19. Thomas Norton and Thomas Sackville, *Gorboduc*, in John W. Cunliffe (ed.), *Early English Classical Tragedies* (Oxford: Clarendon Press, 1912), 3.1.14–15.
20. Early modern preferences intensified the centrality of women in Greek tragedy, but did not create it: see A. W. Gomme, 'The Position of Women in Classical Athens', *Classical Philology* 20.1 (1925), pp. 1–25; Helene P. Foley, *Female Acts in Greek Tragedy* (Princeton: Princeton University Press, 2001). For a recent overview of critical approaches to women's roles on the ancient stage, see Victoria Wohl, 'Tragedy and Feminism', in Rebecca Bushnell (ed.), *A Companion to Tragedy* (Oxford: Wiley-Blackwell, 2009), pp. 145–60.
21. On editions, see Saladin, 'Euripide Luthérien?', p. 164; Hirsch, 'Printing Tradition', pp. 141–3. For a full list of vernacular translations of Greek texts before 1600, see Bolgar, *Classical Heritage*, pp. 508–25.
22. See Hirsch, 'Printing Tradition', pp. 141–3; Bolgar, *Classical Heritage*, pp. 512–25. Aeschylus' plays received considerably less attention in the period because textual corruption and linguistic complexity limited their accessibility.
23. For details of these performances, see the APGRD Database.
24. Margaret Alexiou, *The Ritual Lament in Greek Tradition* (Cambridge: Cambridge University Press, 1974); Christian M. Billing, 'Lament and Revenge in the *Hekabe* of Euripides', *New Theatre Quarterly* 23.1 (2007), pp. 49–57; Foley, *Female Acts*, esp. pp. 21–55, 145–71; Gail Holst-Warhaft, *Dangerous Voices: Women's Laments and Greek Literature* (London: Routledge, 1992), esp. pp. 104–70; Nicole Loraux, *Mothers in Mourning*, trans. Corinne Pache (Ithaca: Cornell University Press, 1998).
25. Billing, 'Lament and Revenge', pp. 50, 51, who argues that 'the audience is led to understand that the pain of bereaved mothers is capable of creating an emotional context within which impassioned calls for revenge may easily be accommodated'. Holst-Warhaft, *Dangerous Voices*, similarly examines (though not in *Hecuba*) 'the threat of female mourning to the state and to male authority' in Greek literature (p. 161).
26. Billing, 'Lament and Revenge', describes the blinded Polymestor as 'a spectacular warning to those who consider female lament to be inconsequential', and adds that Hecuba 'rests safe in the knowledge that Agamemnon's quasi-juridical process sanctioned her actions entirely' (pp. 54, 55). On the traditional understanding in Greek tragedy of revenge as an obligation to help friends and harm enemies, see M. Whitlock Blundell, *Helping Friends and Harming Enemies* (Cambridge: Cambridge University Press, 1989); Anne Pippin Burnett, *Revenge in Attic and Later Tragedy* (Berkeley: University of California Press, 1998).
27. When Jason learns of her murder of his children, Euripides' Medea flaunts

her successful punishment of him: 'For I, as necessary, have attacked your heart in return' (τῆς σῆς γὰρ ὡς χρῆν καρδίας ἀνθηψάμην: *Medea* 1360). Discussing Hieronimo's account of his revenge in *The Spanish Tragedy*, Gordon Braden, *Renaissance Tragedy and the Senecan Tradition* (New Haven: Yale University Press, 1985), identifies his pride with 'the recognition to which Seneca's Medea and Atreus aspire in their last scenes' (p. 211); I suggest that Seneca's model has Euripidean roots. On Seneca's debts to Euripides, see R. J. Tarrant, 'Senecan Drama and its Antecedents', *Harvard Studies in Classical Philology* 82 (1978), pp. 213–63.

28. See Froma Zeitlin, *Playing the Other: Gender and Society in Classical Greek Literature* (Chicago: The University of Chicago Press, 1996), pp. 194–8. I am grateful to David Quint for calling this to my attention. On Renaissance identification of Homer's *Odyssey* with the origins of tragicomedy, see Sarah Dewar-Watson, 'Shakespeare's Dramatic Odysseys: Homer as a Tragicomic Model in *Pericles* and *The Tempest*', *Classical and Modern Literature* 25.1 (2005), pp. 23–40 (esp. 24–8); on Euripides' *Cyclops* in particular as an important model for tragicomedy in the period, see Marvin T. Herrick, *Tragicomedy: Its Origin and Development in Italy, France, and England* (Urbana: University of Illinois Press, 1955), pp. 7–13.

29. Scaliger, *Select Translations*, p. 61.

30. Giraldi Cinthio, *On the Composition of Comedies and Tragedies* (1543), trans. Allen Gilbert, in *Literary Criticism: Plato to Dryden* (New York: American Book Co., 1940), pp. 252–62 (p. 256); Castelvetro, *Castelvetro on the Art of Poetry*, ed. and trans. Andrew Bongiorno (Binghamton, NY: Medieval & Renaissance Texts & Studies, 1984), p. 19.

31. On Renaissance interest in tragic affect as a response to Aristotle's *Poetics*, see Nicholas Cronk, 'Aristotle, Horace, and Longinus: The Conception of Reader Response', in in G. P. Norton (ed.), *The Cambridge History of Literary Criticism* (Cambridge: Cambridge University Press, 1999), vol. 3, pp. 199–204; Timothy J. Reiss, 'Renaissance Theatre and the Theory of Tragedy', in *The Cambridge History* (1999), vol. 3, pp. 229–47; Stephen Orgel, 'Shakespeare and the Kinds of Drama', *Critical Inquiry* 6.1 (1979), pp. 107–23.

32. Francis Bacon, 'Of Revenge', in John M. Robertson (ed.), *The Philosophical Works of Francis Bacon* (New York: Routledge, 1970), famously criticised revenge as 'a kind of wild justice', and insists 'This is certain, that a man that studieth revenge keeps his own wounds green, which otherwise would heal and do well' (p. 740).

33. Mossman, *Wild Justice*, p. 243.

34. On the centrality of maternal lament to tragedy, and on Hecuba as a 'paradigm of mourning motherhood', see Loraux, *Mothers in Mourning*, pp. 27–8, 40.

35. Recent work on classical reception has emphasised the ways in which later periods actively rewrite the past: see Charles Martindale, 'Thinking

through Reception', in Charles Martindale and Richard F. Thomas (eds), *Classics and the Uses of Reception* (Oxford: Oxford University Press, 2006), pp. 1–13. Bruce Smith, *Ancient Scripts and Modern Experience on the English Stage, 1500–1700* (Princeton: Princeton University Press, 1988), has suggested that the term *confluence* might be more apt than influence for describing the reciprocity by which early moderns shaped what they read (p. 6).

36. See Robert S. Miola, 'Euripides at Gray's Inn: Gascoigne and Kinwelmersh's *Jocasta*', in *The Female Tragic Hero*, pp. 33–50. Challenging received opinion that the translators adhered strictly to Dolce's version, Howard Norland, *Neoclassical Tragedy in Elizabethan England* (Newark, DE: University of Delaware Press, 2009), points out that they amplify the emotional intensity of the queen's suffering through expanding her lines and accounts of her sorrows, and cutting material not directly relevant to her (pp. 83–9).

37. George Gascoigne and Francis Kinwelmersh, *Jocasta*, in *Early English Classical Tragedies*, 2.1.92–5.

38. Lodovico Dolce, *Giocasta* (Venice, 1549), is a very close translation: 'Amor non è, che s'appareggia a quello, / Che la pietosa madre a i figli porta: / Ilqual tanto piu cresce, quanti in essi / Scemail contento, & crescono gi affanni' (sig. 14v).

39. Loraux, *Mothers in Mourning*, writes of this and other references that 'a mother owes her pre-eminent position alongside the dead to the unconditional privilege given once and for all by the bond of childbirth. A bond that is without mediation, exacting, painful, and that Euripides's choruses sometimes describe as "terrible": terribly tender, terribly strong, simply *terrible* . . . in order to designate the child as what is both the most precious and the most heartrending possession of a mother, Euripidean tragedy readily calls it the *lókheuma*, the product of childbirth' (pp. 35–6).

40. Although Gascoigne and Kinwelmersh have been seen as drawing exclusively on Dolce's translation, Sarah Dewar-Watson, '*Jocasta*: "A Tragedie Written in Greek"', *International Journal of the Classical Tradition* 17.1 (2010), notes that *Jocasta* draws on information about Theban gates and stage directions found in Rudolph Collinus' translation that does not appear in Dolce's (pp. 22–32).

41. Jane Lumley, *Iphigenia in Aulis*, ed. Harold Child (London: Chiswick Press, 1909 [Malone Society Reprints]), sig. 84v. On Lumley's experimental approach to translation, see Patricia Demers, 'On First Looking into Lumley's Euripides', *Renaissance and Reformation* 23.1 (1999), pp. 25–42; Marta Straznicky, *Privacy, Playreading, and Women's Closet Drama, 1500s–1700* (Cambridge: Cambridge University Press, 2004), pp. 19–47.

42. Lumley had access to Erasmus' dual-language Greek–Latin edition, as well as a Greek edition of Euripides: see Sears Jayne and Francis R. Johnson (eds), *The Lumley Library: The Catalogue of 1609* (London:

British Library, 1956), nos. 1736 and 1591a, cited in Straznicky, *Privacy*, p. 33. I challenge here the longstanding claim that Lumley worked directly from the Latin version and 'shows no knowledge of Greek': see Frank D. Crane, 'Euripides, Erasmus, and Lady Lumley', *The Classical Journal* 39.4 (1944), pp. 223–8 (p. 228).
43. Although precisely when Lumley translated the play is not known, it is typically dated to the early years of her marriage: see Harold Child, 'Introduction', in Harold Child (ed.), *Iphigenia in* (London: Chiswick Press, 1909 [Malone Society Reprints]), pp. v–vii (p. vi); Demers, 'First Looking', pp. 25–6.
44. Elizabeth studied under the Hellenist Roger Ascham; on her translation, which is not extant, see T. W. Baldwin, *William Shakspere's Small Latine and Lesse Greeke*, 2 vols (Urbana: University of Illinois Press, 1944), vol. 1, p. 282. On women's affinity for closet drama and translation, see Straznicky, *Privacy*.
45. Gascoigne and Kinwelmersh, *Jocasta*, p. 159.
46. Stephen Gosson, 'Plays Confuted in Five Actions', in Tanya Pollard (ed.), *Shakespeare's Theater: A Sourcebook* (Oxford: Wiley-Blackwell, 2004), pp. 84–114 (p. 95), (sig. C5v–C6r); see also Marissa Greenberg, 'Women and the Theater in Thomas Heywood's London', in Joan Fitzpatrick (ed.), *The Idea of the City: Early-Modern, Modern and Post-Modern Locations and Communities* (Newcastle: Cambridge Scholars Publishing, 2009), pp. 79–89; Phyllis Rackin, 'Engendering the Tragic Audience: The Case of *Richard III*', *Studies in the Literary Imagination* 26.1 (1993), pp. 47–65.
47. See *A Warning for Fair Women*, ed. Charles Cannon (The Hague: Mouton, 1975), pp. 97–100 (Induction); Thomas Heywood, *Apology for Actors*, in Tanya Pollard (ed.), *Shakespeare's Theater: A Sourcebook* (Oxford: Wiley-Blackwell, 2004), pp. 213–54, depicts the tragic muse Melpomene (pp. 216–18). Rackin, 'Engendering the Tragic Audience', discusses *A Warning* (p. 49); Goodland, *Female Mourning*, discusses the identification of tragedy with tears and the feminine, esp. pp. 175–6.
48. See Jessica Winston, 'Seneca in Early Elizabethan England', *Renaissance Quarterly* 59.1 (2006), pp. 29–58 (p. 43).
49. Jasper Heywood, *Troas* (London, 1559), sig. B3v, quoted in Winston, 'Seneca in Early Elizabethan England', p. 41.
50. On tragedy and tyranny, see Rebecca Bushnell, *Tragedy and Tyrants* (Ithaca: Cornell University Press, 1990). Heather James, 'Dido's Ear: Tragedy and the Politics of Response', *Shakespeare Quarterly* 52.3 (2001), pp. 360–82, explores the relationship among tragic sympathy, rebellion against authority and ultimately regicide.
51. Sidney, *The Defense of Poesy*, p. 151 (sig. F3v, F4r).
52. In *de Alexandri* Plutarch refers to Hecuba's daughter Polyxena, who appears in *Hecuba* but not in The *Trojan Women*: see Mossman, *Wild Justice*, p. 218. Critics typically identify Sidney's passage with *Pelopidas*

and *The Trojan Women*. For identification of the passage in *Pelopidas* as an influence on *Hamlet*, because of its emphasis on the tyrant's guilt, see James Freeman, 'Hamlet, Hecuba, and Plutarch', *Shakespeare Studies* 7 (1974), pp. 197–202; Patricia Gourlay, 'Guilty Creatures Sitting at a Play: A Note on *Hamlet*, Act II, Scene 2', *Renaissance Quarterly* 24.2 (1971), pp. 221–5. However, Gourlay suggests that the *de Alexandri* passage more directly influenced Sidney.

53. *Pelopidas* appears in translations of the *Lives* by both North (1579) and Jacques Amyot (1559), and *de Alexandri* in Amyot's translation of the *Moralia* (1572).
54. Plutarch, 'De la fortune ou vertu d'Alexandre', in *Les Oeuvres Morales & Meslees du Plutarque*, trans. Jacques Amyot (Paris, 1572), sig. 308r–18r (sig. 312r). In his 1603 English translation, Philemon Holland similarly has 'mollified his hard heart and made it melt like a peece of iron in the furnace', taken from Plutarch's own ἐμάλαξεν [*emalaxen*], from μαλάσσω [*malasso*] 'soften': Plutarch, 'On the fortune or virtue of Alexander', trans. Frank Babbitt, in Frank Babbitt (ed.) *Moralia* (Cambridge, MA: Harvard University Press, 1936), vol. 4, pp. 382–487 (p. 424). D. M. Gaunt, 'Hamlet and Hecuba', *Notes and Queries* 16.4 (1969), pp. 136–7, identifies the *de Alexandri* as a source for the Hecuba episode in *Hamlet* by suggesting that Hamlet's reference to being 'muddy-mettled' alludes to the imagery of melting iron.
55. On 'mollify', see *OED*, 'mollify, v', definition 3.
56. George Puttenham, *The Art of English Poesy*, in Tanya Pollard (ed.), *Shakespeare's Theater: A Sourcebook* (Oxford: Wiley-Blackwell, 2004), pp. 135–45 (p. 138).
57. Bushnell, *Tragedy and Tyrants*, esp. pp. 5–7, notes that the historical relationship between playwrights and tyrants was in fact far more complicated than typically imagined by early modern writers.
58. Castelvetro, *On the Poetics*, trans. Allen Gilbert, in *Literary Criticism: Plato to Dryden*, pp. 305–57 (p. 331).
59. Shakespeare mentions Dido, to whom he has been described as 'mysteriously attracted', thirteen times (James, 'Dido's Ear', p. 364); Hippolyta six times (plus four in stage directions, all in *A Midsummer Night's Dream*); and Medea once; Iphigenia, Clytemnestra and Antigone do not feature at all, nor do Oedipus, Orestes, Hippolytus, Thyestes or Atreus. The only classical literary characters who appear more frequently are those with active roles in *Troilus and Cressida*, such as Achilles, Hector, Priam, Agamemnon and Aeneas and demigods such as Hercules.
60. William Shakespeare, *Titus Andronicus*, in *Norton*, 1.1.136–9; 'I have heard my grandsire say full oft, / Extremity of griefs would make men mad; / And I have read that Hecuba of Troy / Ran mad through sorrow' (ibid. 4.1.18–21).
61. William Shakespeare, *The Rape of Lucrece*, in *Norton*, 1447, 1458.
62. William Shakespeare, *Coriolanus*, in *Norton*, 1.3.37–40. Intriguingly, this

quotation suggests a possible verbal echo from Euripides' *Hecuba* (424), in which Hecuba's daughter Polyxena, facing her upcoming sacrifice by Pyrrhus, laments to her mother, 'O chest and breasts, that suckled me sweetly' (ὦ στέρνα μαστοί θ', οἵ μ' ἐθρέψαθ' ἡδέως).

63. William Shakespeare, *Coriolanus*, in *Norton*, 4.2.314–16. References to Hecuba also feature in *Troilus and Cressida* (c.1602), but as the events take place before the Fall of Troy, they do not illustrate her tragic grief.

64. For numerous examples of the more typical images of Hecuba linked with woe, see Westney, 'Hecuba in Sixteenth-Century English Literature'.

65. In 1985, Gordon Braden, *Renaissance Tragedy and the Senecan Tradition* (New Haven: Yale University Press, 1985), held that 'the generally insufficient knowledge of or even interest in Greek tragedy on the part of Renaissance dramatists is hard to deny' (p. 1).

66. Lane Cooper, *The Poetics of Aristotle* (Ithaca: Cornell University Press, 1923), writes that Shakespeare, 'though more Roman than Greek in his dramatic origins, is nearer ... to Aristotle and the spirit of Greek tragedy' (p. 134); and recently Michael Silk, 'Shakespeare and Greek Tragedy: Strange Relationship', in Charles Martindale and A. B. Taylor (eds), *Shakespeare and the Classics* (Cambridge: Cambridge University Press, 2004), pp. 239–58, has similarly argued that 'Against all the odds, perhaps, there is a real affinity between Greek and Shakespearean tragedy. What there is not is any "reception" in the ordinary sense' (p. 241).

67. See Jones, *Origins of Shakespeare*; Douglas B. Wilson, 'Euripides' *Alcestis* and the Ending of Shakespeare's *The Winter's Tale*', *Iowa State Journal of Research* 58 (1984), pp. 345–55; Louise Schleiner, 'Latinized Greek Drama in Shakespeare's Writing of *Hamlet*', *Shakespeare Quarterly* 41.1 (1990), pp. 29–48; Laurie Maguire, *Shakespeare's Names* (Oxford: Oxford University Press, 2007), pp. 97–104; Sarah Dewar-Watson, 'The *Alcestis* and the Statue Scene in *The Winter's Tale*', *Shakespeare Quarterly* 60.1 (2009), pp. 73–80. On Greek romances as transmitting Greek dramatic conventions, see Tanya Pollard, 'Romancing the Greeks: *Cymbeline*'s Genres and Models', in Laurie Maguire (ed.), *How to Do Things with Shakespeare* (Oxford: Blackwell, 2007), pp. 34–53.

68. At a structural level, revenge tragedy in England had many links with Greek models: Shakespeare's well-documented use of contemporary European plays and *novelle* as sources demonstrates that he was familiar with the Continental writers who developed their plays and dramatic theory in dialogue with classical plays and Aristotle's *Poetics*. *The Spanish Tragedy* (1587), to which he was deeply indebted, was heavily shaped by classical study: Kyd quoted Seneca, translated a play by the French neoclassical playwright Robert Garnier, appears to have been influenced by Italian neoclassicists such as Cinthio, and was close friends with Thomas Watson, who translated *Antigone* in 1581.

69. Scholars generally agree that Shakespeare had a standard grammar-school education, which typically included some Greek: see Baldwin, *William*

Shakspere's Small Latine and Lesse Greeke. Beyond Volumnia's evocation of Polyxena's lines apostrophising Hecuba's breasts, the player's account of Pyrrhus' pause before slaying Priam in *Hamlet* – 'neutral to his will and matter' (2.2.484) – closely resembles Pyrrhus' pause before slaying Polyxena in *Hecuba*, where he is 'not willing and willing' (οὐ θέλων τε καὶ θέλων: 566); see Martin Mueller, '*Hamlet* and the World of Ancient Tragedy', *Arion*, 3rd ser., 5.1 (1997), pp. 22–45 (p. 38). In *Titus Andronicus*, Demetrius identifies Hecuba's violent revenge as having taken place in a tent, a detail that appears in Euripides' play but not in Ovid: see J. A. K. Thomson, *Shakespeare and the Classics* (London: George Allen & Unwin, 1952), pp. 57–8.

70. See, for instance, Bate, *Shakespeare and Ovid*; James, *Shakespeare's Troy*; Enterline, *Rhetoric of the Body*. Jones, *Origins of Shakespeare*, rightly notes that 'we are not faced with a choice between Euripides and Ovid, since no one denies Ovidian influence. The choice is between Ovid alone and Ovid together with Euripides' (p. 102). Latin poets' considerable debts to Euripides point to overlapping forms of influence: see Garland, *Surviving Greek Tragedy*, p. 60; Bate, *Shakespeare and Ovid*, who suggests that Shakespeare 'derived a Euripidean spirit from Ovid' (p. 239).

71. Jones, *Origins of Shakespeare*, pp. 102–3.

72. See Bamber, *Comic Women*. Although Shakespeare markedly intensified this trend, he was hardly the first to focus tragedies predominantly on male protagonists. Responding in part to the all-male acting tradition in the schools and universities where classical dramatic genres began to take hold, as well as in the commercial theatres where they eventually took root, male revengers had dominated English tragedies from both their academic origins in *Gorbuduc* and their commercial origins in *The Spanish Tragedy*. On the apparent erasure of mothers, in particular, in Shakespeare's plays, see Mary Beth Rose, 'Where are the Mothers in Shakespeare? Options for Gender Representation in the English Renaissance', *Shakespeare Quarterly* 42.3 (1991), pp. 291–314; Janet Adelman, *Suffocating Mothers* (New York: Routledge, 1992).

73. The proliferation of Hecuba references in *Hamlet* and *Troilus and Cressida* suggests the possible influence of George Chapman, who had just published his translation of seven books of Homer's *Iliad* in 1598: I am grateful to Tania Demetriou for this observation. On literary responses to Chapman's Homer, see Tania Demetriou, '"Essentially Circe": Spenser, Homer, and the Homeric Tradition', *Translation and Literature* 15.2 (2006), pp. 151–76.

74. On Hecuba as an affront to Gertrude's own failure to mourn properly, see Miola, 'Aeneas and Hamlet', p. 284; James, *Shakespeare's Troy*, p. 40.

75. Goodland, *Female Mourning*, esp. 171–2.

76. On critical responses to this preoccupation, and on Gertrude as evoking ambivalence toward the ageing Elizabeth, see Steven Mullaney, 'Mourning and Misogyny: *Hamlet, The Revenger's Tragedy*, and the Final Progress of

Elizabeth I, 1600–1607', *Shakespeare Quarterly* 45.2 (1994), pp. 139–62 (esp. pp. 150–4).

77. Achilles cites Niobe as an analogy for Priam's grief over his (and Hecuba's) son Hector's death (Homer *Iliad* 24.602–14). Curiously, Sophocles' Antigone – who dies a virgin – likens her tearful death to Niobe's (*Ant.* 824–31), though the chorus reminds her that, as a mortal, she is not comparable to the goddess-born Niobe (834–5). Thomas Watson rendered the exchange faithfully in his 1581 Latin translation of the play, which would have been easily available to Shakespeare.
78. In keeping with Claudius' complaints about Hamlet's 'unmanly grief', Gertrude similarly advises him to 'cast [his] nightly colour off' (1.2.94, 68).
79. See Tony Howard, *Women as Hamlet: Performance and Interpretation in Theatre, Film and Fiction* (Cambridge: Cambridge University Press, 2007), p. 1.
80. The play becomes the means for Hieronimo and Bel-Imperia to murder Lorenzo and Balthazar; Vindice's opportunity to kill Lussurioso and his nobles in Thomas Middleton's *The Revenger's Tragedy* (1606); Ferdinand's means to torture his sister in John Webster's *The Duchess of Malfi* (1614); and, perhaps most strikingly, Domitian's stabbing of Paris in Philip Massinger's *The Roman Actor* (1626), to name only a few examples.
81. Dieter Mehl, *The Elizabethan Dumb Show* (London: Methuen, 1965).
82. See John W. Cunliffe, 'The Influence of the Italian on Early Elizabethan Drama', *Modern Philology* 4 (1907), pp. 597–604; and John W. Cunliffe, 'Italian Prototypes of the Masque and Dumb Show', *Publications of the Modern Language Association* 22 (1907), pp. 140–56.
83. In early neoclassical plays, the dumb-show is both structurally and thematically linked with the chorus: the choral odes that close each act immediately precede the dumb-shows that open the next act, so that the two devices frame the action, and typically treat related topics.
84. Euripides *Hecuba* 1042–3: βούλεσθ' ἐπεσπέσωμεν; ὡς ἀκμὴ καλεῖ / Ἑκάβῃ παρεῖναι Τρῳάσιν τε συμμάχους (Should we burst in on them? The moment requires us to stand with Hecuba and the Trojan women as allies). This pattern of considering but refusing action is common in Euripides' choruses. In response to Medea's children's offstage cries for help while their mother attempts to murder them, the chorus of Corinthian women wonders, 'Shall I go into the house? I must prevent the children's death' (παρέλθω δόμους; ἀρῆξαι φόνον / δοκεῖ μοι τέκνοις). Although the children, breaking tragic convention, hear this from offstage and reply, 'Yes, by the gods, help, for it must be done now!' (ναί, πρὸς θεῶν, ἀρήξατ': ἐν δέοντι γάρ), the chorus does nothing but lament (Euripides *Medea* 1275–7). On the varieties of the Euripidean chorus, see Rush Rehm, 'Performing the Chorus: Choral Action, Interaction and Absence in Euripides', *Arion*, 3rd ser., 4.1 (1996), pp. 45–60; Donald J. Mastronarde, *The Art of Euripides: Dramatic*

Technique and Social Context (Cambridge: Cambridge University Press, 2010), pp. 88–152.
85. Like Hecuba, Hamlet is frequently depicted as a mirror in which others see themselves. Ophelia describes him as 'The glass of fashion and the mould of form, / Th'observ'd of all observers' (3.1.152–3).
86. On early modern ideas about mirrors and their audiences, see Herbert Grabes, *The Mutable Glass*, trans. Gordon Collier (Cambridge: Cambridge University Press, 1982), pp. 131–44.
87. Robert S. Miola, *Shakespeare and Classical Tragedy: The Influence of Seneca* (Oxford: Clarendon Press, 1992), pp. 38–9
88. Noting that most tragic choruses are female, Oliver Taplin, 'Comedy and the Tragic', in M. S. Silk (ed.), *Tragedy and the Tragic: Greek Theatre and Beyond* (Oxford: Oxford University Press, 1996), pp. 188–202, suggests that 'Women and weak old men seem to be favoured for choruses partly because of their ineffectuality in action' (p. 193).
89. On the text's relative silence on Gertrude's moral status, and critical tendencies to follow Hamlet's disapproval despite this lack of evidence, see Rebecca Smith, 'A Heart Cleft in Twain: The Dilemma of Shakespeare's Gertrude', in Carolyn Ruth Swift Lenz, Gayle Greene and Carol Thomas Neely (eds), *The Woman's Part: Feminist Criticism of Shakespeare* (Urbana: University of Illinois Press, 1980), pp. 194–210; Richard Levin, 'Gertrude's Elusive Libido and Shakespeare's Unreliable Narrators', *Studies in English Literature* 48.2 (2008), pp. 305–26.
90. See Nona Fienberg, 'Jephthah's Daughter: The Part Ophelia Plays', in Raymond-Jean Frontain and Jon Wojcik (eds), *Old Testament Women in Western Literature* (Conway, AR: University of Central Arkansas Press, 1991), pp. 128–43; Goodland, *Female Mourning*, pp. 188–9.
91. Just prior to writing his play, Buchanan had translated Euripides' *Alcestis* and *Medea* from Greek into Latin. See Wilbur Sypherd, *Jephthah and his Daughter* (Newark, DE: University of Delaware Press, 1948); Debora Shuger, *The Renaissance Bible: Scholarship, Sacrifice, and Subjectivity* (Berkeley: University of California Press, 1994); Paul D. Streufert, 'Christopherson at Cambridge: Greco-Catholic Ethics in the Protestant University', in Jonathan Walker and Paul D. Streufert (eds), *Early Modern Academic Drama* (Farnham: Ashgate, 2008), pp. 45–64.
92. Roger Ascham, *The Scholemaster* (London, 1571), describes the play as one of only two modern tragedies 'able to abide the true touch of Aristotle's precepts and Euripides' examples' (p. 174); Sidney in *The Defense of Poesy* claims that 'the tragedies of Buchanan do justly bring forth a divine admiration' (K3v). The Cambridge performance could have been either Buchanan's or Christopherson's play: see Sypherd, *Jephthah and his Daughter*, p. 15. On Dekker and Munday's play, see R. A. Foakes (ed.), *Henslowe's Diary*, 2nd edition (Cambridge: Cambridge University Press, 2002), pp. 200–3, 296.
93. Although it is the murder of her son Polydorus that ultimately catalyses

Hecuba's revenge on his killer, Polymestor, the sacrifice of her daughter Polyxena lays a foundation for the grief that eventually turns into murderous rage. Shuger, *Renaissance Bible*, notes that 'With the partial exceptions of *Medea* and *Electra*, all translations of Greek tragedy (including both Latin and vernacular) printed before 1560 concern human sacrifice, especially female sacrifice: Euripides's *Hecuba* (1506), *Iphigenia in Aulis* (1506), *Alcestis* (1554), and *Phoenissae* (1560) and Sophocles' *Antigone* (1533)' (p. 129).

94. On the significance of song in shaping her meaning in the play, see Leslie C. Dunn, 'Ophelia's Songs in *Hamlet*: Music, Madness, and the Feminine', in Leslie C. Dunn and Nancy A. Jones (eds), *Embodied Voices: Representing Female Vocality in Western Culture* (Cambridge: Cambridge University Press, 1994), pp. 50–64; Jacquelyn Fox-Good, 'Ophelia's Mad Songs: Music, Gender, Power', in David C. Allen and Robert A. White (eds), *Subjects on the World's Stage: Essays on British Literature of the Middle Ages and the Renaissance* (Newark, DE: University of Delaware Press, 1995) pp. 217–38.

95. Eric Nicholson, 'Ophelia Sings Like a *Prima Donna Innamorata*: Ophelia's Mad Scene and the Italian Female Performer', in Robert Henke and Eric Nicholson (eds), *Transnational Exchange in Early Modern Theater* (Aldershot: Ashgate Publishing Ltd, 2008), pp. 81–98 (p. 93); see also Pamela Allen Brown, 'The Counterfeit *innamorata*, or, The Diva Vanishes', *Shakespeare Yearbook* 10 (1999), pp. 402–26.

CHAPTER 15

'Nursed in Blood': Masculinity and Grief in Marston's *Antonio's Revenge*

Rebecca Yearling

The revenger occupies a unique position among the heroes of tragedy. As John Kerrigan argues:

> Most tragic protagonists are responsible for how they suffer. More than rats in traps, tennis-balls bandied by the stars, they help create the circumstances in which events unfold.... A revenger's position is different. His predicament is imposed on him, and to know this is part of his plight. Injured by another, or urged towards vengeance by a raped mistress or murdered father, he is forced to adopt a role.... [F]or as long as he remains a revenger the proportions of the acts he engages in are determined by an injury he never gave or a request he did not make.[1]

Revengers begin as victims, as survivors of trauma. Typically, they are dazed, disorientated, full of grief. They have been wronged, yet they have no way to find justice through the usual channels. They are thus forced initially into a condition of passivity and impotence that, for a male revenger, can be read as emasculating. Moreover, the male revenger's grief, his inability to forget or overcome his losses, might seem to confirm that emasculation. Mourning was not an exclusively female activity, of course, either in the drama of this period or in reality, but the idea of excessive mourning, of an immoderate, tearful wallowing in sorrow, was seen as connected to the feminine.[2] In *Hamlet*, for example, Claudius reprimands the prince for his 'unmanly grief' over his father, in his refusal to move on from the death, his determination to 'persever / In obstinate condolement' (1.2.92–3).[3]

However, in much literature of this period, revenge is seen as a way to escape from this 'feminine' mode of tearful impotence. In Kyd's *The Spanish Tragedy*, Hieronimo muses that, 'To know the author were some ease of grief, / For in revenge my heart would find relief', and later reflects that 'naught but blood will satisfy my woes' (2.5.40–1; 3.7.68).[4] He imagines that letting the blood of his oppressors will help him to purge his own sorrow and suffering. Similarly, in *The Rape of Lucrece*, Brutus reprimands the weeping, potentially suicidal father and husband of the dead Lucrece, asking them,

> [I]s woe the cure for woe?
> Do wounds help wounds, or grief help grievous deeds?
> Is it revenge to give thyself a blow
> For his foul act by whom thy fair wife bleeds?
> Such childish humour from weak minds proceeds:
> Thy wretched wife mistook the matter so
> To slay herself, that should have slain her foe. (1821–7)

Brutus suggests that mourning is useless; it cannot either cure the pain of bereavement or avenge the dead. To mourn, or to commit violence on oneself, is the act of a weak mind (and, moreover, a mind that is seen here to be weak in a specifically female way: Lucrece herself has taken this option). A true man will not succumb to such things, but will rather 'live to be revengèd' (1778). The revenger may initially be feminised by his victimhood, but in his path to revenge he reclaims his masculinity. One way to read revenge, therefore, is to say that it represents the turning of female grief into manly action: the move from tears to blood.[5]

This essay will explore the treatment of this theme in John Marston's 1600–1 tragedy, *Antonio's Revenge*. As we shall see, *Antonio's Revenge* develops the idea that the movement towards revenge involves a putting aside of the womanly emotions of love, pity and grief in order to dedicate oneself to the single-minded pursuit of violent retribution. Moreover, it is a particularly interesting play because it is virtually the only early modern revenge tragedy in which the revenger and his co-conspirators end the play alive and unpunished for their actions.[6] As Kerrigan puts it:

> Outside a world which believes in Furies ... there is no necessary reason for B or his accomplices to be damaged by their revenge upon A. ... [T]he survival of Antonio and his fellows ... is evidence not just of the sympathy which could flow to outrageously provoked revengers but of the pressure towards tragicomic outcomes created by vengeful plotting.[7]

Kerrigan argues that *Antonio's Revenge* tends towards being tragicomic rather than truly tragic because its conclusion offers a 'double arrangement' of 'opposite fortunes for the good and bad people': the villain Piero is killed, but Antonio and his friends escape largely unscathed.[8] In this play, Kerrigan suggests, revenge is treated relatively sympathetically. Antonio's actions have, in fact, set the world to rights, by removing a vicious tyrant, and so the revengers can be allowed to reconcile with their society, rather than being punished. However, I wonder whether this is really true. There are, I think, aspects of *Antonio's Revenge* which work against us reading it as a play that in any real sense sanctions revenge. Moreover, I would argue that it does not actually endorse the idea that revenge can provide a genuine cure for the anguish of bereavement, by offering a way of escape from the grieving process which allows victimised men to reclaim their lost masculinity. Antonio does indeed ultimately achieve an overtly 'manly' revenge on his oppressor, the wicked Piero – but the horror of the revenge itself, as it is portrayed on stage, and the desolation that overcomes the revengers once the act is complete, serve to undermine the sense that this kind of 'masculine' achievement is in any real way desirable.

The basic plot of *Antonio's Revenge* resembles that of *Hamlet* in a number of aspects. Before the play begins, Antonio's father Andrugio has been secretly murdered, poisoned by the evil Piero, Duke of Venice, who also plans to marry Antonio's mother Maria. Towards the start of the play, before he knows the true cause of his father's death, Antonio appears at risk of being permanently overwhelmed by grief:

MARIA: How now, sweet son; good youth, what dost thou?
ANTONIO: Weep, weep.
MARIA: Dost naught but weep, weep?
ANTONIO: Yes, mother, I do sigh and wring my hands,
Beat my poor breast and wreathe my tender arms. (2.2.141–5)[9]

Antonio refuses to eat or drink, can take no comfort in books of philosophy, and spends much of his time lying face-down on the ground, literally prostrate with misery.

However, in Act 3, scene 1, Antonio is visited by the ghost of his dead father, who tells him the truth of what happened, and urges him to revenge: 'Thou vigour of my youth, juice of my love, / Seize on revenge, grasp the stern-bended front / Of frowning vengeance [...] / Alarum Nemesis, rouse up thy blood ...' (3.1.44–7). Antonio takes these words to heart: he vows to 'suck red vengeance / Out of Piero's wounds', and promptly goes off to commit the first act of his revenge, the murder of Piero's infant son Julio. The cannibalistic image of Antonio 'sucking' Piero's blood is an interesting one in the context of the play. Earlier in the action, Piero himself had used a similar image, when he claimed that, 'I have been nursed in blood, and still have sucked / The steam of reeking gore' (2.1.19–20). Piero is a multiple murderer, having killed both Andrugio and the court satirist Feliche, and his metaphor here suggests that the murders he has committed represent a kind of rebirth for him. He has changed from being an ordinary human, reared on mother's milk, into a new kind of being, sustained and nurtured by blood.

Antonio's Revenge was originally written for the boy actors of the St Paul's theatre company, and Marston's exploration of what it means to be a man builds thematically on this fact. All the play's characters are being performed by adolescent boys, who are themselves not yet fully equipped with adult bodies, and who are therefore forced to act a manliness that they do not literally possess. Marston makes a direct reference to the youth of the actors in the play's second act, in a scene in which the foolish courtier Balurdo enters with a false beard, half stuck on, half falling off (s.d. 2.1.20). Piero asks him, 'What dost thou with a beard?' and Balurdo makes a joke about trying to compensate for having a 'bald wit', but there is a deeper point being made here, which is to remind us, via the metatheatrical joke of Balurdo's beard, that these actors are just boys, too young to grow a real beard. Manliness is therefore something that they must play, rather than something that they naturally 'have' – and we may be led to reflect on the links between that fact and the dilemma that afflicts the play's characters themselves, as they too try to learn how to be 'men'. Throughout *Antonio's Revenge*, there seems to be a sense that masculinity is performative rather than inherent. In order to be a 'real man', one must deliberately cast off the softer emotions. Antonio is, at the start of the play, presented as 'a gentle boy' (3.1.36), and when he encounters Julio, the child actually seems to see him as a kind of mother substitute, innocently remarking that, 'Truth, since my mother died I loved you best' (3.1.154). However, in order to carry out his father's command, Antonio must get rid of, or at least suppress, the element of the 'mother' within him, and become like Piero, a creature nursed in blood, with no emotions beyond rage and revenge.

The idea that people are made up of two sides, the feminine and the masculine, becomes overt in the murder of Julio. Before he kills the boy, Antonio briefly reflects on what he is doing. He has no quarrel with Julio himself; his fury is solely directed at Piero. However, Piero is Julio's father, and so Julio's body is partly made up of Piero: his blood, his essence. As Antonio muses,

> O that I knew which joint, which side, which limb,
> Were father all, and had no mother in't,
> That I might rip it vein by vein and carve revenge
> In bleeding rases! But since 'tis mixed together,
> Have at adventure, pell mell, no reverse!
> . . .
> Thy father's blood that flows within thy veins
> Is it I loathe, is that revenge must suck. (3.1.165–81)

Antonio wishes that he could separate out the male and female elements that make up the infant Julio, and leave only the parts that are male, the parts that belong to Piero. Similarly, in his own quest to become a successful revenger, he needs to remove or suppress the 'womanly', emotional side of his own nature. In this scene, Antonio does not seem yet quite to have achieved his desired level of pure manliness: he hesitates when Julio begs him for mercy, and only continues with the killing when the ghost of his father reappears to again order him to 'Revenge!' (3.1.175). Antonio obeys, but he is still emotionally divided between the desires for revenge and for mercy, and weeps while he kills the child: 'Whilst thy wounds bleed, my brows shall gush out tears' (3.1.186). He has not, apparently, left 'womanly' emotion behind completely.

The association of weeping with femininity, and the related idea that such femininity is a weakness, that it prevents one from being a true or a complete man, continues throughout the play. In Act 4, Pandulpho, the father of the murdered courtier Feliche, who has been trying to maintain a Stoic calm despite his grief, finally breaks down. He begins to cry, and when asked why, he replies that his attempt to force down and deny his misery was only an act. As he says, 'I spake more than a god, / Yet am less than a man' (4.2.74–5). Here, Pandulpho's tears represent his real self, bursting through his Stoic pretence, but nevertheless, he feels that this grief, however natural and true, makes him 'less than a man'. Masculinity is, in this play, a source of anxiety. The male characters seem continually to be trying to reinvent themselves as an ideal or fantasy of true manliness – creatures of action, creatures who do not cry or grieve, creatures who have no 'woman's part' in them – but the play emphasises how difficult it is to achieve such an ideal.

Nevertheless, Antonio does carry out the murder of Julio, and in return, the ghost of Andrugio congratulates him, announcing, 'Here stands Andrugio's son, / Worthy his father' (3.1.197–8). Antonio the gentle boy has, implicitly, become Antonio the man, a worthy successor to the dead patriarch; and he embraces his own success, announcing, 'Lo, thus I heave my blood-dyed hands to heaven, / Even like insatiate hell, still crying: "More! / My heart still thirsting dropsies after gore"' (3.1.212–14). The final revenge can then be seen as the ultimate victory for Antonio's manliness. In the play's last scene, just before the murder of Piero, he announces, 'Now, therefore, pity, piety, remorse, / Be aliens to our thoughts: grim, fire-eyed rage / Possess us wholly' (5.3.90–2). In this part of the revenge, there will be no womanish tears or regret. Antonio and his helpers (a collection of other characters who have also been abused by Piero) enter the court disguised as masquers, before revealing their true identities. They then tie Piero to a chair, cut out his tongue, taunt him with a dish containing Julio's severed limbs, and proceed to stab him multiple times, until he is dead. As Mark Albert Johnson comments, Antonio has by this stage become a 'hyper-masculine revenge hero', who 'accesses a martial virility surpassing ... that generated by the arch-villain Piero'.[10] Piero, by contrast, is in the course of the revenge thoroughly *un*manned, rendered both helpless and voiceless by the revengers.

The revenge itself is excessively violent and shocking, but what happens immediately afterwards is perhaps even more striking. As I commented earlier, in almost every other revenge tragedy of this period, the successful revenger dies, either during or immediately after his revenge: a fate which reflects the early modern ambivalence towards revenge itself. As has been often noted, while early modern audiences might have been sympathetic towards the emotional desire for revenge, they would also have been aware of the Biblical prohibitions against it. However, *Antonio's Revenge* provides the apparent exception. After the death of Piero, Antonio is not punished in any way; rather, he is hailed as a conquering hero by a chorus of senators who enter the play at this point. The senators call him 'another Hercules', and thank him for his murder of Piero, by which act he has 'ridd[en] huge pollution from our state' (5.3.129-30).

The fact that Antonio and the other revengers meet with no retribution at the end – and are, in fact, celebrated for their actions – is one of the play's most troubling aspects. Charles and Elaine Hallett argue that Marston, in his desire to reverse dramatic convention, has produced an unsatisfying resolution to the work. While other dramatists, such as Kyd, had explored the complexities of the revenger's situation, the way in which the revenging drive is a kind of madness, a surrender of self-control to chaotic passion, Marston 'deliberately counteracts this trend', by trying to suggest that the revenge itself may be a sane and necessary act, that it can indeed cleanse society and that the revenger can walk away afterwards. Marston thus understands, they write, 'the *experience* of revenge but not its *implications*': while able vividly to convey the revengers' emotional states, he oversimplifies the moral issues involved.[11] By this reading, *Antonio's Revenge* has an amoral and gratuitous conclusion, in which we the audience are encouraged to revel in the psychological and physical torture of Piero. Marston appears to be endorsing this kind of ruthless, sadistic revenge in an unequivocal fashion, suggesting that Antonio really is a hero for his murders of Julio and Piero.

However, the trouble with this reading is that it assumes that the audience were intended to accept the rightness of this conclusion without question, seeing the torture and murder of Piero as in some sense a legitimate means to a necessary end. In practice, I would argue, the conclusion of *Antonio's Revenge* invites a rather more complicated set of audience responses. The spectators may indeed want to see Antonio kill Piero: throughout this play and its prequel, *Antonio and Mellida*, Piero has revealed himself as a murderous psychopath, who appears to deserve whatever nasty comeuppance he gets. Nevertheless, the hyperbolic cruelty of the final revenge seems likely to work against the possibility of an audience wholeheartedly endorsing Antonio's actions. The focus of the scene is explicitly on the sadism of the revengers. After binding Piero and removing his tongue, Antonio and his followers mock him with Julio's death – 'Here lies a dish to feast thy father's gorge. / Here's flesh and blood which I am sure thou lov'st' – while the duke, in a stage direction, '*Seems to condole his* [dead] *son*' (s.d. 5.3.80-1). They enjoy his grief: 'He weeps. Now do I glorify my hands; / I had no vengeance if I had no tears' (5.3.76-7). A stage direction indicates that they '*offer to run all at PIERO and on a sudden stop*', which suggests that they are reluctant to actually kill their victim, preferring instead to prolong his agony for as long as possible. As Pandulpho says, their desire is to: '[L]et him die and die, and still be dying. / And yet not die till he hath died and died / Ten thousand deaths in agony of heart' (5.3.105-7). In bringing about the revenge, Antonio has, in a manner typical of revenge heroes, effected a reversal, in which he 'transforms his enemy into the kind of victim he once was'.[12] Piero is now the one who is helpless, tearful, impotent in his grief. But in this scene, we do not, I think, feel contempt for the villain who has failed at 'manliness'; we rather feel pity for him, and revulsion at what the revengers are doing. Antonio's own form of 'manliness' here seems not far from psychosis.

One might, of course, argue this this is an anachronistic reading of the play. The original Renaissance spectators might have felt differently; they might have been more comfortable with the idea of blood revenge, and more relaxed about the idea that torture and violence could be a source of unproblematic entertainment. However, I would argue that there are aspects of the revenge that seem designed to create a sense of unease in early modern spectators. However they might feel about the ultimate treatment of Piero, it seems likely that they would find the murder and cannibalistic 'serving up' of the child Julio problematic. Janet Clare notes the origins of this plot device in Seneca's *Thyestes* and Shakespeare's *Titus Andronicus*. However, she comments, the horror created by Marston's use of the device exceeds that of his sources: 'There is a primitive justice at work in *Titus Andronicus* [in which Chiron and Demetrius, the two victims of Titus' cannibalistic plot, are themselves unrepentant rapists]. In Seneca the horror is muted by its report through the Chorus.'[13] The death of Julio, however, occurs both onstage and to an innocent victim. Furthermore, as Clare goes on to point out, while much of *Antonio's Revenge* feels playful and parodic in its treatment of revenge tragedy conventions, the murder of Julio is played relatively 'straight', with no comic undercutting: 'Even in a play where so much is sent up, it would be difficult to mock an innocent, trusting victim.'[14]

Moreover, even if the theatre audience has felt some sense of vicarious excitement and pleasure at the scene of Piero's torture and death, Marston works deliberately to dissipate the sense of triumph in the scene that follows. *Antonio's Revenge* does not end on the senators' praise for the murder but on the reactions of the revengers themselves, and their state after the revenge is one of desolation. When asked what they will do now, Pandulpho replies,

> We know the world, and did we know no more
> We would not live to know; but since constraint
> Of holy bands forceth us to keep this lodge
> Of dirt's corruption till dread power calls
> Our souls' appearance, we will live enclosed
> In holy verge of some religious order,
> Most constant votaries. (5.3.147–53)

According to Pandulpho, the revengers would actually welcome the death that dramatic tradition has established as the fit end for men like them, but they know that suicide is a crime. Therefore, all they can do is retreat to a monastery, to mourn away the rest of their days. The main impression of these lines is a sense of hopelessness: the death of Piero has not really solved the revengers' problems or relieved their grief. The play thus seems deliberately to end on an unsettling note. It has concluded the way that a revenge tragedy 'ought' to conclude, with a bloodbath, and the death of the villain. Antonio has overcome his feminine 'weaknesses' and triumphed as a particular kind of hyper-masculine revenger. However, it does not feel like a triumph; instead, it feels ugly and disturbing.

Antonio's Revenge demonstrates Marston's complex handling of genre and his skill in crafting problematic endings. Such techniques are evident elsewhere in Marston: in, for example, the ending of his most famous play, *The Malcontent* (c.1603). *The Malcontent* is a satirical tragicomedy about a corrupt Italian court, and the efforts of the deposed Duke Altofront to regain power and bring back order to his society. As Jacqueline Pearson puts it:

> the play opens with a striking image of discord, as the 'vilest out-of-tune music' (1.1.initial SD) is heard from the malcontent's chamber. It ends with the reimposition of harmony in masque and dance, and with Altofront's return to his real identity as philosopher-king.[15]

However, the extent to which Altofront really does reimpose harmony, or restore social order, is debatable. In his final speech, he appears to deal out justice to all who deserve it, but his criticisms are mild and his penalties lenient. The murderous usurper Mendoza is banished rather than being executed; the adulterous Aurelia is ordered simply to be faithful to her husband in future; the pompous flatterer Bilioso is mocked but receives no punishment; the bawd Maquerelle is banished from the city centre but not ordered to end her trade; and the rest of the characters receive no punishment whatsoever. The lecherous Ferneze, for example, who began the play's series of plots and intrigues through his affair with Aurelia, is shown to have learned nothing from what has occurred, as he ends the play flirting with Bilioso's wife Bianca, beseeching her to 'let me enjoy you tonight, and I'll marry you tomorrow fortnight, by my troth, la' (5.5.96–8).[16] There is not much sense that the citizens of this society will be more virtuous or well-behaved now that Altofront is back than they were in his absence.

One could argue that Altofront's failure to provide harsher punishments for the foolish or villainous courtiers is merely evidence of Marston's fidelity to his play's genre.[17] *The Malcontent* is a kind of revenge play, charting Altofront's schemes to get even with his usurpers, but it is structured as a tragicomedy, not as a tragedy, and, according to the contemporary Italian playwright Giambattista Guarini – the first literary theorist to discuss tragicomedy – 'Punishment ... is unfitting to tragicomic poetry, in which according to comic custom, the bad characters are not chastised.'[18] However, there are problems with reading the play as a tragicomedy in the strict Guarinian mould. According to Guarini, tragicomedies mingled tragic and comic events throughout but ended happily, and their aim was to 'purg[e] with pleasure the sadness of the hearers ... freeing the hearers from melancholy'.[19] Marston's play, however, does not have a straightforwardly 'happy ending', and it seems more likely to leave the audience feeling disturbed than 'purged'. Throughout, the play has presented not just the court but the world as a whole as a place of corruption and degeneracy. As Altofront describes it, this earth is the only grave and Golgotha wherein all things that live must rot ... the very muckhill on which the sublunary orbs cast their excrements. Man is the slime of this dung-pit, and princes are the governors of these men. (4.5.123–9)

Coming after the horror of this vision, it is hard for an audience to believe that Altofront's return to power has really put everything right.

Again, therefore, Marston seems to be playing games with genre and with his audience's expectations. In *Antonio's Revenge*, he encourages us to feel how unsatisfactory a revenge tragedy ending can be. In *The Malcontent*, he takes the opposite extreme, giving us a comic ending which *also* feels unsatisfactory, having none of the sense of optimism that we would expect from the end of a true comedy or even from a Guarinian tragicomedy. Both of these plays seem designed to please their audiences on a superficial level, by appearing to follow a conventional dramatic structure, but yet within that structure they are works which aim to unsettle and provoke, as Marston undercuts the sense of security that the traditional comic or tragic forms would otherwise engender. This approach is, in fact, typical of Marston's dramatic work. His plays are frequently structured as, in effect, two plays in one: a superficially conventional drama, which offers the spectators what they expect, based on established dramatic and generic conventions, and a second drama that undercuts or works against this first drama, that questions its assumptions and problematises its conclusions.[20]

Rick Bowers, while recognising the way in which Marston repeatedly subverts and parodies theatrical and generic conventions in his drama, argues that Marston has no particular moral purpose in doing this. 'In Marston's plays', he writes, 'the thrust of action is basically sensational, not moral; a matter of contemporary theatrical and popular culture, not ethical consistency excavated from the classics.'[21] For Bowers, the emotional excess, moral inconsistency and subversions of dramatic convention within Marston's plays are intended simply to 'surprise, entertain, and emotionally unsettle' the spectators, and so he expresses doubt 'that *Antonio's Revenge* represents much in the way of moral arguments against revenge'.[22]

However, the fact that a text is sensationalist, self-conscious and metatheatrical (as this play undoubtedly is) does not necessarily mean that it has nothing serious to say. On the one hand, *Antonio's Revenge* can be seen as a kind of parody of contemporary revenge dramas, which deconstructs and mocks the conventions of the genre. On the other hand, though, in so doing it also works as a moral critique of the assumptions that seem to lie behind many of these dramas. It superficially appears to restate some conventional beliefs about revenge: that the pursuit of vengeance can free individuals from debilitating and effeminising grief; that it can empower the disempowered and provide a way for victims of brutality to regain their self-determination and self-respect. However, at the same time, Marston works to undermine this reading of revenge, by emphasising both the horror of the revenge act itself, and the ultimate inadequacy of revenge as a cure for emotional trauma. Revenge tragedy conventionally requires blood to be spilt, but Marston takes this convention to its limits, and in doing so, raises questions about the moral limitations of the revenge tragedy genre, as well as the mindset that sees such revenge as the ultimate statement of manly honour and masculine self-assertion.[23]

NOTES

1. John Kerrigan, *Revenge Tragedy: Aeschylus to Armageddon* (Oxford: Clarendon Press, 1996), p. 12
2. See, for example, Andreas Hyperius, who remarks that 'it is very uncomly and wommanish to lament without measure'. Hyperius, *The Practice of Preaching, Otherwise Called the Pathway to the Pulpit* (London: Thomas East, 1577), pp. 171–2, quoted in Jennifer C. Vaught, *Masculinity and Emotion in Early Modern English Literature* (Aldershot: Ashgate, 2008), p. 1, n. 1.
3. William Shakespeare, *Hamlet, The Oxford Shakespeare – The Complete Works*, ed. John Jowett, William Montgomery, Gary Taylor and Stanley Wells, 2nd edition (Oxford: Oxford University Press, 2005). All further references to the works of Shakespeare are to this edition.
4. Thomas Kyd, *The Spanish Tragedy*, ed. Philip Edwards, The Revels Plays (London: Methuen, 1959).
5. Thomas Rist, *Revenge Tragedy and the Drama of Commemoration in Reforming England* (Aldershot: Ashgate, 2008), pp. 25, 60–7, suggests that in many of the earliest English revenge tragedies (*The Spanish Tragedy, Hamlet, Titus Andronicus* and, to an extent, *Antonio's Revenge*) the extreme grief of the revengers is actually defended as 'proportionate' rather than excessive and debilitating. In his account of *Hamlet*, for example, Rist argues that the play stresses the importance of remembering the dead properly, through the old rituals of mourning associated with Catholicism, whereas the wicked Claudius is associated with the 'Reformed' Protestant attitude that insists that the dead are dead and the living should move on with their lives. However, this argument largely overlooks the fact that Hamlet is already mourning his dead father before the ghost appears to him. The ghost does not need further grief from his son; what he needs is for him to transform that grief into action. His parting command to his son to 'Remember me' thus becomes synonymous with his first command, 'Revenge [my] foul and most unnatural murder' (1.5.91, 1.5.25).
6. The only other exceptions are Cyril Tourneur's *The Atheist's Tragedy*, ed. Brian Morris and Roma Gill (New York: W.W. Norton, 1989; first published in 1611), in which the 'revenger', Charlemont, does not actually carry out his revenge against the villain D'Amville himself, but rather leaves it in the hands of God, and Thomas Heywood's *A Woman Killed With*

Kindness, ed. R.W. Van Fossen (London: Methuen, 1961; first published in 1607), in which the cuckolded husband Frankford 'revenges' himself on his wife by ostracising her. Although Anne Frankford does die at the end of the play, the cause is self-starvation, rather than physical violence from her spouse. *Antonio's Revenge* is thus the only contemporary revenge tragedy in which a violent revenger meets with no ultimate retribution.

7. Kerrigan, *Revenge Tragedy*, pp. 209–10.
8. Ibid. p. 208, who quotes Aristotle, *Poetics* 1354a.
9. John Marston, *Antonio's Revenge*, *The Selected Plays of John Marston*, ed. by Macdonald P. Jackson and Michael Neill (Cambridge: Cambridge University Press, 1986). All further references to Marston's drama are to this edition.
10. Mark Albert Johnston, *Beard Fetish in Early Modern England: Sex, Gender, and Registers of Value* (Burlington, VT: Ashgate, 2011), pp. 225–6.
11. Charles A. and Elaine S. Hallett, '*Antonio's Revenge* and the Integrity of the Revenge Tragedy Motifs', *Studies in Philology* 76.4 (1979), p. 366. Italics original. Other critics who have found fault with the conclusion of *Antonio's Revenge* on moral grounds include H. Harvey Wood, 'Introduction' to *The Plays of John Marston* (London: Oliver and Boyd, 1934), vol. 1, p. xxxv; Fredson Bowers, *Elizabethan Revenge Tragedy 1587–1642* (1940; reprinted Princeton: Princeton University Press, 1966), pp. 118–25; T. B. Tomlinson, *A Study of Elizabethan and Jacobean Tragedy* (1964; reprinted Cambridge: Cambridge University Press, 2011), pp. 219–20.
12. Kerrigan, *Revenge Tragedy*, p. 6.
13. Janet Clare, *Shakespeare's Stage Traffic: Imitation, Borrowing and Competition in Renaissance Theatre* (Cambridge: Cambridge University Press, 2014), p. 179.
14. Ibid. p. 179.
15. Jacqueline Pearson, *Tragedy and Tragicomedy in the Works of John Webster* (Manchester: Manchester University Press, 1980), p. 48.
16. Marston, *The Malcontent*, in Jackson and Neill (eds), *The Selected Plays of John Marston*.
17. This position is taken by, for example, Jason Lawrence, 'Re-Make/Re-Model: Marston's *The Malcontent* and Guarinian Tragicomedy', in Michele Marrapodi (ed.), *Italian Culture in the Drama of Shakespeare and His Contemporaries* (Aldershot: Ashgate, 2007), pp. 155–68, p. 166; Lucy Munro, *Children of the Queen's Revels: A Jacobean Theatre Repertory* (Cambridge: Cambridge University Press, 2005), p. 111.
18. Giambattista Guarini, *The Compendium of Tragicomic Poetry* (1599), trans. Allan H. Gilbert, in *Literary Criticism: Plato to Dryden*, ed. Allan H. Gilbert (New York: American Book Company, 1940), p. 527.
19. Ibid. p. 524.
20. I explore this aspect of Marston's plays more fully in my book *Ben Jonson, John Marston and Early Modern Drama: Satire and the Audience* (London: Palgrave Macmillan, 2016).

21. Rick Bowers, *Radical Comedy in Early Modern England* (Aldershot: Ashgate, 2008), p. 72
22. Ibid. pp. 74, 82.
23. In the production of the play that I saw in 2006, performed by students from the London Drama Centre, the audience was laughing at the start of the revenge, as Antonio and his friends performed their 'masque', seizing Piero and forcing him to dance with them. However, the spectators gradually fell silent as the revengers proceeded to hold the duke down, cut out his tongue, stuff his mouth with the intestines of his dead infant son (in an addition to the printed text), and then stab him repeatedly in the chest and groin.

    Barbara J. Baines, '*Antonio's Revenge*: Marston's Play on Revenge Plays', *Studies in English Literature* 23 (1983), pp. 277–94, has argued that the spectators at the conclusion of *Antonio's Revenge* may feel a sense of guilt for their emotional participation in the revenge. She describes the structure of the play as one which repeatedly encourages a 'dual response' from its audience – emotional engagement versus moral judgement – and sees the final scene as the climax of this technique, as the audience is allowed the cathartic release of the expected murder, and is then confronted with a sense of moral unease at what they have seen. 'As the audience watches the deficiencies in the sensibilities of these characters, it becomes aware of the deficiencies of its own perception and response, or perhaps more specifically the deficiencies of its taste for revenge tragedy' (p. 281).

CHAPTER 16

Outfacing Vengeance: Heroic Dying in Webster's *The Duchess of Malfi* and Ford's *The Broken Heart*

Lesel Dawson

Revengers, as has been frequently observed, are 'surrogate artists' who devise intricate tortures both to overreach the crimes that have come before and to invest their acts of violence with specific meanings.[1] But what happens when the revenge does not go to plan? Both John Webster's *The Duchess of Malfi* (1612–13) and John Ford's *The Broken Heart* (1633) feature victims of revenge who take charge of their suffering, seizing theatrical power in a manner that challenges the meaning of their punishment. In *The Duchess of Malfi* Ferdinand devises a series of spectacles to torment his twin sister before killing her; however, the duchess reacts to these with indifference, exhibiting a Christian confidence which upstages Ferdinand's revenge and spoils his satisfaction. And in *The Broken Heart*, when Orgilus imprisons Ithocles in a trick chair before murdering him (a contraption which prevents him from defending himself), Ithocles is able both to challenge Orgilus' role of onstage playwright and to reconfigure the symbolic meaning of the chair in which he is trapped. Ithocles' stoical self-resolve, like that of the duchess, exemplifies the battle for meaning at the heart of many revenge plots, and the way in which heroic dying can serve as a form of resistance and protest. Because the duchess and Ithocles seize control, their deaths appear self-authored, and they are able to counter the revenger's fantasies of power and his or her narrative control.

The shift in focus encountered in *The Duchess of Malfi* and *The Broken Heart* – away from the witty plotting of the revenger and towards the courage of the victim – corresponds to a wider shift that Mary Beth Rose has identified in the construction and gendering of heroism. According to Rose, during the early modern period there is a move away from the 'heroics of action' towards the 'heroism of endurance', an ideal that privileges 'not the active confrontation with danger, but the capacity to endure it, to resist and suffer with patience and fortitude'.[2] The variety of sources for this model (which include, for example, 'Seneca and the stoics, the lives of the Catholic saints, the continuing popularity of medieval treatises on the art of dying, Patient Griselda stories, and the careers and tribulations of both Protestant and Jesuit martyrs') suggests that both men and women can embody this ideal. Nevertheless, as Rose argues, 'the terms which constitute the heroics of endurance are precisely those terms used to construct the early modern idealization of women: patient suffering, mildness, humility, chastity, loyalty, and obedience',[3] which led to the emergence of a new model of masculinity and of the revenge narratives in which men feature.

Because the qualities associated with the heroism of endurance correspond to a highly conventional female role, this particular form of bravery is one that has been consistently open to women and to female literary figures across time; as is made especially clear in revenge tragedy from ancient to early modern literature, women have been admired for their ability to suffer patiently, to put others first and to die well. For men, however, the heroism of endurance is less straightforward. While men are frequently depicted as meeting their end nobly on the battlefield or in suicide, the 'good' death displayed by female revenge victims is less common, as men are expected to fight their enemies. So how might male revenge victims display stoical fortitude in death? How can a man's choosing to die rather than fight the revenger be seen as an act of bravery rather than cowardice? In this chapter, I will address these questions, exploring the difference that gender makes in the representation of the heroics of endurance and the narrative structure of revenge. Comparing the ways in which the deaths of the Duchess of Malfi and Ithocles are imagined and constructed within the plays, I will argue that the heroics of endurance are indeed gendered in these texts. While for both characters heroic dying functions as a form of self-authorship which resists the revenger's power and narrative control, nevertheless the lengths to which Ford goes to reinscribe Ithocles' death back into a language of martial combat suggest the extent to which masochistic self-sacrifice is perceived to be natural for women and unnatural for men.

TRAP PLOTS AND TRICK CHAIRS

For those individuals whose honour has been destroyed, whose loved ones have been killed, and whose sense of self and world have been shattered, vengeance becomes a perverse means of seizing ideological and narrative control: it appears – at least momentarily – to bring the world back into a coherent design, granting the revenger a renewed sense of agency and authorship.[4] Revengers are concerned not only with finding 'fitting' forms of punishment (overtopping their enemies and matching the punishment to the crime), but also with ensuring that their victims know why they are being punished and by whom. Bacon, observing the tendency by revengers to reveal the reasons for their actions, sees this as the 'more generous' approach, 'For the Delight seemeth to be, not so much in doing the Hurt, as in Making the Party repent.'[5] Repentance, however, is rarely the goal of such behaviour. Instead, revengers find satisfaction not only in their victim's physical pain, but also in their awareness of its cause and source, so that bodily harm is concurrent with (and acts as a trigger for) the suffering imagined to take place in the victim's mind. The victim, in this respect, not only functions like an actor in the revenger's plot, but also serves as an audience, in scripts designed to elicit pain and impose on the victim the plot's designated meaning.

The importance of the victim 'playing their part', and the revenger's need to control the meaning of the onstage play, often results in the victim being imprisoned or silenced in some way: hands are tied, mouths are gagged, and tongues are nailed down or cut out. At times, restraint gives an individual time to explain his or her reasons for the revenge and to ensure that the murder is accomplished. Trick chairs, which provide a more inventive way of trapping the victim, are also sometimes used; they feature in both Barnabe Barnes' *The Devil's Charter* (1607) and John Ford's *The Broken Heart*. The real-life account of Simone Turchi's murder of Geronimo Deodati in 1551, which is described in Matteo Bandello's *Novella* (Part IV, novel 27) and translated into French,[6] is one possible source of this theatrical device.[7] In certain respects, Simone's decision to use a trick chair is pragmatic. Simone is 'gouty and weak of arm and hand' and therefore 'not strong enough to commit the murder himself', needing both the chair and his servant Giulio to assist him.[8] However, the device also appeals to Simone's vicious disposition, satisfying his desire to imitate 'the barbarous cruelties of certain tyrants' (pp. 304–5). In fact, when it comes to the murder, Simone finds he has neither the strength nor stomach for the task. After forcing Geronimo to sign papers that will clear his name and suggest he owes him money, Simone either 'Feeling pity for the wretched man, or else wanting strength to do the deed' throws down his dagger and walks away (pp. 308–10). It is left for the servant, Guilio, to kill Geronimo, stabbing him a number of times in the head and chest.

In *The Devil's Charter*, a play which dramatises the scandalous stories that circulated about the lives of the Borgia family, Lucretia's use of the trick chair emphasises her ingenuity as well as her viciousness. Lucretia, the illegitimate daughter of Rodrigo Borgia (who became Pope Alexander VI), uses the trick chair to kill her husband, Gismond, who has slandered her (accurately, in this version) for being unchaste. Lucretia epitomises Chloe Kathleen Preedy's description of the female revenger whose 'literacy and classical knowledge play a crucial role in scripting vengeance'.[9] Placing herself in a line of female revengers, she readies herself for the murder by calling to mind the deeds of Medea, Clytemnestra, Procne and Danaus, and calling on the Furies. Lucretia also references the Roman god Vulcan, who traps his mother Juno in a chair to punish her for abandoning him as an infant, boasting that she has 'devised such a curious snare / As jealous Vulcan never yet devis'd'.[10] Bandello is an equally important source for this scene. Like Simone, Lucretia uses the trick chair to force her victim to sign papers which will exonerate her name and clear her from any charge of murder. After releasing a mechanism which traps Gismond in the 'curious snare', Lucretia *'pulleth out his dagger'*, *'gaggeth him'* and then forces him to sign the papers, promising that if he does so she will not kill him (s.d. 1.5, pp. 22, 25). Once Gismond has acted his part, however, Lucretia reveals this promise to be a lie:

> So now that part is play'd, what follows now?
> Thou ribald, cuckold, rascal, libeller,
> Pernicious lecher, void of all performance!
> Take this for sland'ring of his Holiness,   *She stabbeth*
> My blessed father, and my brother Caesar
> With incest. Take this for my brother Candy!   *[Again]*
> And this for noble Sforza, who thou wrongest!   *[Again]*
> And since the time is short, I will be short:
> For locking up of me, calling me whore,
> Setting espials tending at my tail,   *Three stabs together*
> Take this, and this, and this, to make amends
> And put thee from my pains. (1.5, p. 25)

The stage directions highlight the way in which Lucretia invests murder with meaning. Stabbing her husband six times, she delivers each blow so that it punctuates (and corresponds to) a particular crime of which Gismond is accused. However, while Lucretia might seem to offer an attractive image of a powerful female revenger, she in many ways exemplifies Alison Findlay's warning that 'violence by female revengers is deeply problematic ... since it often reproduces masculine codes of oppression and possibly even dominant values of patriarchy'.[11] Labelling Gismond as a 'ribald, cuckold, rascal, libeller' and stabbing him on behalf of her father, brothers and herself, she resembles those violent men who kill to preserve family honour and enforce patriarchal codes of honour (1.5, p. 25). Insulting Gismond's sexual ability (as 'void of ... performance'), she is, like Evadne, 'a monstrous parody of phallic power'.[12]

Nevertheless, if Lucretia is 'a monstrous parody of phallic power', the parodic aspect is crucial. Gismond's accusations are, of course, all true, so that while she appears to uphold the 'dominant values of patriarchy', she is in fact exploiting these conventions to her own ends (suggesting that she is defending her family's honour as a means of getting rid of a tiresome husband). The unusually detailed stage directions reveal her theatrical skills, indicating how she stage-manages her husband's dead body in order to make the murder look like a suicide and to clear her name: 'She unbindeth him, layeth him on the ground, putteth the dagger in his hand, a paper on his knee, and taking certain papers out of his pocket, putteth in others in their stead; and conveyeth away the chair' (1.5, p. 25). Lucretia, known historically for her cleverness and education, here uses her learning to manipulate the visual and verbal codes, forging letters and displaying them to control the interpretation of Gismond's death. Stepping back to admire her artistry, Lucretia looks forward to how her father and brothers will praise her handiwork, anticipating that they will say that 'Lucrece hath perform'd a cunning part' (1.5, p. 26).

Gismond's murder in many ways epitomises what early modern playwrights found so despicable about trick chairs; such devices highlight the revenger's duplicity (like poison, trick chairs are seen as a particularly cowardly and underhanded way of attacking an enemy), sadism (in that the revenger is able to extend and relish in the victim's suffering), and desire for total control over the victim, over the action and over the interpretation of events more widely. For Lucretia, revenge enables her to dispatch with a problematic husband, while simultaneously presenting herself as a wronged wife and the proud defender of her family's honour. Vengeance in this context is not only about punishing the victim but also about obtaining narrative control: the revenger shapes the world, like the bodies on stage, into a design which accords with his or her own wished-for meaning. The elaborate nature of these punishments, their very theatricality and intricacy, transforms murder into its own macabre art form: bodies are raped, dismembered, tortured and eaten for specific aesthetic and psychic ends.

UPSTAGING TYRANNY IN *THE DUCHESS OF MALFI*

There are, however, circumstances in which the victim of revenge can refuse to play his or her part, challenging the revenger's interpretation of events. In John Webster's *The Duchess of Malfi* the duchess' stoical behaviour during her imprisonment by her psychotic brother, Ferdinand, functions as a form of resistance to his tyrannous design, contesting his interpretation of her life and punishment. The duchess' behaviour during her imprisonment and at her death not only grants her heroic stature and invites sympathy, but also challenges Ferdinand's role as a revenger. She recognises and rejects the part that has been devised for her – 'I account this world a tedious theatre, / For I do play a part in't 'gainst my will'–eventually taking control of the theatrical action in a manner which disturbs Ferdinand's power as onstage playwright.[13]

From the outset, the duchess exhibits a stoical indifference to her suffering. Bosola describes how 'She's sad, as one long us'd to't', exhibiting 'a behaviour so noble / As gives a majesty to adversity' (4.1.3, 5–6). Ferdinand is infuriated by her lack of response and devises a series of sadistic spectacles to drive her to madness and despair. It is in these scenes that we see most forcefully the way that Ferdinand acts as a 'surrogate artist', acquiring props, writing scripts and treating Bosola as his actor.[14] In Ferdinand's case, if he can have his sister manifest the very perverse sexuality that he ascribes to her, he will be able not only to justify his sadistic behaviour but also to reattribute its origin. His 'masques of common courtesans' and mad men are, in this way, not only a form a torture meant to drive her mad, but also, as Christy Desmet suggests, 'a rhetorical production, intended to persuade the Duchess to adopt Ferdinand's debased image of her' (4.1.124).[15] The duchess' refusal to play this part, and her confidence in herself – 'I am Duchess of Malfi still'– thus calls into question the meaning of Ferdinand's actions and his misogynistic fantasies about her sexuality (4.2.141).

The duchess' ability to resist the part scripted for her is most forcefully depicted in the scenes in which Bosola, disguised as an old man, presents her with the ropes that will strangle her and the tomb in which she is to be buried. Bosola, assuming that she will be terrified ('Yet, methinks, / The manner of your death should much afflict you'), is impressed by her indifference (4.2.210–11). She instructs Bosola, 'tell my brothers / That I perceive death, now I am well awake, / Best gift is they can give, or I can take' (4.2.221–3). The duchess' words reconfigure her death, transforming it from a punishment to a gift that she can willingly and actively receive. Similarly, it is she who commands the executioners to act with words that resonate, not with revenge, but with Christian martyrdom:[16] 'Pull, and pull strongly, for your able strength / Must pull down heaven upon me' (4.2.228–9). Her bravery and humility have their effect not only on Bosola, but on Ferdinand too. Unlike revengers such as Hieronimo, Titus and Vindice who revel triumphantly in their victims' murder, Ferdinand is instead stunned and confused. Looking on her face, he famously remarks: 'Cover her face: mine eyes dazzle: she died young' (4.2.262). Even in death, the duchess retains an integrity and alterity that Ferdinand cannot simply co-opt or possess.

Having failed to create a persuasive narrative of his sister's whorishness, Ferdinand is left instead with his own barbarity; as a result, his projections regarding his sister come back to haunt him, in both his lycanthropy (a form of madness in which he believes himself to be a wolf) and his guilt. Having previously seen his sister as the contaminated part of himself, after her death he returns to an idealised vision of her. Although this shift in no way challenges a polarised view of women (which constructs them as either chaste angels or whorish devils), it does nonetheless relocate Ferdinand's own sense of crisis, so that the division he identified with his twin is now experienced as self-division. If the victim of revenge is in many ways the revenger's double, experiencing the revenger's suffering and playing the role that he or she formally had, then Ferdinand curiously becomes his own double. Feeling like he is both guilty murderer and wronged party, he comes to occupy, perversely, the roles of revenger and victim simultaneously, a self-division dramatised when he attacks his own shadow as his enemy.

The duchess' noble behaviour thus challenges Ferdinand's narrative of events, throwing back the responsibility for her death onto him and Bosola. Although both of these men try to evade their guilt (each blaming the other), the duchess' ability to exert control even at her most downtrodden gives the lie to those individuals who relinquish moral authority to social superiors and to fate. The duchess' actions imply that one always has some sort of a choice. Bosola may claim 'We are merely the stars' tennis-balls', but it is not in the stars, but in himself that he is a murderer (5.4.54).

Critics have emphasised the way in which the duchess' stoical courage at her death aligns her with 'traditional discourses of womanhood'.[17] Lisa Jardine, for example, points out that the female hero 'is most reassuring and admirable when associated with patient suffering', seeing her transformation from an independent, strong woman to 'the safe composite stereotype of penitent whore, Virgin Majestic in grief, serving mother, and patient and true turtle-dove mourning her one true love' as reassuring to male audience.[18] And Theodora Jankowski, while arguing that the duchess is subversive politically and in terms of her marriage, nonetheless suggests that the 'final representation of Webster's protagonist is not as ruler, but as idealized suffering wife / mother / woman' in accordance with a "martyred" view of womanhood' in which 'a talent for suffering nobly (and quietly) becomes the only means by which a woman can be viewed as "heroic"'.[19] While I agree that the duchess' behaviour fits a traditional model of femininity, a fact that diminishes the radicalism of her actions, I would nevertheless argue that the duchess' behaviour while imprisoned is not a swerve from her earlier efforts at self-determination, but a crucial extension of it.[20] Read in this manner, her submissive acquiescence at her death is simultaneously a form self-authorship, marking a new phase (as suggested by Rose) in which female-gendered attributes are increasingly valorised over those of martial strength. Rather than seeing the duchess as dwindling from self-determining prince to self-effacing martyr, Webster's narrative offers one example of the way in which qualities of patience, humility and stoical endurance increasingly come to define the heroic.

AUTHORING DEATH IN *THE BROKEN HEART*

John Ford was clearly an admirer of Webster, with whom he collaborated, and of *The Duchess of Malfi* in particular. He wrote a poem in praise of the play for the earliest printed edition of 1623, and in several of his works he reconfigured, in different ways, its central brother–sister relationship, its portrayal of sexual jealousy and the duchess' dignified end. Like *Othello* (another key text for Ford), *The Duchess of Malfi* also features a man killing the woman he loves, one of Ford's central preoccupations. And if from Shakespeare Ford drew upon the intimacy and eroticism of such deaths, from Webster he learned how the tragic subject can take charge of their suffering to exert some control over its meaning.

In *The Broken Heart* Ford uses the trick chair as a means of granting the male revenge victim a heroic death: the same chair which imprisons Ithocles simultaneously releases him from the need to display martial valour, allowing him to exhibit the kind of heroic self-display normally reserved for women. In making this change Ford also reimagines the function and meaning of the trick chair. Whereas physical bondage in revenge tragedies is typically associated with the revenger's physical weakness or sadism, here it becomes part of a tableau in which death is the supreme theatrical moment of self-display which crowns life; as Michael Neill argues: 'death becomes the chosen instrument by which the protagonists fashion themselves into a display of marmoreal perfection'; it becomes, paradoxically, 'a powerfully individuating experience, the supreme occasion for exhibitions of individual distinction'.[21] The lengths to which Ford must go to make Ithocles' willing death as a revenge victim noble, however, says something about the way that the heroics of endurance run counter to traditional expectations of masculinity.

Ford, whose admiration for stoicism is expressed in his prose tracts *The Golden Mean* (1614) and *A Line of Life* (1620), would have found the duchess' dignified death appealing. Following familiar stoical principles, Ford advocates that men 'live with an expectation of death', envisioning death as 'a passage to glory' whereby individuals can either secure everlasting fame or counterbalance a questionable reputation with a noble end.[22] Sir Walter Raleigh, for example, whose life Ford describes as 'unsteaddie' with 'many changes of *resolution*', nevertheless exhibits admirable '*Wisdome* and *Courage* ... in his last demeanour' so that '*he strove to be so great in his resolution when he came to bee nothing*'.[23] That Raleigh's bravery at his death helps to secure his reputation follows the precept that the way in which the dying person behaves demonstrates something important about the nature of their life and being. Death, in this context, is treated as a dramatic performance which secures one's good name. As Seneca explains:

> It fareth with our life as with a stage-play, it skilleth not how long, but how well it hath been acted. It importeth nothing in what place thou makest an end of life: die where thou wilt, think only to make a good conclusion.[24]

Within this context, death becomes the sublime theatrical moment in which individuals could display their courage and strength of mind.

Ford's *The Golden Mean* and *A Line of Life* illustrate how stoical philosophy advocates the 'heroism of endurance' as described by Rose, which celebrates 'not the active confrontation with danger, but the capacity to endure it, to resist and suffer with patience and fortitude'.[25] Ford writes that to 'live well', men need not only 'ACTION', but also 'PERSEVERANCE IN ACTION' and 'SUFFERANCE IN PERSEVERANCE'; as Gilles Monsarrat points out, Ford's stoical tracts advocate an ideal of behaviour in which 'temperance, self-control, constancy, measure, and tranquillity of mind' are central and thought to be 'different facets of a single attitude and virtue'.[26] The heroics of endurance are most commonly displayed by Ford's female tragic characters, who are typically murdered by their lovers and husbands, and who confront death with calm self-assurance. While directors have scope to vary these performances, most of these female characters, at the very least, verbally acquiesce with their lovers' murderous intents. More frequently they can be seen to embrace their death in a manner which is eroticised. Susan in *The Witch of Edmonton* (1621), discovering that her marriage to Frank is bigamous, does not turn from the knife with which Frank threatens her, but rather figures death as a husband she will love and 'embrace'.[27] In *Love's Sacrifice* (1633), Bianca bates her husband, the duke, in order that he kill her, offering to run 'to the point / Of thy sharp sword with open breast'.[28] Annabella too in *'Tis Pity She's a Whore* tries to goad Soranzo into killing her, before eventually being murdered in bed by her brother–lover.[29]

Men in Ford are also depicted as facing death with dignified self-control, but more frequently this is on the scaffold rather than as revenge victims. In *The Witch of Edmonton* Frank's penitence when facing his execution reconciles him to the wider community, and in *Perkin Warbeck* and *The Broken Heart* Perkin and Orgilus are similarly admired for their courage when facing execution. Suicide also provides opportunities for male characters to display their bravery and self-possession, as in the case of both Caraffa and Fernando from *Love's Sacrifice*, who compete over who will achieve the best death and be worthy of the dead Bianca. Ithocles in *The Broken Heart*, however, is distinct in displaying such courage when confronting death as a male revenge victim. The uniqueness of this representation – not only to Ford's works, but to early modern revenge plays more generally – suggests how problematic this stance is for men, who are expected to fight their enemies, exposing the tension between martial valour and a new conception of the heroic which values endurance and constancy.[30]

In *The Broken Heart*, the central revenge plot springs from action that has preceded the play. After the death of their father, Ithocles has broken off the love-match between Penthea and Orgilus, so that his sister can marry Bassanes, who is, as Orgilus describes, 'a nobleman in honour / And riches ... beyond my fortunes' (1.1.45–6).[31] The Ithocles at the play's opening, however, is an older and more mature figure, who regrets his former actions and seeks his sister's forgiveness. Now in love with Princess Calantha, Ithocles also understands in emotional terms the devastation he has caused. Orgilus initially seems prepared to forgive Ithocles. Things change, however, when Penthea's lovesick melancholy becomes acute and she decides to end her life: feeling that her marriage is a betrayal of her former love for Orgilus and a form of adultery, Penthea starves herself and becomes mad.[32] When, during a mad episode, Penthea points to Ithocles as the cause of her unhappiness, Orgilus interprets this as her instruction to return to a path of revenge; 'Some powerful inspiration checks my laziness', he remarks (4.2.125).

Orgilus arranges each detail of his revenge in order to convey the meaning and justice of his actions. Central to his plan is the mechanical chair, which functions as the key symbol of his design. Timing Ithocles' murder so that it follows directly after Penthea's suicide, Orgilus' uses his beloved's corpse as a prop: Penthea's body is brought on stage in a chair, her face covered with a veil, and a chair is placed on either side of her. Orgilus instructs Ithocles: 'Take that chair. / I'll seat me here in this. Between us sits / The object of our sorrows' (4.4.16–18). '*Ithocles sits down, and is catcth in the engine*' (s.d. 4.4). The stage picture, in which the dead Penthea sits between Ithocles and Orgilus, suggests the symmetry of revenge while also anticipating the escalating violence: Ithocles' life will pay for that of Penthea, just as Orgilus' will eventually pay for that of Ithocles. Beckoning Ithocles to turn away from his imagined marriage and towards the devastation wrought by his youthful ambition, Orgilus lifts

Penthea's veil, instructing him to 'Survey a beauty withered by the flames / Of an insulting Phaethon, her brother' (4.4.25–6).

Ithocles regards Orgilus' use of the trick chair as cowardly and ignoble; 'Thou meanest to kill me basely?' (4.4.27), he asks. His question, however, fails to take into account the symbolic meaning Orgilus ascribes to it. Immobilised by the chair, Orgilus tells him: ''Tis thy throne of coronation, / Thou fool of greatness', asking:

> You dreamed of kingdoms, did 'ee? How to bosom
> The delicacies of a youngling princess;
> How with this nod to grace that subtle courtier;
> How with that frown to make this noble tremble;
> And so forth; whiles Penthea's groans and tortures,
> Ne'er touched upon your thought. (4.4.23, 30–6)

In Orgilus' theatrical design the chair becomes an ironic symbol of Ithocles' aspirations for power, offering a tantalising vision of happiness that will soon be snatched away. The mechanical chair also functions as a symbol of Penthea's unhappy marriage, which is repeatedly described as a kind of 'torture' and life-in-death entrapment (1.1.49).[33] Married to the insanely jealous Bassanes, Penthea is 'buried in a bride-bed': she is kept under lock and key and 'Compelled to yield her virgin freedom up / To him who never can usurp her heart' (2.2.38; 1.1.51–2). Orgilus thus designs his revenge so that Ithocles can experience something of Penthea's 'tortures' and 'agonies' before he dies: just as Penthea is 'yoked / To a most barbarous thraldom' so too is Ithocles immobilised in the trick chair (1.1.53–4).

Lisa Hopkins argues that Orgilus' careful crafting of the visual stage picture and use of emblems to convey the meaning of his revenge is typical of Ford's characters: 'as language becomes increasingly distrusted by the characters in his plays as a reliable medium for the accurate conveying of thought, they turn more and more towards visual signifying systems such as the use of gesture, ritual, emblem and tableau'.[34] This accords with Orgilus' own explanation for the trick chair. As he later explains, he uses the 'engine' not because of 'a slavish fear to combat / Youth, strength, or cunning', but rather because he does not want to leave the meaning and outcome of his revenge to chance: he 'durst not / Engage the goodness of a cause on fortune, / By which his name might have out-faced my vengeance' (5.2.140–4). However, if Orgilus hopes that by turning from the verbal to the visual, from words to stage pictures, he will be able to control the meaning of his revenge, such visual signifying systems turn out to be just as unreliable and open to reinterpretation as language.[35] Even as a bound revenge victim, Ithcoles is able to reject the part scripted for him. Like Webster's duchess, he refuses to act the part of the terrified victim:

> Orgilus: Behold thy fate, this steel.
> Ithocles: Strike home. A courage

As keen as thy revenge shall give it welcome.
But prithee faint not. If the wound close up,
Tent it with a double force, and search it deeply.
Thou lookest that I should whine and beg compassion,
As loath to leave the vainness of my glories.
A statelier resolution arms my confidence,
To cozen thee of honour (4.4.39–46)

Shown the dagger that will kill him, Ithocles commands 'Strike home', appropriating the words of the revenger and completing Orgilus' line. Like the duchess who commands 'pull' to her executioners, it is a rhetorical move which appears to relocate the authorship of this moment, allowing Ithocles to exert control over the meaning of his death. Describing his dreams for the future as 'the vainness of my glories', Ithocles also appropriates Orgilus' political language. He proclaims that he is now armed with a 'statelier resolution' which will 'cozen thee of honour', recasting the revenge as a competition between two foes, so that it sounds more like an honourable duel than a murder. If part of what revengers crave is their own sense of heroic achievement, Ithocles' courageous death offers a direct challenge to this: despite Orgilus' careful planning, Ithocles outfaces Orgilus vengeance, imposing his own narrative on events which re-establishes his good name.

Ithocles' fortitude allows him to move from an actor in Orgilus' script to a collaborator in his final end. Indeed, as the two men begin to work together, it is Ithocles' interpretation which takes precedent, with Orgilus praising Ithocles' 'goodly language' and promising that he will 'report thee to thy mistress richly' (4.4.52, 53). The trick chair, which is initially used to symbolise Penthea's torturous marriage and to mock Ithocles' erotic and political aspirations, is thus transformed into a sincere symbol of Ithocles heroic fortitude – it becomes a 'throne of coronation' on which his theatrical death is his crowning achievement;[36] or, as Orgilus puts it, Ithocles would have been 'butchered, had not bravery / Of an undaunted spirit, conquering terror / Proclaimed his last act triumph over ruin' (5.2.40–3).

Recent scholars have criticised Ithocles' acceptance of his death, seeing it as a product of Sparta's deadening and repressive stoical philosophy that entraps and immobilises all of the characters in the play.[37] William D. Dyer, for example, who sees the play as a 'psychological and emotional graveyard', believes that Ithocles' stoical death is motivated by his 'desire for unconsciousness', so that 'although Ithocles' passive resistance achieves some nobility, he has largely given up'.[38] And Naomi Baker argues that Spartan self-control is 'indistinguishable from self-petrification', arguing that the 'the play depicts beauty as a metaphysical ideal ... which poisons the characters' ability to embrace life in the material world'.[39] Within this context, the mechanical chair 'is appropriate as a symbol for the whole play', suggesting the way that 'human emotion has been radically circumscribed' in a Sparta which is both 'blighting and blighted'.[40] Penthea's tragedy here springs not only from the way her brother thoughtlessly traffics her in marriage, but also from how she accepts and internalises her society's cultural norms, similarly adhering to a stoical philosophy which is deadening.

Critics are right to recognise the masochistic nature of the Spartan stoical ideal and to note that Ford's characters' efforts at self-control are self-destructive. However, I agree with Michael Neill and Cynthia Marshall, who also see such behaviour as constructive; I would add to Neill's observation that they provide 'a temporary sense of mastery to the unshaping hand of time', an emphasis on how they impact revenge structures and function politically.[41] For example, while Penthea's adherence to Spartan cultural codes is self-destructive in the way that it prompts her to reject Orgilus and results in her starvation and lovesickness, her masochistic behaviour is also a form of expression which purposely influences the action of the play. Like lamentation, her melancholy expresses her anger and keeps the past alive, instigating (along with her suicide) Orgilus' revenge. Her suffering, as Hamilton observes, thus has a 'vengeful side'.[42] It also makes visible the emotional devastation wrought by such marriages; it is in part her example which prompts Nearchus to step aside in his courtship of Calantha. Ithocles' behaviour, similarly, is not simply a mechanised enactment of society's codes but a purposeful action taken to counter Orgilus' revenge narrative. Like Penthea's starvation, his behaviour at his murder acts as a form of self-authorship and resistance, achieving, in Cynthia Marshall's words, 'a kind of mastery through submission to suffering', politically as well as personally.[43]

In early modern executions, the ability to endure physical torture and to display one's repentance was often the only 'action' available to the condemned. At times the accused's contrition and wholehearted acceptance of the punishment could paradoxically draw attention to its barbarity, undermining the execution's intended meaning.[44] A particularly striking example of this is found in Bandello's story of Simone Turchi and Geronimo Deodati, one of Ford's source texts. Although a number of critics have suggested that the trick chair in *The Broken Heart* is based on the one used in Geronimo's murder, none, as far as I am aware, have pointed out that Ford also draws on Simone's behaviour at this execution in his representation of Ithocles' death and that of Orgilus.[45] Indeed, it could be argued that Ford's innovative use of physical restraint in a revenge killing (in which it highlights Ithocles' courage rather than Orgilus' sadism) results from him combining Simone's use of a trick chair with his noble demeanour at his death.

Simone's brave behaviour at his execution may have been what drew Ford to this story, as it offers a vivid account of how heroic dying could provide a means of self-authorship, functioning, at times, as a form of resistance and even political protest. In the case of Simone's execution, the scaffold acts like a theatrical stage on which competing interpretations of the violent spectacle vie for dominance. The details of Simone's death are grisly and Bandello's account of it is factually accurate.[46] After being apprehended for Geronimo's murder, Simone is sentenced to die in a manner that resembles an early modern revenge plot: Simone is 'to be burned publicly in the marketplace of Antwerp before a slow fire' (p. 320),[47] imprisoned in the very trick chair that he had used to trap and kill Geronimo. Although initially terrified, on the day itself Simone behaves with admirable fortitude. While the ministers of justice 'gradually fed with fagots when necessary, being careful not to let the flames become too fierce, so that for his greater torment the wretched Turchi might be slowly roasted', Simone remains calm, continuing to answer the friar's call that 'now is the fruitful time of repentance', with 'Ay, father, ay, father . . . So far as one could judge by his gestures, the unhappy culprit showed the utmost patience and contrition, meeting his cruel and shameful death without a murmur' (pp. 320–1).

Like Ithocles and Orgilus, Simone is able to take charge of his suffering in a manner which challenges its authorised meaning. This is made explicit by the narrator, who steps out of the narrative to reflect on Simone's bravery and how this might open up alternative ways of interpreting the meaning of his execution. After his death, Simone's body is taken outside the city and chained to a stake in the middle of the main road. Although his gruesome death and the display his corpse is meant to encode his dishonourable end, 'so that all might see how shameful had been the death of so cruel a murderer', the narrator questions such a reading:

> I am fain to believe that as the wretched Simone repented of his sins and showed himself ready for death, since die he must, it mattered little to him what sort of death were his, if only this had been without shame, as it is not the quality of the punishment, but the cause for this, which makes death abominable and ignominious. Virtue, in truth, can invest any sort of death with honour, whereas death, of whatever kind it be, may never avail to put on virtue any stain. (pp. 321–2)

Simone's behaviour at his death offers one example of the way in which an individual's performance on the scaffold could undermine the state's intended meaning of the punishment. The narrator moves in an interesting way away from the public handling of the body, of the sense of shame that this is meant to encode, towards the belief that it is the reason for the execution, the murder of Geronimo, which makes this death shameful. One should not get so caught up in such violent displays, he seems to be saying, that one forgets the reason they are taking place. Nonetheless, while he expresses scepticism towards the crude literalism of such executions, he nonetheless responds to Simone's own bodily fortitude as meaningful, and sufficient to counter the state's interpretation of his punishment. Simone's preparedness for death, fortitude and repentance, not only draws attention to the brutality of the state, but also offers a powerful counter-narrative in which 'virtue . . . can invest any sort of death with honour'; or, as Malcolm says of the disgraced Thane of Cawdor in Shakespeare's *Macbeth*, 'Nothing in his life / Became him like the leaving it'.[48] Simone's execution makes him appear less like a Machiavellian murderer than a brave and contrite Christian; in such instances it is difficult to know if public executions are better at exposing criminals or at making martyrs.

Simone's execution highlights the way that heroic dying can act as a form of power for the powerless, in which the subject achieves self-mastery at the very moment that self is destroyed. In this respect, it resembles Andrew Bennett's description of suicide, which as well as being 'the most self-defeating of acts' also constitutes 'the ultimate assertion of power, of autonomy, of sovereignty – even over death, since it is the only act that allows death to be, or appear to be, mastered'. In that it can offer an interpretation of that death that runs counter to that envisaged by the revenger or state, it can also be seen as 'a singular political act, as a "form of resistance" to authority'.[49] As Phoebe S. Spinrad observes, 'Above all, heroic dying becomes not only a spiritual victory but a temporal one as well; it can foil tyrants as well as devils when men die cheerfully in the teeth of unjust persecution.'[50] The duchess' and Ithocles' heroic deaths function in just this fashion. Despite their being murdered, their ends appear self-authored, allowing them to resist the revenger's overarching design and advance their own narrative of their lives and deaths. These efforts are successful: Ferdinand finds his delusive fantasies about his sister shattered, and Orgilus' envisaged moment of victory becomes Ithcoles' 'triumph over ruin' (5.2.43).

The duchess' and Ithocles' courage in facing their deaths suggest a move toward the heroics of endurance, in which 'rather than acts of killing and conquest, the patient suffering of error, misfortune, disaster, and malevolence is idealized'.[51] However, while this model opens up a space for new female heroes, the very fact such forms of self-assertion fit into conventional ideas of femininity, ultimately makes such figures less radical then they might first appear. For men, on the other hand, the heroics of endurance offer an opportunity for writers to reimagine the basis of what constitutes male valour. Nevertheless, while Ford is clearly drawn to this ideal, any radical possibilities of this model are foreshortened by the way that the heroics of endurance are inflected by gender. Unlike Ford's female revenge victims, whose deaths are typically intimate and eroticised, and unlike the duchess' death which invokes a language of Christian martyrdom, Ithocles' death is staged like a quasi-execution and described in the language of duelling and martial combat. Thus, while Ford's deployment of the trick chair in Ithocles' murder is innovative in terms of the way that bondage is typically used in revenge plays, when it comes to gender, this scene has a conservative effect, reinscribing the heroics of endurance back into a language of 'killing and conquest'.[52] Heroic dying may provide even the most downtrodden revenge victims with a powerful means to outface vengeance, but the subtle differences in how the duchess and Ithocles meet their ends suggests the persistence of a model in which masochistic self-sacrifice is seen as essential to women, and bad for men.[53]

NOTES

1. John Kerrigan, *Revenge Tragedy: Aeschylus to Armageddon* (Oxford: Clarendon Press, 1996), p. 17.
2. Mary Beth Rose, *Gender and Heroism in Early Modern English Literature* (London: The University of Chicago Press, 2002), pp. xii, xxi.
3. Ibid. p. xv.
4. For the therapeutic benefits of revenge, see Robert N. Watson, *The Rest is Silence: Death as Annihilation in the English Renaissance* (Berkeley; London: University of California Press, 1994), pp. 55–73; Deborah Willis, '"The Gnawing Vulture": Revenge, Trauma Theory, and *Titus Andronicus*', *Shakespeare Quarterly* 53.1 (2002), pp. 21–52.
5. Francis Bacon, 'Of Revenge', in Michael Kiernan (ed.), *The Essayes or Counsels, Civill and Morall* (Oxford: Clarendon Press, 1985), p. 17.
6. Carsaniga, 'The Truth', p. 346, notes that the story is 'recorded in the Antwerp archives and is mentioned by several writers', including Girolamo Cardano (*De rerum varietate* [1580], XI, liii), and Jehan Leblond, the translator of *Les chroniques de Jean Carion philosophe* (Paris, 1553), p. 329 r. Although the story does not seem to have been translated into English, Ford could have read the original, Matteo Bandello, *La quarta parte de le novelle del Bandello* (Lyon: Alessandro Marsilii, 1573), pp. 118–26, or the French translation: Bandello, *Dernier volume des novvelles de Bandel* (Lyon: Alexandre Marsilii, 1578), histoire xxvii.
7. Alexander Dyce in his additions to Gifford's edition of Ford's works, *The Works of John Ford*, ed. Alexander Dyce and William Gifford, 3 vols (London: James Toovey, 1869), vol. 1, pp. cxii, 348, was the first to suggest that the trick chair featured in Bandello was a source for Ford's use of it in *The Broken Heart*. See also C. R. Baskervill, 'Bandello and *The Broken Heart*', *Modern Language Notes* 28.2 (1913), pp. 51–2. Giovanni M. Carsaniga, '"The Truth" in John Ford's *The Broken Heart*', *Comparative Literature* 10.4 (1958), pp. 344–8, argues that the story of Geronimo's murder is the 'Truth' that Ford refers to in the Prologue of *The Broken Heart*. In T. J. B. Spencer, 'Appendix B', in John Ford, *The Broken Heart*, ed. T. J. B. Spencer (Manchester: Manchester University Press, 1980), 224–8, Spencer discusses Ford's engagement with Bandello's novellas and provides a history of the use of the trick chair in fictional texts and in reality.
8. I am using Percy Pinkerton's translation: Matteo Bandello, *Twelve Stories Selected and Done into English with a Memoir of the Author*, trans. Percy Pinkerton (London: John C Nimmo, 1895), p. 305. An online version of Bandello's rendition of the story can be found at: <https://it.wikisource.org/wiki/Novelle_(Bandello)/Quarta_parte/Novella_XXVII> (last accessed 3 July 2017).
9. For the way that female revengers used their education to achieve their revenge, see Chloe Kathleen Preedy's essay in this volume.

10. Barnabe Barnes, *The Devil's Charter*, ed. Nick de Somogyi, Globe Quartos (London: Nick Hern Books, 1999), 1.5, p. 22. For versions of the classical myth, see Pausanias 1.20.3; Hyginus *Fabulae* 166.
11. Alison Findlay, *A Feminist Perspective on Renaissance Drama* (Oxford: Blackwell Publishers, 1998), p. 72.
12. Ibid. p. 73.
13. John Webster, *The Duchess of Malfi*, ed. John Russell Brown, Revels Plays, second edition (Manchester: Manchester University Press, 1963), 4.1.84–5. All subsequent references will be to act, scene and line numbers in this edition.
14. Andrea Henderson, 'Death on Stage, Death of the Stage: The Antitheatricality of *The Duchess of Malfi*', in Dympna Callaghan (ed.), *The Duchess of Malfi* (Basingstoke: Macmillan Press, 2000), pp. 61–79, points out that the cardinal also acts as a kind of 'playwright', observing that when the cardinal and Ferdinand 'are not forcing others to play the role of passive spectator, the brothers require them to participate in their shows, to speak according to their scripts' (p. 62).
15. Christy Desmet, '"Neither Maid, Widow, nor Wife": Rhetoric of the Woman Controversy in *Measure for Measure* and *The Duchess of Malfi*', in Dorothea Kehler and Susan Baker (eds), *Another Country: Feminist Perspectives on Renaissance Drama* (Metuchen, NJ: Scarecrow Press, 1991), pp. 71–92 (p. 82).
16. T. F. Wharton, '"Fame's Best Friend": Survival in the *Duchess of Malfi*', in James Hogg (ed.), *Jacobean Miscellany I* (Salzburg: Institut fur Englische Sprache und Literatur, 1980), pp. 18–33, argues that the duchess adopts the discourse of a religious martyr in which her death appears 'not a defect, but an award' (p. 22).
17. Theodora A. Jankowski, 'Defining/Confining the Duchess: Negotiating the Female Body in John Webster's *The Duchess of Malfi*', *Studies in Philology* 87.2 (1990), pp. 221-45 (p. 242).
18. Lisa Jardine, *Still Harping on Daughters: Women and Drama in the Age of Shakespeare* (Brighton: Harvester, 1983), pp. 71, 91.
19. Jankowski, 'Defining/Confining the Duchess', p. 243.
20. My reading here is in line with that of Charlotte Spivack, '*The Duchess of Malfi*: A Fearful Madness', *Journal of Women's Studies in Literature* 2 (1979), pp. 122–32, who argues that the duchess' power and authority is in part derived from her 'supreme rational and conscious control', which is manifested in her ability to remain unshaken when confronted with her death (p. 125).
21. Michael Neill, *Issues of Death: Mortality and Identity in English Renaissance Tragedy* (Oxford: Clarendon Press, 1997), pp. 34, 47–8. See also, Michael Neill, 'Ford's Unbroken Art: The Moral Design of *The Broken Heart*', *The Modern Language Review* 75.2 (1980), pp. 249–68.
22. John Ford, *A Line of Life*, in Gilles Monsarrat, Brian Vickers, and R. J. C.

Watt (eds), *The Collected Works of John Ford* (Oxford: Clarendon Press, 2012), vol. 1, pp. 565–616 (p. 569).
23. Ibid. p. 587.
24. Seneca, *The Workes of Lucius Annaeus Seneca both Morall and Naturall*, trans. Thomas Lodge (London, 1620), Epistle LXXVII, p. 323. Quoted in Neill, *Issues of Death*, p. 35.
25. Rose, *Gender and Heroism*, p. xv.
26. Ford, *Line of Life*, p. 571; Gilles Monsarrat, 'Introduction: *The Golden Meane*', in Monsarrat et al. (eds), *Collected Works*, p. 433.
27. William Rowley, Thomas Dekker and John Ford, *The Witch of Edmonton*, in Peter Corbin and Douglas Sedge (eds), *Three Jacobean Witchcraft Plays: Sophonsiba, The Witch, The Witch of Edmonton*, Revels Plays (Manchester: Manchester University Press, 1986), 3.3.49.
28. John Ford, *Love's Sacrifice*, ed. A. T. Moore, Revels Plays (Manchester: Manchester University Press, 2002), 5.1.159.
29. Lisa Hopkins, *John Ford's Political Theatre* (Manchester: Manchester University Press), p. 156, makes this same point.
30. A more conventional depiction of a male revenge victim, whose willingness to die is perceived as cowardly, can be found in George Chapman's *The Revenge of Bussy D'Ambois* (1613), in Katharine Eisaman Maus (ed.), *Four Revenge Tragedies: The Spanish Tragedy, The Revenger's Tragedy, The Revenge of Bussy D'Ambois, The Atheist's Tragedy*, World's Classics (Oxford: Oxford University Press, 1995). When Montsurry initially lies down rather than fighting, Clermont is disgusted, describing Montsurry as a 'beast' who needs to recover 'the spirit of a man' (5.5.23–4).
31. Ford, *The Broken Heart*. All subsequent references will be to act, scene and line numbers in this edition.
32. For an exploration of how Ford's female characters are represented as simultaneously innocent and guilty and the way that this informs 'Ford's ironic perspective on action', see Thelma N. Greenfield, 'John Ford's Tragedy: The Challenge of Re-Engagement', in Donald K. Anderson (ed.), *'Concord in Discord': The Plays of John Ford, 1586–1986* (New York: AMS Press, 1986), pp. 1–26 (p. 4).
33. Brian Morris also makes this point; see 'Introduction', in John Ford, *The Broken Heart*, ed. Brian Morris (London: Ernest Benn, 1968), pp. xxiv–xxv.
34. Hopkins, *Ford's Political Theatre*, p. 162. Hopkins sees Ford's use of symbols as evidence of a Catholic sensibility, an argument rejected by Monsarrat ('Introduction: *Christes Bloodie Sweat*', in Monsarrat et al. [eds.], *Collected Works*, p. 33). Sara Eaton's chapter in this volume sees Giovanni's desire to seize his sister's heart at the end of the play as driven, in part, by a distrust of language and of the heart, both of which are ultimately unable to encode emotion and meaning adequately. R. J. Kaufmann, 'Ford's "Waste Land": *The Broken Heart*', *Renaissance Drama* 3 (1970), pp. 167–87, observes that Ford's characters are often

'compelled to express their deepest impulses through symbolic gesture' (p. 178).
35. Eaton's chapter in this volume makes similar claims in relation to Giovanni's attempts to know the meaning of Annabella's heart.
36. Citing Pierre Charron, *Of Wisdome: Three Books*, trans. Samson Lennard, 2nd edition (London, 1630), pp. 121, 345–6, that 'He that judgeth of the life of a man, must look how he carrieeth himself at his death; for the end crowneth the work', Neill, *Issues of Death*, argues that 'the memorializing art of the dramatist collaborates with the characters' art of dying to produce a brilliant troping of the tag with which the tragedy of the period so often signals the human transcendence of death: *finis coronat opus* ("the end crowns all")' (pp. 36, 47).
37. Kaufmann, 'Waste Land', famously sees the play as an emotional waste land, a view shared by Sharon Hamilton, '*The Broken Heart*: Language Suited to a Divided Mind', in Anderson (ed.), *Concord in Discord*, pp. 171–93, who argues: 'the Spartan creed encourages a stoicism that is both sterile and hollow'; it is 'flawless only superficially. Within, it is hollow, arid, doomed' (pp. 171, 180). See also Patriacia A. Cahill, 'Going through the Motions: Affects, Machines, and John Ford's *The Broken Heart*', in Ronda Arab, Michelle M. Dowd and Adam Zucker (eds), *Historical Affects and the Early Modern Theater* (London: Routledge, 2015), who explores the characters' automated movements and the 'technological imaginary' of the play and of the trick chair scene in particular (p. 16).
38. William D. Dyer, 'Holding/Withholding Environments: A Psychoanalytic Approach to Ford's *The Broken Heart*', *English Literary Renaissance* 21.3 (1991), pp. 401–24 (p. 403).
39. Naomi Baker, 'Apollo's Deception: The Will to Beauty and *The Broken Heart*', *Literature and Philosophy* 41.2 (2016), p. 1.
40. Kaufmann, 'Waste Land', pp. 175, 178. 187.
41. Neill, *Issues of Death*, pp. 34, 47–8.
42. Hamilton, 'Divided Mind', p. 184.
43. Cynthia Marshall, *The Shattering of the Self: Violence, Subjectivity, and Early Modern Texts* (London: Johns Hopkins University Press, 2002), p. 157.
44. While J. A. Sharpe, '"Last Dying Speeches": Religion, Ideology and Public Execution in Seventeenth Century England', *Past and Present* 107 (1985), pp. 144–67 is right to observe that executions in early modern England was 'one of the principle methods by which the power of the state was demonstrated', such occasions were also open to carnivalesque inversions and switches in sympathy (p. 161). As M. Lindsay Kaplan, *The Culture of Slander in Early Modern England* (Cambridge: Cambridge University Press, 1997), observes: 'the cruelty and humiliation of public executions could ... redound to the infamy of the state and not the criminal' (p. 26). Some executed for their religious beliefs, for example, were seen to meet

their end with such dignity and self-assurance that, rather than appearing like traitors to God and country, their behaviour (at least for some) seemed to validate their beliefs, transforming them from heretics into religious martyrs.
45. For critics who suggest that Ford may have drawn on Bandello's description of the trick chair, see note 7 above.
46. For the historical accuracy and sources of Bandello's story, see Mario Mazzolani, 'Simone Turchi: Sstoria di un delitto famoso e commento ad Bandello', in *Bollettino Storico Lucchese* 7.3 (Lucca, 1937), pp. 125–62.
47. Bandello, *Twelve Stories Selected and Done into English with a Memoir of the Author*.
48. William Shakespeare, *Macbeth*, ed. A. R. Braunmuller, *The New Cambridge Shakespeare* (Cambridge: Cambridge University Press, 1997), 1.4.7–8.
49. Andrew Bennett, *Suicide Century: Literature and Suicide from James Joyce to David Foster Wallace* (Cambridge: Cambridge University Press, 2017), p. 2.
50. Phoebe S. Spinrad, *The Summons of Death on the Medieval and Renaissance English Stage* (Columbus: Ohio State University Press, 1987), p. 39.
51. Rose, *Gender and Heroism*, p. xii.
52. Ibid. p. xii.
53. My concluding statement paraphrases a claim made by Gayle Rubin in her influential essay, 'The Traffic in Women: Notes on the "Political Economy" of Sex', in Rayna Reiter (ed.), *Toward an Anthropology of Women* (New York: Monthly Review Press, 1975), pp. 157–210. In her ambitious attempt to locate some of the key social, economic and cultural reasons for the longevity of the sexual double standard, Rubin suggests that aspects of psychoanalysis support a traditional view of gender in which 'masochism is bad for men, essential to women. Adequate narcissism is necessary for men, impossible for women. Passivity is tragic in man, while lack of passivity is tragic in a woman' (p. 202).

List of Contributors

Alessandra Abbattista wrote her PhD on animal metaphors and the depiction of female avengers in Attic tragedy at the University of Roehampton. Her main research interests are ancient Greek language, literature and drama.

Anne Baden-Daintree is a Teaching Fellow and Research Associate at University of Bristol. Her research interests include elegy, medieval lyric poetry, and late medieval reading and devotional practices.

Janet Clare is Professor of Renaissance Literature at the University of Hull. She is the author of *Shakespeare's Stage Traffic: Imitation, Borrowing and Competition in Renaissance Theatre* (Cambridge University Press, 2014 and 2017), *Revenge Tragedies of the Renaissance, Writers and their Work* (Northcote House/British Council, 2006), *Drama of the English Republic 1649-1660* (Manchester University Press, 2002 and 2005), *'Art Made Tongue-tied by Authority': Elizabethan and Jacobean Dramatic Censorship* (Manchester University Press, 1999 and 1990). She has also edited many collections, including *Republic to Restoration: Legacies and Departures*, which will be published by Manchester University Press in 2018.

Lesel Dawson is a Senior Lecturer in English at the University of Bristol. She is the author of *Lovesickness and Gender in Early Modern Literature* (Oxford University Press, 2008) as well as articles on early modern drama, misogyny, menstruation and cruentation. Her research interests include Renaissance psychology and medicine, and she is currently working on a project on early modern ideas about vision, cognition and grief.

Sara Eaton was Professor of English Emerita at North Central College in Naperville, Illinois until her death in 2016. She was twice recognised with the Dissinger Award for Distinguished Teaching and Service and she is the author of many articles on early modern drama, gender and courtly love.

Ian Felce is the author of *William Morris and the Icelandic Sagas* (Boydell & Brewer, forthcoming) and several articles on medieval literature and its reception in post-medieval English literature. He is particularly interested in how medieval narratives have been transformed to meet the needs and priorities of later writers.

Alison Findlay is Professor of Renaissance Drama at Lancaster University. She is the author of *Women in Shakespeare: A Dictionary* (Continuum, 2010), *Playing Spaces in Early Women's Drama* (Cambridge University Press, 2006), *Women and Dramatic Production, 1550-1700* (Longman, 2000), *A Feminist Perspective on Renaissance Drama* (Blackwell Publishers, 1998), *Illegitimate Power: Bastards in Renaissance Drama* (Manchester University Press, 1994) as well as a number of edited collections.

Edith Hall is Professor in the Classics Department and Centre for Hellenic Studies at King's College London. She is the author of *Introducing the Ancient Greeks* (Bodley Head, 2014), *Adventures with Iphigenia in Tauris: A Cultural History of Euripides' Black Sea Tragedy* (Oxford University Press, 2012), *Greek Tragedy: Suffering under the Sun* (Oxford University Press, 2010), *The Return of Ulysses: A Cultural History of Homer's Odyssey* (Johns Hopkins University Press, 2008), *The Theatrical Cast of Athens* (Oxford University Press, 2006), *Greek Tragedy and the British Theatre 1660-1914* (Oxford University Press, 2005, co-authored with Fiona Macintosh), *Aeschylus' Persians*, edited with translation, Introduction and Commentary (Aris & Phillips, 1996), *Inventing the Barbarian: Greek Self-Definition through Tragedy* (Clarendon Press, 1989) as well as a number of edited collections. Her new book, *Happiness: Ten Ways Aristotle Can Change Your Life*, will be published by Bodley Head in 2018.

Lydia Matthews is a researcher in Ancient History at Oxford University. Her research interests include Roman history, ancient sexuality and gender, ancient medicine and ancient ethnography.

Fiona McHardy is Professor of Classics at the University of Roehampton. She is author of *Revenge in Athenian Culture* (Duckworth, 2008) and has co-edited three volumes: *Women's Influence on Classical Civilization* (Routledge, 2004), *Lost Dramas of Classical Athens* (University of Exeter Press, 2005) and *From Abortion to Pederasty* (Ohio State University Press, 2014). She is currently writing a book on gendered violence in ancient Greece with Susan Deacy covering such topics as infanticide, rape, uxoricide and domestic violence.

Andreas N. Michalopoulos is Professor of Latin at the Classics Department of the National and Kapodistrian University of Athens. He is the author of *Ovid, Heroides 20 and 21: Introduction, Text, Translation, and Commentary* (Papadimas, 2013), *Ovid, Heroides 16 and 17: Introduction, Text and Commentary* (Francis Cairns Publications, 2006) and *Ancient Etymologies in*

Ovid's Metamorphoses: A Commented Lexicon (Francis Cairns Publications, 2001). He has also written two books with Charilaos N. Michalopoulos: *Roman Lyric Poetry: Horace Carmina* (HEAL Link, 2016) and *Roman Love Elegy* (HEAL Link, 2016). His research interests include Augustan poetry, ancient etymology, Roman drama, Roman novel and modern receptions of classical literature.

Tanya Pollard is Professor at Brooklyn College and the Graduate Center, City University of New York (CUNY). She is the author of *Greek Tragic Women on Shakespearean Stages* (Oxford University Press, 2017) and *Drugs and Theater in Early Modern England* (Oxford University Press, 2005). She is also the editor of a number of scholarly editions and essay collections, including two collections with Tania Demetriou: *Homer and Greek Tragedy in Early Modern England's Theatres*, a special issue of *Classical Receptions Journal* 9.1 (2017) and *Milton, Drama, and Greek Texts*, a special issue of *The Seventeenth Century Journal* 31.2 (2016). She is currently co-editing with Marcus Nevitt *Reader in Tragedy: An Anthology of Classical Criticism to Contemporary Theory* for Bloomsbury.

Chloe Kathleen Preedy is a Lecturer in Shakespeare and Renaissance literature at the University of Exeter. She is the author of *Marlowe's Literary Scepticism: Politic Religion and Post-Reformation Polemic* (Bloomsbury, 2013). Her new book project explores how sixteenth- and seventeenth-century playwrights utilised aerial and atmospheric imagery to conceptualise theatrical space, and she is currently co-developing a collaborative research project which investigates the twentieth- and twenty-first-century cultural afterlives of those associated with the Blackfriars Theatre.

Irene Salvo is a Research Associate at the University of Göttingen in the Collaborative Research Centre 1136 'Education and Religion'. Her research focuses on Greek social and cultural history, with a particular focus on: gender and magic, religious knowledge, ideas of purity and pollution, homicide, and the anthropology of feuding and emotions. She is currently working on a monograph entitled *Unclean Hands: Homicide, Revenge, and Civic Purification in Greek Inscriptions and Culture*.

Marguerite A. Tassi is the Martin Distinguished Professor in English at the University of Nebraska at Kearney. She is the author of *Women and Revenge in Shakespeare: Gender, Genre, and Ethics* (Susquehanna University Press, 2011), *The Scandal of Images: Iconoclasm, Eroticism, and Painting in Early Modern English Drama* (Susquehanna University Press, 2005), and numerous articles on Shakespeare, classical mythology and Mary Queen of Scots. Her *Poetry for Kids: William Shakespeare*, an illustrated introduction to Shakespeare for younger readers, was published by MoonDance Press in 2008.

Kathrin Winter is a Lecturer in Latin at the University of Heidelberg. She is the author of *Artificia mali: Das Böse als Kunstwerk in Senecas Rachetragödien* (Universitätsverlag Winter, 2014) and is co-editor of *Horace and Seneca: Interactions, Intertexts, Interpretations* (De Gruyter, 2017). Her research interests include ancient drama, Augustan and early imperial literature.

Rebecca Yearling is a Lecturer in English literature at Keele University. She is the author of *Ben Jonson, John Marston and Early Modern Drama: Satire and the Audience* (Palgrave Macmillan, 2016) as well as articles on parent–child rivalry in Shakespeare's late plays, *Hamlet* and cognitive narratology, and early modern homoeroticism. Her research interests include Renaissance satire, early modern drama on stage, theatrical violence, and early modern psychology and medicine. She is currently working on a new project on depictions of violence in Shakespeare, tentatively titled *Shakespeare's Violence and the Early Modern Spectator*.

Index

Page numbers in *italics* refer to illustrations and those followed by n refer to notes. Titles of texts are listed under the author's name.

Achilles (character), 153–4n, 292n
   compared to lion, 205, 215
   killed by Paris, 250n
   revenge and eating, 46
   The Trojan Women, 16
   'wrath', 10, 160, 209
Acker, Paul, 8
Aegisthus (character), 15, 41, 43, 111–12, 165–7, 205, 208–11
Aeschylus
   Agamemnon, 41, 203–4, 208–11, 212, 215–16
   Choephori, 13, 111–12, 166–7
   Clytemnestra and Erinyes, 33
   Clytemnestra as lioness, 10, 203–4, 206, 208–11, 215–16, 217n
   Clytemnestra as 'man-minded', 1, 208
   Eumenides, 33, 36, 39–41
   Oresteia, 45, 47, 49–50, *49*, 119
   Phineus, 40–1
   plays, 285n
   Seven against Thebes, 38
Agamemnon (character), 16, 43, 177n
   Electra's grief for, 15
   Electra's revenge, 112
   Hecuba, 221–2, 224, 227, 268, 285n
   killed by Clytemnestra, 1–2
   and lions, 208–11

Ajax (character), 205
Alcmaeon (character), 55n
Alexiou, Margaret, 14, 27–8n
Allen, Danielle, 4, 22n
Allman, Eileen, 8, 25n, 183, 190
Altman, Joel, 192
American Conservatory Theatre, 123
amphora fury, 40
Anderson, Craig A., 56n
Andromache (character), 15
Antigone (character), 15, 151n, 280, 292n
Antiphon, 160, 164, 171
   On the Poisoning by the Stepmother, 164–5
Apollo (god), 40, 142, 209, 245, 249n, 250n
   and medicine, 243–4, 249n
Apostolos-Cappadona, Diane, 17
Aquinas, Thomas, 124
Aristogeiton, 162, 171, 172
Aristophanes, 167
   Wealth, 47, 171
Aristotle, 35–6, 124, 269, 293n
   Poetics, 286n, 272–3, 290n, 305n
   Politics, 175n
   Rhetoric, 64
Armstrong, Dorsey, 258, 260

INDEX 331

Árnason, Vilhjálmur, 22–3n, 93
Artemis (goddess), 36, 209, 212, 217n
Ascham, Roger, 280, 293n
Atreus (character), 268, 286n
Aubriot-Sévin, Danièle, 151n
Austin, J. L., 126–7
avenging daughter, 111–21

Bacon, Francis
  lamentation, 15
  public revenge, 118
  revelation, 308
  'wild justice', 58, 183, 286n
  witch and revenger, 65, 228
Baden-Daintree, Anne, 262n
Baker, Naomi, 316
Bamber, Linda, 9, 26n
Bandello, Matteo, 309–10, 318–20
Barnes, Barnabe, *The Devil's Charter*, 309–11
Bartlett, Robert, 263n
Bates, Catherine, 131–2
beards, 91–2, 254, 257, 263n, 298
Beaumont, Francis
  Love's Cure (with John Fletcher), 184
  The Maid's Tragedy (with John Fletcher), 190, 194, 231–3, 310
Beckwith, Sara, 134–5n
'becoming-animal', 207
Bennett, Andrew, 320
Beowulf, 8, 18, 25n
Beowulf (character), 18
bereaved mothers, 268, 273, 281, 285n
Bicks, Caroline, 198n
Bilgames and the Netherworld, 43–4
Billing, Christian, 268, 285n
birth and female generation, 77n, 99–102, 104, 269–70, 287n
Bloom, Gina, 67
Boedeker, Deborah, 100
Bongie, Elizabeth, 10
Borgias, 309–10
Bouguereau, William-Adolphe, 1, 2, 21
Bowers, Fredson, 61, 63
Bowers, Rick, 303
Bradley, Edward M., 240
Braidotti, Rosi, 10, 203–4, 206–8, 212, 215–16
Braithwaite, Richard, 227

Bremmer, Jan N., 152n
Briem, Ólafur, 22n
Brooke, Nicolas, 64
'brother unkind', 122–40
Broude, Ronald, 23n
Bucer, Martin, 17–18
Buchanan, George, 293n
  Jephthes sive votum tragoedia, 280
Burnett, Anne Pippin, 4, 203
Bush, Geoffrey, 121n
Butler, Judith, 3, 87
Byron, *Don Juan*, 33, 52

Calvin, John, 124
Calydonian boar hunt, 47–8
Cannon, Christopher, 254
Carey, Christopher, 170–1, 178n
Casali, Sergio, 248–9n
Cassandra (character), 208, 209–11, 243, 249n
Castelvetro, 269, 272–3
Catholicism, 134n
Cavell, Stanley, 126–7
Chaereas (character), 168–9, 171–2
Chance, Jane, 8
Chaniotis, Angelos, 146
Chapman, George, 291n
  Bussy D'Ambois, 192–3
  The Revenge of Bussy D'Ambois, 13, 33, 184, 191–5, 199n, 323n
Chariton, 13, 168–9
Charlebois, Elizabeth, 132n
Charron, Pierre, 324n
Cheek by Jowl, 133n
Christianity, 5–6, 17–18, 93
Christopherson, John, *Jephthah*, 280, 293n
Cicero, 16, 58, 58–9
Cinthio, Giraldi, 269
'civic retraint', 4, 22n
Clare, Janet, 183, 190, 194, 301
Clark, David, 4, 93, 253
Clemen, Wolfgang, 29n
Cleopatra (character), 128
Clover, Carol, 87, 252–3, 254, 262n
Clytemnestra (character)
  cursing, 143
  Electra's grief, 15
  Erinyes, 41, 48–9

332 INDEX

Clytemnestra (character) (*cont.*)
  gossip, 165–7
  grief and revenge, 268
  Iphigenia, 270
  killed by Orestes, 1–2
  as lioness, 10, 203–4, 206–16, 217n, 219n
  Orestes and Electra, 112
  she-avenger, 33, 309
  tricks and deception, 154n
Cohen, David, 22n
'conditional self-curse', 149–50
Congreve, William, *The Mourning Bride*, 34–5
Conn Liebler, Naomi, 9–10
corpus linguistics, 60–3
Corythus (character), 243
costume and mask makers, 39–41
CQPweb, 62, 78n, 80n
crime and punishment, 36–7, 108n, 146–7, 149–50
Crosbie, Christopher, 23n
Crown, John, *Caligula: A Tragedy*, 64
curse tablets, 12, 26n, 27n, 36
curses, 11–14, 12, 27n, 48–9, 229–30, 241–3, 245, 248n
cursing-prayers, 141–59, 229
Cybele (goddess), 204, 217n

Dawson, Lesel, 122, 194
de Vries, Hent, 126–7, 130
deinon, 270
Dekker, Thomas, 280
  The Witch of Edmonton, 314–15
Deleuze, Gilles, 62
Demosthenes, 171, 172
  Against Aristogeiton I, 162
Deodati, Geronimo, 309, 318–20
Derderian, Katharine, 27n
Desmet, Christy, 311
Dessen, Alan, 133n
DeWall, C. Nathan, 56n
Dionysus (god), festival of, 203–4
dogs, 36, 56n
Dolan, Frances, 230–1
Dolce, Lodovico, 287n
  Giocasta, 269–70
Dollimore, Jonathan, 64
Dubrow, Heather, 121n

Dué, Casey, 14
Dyer, William D., 316

Early English Books Online (EBBO), 11, 61–3, 77n, 78n, 80n
Eastwood, Adrienne, 123, 133n
Eck, Bernard, 154n
education, 181–202
Eidinow, Esther, 12, 163, 165
Electra (character), 15, 28n, 111–12, 115, 119, 166
English Civil Wars, 61, 63, 68–70, 80n
The English Gentlewoman, 227
Epicasta (character), 143
epigraphic documents, 144–50
Erasmus, 224, 266–7, 270–1, 283n
Erinyes
  Alcmaeon, 55n
  curse-prayers, 142–3
  dogs, 56n
  femininity of, 7–8, 33–57, 59, 63–4, 67, 76, 109n, 250n
  'The Kindly Ones', 70–2
  and lions, 204–5, 217n
  Medea, 66, 75, 106n, 228–9
  Orestes, 1
  sleeping, 198n
Eriphyle (character), 143
Ester hath hang'd Haman, 183
Euripides
  Alcestis, 167
  Andromache, 13, 165, 166, 205
  The Bacchae, 71, 165
  Electra, 1, 112, 166
  female avengers, 182–4
  Hecuba: cursing, 12; fate, 235n; female avenger, 234; and *Hamlet*, 19–20, 264–6; lamentation, 15; Polydorus (character), 284n, 293–4n; and Shakespeare, 266–94; translation and performance, 224–5
  Hercules Furens, 36
  Hippolytus, 161, 164, 167–8, 171–2
  Iphigenia in Aulis, 15, 266–8, 270–1, 280
  lioness, 203–4, 206, 217n
  Medea, 10, 212–16: birth and female generation, 102–3; character underestimated, 109n; female

avengers, 182; feminine and masculine aspects, 107n; lioness, 203–4, 215–16; Seneca read, 97–8, 106n; Themis (character), 212
The Phoenician Women, 269–70
The Suppliants, 15
The Trojan Women, 15, 272, 288–9n
Ewbank, Inga-Stina, 67
executions, 123, 130, 188, 312, 315, 317–20, 324–5n

Faraone, Christopher, 36, 145–6
Fatal Attraction, 33
Fawcett, Mary Laughlin, 187
female fury, 1–32
female revenger, 7–11
Fetherstone, Christopher, *A dialogue agaynst light, lewde, and lasciuious dauncing*, 182
Findlay, Alison, 9, 183, 310
Finglass, Patrick J., 41
Fletcher, John
  Love's Cure (with Francis Beaumont), 184
  The Maid's Tragedy (with Francis Beaumont), 190, 194, 231–3, 310
Foakes, R. A., 121n
Foley, Helene, 9, 10, 15, 107n, 109n, 204–5
Ford, John
  The Broken Heart, 307–25
  The Golden Mean, 314
  A Line of Life, 314
  Love's Sacrifice, 314–15
  Perkin Warbeck, 315
  'Tis Pity She's a Whore, 7, 80n, 122–40, 314–15, 323n
  The Witch of Edmonton, 314–15
Fraenkel, E., 211
France, 227–8
Frontisi-Ducrox, Françoise, 154n
Fulkerson, Laurel, 240, 248n
Furies *see* Erinyes

Gagarin, Michael, 170–1
Gascoigne, George, *Jocasta*, 269, 270–1, 278, 287n
Gauer, Denis, 124
gender hybridity, 70–6

Geoffrey of Monmouth, *Historia Regum Britanniae*, 113, 114
Gill, Chris, 103, 109n
Gísla saga Súrssonar, 93
Goffe, Thomas, *Orestes*, 61
Goldhill, Simon, 208
Golding, Arthur, 223, 235n
Goodland, Katharine, 17, 275
Goodsell, Judith, 28n
gossip, 13, 160–80
Gosson, Stephen, 271
grief, 18–19, 29n, 250n, 267–8, 292n
Griswold, Wendy, 25n, 61
Guarini, Giambattista, 302–3
Guattari, Felix, 62
Guðrún Poems, 4

Haas, Renate, 256, 261n
Hainsworth, Bryan, 153n
Hall, Edith, 161, 168, 208, 213
Hallett, Charles A., 24n, 300
Hallett, Elaine S., 24n, 300
Hamel, Mary, 259
Hamilton, Sharon, 318
Hardie, Andrew, 62, 78n
Harpies, 40–1, 71
Harrison, Jane Ellen, 37–40, 56n
Hart, F. Elizabeth, 65
Hawley, John Stratton, 17
Heaney, Seamus, 8
Heath, Malcolm, 223
Heavey, Katherine, 60, 66
Hecate (character), 36
Hector (character), 46, 205, 215
Hecuba (character), 221–9
  desire for revenge, 160
  dream, 41, 249n
  fate, 235n
  female avenger, 46, 234
  and *Hamlet*, 20, 264–6
  lamentation, 14–16, 285n
  and Shakespeare, 264–94
  in sixteenth-century Europe, 266–73
  stabbing, 184
Heiðarvíga saga, 17
Helen (character), 217n, 241–3, 245, 248n
Henderson, Andrea, 322n
Hercules (character), 29n, 164, 167

Herman, Gabriel, 22n
Hermanson, Anne, 72
Herodotus, 217n
heroic dying, 307–25
'heroics of endurance', 20, 307–8, 314, 320
Hesiod, 35, 43–6, 162
   Theogony, 7, 43–5
Heywood, Jasper, 304–5n
   Apology for Actors, 271
Heywood, Thomas
   A Warning for Fair Women, 271
   A Woman Killed With Kindness, 304–5n
Higgins, John, *The Mirour for Magistrates*, 114
Hirschfeld, Heather, 24n, 50
Hobbes, Thomas, *Rhetoric*, 64
Holinshed, Raphael, *Chronicles of England, Scotlande, and Irelande*, 114
Holland, Philemon, 289n
Holmes, Lucy, 35, 52
Holofernes (character), 20, 227–8, 232
Homer
   Clytemnestra, 208
   cursing, 142–3, 153n
   desire for revenge, 53n
   Erinyes, 39
   grief, 27n
   Hecuba, 291n
   Iliad: Ajax (character), 205; Althaea (character), 47–8, 142–4, 151n, 153n, 154n; Amyntor (character), 48–9, 153n; Chryses (character), 142; cursing, 142–3, 153n; grief, 224; Hecuba (character), 276, 291n; Heraclitu (character), 143; lack of female avengers, 35; Meleager (character), 14–18, 142–3, 152n, 152–3n, 154n; mourning, 15; Patroclus (character), 205, 215; Phoenix (character), 47–9, 153n; revenge and eating, 46–9
   lamentation, 15, 28n, 48
   lions, 204–6, 213, 215
   Odyssey, 41–2, 143, 152n, 163: Nausicaa (character), 163; Penelope (character), 143, 204–5, 210;

Polyphemus (character), 268; Telemachus (character), 143, 204
'honorary man', 269
Hopkins, Lisa, 127–8, 316
Horsman, Yasco, 126
Hughes, Thomas, *The Misfortunes of Arthur*, 59
human sacrifice, 16, 36, 294n
   Hamlet, 279–81
   Hecuba, 222, 268, 280, 290n, 294n
   Iphigenia, 2, 43, 208, 211, 270
   Jephthah (character), 279–80
   Titus Andronicus, 225
Hunter, Virginia, 161, 162–3
hvǫt scenes, 17, 252–4, 259–60, 262n
Hyperides, *On the Defence of Lycophron*, 163–4
Hypsipyle (character), 241, 248n

Icelandic literature, 4, 14, 16–17, 22–3n, 24n, 29n
Icelandic sagas, 252–3, 257
Ide, Richard, 191–2
identity and alterity, 108–9
illegitimate children, 163–4
infanticide, 212–15, 229
Inns of Court, 59, 80n
Iphigenia (character), 2, 15, 208–9, 211, 224, 270, 280
Isaeus, *On the Estate of Pyrrhus*, 162–3
Íslendingasögur, 86–8, 92, 93

Jakobsson, Ármann, 91
James, Heather, 186
Jankowski, Theodora, 313
Jardine, Lisa, 185, 312–13
Jason (character), 99–105, 109n, 120n, 212–15, 228, 241, 285–6n
Jephthah (character), 279–80
Jocasta (character), 227
Johnson, Mark Albert, 299
Johnstone, Steven, 172
Jones, Emrys, 225, 273, 274
Judith (character), 20, 227–8, 232

Kahn, Coppélia, 186, 187
Kaufmann, R. J., 324n
Kerrigan, John, 4, 61, 64, 181, 223, 295–6

King, Christine M., 29n
King Leir (character), 113–14
Kinwelmersh, Francis, *Jocasta*, 269, 270–1, 278, 287n
Kipling, Rudyard, 33
Knidos, Turkey, 12–13, 59, 144–50, 156n, 157n, 158n
Knowles, Richard, 112–13
Knox, P. E., 209, 212, 249n
Konstantinou, A., 205–6, 211, 213
Kordecki, Lesley, 121n
Koskinen, Karla, 121n
Kyd, Thomas
  Erinyes sleeping, 198n
  self-control, 300
  Seneca's influence, 264
  Soliman and Perseda, 189
  The Spanish Tragedy: Bel-Imperia (character), 13, 59, 60, 189–92, 194–5, 292n; education, 13, 184, 189–91, 194–5; grief, 224–5; Hieronimo (character), 59, 60, 64, 189–91, 195, 224–5, 286n, 292n, 295–6; Horatio (character), 59, 189, 224–5; Isabella (character), 20, 224–5; letters, 59–60; Lorenzo (character), 190; male revengers, 291n; masculinity and vengeance, 295–6; maternal grief, 275; mourning, 20; play-within-the-play, 278; self-revelation, 64; Seneca, 264, 290n; vegetative soul, 23n
  A Warning for Fair Women, 271

lamentation, 3, 11, 14–21, 27–30n, 36, 238–325
Laqueur, Thomas, 87
Larran, Francis, 162
law courts, 162
Laxdæla saga, 4–5, 85–96
Leach, Colin Wayne, 51
Lee, Mary, 73, 74
letters, 16, 60–3, 191–5
Linear B, 42
lions, 203–20, 217n
Llewellyn, Kathleen, 227–8
Loraux, Nicole, 273, 287n
Low, Jennifer, 127, 128, 135n

Lumley, Jane, 270–1, 287–8n
  Iphigeneia, 224
Luther, Martin, 124
Lyne, Adrian, 33
Lysias, 163
  On the Murder of Eratosthenes, 13, 161, 169–73, 178n, 179n

McCabe, Richard, 128
McClure, Laura K., 161
McConachie, Bruce, 65
McHardy, Fiona, 208, 212
McLuskie, Kathleen, 117
madness, 24n
male devotion and vengeance, 85–96
'male-like' Cordelia, 6
Malory, Thomas, 251
Manuche, Cosmo, *The Bastard*, 65, 70–2, 80n
Marshall, Cynthia, 317
Marston, John, 20
  Antonio and Mellida, 300
  Antonio's Revenge, 19, 295–306
  The Malcontent, 302–3
Martin, John, 124, 125, 126, 134n
Martínez, Zenón Luis, 128
'masculine' values, 2
masculinity
  and grief, 295–306
  and vengeance, 1–32
maternal curses, 143–4, 153n, 154n
maternal uncles, 151n, 152n
Maus, Katherine Eisaman, 199n
Mazzio, Carla, 124–5, 134n
Medea (character)
  Althaea compared to, 143
  avenging daughter, 120n
  The Bastard, 71–2
  cruelty, 268
  family roles, 6
  female revenge, 65–8, 73, 75–6
  gender, identity and revenge, 97–110
  gender and, 59–60, 77n
  gossip, 163
  heroic, 10–11, 26n
  infanticide, 292n
  letters, 241, 248n
  as lioness, 203–4, 206, 207–8, 212–16
  punishment, 285–6n

Medea (character) (cont.)
  retaliatory mother, 33, 61, 76
  stabbing, 184
  stoicism, 191
  as victim, 74
  violent passion, 228–9, 245
  as a warning, 182
Melancthon, Philip, 124, 267
Melville, Herman, 46
Menander, 164
Menelaus (character), 205, 241–2, 248n
metamorphoses, 102, 206–15
Meulengracht Sørensen, Preben, 86–7, 92
Middleton, Thomas, 80n
  The Second Maiden's Tragedy, 190
Miles, Geoffrey, 191
Miller, William Ian, 4, 17, 22n, 29n, 94
Minturno, Antonio, 267
Miola, Robert S., 67, 279
'mirror neurons', 65, 79n
Monsarrat, Gilles, 314
Mossman, Judith, 223–4, 269, 285n
Mother Earth, 37–8
mourning, 30n
Mullaney, Stephen, 24n
Müller, Karl Otfried, 41–2
Munda, Constantia, 182, 183
Munday, 280

Nashe, Thomas, 182
Nature journal, 51–2
Neill, Michael, 123, 130, 313, 317, 324n
Neoptolemus (character), 166, 205
net, 209, 210, 213
Newton, Charles T., 145
Nicholson, Eric, 280
Niobe (character), 101, 276, 292n
Njáls saga, 4–5, 85–96, 252–3, 257, 262n
Norland, Howard, 287n
Norton, Thomas, 267
  Gorboduc, 59, 267, 278, 291n
Nussbaum, Martha, 222

Odysseus (character), 16, 41–2, 152n, 163, 171, 205, 268
Oedipus (character), 27n, 38, 142–4, 227

Oenone (character), 16, 239–50
Ogle, M. B., 166
'On Revenge', 228, 286n
Ophelia (character), 6, 225, 275, 279–81, 293n
Orestes (character)
  Clytemnestra, 211
  Electra, 28n, 111–12
  Erinyes, 1–2, 2, 55n
  gossip, 166–7
  lions, 208
  masculinity and vengeance, 4, 21, 177n
Orestes Pursued by the Furies, 1, 2, 21
Ortner, Sherry, 35
Otherness, 9, 103
Ovid
  Hecuba, 266, 274, 291n
  Heroides, 16, 186, 245, 246n, 250n
  lamentation, 28n
  Metamorphoses, 184–8, 195, 223–4
  Oenone Paridi (*Heroides* 5), 239–50, 243
Oxford English Dictionary, 77n

Packard, Bethany, 187
Pacuvius, 16
Palmer, A., 240
Pálsson, Hermann, 22n
Panoussi, Vassiliki, 29n
Paris (character), 16, 41, 205, 239–6, 248n, 249n, 250n
Parker, Matthew, 17–18
passivity, 11, 190, 231, 295, 325n
Patten, Kimberley Christine, 17
Pausanias, 42–3
Peaps, William, *Love In Its Extasie*, 68–70, 80n
Pearson, Jacqueline, 302
Petit-Sens, Jean-Antoine, 33
Phillippy, Patricia, 19, 30n
Philoctetes (character), 205
Pindar, 41, 165
Pix, Mary, *The False Friend or the Fate of Disobedience*, 74–5
Plato, 143–4, 271
play-within-the-play, 272, 278, 292n
Plutarch, 15, 143
  Life of Pelopidas, 272, 288–9n

On the Fortune of Virtue of Alexander the Great, 272
Poetic Edda, 4, 253
Pollard, Tanya, 222
Polymestor (character), 12, 222–4, 226, 268, 279, 285n, 294n
Porter, John R., 161, 170–1
posthuman, 206–7, 215–16
posthumanism, 10
prayers, 12–13, 59, 144–50, 155n
pregnancy imagery, 75, 101–2, 125, 266, 270, 282–3n, 283n
Priam (character), 46, 215, 264–5
Prosodion, 147–8
prothesis vase, 39
'prototragedies', 47–8
punishment, 308–9
Puttenham, George, 272
Pye, Christopher, 60, 64, 67–8
Pythagoras, 35–6

Quilligan, Maureen, 116, 121n

Rabinowitz, Nancy Sorkin, 1
Raleigh, Sir Walter, 314
Rawlings, Elizabeth Trapnell, 28n
The Rebellion of Naples, 68
Reformation, 17–18, 124
regicide, 232–3, 272
Renaissance Revivals, 61
revenge and eating, 46–7
revenge inscriptions, 59–60
revengeful wife, 230–1
'revenging home', 7
Rikhardsdottir, 30n
Rist, Thomas, 304n
Roisman, Hanna M., 161, 168, 172
Roman literature, 5, 16, 106–7n
Rose, Mary Beth, 20, 307–8, 314
Rosenbloom, David S., 171
Ross, Margaret Clunes, 86
Rowley, William, 80n
  The Witch of Edmonton, 314–15
Rubin, Gayle, 325n
Ruyer, Raymond, 62

Sackville, Thomas, 267
sagas, 16–17, 22–3n, 29n, 252–3
Salvo, Irene, 59

Samia, 164
Sanders, Ed, 165
Saul, Nigel, 5
Scaliger, Joseph, 267, 269
Schierl, Petra, 16
Schiesari, Juliana, 30n
Scourfield, John H. D., 168
scripting vengeance, 189–91
self-control, 1–2, 5, 300, 314–17, 322n
self-harm, 15
Seneca
  Erinyes, 59
  ghosts triggering revenge, 18–19
  Hecuba, 268–9
  horror, 72
  influence, 181, 191–2, 264
  King Lear, 115
  lamentation, 14–16, 29n
  Medea, 97–110: Appamia (character), 75; avenging daughter, 120n; birth and female generation, 77n; female revenger, 10–11, 59–60, 228; *The Maides Revenge*, 66–7; passionate emotion, 5
  recognition, 286n
  Stoic philosophy, 314
  Thyestes, 301
  translation and performance, 224
  Troas, 271, 279
  The Trojan Women, 14–16
Seneca: His Tenne Tragedies, 59–60
Settle, Elkanah, *Love and Revenge*, 72–4
sexual jealousy, 161–5
Shakespeare, William
  The Broken Heart and, 313
  Cleopatra, 128
  comedy, 182–3, 197n
  Cymbeline, 273
  family roles, 6–7
  female revengers, 11–13
  female victims, 26n
  Hamlet: *Antonio's Revenge*, 297; Claudius (character), 232, 266, 272, 279, 280, 292n, 295, 304n; education, 181; Gertrude (character), 20, 266, 275–6, 281, 291n, 292n; Hamlet (character), 20, 72–3, 181, 221–2, 232, 264–6, 272, 275–81, 293n, 304n; Hecuba,

Shakespeare, William (cont.)
  Hamlet: Antonio's Revenge (cont.)
    221–2, 224–5, 264–81, 288–9n;
    lamentation, 20; Love and Revenge,
    72–4; mourning, 304n; Ophelia
    (character), 6, 225, 275, 279–81,
    293n; Polonius (character), 221,
    234, 265, 279; regicide, 232;
    'unmanly grief', 295
  Hecuba, 273–4
  Henry VI trilogy, 12, 20, 225–7,
    229
  King Lear, 6–7, 12, 111–21, 121n
  Macbeth, 67, 115, 319
  mourning, 19–20
  Much Ado About Nothing, 11
  Othello, 123, 313
  Otherness, 9–10
  The Rape of Lucrece, 273, 296
  Richard III, 226, 229
  The Tempest, 12
  Timon of Athens, 12
  Titus Andronicus: Aaron (character),
    12, 185–6, 188, 195, 198n;
    Bassianus (character), 185;
    education, 13, 194–5; Erinyes,
    33; female revenger, 20, 192,
    198n; Hecuba (character), 225–7,
    234, 273; horror, 301; Lavinia
    (character), 13, 185–8, 195, 198n,
    226, 273; Marcus (character),
    186–8; maternal grief, 275; and
    Ovid, 185–9; Philomel (character),
    185–8, 195; Procne (character), 184,
    185, 187–8; Tamora (character), 20,
    33, 185–8, 195, 225–7, 273; Titus
    (character), 129, 185–8, 189, 198n,
    225
  Troilus and Cressida, 275, 290n,
    291n
Shenandoah Shakespeare, 123
Shirley, James
  The Maides Revenge, 65–70
  The Schoole of Complement, 66
  The Triumph of Beautie, 66
Shrank, Cathy, 198n
Shuger, Debora, 294n
Sidney, Philip
  Astrophil, 131

Buchanan, 293n
Hecuba (character), 271–2, 288–9n
Hecuba, 224, 267, 280, 284n
Simone Turchi, 309, 318–20
'sincerity', 134–5n
Singer, Tania, 51–2
Smail, Daniel Lord, 23n
Smith, Bruce, 287n
Solon, 15
Sommerstein, A. H., 205
Sophocles
  Ajax, 15
  Antigone (character), 15, 151n, 292n
  Antigone, 15
  Electra (character), 28n, 111–12, 119
  Electra, 15, 41, 166
  Inachos, 217n
  lamentation, 15
  passivity, 212
  Philoctetes, 47
  Trachiniae, 164
  translation and performance, 267
Sowernam, Ester, 182, 183
Spacks, Patricia M., 162
Speght, Rachel, 183–4
Spenser, Edmund, The Faerie Queen,
  114
Spinrad, Phoebe S., 320
Stainton, Robert J., 65
Stanavage, Liberty, 186
Steenbergh, Kristine, 5, 23n, 59, 80n
Stephens, Scott Manning, 124
stereotypes, 13–14, 51, 102, 104, 154n,
  171
Stiblinus, Gasparus, 267
stoicism
  Antonio's Revenge, 299
  The Broken Heart, 316–17, 324n
  The Duchess of Malfi, 312–14
  Hercules Furens, 29n
  The Revenge of Bussy D'Ambois,
    191–2, 195
  self-control, 5
Studley, John, 66, 228
  Seneca: His Tenne Tragedies, 59–60
suicide, 245, 250n, 315, 320
Sumerian text, 43–4
'surrogate artist', 181, 307, 311
survoler, 62

Suter, Ann, 14, 27n, 28n
Svavarsson, Svavar Hrafn, 87, 94
Swetnam, Joseph, 182, 183–4
    Arraignment of Lewd, Idle, Froward, and Unconstant Women, 182–3

'table of opposites', 35–6
Tantalus (character), 101
Tassi, Marguerite A., 67, 120n, 182–3, 197n, 222, 227
Taylor, Gary, 121n
Thesmophoria, 13, 146
Thomson, G., 208–9
tiger, 228
torture and violence, 300–1, 306n, 311–12, 318
Tourneur, Cyril, *The Atheist's Tragedy*, 304n
The Tragedy of that Famous Roman Oratour Marcus Tullius Cicero, 58–9, 60
tragicomedy, 269, 302–3, 306n
trick chairs, 308–11, 313–14, 316, 318–19, 324n
Trojan War, 209–11, 264–5, 267

Underworld Painter, 37

Versnel, Henk, 155n
Virgil, 264–6, 274
    Aeneid, 29n

'wailing for the dead', 17–18
Walsh, Lisl, 99, 102, 104, 107n, 109–10n
Watson, Thomas, 292n
Webster, John
    The Duchess of Malfi, 307–25
    The White Devil, 225, 230
weeping, 298–9
West, Richard, 224, 235n
'The Wife's Lament', 28n
Wilamowitz-Moellendorff, Ulrich von, 60, 97–8
wild cat imagery, 228–9
Wilkinson, Kate, 132n
Williams, Raymond, 62
Willis, Deborah, 185
Winston, Jessica, 271
Wiseman, Susan, 126, 129, 136n
witch and revenger, 228
Wohl, Victoria, 9
Wolff, C., 205
Wolpert, Andrew, 179n
women transmogrified, 202–38
Woodbridge, Linda, 61, 63, 112
Woods, Gillian, 125, 126, 134n, 135n

Zechariah, 61–2
Zeitlin, Froma, 9, 10–11, 50, 102–3, 268
Zeus (god), 38, 46, 48–9
Žižek, Slavoj, 7, 129–32, 136n
Zobia, 162, 172

EU representative:
Easy Access System Europe
Mustamäe tee 50, 10621 Tallinn, Estonia
Gpsr.requests@easproject.com

www.ingramcontent.com/pod-product-compliance
Lightning Source LLC
Chambersburg PA
CBHW061706300426
44115CB00014B/2578